The Last voyage of the *Lucette*

The Last Voyage of the *Lucette*

Douglas Robertson

SEAFARER BOOKS

SHERIDAN HOUSE

© Douglas Robertson 2005

First published in the UK by:
Seafarer Books
102 Redwald Road
Rendlesham
Woodbridge
Suffolk IP12 2TE

2nd impression 2005

And in the USA by:
Sheridan House Inc.
145 Palisade Street
Dobbs Ferry
N.Y. 10522

UK   ISBN   0 95427 508 X
USA ISBN   1 57409 206 5

British Library Cataloguing in Publication Data
Robertson, Douglas
  Last voyage of the Lucette
  1.Robertson, Douglas – Travel 2.Robertson (Family)
  3.Lucette (Ship) 4.Shipwrecks – Pacific Ocean 5.Survival
  after airplane accidents, shipwrecks, etc. 6.Voyages around
  the world 7.Sailing
  I.Title
  910.`9 `164

   ISBN 095427508X

A CIP catalog record for this book is available from the
Library of Congress, Washington, D.C.

Typesetting and design by Julie Rainford
Cover design by Louis Mackay

Illustrations by Douglas Robertson, Emma Smith
and Alexandra Deacon
Maps by Douglas Robertson and Alexandra Deacon
Photographs from the Robertson family archive

Printed in Finland by WS Bookwell OY

In memory of

Dougal Robertson
1924–1991

Linda Robertson
1919–1998

Dedicated to Anne, Douglas, Neil, Sandy, Keywan, Zana, Lisa, Douglas Jnr, Kieran, Alexander, Shilan, Sara-Jayne, Duncan, Charlotte, Jimmy, Elizabeth, Joshua, Cameron, Lucette, Anna, Hugh, Tim and Jack and their successive generations of offspring, none of whom would have been born but for the outturn of the real-life events depicted in this book.

Contents

Foreword by Sir Robin Knox-Johnston 9
Preface 11
Acknowledgements 13

Prologue, 1942: The loss of the *Sagaing* 15

Part 1: To round the world we set our sails
1: New horizons 29
2: Atlantic crossing 42
3: The Windward Islands 62
4: The Bahamas 76
5: American affairs 101
6: To Jamaica 114
7: The Spanish Main 138
8: Pacific blues 160
9: Under attack 166

Part 2: Shipwreck in the Pacific
10: Castaways 189
11: Incredible journey 265
12: Safety 336

Epilogue, 1975: Amen to the *Ambassador* 351

Ode to the frigatebird 358

Appendix 1: The SY Lucette 360
Appendix 2: Voyage plan, 27 January 1971 – 31 August 1972 367
Appendix 3: Glossary of sailing terms 369

Afterword 371

Foreword

I have always thought that the ideal family partnership skills for survival in a boat or raft had to be a Master Mariner and a State Registered Nurse. Dougal and Lyn Robertson were therefore ideally qualified for their ordeal of 38 days in a life raft, with their three children and another youngster, when their yacht was struck by killer whales and sank. But their survival had as much to do with the whole family's determination and improvisation.

Many years ago I remember being enthralled by Dougal Robertson's book, *Survive the Savage Sea*. For all any seaman knows, his or her boat might sink any time, so it made sense to try and learn from the experiences of others how they had survived. I can remember meeting them at a Boat Show and being frustrated that there were too many interruptions to have a really good chat, so my desire for more information was confined to the book.

But the loss of their yacht and their amazing survival is only part of the whole story. Here Douglas, who was eighteen years old at the time, recounts the full adventure. It starts with their purchase of the boat, goes through those difficult early days as everyone learns how to live in the confined spaces of a small yacht, their adventures as they crossed the Atlantic and the Caribbean, to their eventual passage through the Panama Canal on their proposed east-to-west circumnavigation. The Pacific Ocean is huge and did not experience the shipping traffic of the Atlantic in those days so once their yacht sank the chances of being sighted and rescued were much reduced. They were lucky, but it was not all down to luck and that is why this book, and Dougal's original book, should be compulsory reading for anyone planning a world cruise. Modern communications have made the oceans safer, but many of the basic lessons to be found in this book still apply. The fact that this is real live adventure and both books are an easy read makes this a pleasure, not a chore.

Robin Knox-Johnston
October 2004

Preface

Dougal Robertson and his family survived the marauding attack of a pod of killer whales, which forced them to abandon their yacht *Lucette* halfway across the Pacific Ocean. After the raft's inflation bellows failed, the inevitable sinking of their rubber survival craft followed on the seventeenth day adrift. Faced with no other choice, the castaways took to their fibreglass dinghy in a last-ditch effort to save themselves and their small children. Crammed into a three-man open boat, the six castaways then embarked upon one of the most audacious survival exploits ever, completing a further twenty-one days sailing across the ocean in an open boat without either navigational equipment or stocks of supplies, catching food and water from the sea in order to survive.

Whilst thirty-eight days was not the longest in terms of days spent adrift, their ordeal in the face of tremendous adversity was one of the most demanding and perilous feats of seamanship and survival known to mankind. In his book *Survive the Savage Sea*, first published in 1973, Dougal Robertson wrote an account of his survival and that of his family. In 1992 a film of the same name was released by Warner Brothers, starring Robert Urich and Ali McGraw. The book *Survive the Savage Sea* is now part of the US school curriculum and is also studied in places of learning around the world.

As Dougal's eldest son and the last remaining survivor who experienced all these events first-hand from an adult's perspective I receive, even to this day, numerous letters and emails asking me questions about our trip aboard *Lucette*, and requests for further information about our incredible journey home.

This book incorporates most of the text of *Survive the Savage Sea*, expanded with new information, as well as a complete record of our trip aboard the *Lucette*. My father's book sought to establish the facts of the shipwreck and how we survived, whereas I have tried to give the reader an insight into the emotional highs and lows we encountered as a family, both before and after the sinking of the *Lucette*. In writing this book I have drawn on discussions with my parents, and on my father's notes and newspaper articles, as well as the recollections of my brothers and sister, but most of all from my own memories of the trip. There is another reason for telling the story, though, and that is a deathbed promise to my father, who asked me to tell it in full after he had died.

I have written from Dougal's perspective because essentially it is Dougal's story. He wrote *Survive the Savage Sea*, and all of the story he told there is included in this book; the contemporaneous notes about the voyage of the *Lucette* were also written by him (the rest of us were too busy having a good time).

Looking back as a father myself I can only imagine the delight of my parents as they witnessed the coming to terms and indeed blossoming beyond years of their young children as they revelled in the adventure they had risked all to provide. As I look at the faces of my own children today I shiver at the torment I know Dougal and especially Linda must have endured after the shipwreck as they beheld our struggle for life over death, feeling the full weight of such an awesome responsibility, to say nothing of the despairing guilt, as they fought against the odds to get us all home.

To this day I am still amazed that we set off from Falmouth with so little preparation. My father was an experienced sailor on big ships and my sister had been introduced to sailing on the trip from Malta, but the rest of us had no previous experience, not even so much as a practice sail around the bay before we set off into the teeth of a Biscay storm. We coped, however, and carried on coping, sometimes in the most adverse of circumstances. Even before our fateful meeting with the killer whales in the mid-Pacific we had learned many lessons in survival. I can let my thoughts about lack of planning, preparation and training colour my view but that would be wrong. We had so little money and, as Dougal believed in training on the job, we had little choice but to accept his blinkered views and seemingly haphazard methods. In many ways it was exactly such blinkered determination and tireless resolve that allowed him to keep going, long after any normal man would have thrown in the towel.

On reflection it is easy to think we should never had made it home; it is even easier to say Dougal should not have risked his and our lives in such a foolhardy venture. As one of the beneficiaries of his slightly eccentric methods, however, I can only offer him my undying gratitude – not only for giving us such a wonderful adventure but also for never giving up in the face of such extreme adversity. Indeed, for his superhuman efforts in getting us all home in one piece, and for giving us those two short years aboard *Lucette*, I shall thank him every day of my life.

Douglas Robertson
September 2004

For further information on the events
described in this book see the websites

www.survivethesavagesea.com

and

www.lastvoyageofthelucette.com

Acknowledgements

I would like to thank the many advisers and assistants who have helped me at various times throughout the writing of this book and whose help has ultimately made its production possible. Especially I would like to thank my long-suffering family, as well as my sister Anne and my brothers Neil and Sandy, whose valuable recollections helped make the picture complete. I would like to thank Bernadette Dyson for work in the early stages, Emma Smith for the additional illustrations and Alexandra Deacon for the digital re-mastering of many of the images. I would also like to take this opportunity to thank Sir Robin Knox-Johnston, who was my father's original inspiration for embarking on the trip, for writing such a wonderful foreword. Finally I would like to thank Hugh Brazier for his excellent editing of the original work to the degree where the text is a joy to read, and Patricia Eve of Seafarer Books for her vision and advice throughout.

Prologue
1942: The loss of the *Sagaing*
Dougal Robertson

The celebrations welcoming the Chinese New Year of the Horse had ceased early for the crew of the SS *Sagaing*, following her hasty departure from the war-troubled city of Glasgow in Scotland. Approaching journey's end almost a month later, we were navigating by soundings alone, in fog-ridden and congested waterways, as our weary old steamship picked her way through the dangerous and crowded waters off the Ceylonese coast. We had been forced close inshore in a deadly game of cat and mouse, in order to avoid detection by a Japanese carrier group patrolling the northern limits of the Malacca Straits. During the hours of darkness our ship's progress had been slow, as she threaded her way through hundreds of trading dhows and small fishing boats, lit only by the briefest flashes of light as weary fishermen alerted the *Sagaing*'s watch-keepers to their presence by holding aloft flaming torches fashioned from oily rags and old newsprint.

Powering our way through the glassy swells of the Bay of Bengal, we had made better progress since dawn. Diverted from our original destination of Rangoon in southern Burma, we were closing rapidly with an offshore waypoint that marked the beginning of the final approach course into the ancient city of Trincomalee in eastern Ceylon. As Junior Third Officer on board, I was responsible for the eight-to-twelve bridge watches each day. The date was early April 1942 and though our ship's chronometer read just before midnight Greenwich Mean Time, local time placed us nine hours ahead at three minutes to nine. It was a sweltering hot morning, the dust haze merging the horizons of both sea and sky into an indiscernible screen of grey mist that ascended into the early-morning sunshine.

The *Sagaing* was an old ship by any standards. Built by Denny's of Greenock on the banks of Scotland's River Clyde in 1924, to the order of the Henderson Line, she was one of a fleet of twin-hatched passenger cargo ships. Equipped with only light-duty union purchase derricks on her cargo hatches, with no heavy lift capacity, she had been designed specifically for the Far East liner trade, more commonly referred to by those who sailed it as 'the Road to Burma'. Her triple-expansion steam engine, cranked up to maximum revolutions under a full head of steam, was producing her top speed of just over 14 knots. Her disproportionately large midships accommodation was home to her officers and provided cabins for 137 immigrant passengers in spacious if somewhat dated comfort. Her accommodation structure was crowned by a tall, black, slightly raked funnel, making her high freeboard and bluff lines appear top-heavy, especially when viewed from aft, at the point where the vertical sides of her joggle-plated hull shaped abruptly to form her wide fantailed counter. Though she was not repulsive to look at, she could not by any stretch of the imagination be called graceful. In contrast to her glistening varnished brightwork and shiny polished fittings, her steel superstructure hadn't seen a lick of paint in years. Her once-gleaming white deck structures, browned over with a heavy film of rust, were pockmarked with weeping paint blisters interlaced by large areas of corroding decay. Earmarked for transfer to the Burma Steamship Company by her owners, it was intended to sail her under the Burmese flag, where the stringent Board of Trade regulations regarding safety at sea would no longer be enforceable. As a result the Browning anti-aircraft gun originally destined for the poop deck remained unfitted and almost all her safety equipment and emergency spares had already been removed. Though she retained her British officers, her replacement crew of over 120 ratings and petty officers consisted of Hindus and Muslims on deck, Lascar firemen below and a Chinese carpenter. A hotchpotch of several different religions and castes, crammed together in the tropical heat below decks, where they lived two or more per cabin. All in all, the *Sagaing* carried an incredibly large number of souls, for a ship of only 455 feet in length and 7,994 gross registered tons.

I stepped forward from the curtained-off chartroom into the bridge, feeling professionally satisfied with my foresight in obtaining a fix earlier than was usual, from what had been a clean sharp horizon. Not long after I had completed my observations the distortions created by the rising airs had made any sort of solar observation impossible. With our position marked on the chart, I instructed the helmsman in my best Hindustani to make a one-and-a-quarter-point course alteration to the west, in order to negate the effects of the northeasterly set encountered during the night. On account of the progressive reduction in visibility since breakfast, I had also ordered the standby lookout to the forward watch post situated on the fo'c'sle. In truth, the poor wretch was only too happy to be relieved from the tedious polishing and repolishing of the already gleaming brass telegraphs and voice pipes, as prescribed in the job rota of the Master's night order book.

Turning the bulkhead fans up to full power, I relaxed in front of them for a while, trying to glean what relief I could from the already baking heat inside the wheelhouse. I tapped the barometer and observed that the needle remained steady. After scrutinising the adjacent hydrometer, and noting its reading was edging perilously close to that of the dew-point temperature, I decided to rouse the captain from his early morning slumbers. Calling Captain O'Hara on the bridge voice pipe, I put him on notice that the visibility was deteriorating rapidly into a blanket of thick fog. Baffled sleep-ridden tones came back from the mouthpiece, ordering me to post additional lookouts and to keep a sharp lookout myself. I slid back the port-hand door leading onto the leeward bridge wing, just as two bells of the forenoon watch were struck on the large brass clock located at the aft end of the bridge. A fine layer of salt crystals caked the windowpanes and varnished woodwork of the solid teak door, making the surface glisten with superimposed rainbows in the bright sunlight, which in turn made the fresh morning air sparkle like diamonds. At the far end of the deck, the gyro compass repeater whirred and clicked like a robot, in time with my ritualistic pacing back and forth along the holystoned deck planks. In the background, the rhythmic pulsing of the main engine punctuated the morning air and the pistons laboured under the increased head of steam in a soft continuous beat. I finally took up position on the starboard bridge wing, lodging my elbows against the canvas wind dodger where I refocused my binoculars towards the horizon. The tight flat awning overhead, bleached white by the sun, shielded the deck underfoot from the black carbon ash blasting skywards from the funnel top. The engineers, located deep within the bowels of the ship, were blowing the boiler tubes clean with high-pressure steam, in an effort to improve the engine's efficiency. I scanned the murk ahead, looking for a first sight of the coast that would indicate our safe arrival, thankful to have evaded the clutches of the Imperial airborne patrols that sealed the eastern route to Singapore. Un-alarmed by the lack of marine traffic, I had failed to make the connection between the lack of shipping and the hand-carried 'top secret' orders, issued to us under a heavy cloak of secrecy by the Allied chief of staff, back in the United Kingdom.

The sealed documents served on us there had requisitioned the *Sagaing* to load a secret war cargo for the Allied forces, following which we were instructed to proceed to Rangoon in Burma 'direct and with all haste'. We carried 20,000 cases of Allsops beer and a similar volume of Johnny Walker Red Label whisky, and this was the only cargo mentioned in signals. Though much to be appreciated by its consignees, it was merely a cover for our 'secret war cargo', which was in fact a consignment of munitions consisting of Hurricane aircraft, a large quantity of ammunition, mines and depth charges, the latter being secured along each side of the forward main decks. Loaded overnight immediately after the cargo holds had been sealed, the large cylindrical charges, each about the size of a fifty-gallon oil drum, had been secured in quick-release sledges so that they could be ditched instantaneously in the event of an emergency. Depth charges were especially dangerous to carry, as a fire aboard would cause them to explode on the ship, whilst jettisoning them overboard without first neutralising the hydrostatic charges would detonate them in the water, killing escaping personnel in the vicinity and tearing apart the hull plating beneath the waterline. In order to avoid just such an eventuality, the heavy metal sledges were lashed atop wooden slip towers, which were then secured with stenhouse slips shackled to the deck and rigged with lattice pull-wires. These wires were in turn attached to inboard multiplication levers, allowing arming and disarming of the hydrostatic detonators for all the depth charges on any particular sledge with a single press of the lever. A ratchet mechanism located on the charges themselves reset the detonators with a second press of the same lever. I looked down on the main deck beneath me and surveyed the towering stacks of sledges, shivering involuntarily as I counted their lethal bulk. In all, there were 23 sledges per side, with 50 units per sledge. I recall thinking that were we to come under attack and the munitions explode, then, together with the inflammable alcoholic cargo stowed below decks, the resulting cataclysm would be as devastating as it would be colossal. We had been warned by countless telegrams from the admiralty that the chances of an attack on our vessel remained high. The Japanese army had already taken Singapore and was advancing in the face of an ineffective and fractured Allied defence, which had been caught completely wrong-footed, having deployed defensive artillery posts with their guns pointing out to sea, away from the advancing enemy, in the mistaken expectation of a seaborne offensive. Talk aboard was that the Japanese would first consolidate their hold on Burma, followed by the entire East Indies and finally Australia, having already secured much of China and Malaya in their relentless stampede south.

The youngest of eight children, I had already left school by the time I reached the age of sixteen, and I had temporarily found work in a lawyer's office. Becoming quickly disillusioned, I then ran away to sea to work as an indentured navigating apprentice, hoping not only to see the world but also eventually to qualify as a deck officer or even a ship's master. I had readily signed the initial two-year indenture but, through what some considered a loophole in the wording, I had been retained under a continuance for a further two years. Because of the heavy losses suffered by the merchant navy since the onset of the war the Board of Trade had circumvented the minimum manning requirements by issuing foreign-going certificates of competency without even requiring the recipients to take the exams they had studied so hard for. Indeed, many of the officers' licences still bore an indelible red stripe to warn ships' masters that they were not officially qualified. So at the tender age of only eighteen I found myself promoted to the rank of a junior watch-keeping officer aboard the *Sagaing*, without the proper qualifications or experience and almost two years before the legal minimum age that would have applied in peacetime. Nevertheless, I proudly sported the gold stripes on the epaulettes of my uniform and for the first time had control of the bridge for the period of my watch. My best pal and closest friend Red, so named because of his flowing locks of dark red hair, had also been promoted at the same time and was in charge of the twelve-to-four watches, immediately following mine. Red and I had joined the merchant navy at the same time and sailed for almost two years aboard our first ship together. A pair of destitute and naive first-trippers, we had shared our cabin as well as our clothes and our youth, each mastering our chosen profession whilst supporting each other through the rigours of the war, finally coming to love each other as brothers. Then I had met Jessie.

It wasn't unusual for sailors, away from home for years at a time, to take on a coast-wife who would sail for the duration of the trip, sharing a man's cabin and his life and living in hope that her man would take her home with him at the end of the voyage. If not, then she would seek out another prospective mate until she managed to better her lot, or until her time and good looks finally ran out. From the sailor's point of view these girls were little better than whores and were treated as good-time girls. 'Don't make them pregnant and never fall in love,' had been O'Hara's watchword when I had first joined the *Sagaing*, advice I had cast aside from the moment I set eyes on Jessie. We had met in a bar in Singapore and under the moonlight on Sentosa Island we had pledged our love for each other in a lifelong oath. Jessie was half Japanese and half American. Her oval face was adorned with long black hair, large brown eyes and full red lips, and her lithe figure made her allure complete. Brought up by her uncle, she had been condemned to a life in the brothels, from a time before she had even reached puberty. My mother would never have approved of the union, and neither did Red. After trying to talk me out of it, he showed his true colours some months later by helping me smuggle her and my baby son Duncan aboard ship, and again later when we had explained to Captain O'Hara what we had done. With the aid of the Old Man's 'blind eye' I had ensured their escape from the ordeals of the war by keeping them aboard ever since.

The grating footsteps of Captain O'Hara interrupted my thoughts as he stepped anxiously onto the bridge wing from the starboard aft stairwell leading directly up from his cabin. Imperious and resolute, O'Hara had a name for fairness and compassion and had been affectionately nicknamed 'Old Iron Balls' by the crew. Standing at over six feet six inches in height, he was over sixty years of age and sported a heavy paunch. A small perfectly round and balding head topped his large frame, and bristling eyebrows shielded his piercing blue eyes. His weather-beaten face, pugnacious and pockmarked, was covered by a darkly tanned skin, which was half buried beneath a profuse and bushy grey beard. He had guided us through many a scrape both ashore and afloat and, as captain aboard our first ship, Red and I had regarded him as a surrogate father – whilst he treated us as the sons he had never had. Nicknamed 'Robbie', I formed an unlikely trio with Red and O'Hara. Others recognised our bond of deep respect and friendship and had christened us 'the A Squad'. My eyes strayed fondly to his peaked navy hat, the only remaining relic of the grander life he had once lived. Crinkled with age and slightly askew, its laurel-leaved badge was still adorned with the old Henderson Line tricolour, the scrambled-egg braiding festooned along its peak having become heavily tarnished with age. He hadn't bothered with a shirt that morning. His tanned barrel chest, covered in an uneven layer of fine curly hair, seemed perched atop his bulbous gut, which overhung his long white shorts. It was a constant source of amazement to those on board that he managed to remain totally credible whilst looking completely ridiculous, all at the same time.

Like many of the senior officers on this ship, O'Hara had been given his last of last chances, and between bouts of drunkenness was desperately trying to hang onto his command. He had served his time and qualified as an Extra Master under sail, even before I had been born, and after a lifetime of exemplary service he had been condemned to serve the rest of his career aboard ships like the *Sagaing*, because of a catastrophic grounding in Hong Kong harbour aboard the company's flagship. Not just an error in judgement, he had run the ship directly onto the rocks of Lan Tao Island, so hard that even her propeller was clear of the water by the time she had come to rest. He had been drunk at the time, his senses clouded after a seven-day binge ashore. He had risen from practically unconscious sleep to take his ship out to sea. Dressing himself in his white short-sleeved uniform shirt and shorts, he had entered the bridge still wearing his shore-going suit underneath. Bedraggled and unkempt, dressed more like a scarecrow than a ship's captain, he looked the epitome of ridicule as, locked in a drunken daze, he dismissed the pilot from the bridge just as his speeding charge was entering Hong Kong's outbound channel. Convinced he was still leaving Manila in the Philippines, his previous port of departure, he suddenly and inexplicably ordered a sharp turn to starboard and headed his ship for an imaginary shortcut. The vessel struck the rocks of Lan Tao Island at over 18 knots, in full view of the teeming bands of tourists visiting Aberdeen Harbour. His ship had remained stuck high and dry for over four and a half months with her bottom literally ripped out. 'Make fast fore and aft,' had been O'Hara's bizarre response as he stepped off the bridge wing onto the rocks immediately below. Old Iron Balls had only the severe personnel shortages caused by the war to thank for still having a command at all. After a time without work, he had managed to persuade an old friend, newly promoted to the rank of marine superintendent, to give him one last chance. That was the *Sagaing*, a decrepit old rust bucket eking out a living as a tramp ship, carrying immigrants and such demeaning cargoes as empty bottles, scrap iron and putrid sacks of dogs' droppings, until the onset of the war had also bought her a reprieve.

It was not long after sighting Ceylon's eastern coast that the fog lifted and we embarked our pilot, who shepherded us into the broad bay of Trincomalee and then to our allocated spot in the munitions anchorage near Malay Cove. A restless interlude ensued as we waited for orders from ashore indicating which military bridgehead was to receive our sinister cargo. At anchor watch, it was amongst my duties to ensure that we remained in our charted position and that all boats coming alongside from the port were authorised and checked. Ever-changing reports of the Japanese advance, supplemented by rumour and counter-rumour, made our torrid stay in the anchorage nerve-racking in the extreme. Even with additional lookouts posted, O'Hara became increasingly tense as we suffered a string of oppressively hot and windless days, where every movement of mind and limb was an almighty effort in the sticky humid air, leaving us soaked to the skin in sweat from the moment we stepped out on deck.

It was on 9 April, following a stand-down after another of the repeated false alarms, that O'Hara remained on the bridge after the 'all clear' had been sounded to raise the issue of the lookout's effectiveness with me. We leant on the dodger side by side, and watched in silence as Jessie appeared on the foredeck below, carefully holding young Duncan's outstretched arm as they commenced their constitutional meander around the deck. Jessie's bright blue kimono flapped unmanageably in the wind as she tried to control her long black hair in the blustery sea air. Duncan's golden curls crowned his smiling face as he and his mother struggled hand in hand against the light headwind, making their way forward towards the forecastle where they often sat and played. At the break of the well deck, they both turned and Jessie helped our little boy wave in my direction. I waved back until they had disappeared from view down the companionway stairs behind the well deck bulkhead. 'They canna stay on board much longer, Robbie,' asserted O'Hara with a deliberate shake of his head. I was stuck between a rock and a hard place. Remaining on board in wartime was a risk but Jessie's distinctive Japanese features made it impossible for me to send her back home, at least until the war had ended, and the presence of my young son made it impossible for my family to remain on board. It was only a matter of time before head office found out and then, well, I just had to find a solution before they did.

I was about to speak, when the blood seemed to freeze in my veins, my eyes catching the unmistakable glint of metal in the skies above. A fleeting instant later, we both heard the sickening whine of Japanese aircraft, accompanied almost simultaneously by the shrill whistle of falling bombs. Seconds afterwards, loud explosions erupted forward and aft, followed immediately by heavy blast waves laden with splintered debris, which slammed us both against the bulkheads before knocking us to the deck, pounding our eardrums and reverberating the air about us. The decks shuddered as a second series of explosions rent the air from deep within the bowels of the hull. O'Hara lay motionless in a twisted heap next to me, his face buried in the deck, his peaked cap several feet away, upended and filled with a pool of blood. Mustering his last ounce of strength, he reached towards me and pressed a key into my blood-soaked hand. His barely comprehensible order, muttered as I cowered next to him, was to be the last of his command. Tears blotted my eyes, as dark clouds of dense billowing smoke, interlaced with flame, turned day into night with another sequence of eruptions that enveloped the entire afterdeck. I squinted into the sun, tracking the planes and observing the large circular decal of the Japanese Imperial Air Force on the upper sides of the wings, just as the first of a line of three aircraft banked sharply to the left before blipping its throttles and disappearing into the glare of the sun. They were coming back for a second run-in, their attack clearly not yet over. I fled from the cover of the wheelhouse, jumping clear of the bridge deck just as the first of the machine-gun bullets tore into the ship's structure all around me. I darted into the captain's cabin in fulfilment of his final order. The starched linen sheet was thrown back where he had pushed it aside when the alarm had called him just a few minutes earlier, the pillow still depressed where his head had lain. I yanked open the heavy door of the safe with the key he had pressed into my hand and took out a tightly wrapped scroll. It bore the zinc seal of the Ministry of War. Next to the scroll there was a camera too, its heavy leather case fitted with a stout canvas strap. Neither was to be allowed to fall into the possession of enemy forces.

With the floor tilting noticeably under my feet I shouldered the camera and bolted for the open decks. I had to find Jessie and Duncan and get them to the boats. Diving for cover beneath the lifeboat winch housing, I crouched low, doubled up in a tight ball as the planes passed overhead, spitting intermittent bursts of cannon fire with deadly accuracy as they neared their closest point of approach. Their engines gunned with a mind-gripping roar as they receded into the distance once more, indicating that they were already turning, unseen, for a third run-in. It was clear that they did not intend to leave until they had finished what they had started.

The *Sagaing* was already listing to starboard and trimming by the head as I leapt downwards from companionway to companionway, taking cover behind the large wooden deck lockers, until I arrived at the main deck. Turmoil reigned as panic-stricken crew members, some badly wounded with gaping strips of flesh torn from their arms and legs, poured onto the decks from the doors leading up from the accommodation below. Reports quickly spread that the engine room doors had jammed shut from the shear forces set up in the hull and the flood water from the duct keel had filled the machinery spaces below. Screams of terror chilled the air, as desperate men tried in vain to force open the doors, unable to escape from the sealed compartments below. With feverish hands I un-dogged the main watertight door in the forward bulkhead which led through to the cargo deck. Not waiting to hook it back, I scurried forward in a sickening panic, my heart filled with fear and apprehension. The menacing sledges of depth charges, stacked high overhead in their wooden framework towers, looked like waiting funeral pyres – and I suddenly made the connection. They were the reason we were being subjected to such close attention from the air. Again, the machine guns chattered into life, tearing up the deck and ricocheting from the steel bulwarks, shattering cavernous holes directly in my path and forcing me to dart for cover behind a cluster of cargo drums. The sledges themselves were now hidden in billowing black clouds of impenetrable, acrid and suffocating smoke, pulsating upwards in large plumes from a yawning hole blasted through both hatch covers forward of the bridge. A mental note flashed through my mind as the smoke settled about me in a choking blinding fog that rapidly covered the entire vessel: it was in those holds that the whisky was stowed.

One last frantic dash brought me to the break of the forward well deck. A few seconds later my heart began to pound as I gulped the air in shallow rapid gasps, my greatest fear suddenly a reality. Jessie lay face down under the break of the number one hatch coaming. Her body, limp yet strangely rigid, was unresponsive to my touch. I dropped on my knees to the deck, slumping over her lifeless body, trying in vain to cover her gaping wounds with the tattered shreds of what had been her best white blouse. 'Don't leave me, my love,' I wept, pulling her head into my chest as I held her tightly in my arms. I did not want to let her go, but for my sweetheart, and the dearest mother of my son, it was already too late. My son! I scoured the immediate vicinity, then my eyes caught sight of a compressed bundle jammed beneath the spare anchor on the forecastle bulkhead. His round white face, frozen in his moment of death, was already cold, etched as in the marble of a finely carved sarcophagus, his once blonde curls already turned black where his precious lifeblood had matted his golden locks. In the blinking of an eye, my life had been changed forever. My head spun as I wretched the very bile from my stomach and wept, my life's hopes and aspirations suddenly in tatters about me.

I could not recall how long I had stayed there, because I had lost all reckoning of time and events, then I slowly became aware of a rapid shaking in my right shoulder. It was Prakash, the chief petty officer. He too had been weeping, his dark tanned skin ashen white and clammy, the stench of vomit redolent on his breath. 'The planes have gone, sahib, and you must help us now,' he stammered in heavily accented English, brushing aside my pleas for help with Jessie's body as he tried desperately to re-establish control over himself. The Serang stood beside him, shaking and stammering as he made a disjointed and breathless report in a garble of Hindustani. 'We are on fire and sinking, sahib; and the depth charges, sahib, they will kill us all if you don't help us fix them, sahib.' Translating as he went, Prakash pleaded insistently into my face as the remnants of the crew, a ragged gang of frightened men, gathered at the top of the companionway. The black smoke belching skywards from below was now interspersed with bright blue flames, springing from the fractured hatchways as the fires inside the holds began to burn ever more fiercely, gathering new energy as they enveloped the crated whisky.

Struggling to gather my shattered wits, half shouting and half sobbing, I strove to take charge of the assembled working party marshalled by the carpenter. I detailed them to start unpinning the neutralising levers on the depth charges. I then formed a second group to help me disarm the charges and, gripping a nearby fire axe, stood by as the stenhouse slips were broken open, in order to release the sledges overboard the moment they had been made safe. It was a race against time. If the depth charges were not neutralised before the *Sagaing* went under or the advancing wall of flames enveloped them, they would explode, preventing us from getting the lifeboats away and killing any personnel left aboard or survivors still in the water. The flames spread rapidly from the hatchways and raced along the decks towards the accommodation. They were already lapping through the scupper doors, leaving not a second to lose. After sending Prakash up to the boat deck to assist the boat parties prepare the lifeboats for launching, I organised the rest of the men to search the vessel and seek out any remaining survivors and direct them to the boats. The Serang and I then turned as one to start jettisoning our deadly cargo. As he pulled the lever on the first of the sledges, I brought the axe down with a hefty swing. To our great relief the sledge slid immediately and harmlessly overboard. Together we systematically despatched sledge after sledge, progressing at a feverish pitch, until the Serang suddenly stopped dead in his tracks. Raising his arm, he groaned in desperation, exclaiming that he had forgotten whether he had pressed the lever or not. Pressing the lever for a second time would reset the charges and blow us out of the water. I had to make a judgement call that would affect the lives of everyone. 'Press it,' I urged, bringing the axe down with a mighty blow. We watched with bated breath as the sledge and its deadly contents slipped safely over the side. Luck seemed to have changed sides at last.

Just fifteen minutes later, we slipped the last of the sledges over the side, before the swirling flames and searing heat forced us from the deck. Leaving Jessie's remains to the all-consuming flames, I rushed up to the boat deck with my son's lifeless body held tightly onto my chest, my feelings of fear rapidly being replaced by those of anger and grief. I arrived at the boat deck, where chaos reigned amid restrained shouts of nervous anticipation as officers and men carried out the final preparations, prior to launching the out-swung lifeboats. Blood-soaked wounded were being carried aboard, my dear friends Red and O'Hara amongst them. I stammered Jessie's name out loud but nobody heard me or stopped to listen. Prakash caught my eye and with a shake of his head gently cajoled me into the boat. My heart sank and my mind swam in turmoil as I leapt clear of the deck and the lifeboat was ordered away, before the increasing angle of heel made it impossible to lower at all.

Our lifeboat struck the ship's side with a sickening jolt, the steel plating already glowing bright red from the furnace-like heat within, as she settled slowly by the head, the pall of smoke now towering thousands of feet skywards. The *Sagaing* seemed to right herself for a moment, before suddenly listing more heavily to starboard as increased volumes of water flooded into her holds below. Loud metallic groans of twisting steel, snapping and bending, gradually intensified before a loud crash of tumbling metal rent the air and the heavy anchor chains plummeted across the chain-locker floors. The fearsome crackle of the flames stopped abruptly as the lower holds flooded with seawater. A few seconds later the eerie and surreal silence was punctuated by loud blasts of venting air from the forecastle, forming huge brown clouds of dried mud mixed with fragmented flakes of rust as the residual air, compressed by the rising waters below, tore the deck plates asunder and burst free.

The rope falls disconnected automatically and swung dangerously over our heads as the lifeboat dropped heavily onto the surface of the water. The engineers had been unable to get the motor to start so, struggling to make myself heard, I crouched low and snapped the rowlock into place; taking up the stroke oar I gripped the wooden shaft and ordered the rest of the crew to assume rowing formation. 'Pull,' I bellowed without waiting for the frightened men to respond. I bent my oar into the water, yelling, 'Fend her off and keep clear in case she takes us with her as she blows.' We heaved the boat clear of the area and waited for survivors to arrive, but they never came. Without warning, the *Sagaing* exploded with a shattering roar, the munitions still aboard detonating in a coordinated series of thunderous, ear-splitting eruptions. Glowing superheated fireballs blasted lethal tentacles of flame in all directions. In a massive and powerful explosion, the sea erupted skywards, thrown to the air in white plumes of pulverised water and emanating powerful shockwaves which slammed into us from beneath. 'Row,' I shouted, 'row for your lives.' For ten torturous minutes we pulled on the oars like demons, our stunned minds failing to comprehend or believe what we were saying or doing. When I looked again, our old ship had disappeared. Abandoned to drift helplessly shoreward, she had become lost in the swirling clouds of smoke suspended over the place where she had been so savagely hit.

Our ship was gone, Jessie and Duncan were gone, Red and O'Hara were mortally wounded, and most of the crew that had escaped the flames were perishing in the water that exploded and erupted around us. Less than thirty minutes before I had been standing on the bridge, part of the life and soul of the *Sagaing*. Now, as we raced to rescue the helpless survivors, I rowed in a raging fury with an energy and strength summoned from the very depths of hell itself. I looked back to the fading cloud of smoke and up to the sky from whence we had been struck this mortal blow, my hatred turning to anger and my anger to an oath of vengeance.

The diesel engine finally kicked into life and, completely spent, I slumped back into the stern of the boat. Leaving the receding coastline behind us, we were alone in an empty sea under a silent sky. In fulfilment of my duty, I instructed Prakash on the use of the camera and ordered him to take a picture of me holding the Ministry of War scroll, before consigning it to the deep to prevent it from falling into enemy hands. I tried to share in the euphoria of my shipmates, but as I beheld the tattered little corpse of my son, lying in the bottom of the boat, I turned my head towards the clouds. Reduced to a grimacing wreck, my heart full of abhorrence, detestation and hatred, I screamed at the heavens and shook my fist. I would exact my revenge, and I would never forgive them for what they had taken from me.

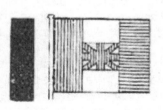

HOUSE FLAG :
Red, White and Blue vertical Tricolour, with Union Jack in centre.

Part 1

To round the world
we set our sails

CHAPTER 1

New horizons

It was a Sunday morning in the autumn of 1968, sixteen years after I had left the sea for good. Returning to Scotland after the loss of the *Sagaing*, I had spent the rest of the war delivering Liberty ships across the North Atlantic, finally moving back out to the Far East, where I had sailed for the China Navigation Company, first as a second mate and then as a chief officer. I met and married Linda (generally known as Lyn) in Hong Kong in 1952, when after gaining my 'Master's Ticket' I finally swallowed the anchor and took up a living from the land, in one of the remoter parts of Staffordshire.

Memories of Jessie and Duncan and my dear friends Red and Captain O'Hara, who did not survive the war, though kept alive in my thoughts and prayers for many years, had long been consigned to the deepest recesses of my consciousness. I watched the milk wagon pull out of the yard on its morning collection round, and sighed resignedly as I walked slowly towards the farmhouse. Yields were down again and fifteen years on an upland dairy farm in north Staffordshire had diminished to extinction my enthusiasm for an agricultural way of life. My interest in progressive farming techniques had changed from an ambitious dream into a grim determination to endure the steady deterioration in living standards which had reduced the number of small dairy producers in England by fifty per cent in the preceding ten years.

I paused where the cobbled road wound round the back of the farmhouse. With a heavy heart I glanced back at the concrete yard surrounding the cowsheds, recently converted to a modern milking parlour, then to the square unpretentious farmhouse, grey-green lichen mellowing the red sandstone and giving the thick 300-year-old walls the appearance of having grown from the soil, rather than having been built upon it. Crossing the stone flags fronting the house, I opened the door to the kitchen, whereupon the welcoming sound of the children's voices filtered in high-pitched chatter from the upstairs bedrooms. During the week, my wife Lyn commuted some six miles to the market town of Leek by motorised cycle to carry out her duties as a sister in the town's only maternity hospital. On Sundays, though, she took one of her two days 'off duty' to be at home with the children during their weekend's break from school. Sunday had evolved not so much as a day of rest for the Robertson

family as a day of family communion, when the previous week's
happenings were recounted and the coming week's plans discussed.
A day for visits from friends and relatives and for lying abed late,
except for Dad who had the privilege of rising early to pursue his
chosen way of life, along with 70,000 other servile dairymen around
the country.

The idyllic air of rustic content was no longer able to mask the
gnawing worries and financial burdens or the hard unyielding routine
of farm labour, which had allowed me fourteen days' holiday in
fifteen years. Neither was it able to allay the discontent which
resulted from the frustration of seeing hopes and visions crumble
under the crude realities of economic necessity. That Sunday
morning stands out in my memory as one of the nice days, however.
I had put the kettle on the hot plate of the solid-fuel Aga cooker and
while waiting for it to boil I switched on the radio to listen to the
news, which amongst other items was commentating on the Round
the World yacht race. I carried the mugs of tea upstairs on a tray,
calling to Anne, our sixteen-year-old daughter, to come through to
our room where our nine-year-old twins Neil and Sandy rocked with
laughter as they lay in bed on either side of their mother, watching
our eldest son Douglas perform one of his slapstick comedy acts. As
Douglas rolled his eyes and cavorted round the bedroom in stiff-
legged imitation of a disabled robot, Neil's face reddened and he
hugged his teddy bear closely as he laughed the breath from his
lungs; even the more serious-minded Sandy chuckled in ecstasy as
he watched his fourteen-year-old brother's antics.

Anne followed me into the bedroom yawning widely, her long
golden hair flowing in tumbled profusion across the shoulders of her
dressing gown. She thumped Douglas with her fist in passing, then,
before he could retaliate, jumped quickly into bed beside her mother.
Slowly their laughter quietened as we talked of school, of Douglas's
rugby, of Anne's rock-climbing and of the twins' new teacher; finally
we touched on the yacht race. The children listened interestedly as I
told them of the dangers and privations which faced lone yachtsmen
in mid-ocean, but I found it difficult to describe the hostile character
of an ocean environment to youngsters who had been no nearer the
sea than the seaside and whose perception of a large stretch of
water approximated the local reservoir. Neil and Sandy fell silent,
while Anne and Douglas asked questions, and Lyn talked of our
sailing adventures in Hong Kong before we had started farming.

Entering into the spirit of the conversation, Neil unexpectedly
shouted 'Daddy's a sailor, why don't we sail around the world?' Lyn
burst out laughing. 'What a lovely idea!' she exclaimed, 'Let's buy a
boat and sail round the world.' I realised that Neil, who thought the
city of Manchester was one of the four brown corners of the earth,
had no conception of the meaning of his remark, and that his mother
was merely entering into the spirit of things. But suddenly, to me, it

was not just a throwaway remark. Why not sell up and circumnavigate the world? I looked at Anne and Douglas, both handsome children, but with the horizons of their minds stunted by the limitations of their environment. In two years they would both have reached school-leaving age and neither had shown any great leaning towards exceptional academic aptitude, whilst the twins, already backward compared with their contemporaries in town, were unlikely to blossom into sudden educational prodigies. In the same two years they would finish their primary schooling, and then ... Well, why not indeed?

We were reasonably well qualified to undertake such a voyage. In my twelve years at sea I had gained a Foreign-Going Master's certificate, and Lyn was a practising midwife and a State Registered Nurse, with additional qualifications in fever nursing. She could make herself understood in rather rusty Arabic and Cantonese, while I could stumble along in equally rusty Hindustani and French. After fifteen years of hard living as un-gentlemanly farmers, we were in tough physical condition and the children had a good background of practical training, begotten from helping with the farm work.

For the next two years, talk at the Robertson household centred round our proposed maritime adventure, the mundane reality of schoolwork and farming banished to a back seat. In the summer of 1970, we each had our appendix removed in the name of preventive medicine and Anne and Douglas took their school-leaving exams, with a new sense of purpose and direction. That same summer we sold our farm business and realised our entire holdings in stock and land. Though we then had sufficient funds to embark on the initial stage of our planned voyage, we had been unable to find a suitable vessel in which to undertake it. Staying with friends and relations whilst we continued our search, we scoured the broker's lists with renewed urgency and looked at boats of all kinds, located throughout the length and breadth of the country. When an envelope containing written specifications of a classic wooden schooner, described as a 'world girdler', came through the door one day, I knew our search was over.

We purchased the fifty-year-old, nineteen-ton, forty-three-foot schooner *Lucette* in Malta and subjected her to a rigorous survey. Originally built by Kings Yacht Builders at Burnham on Crouch in 1922, her specification was impressive. Though old, her hull was fabricated from grown oak frames, covered with thick inch-and-a-quarter pitch-pine planking fastened with copper nails; she also had the benefit of a long lead keel some three tons in weight as well as one and a half tons of movable iron ballast. Though my 1930 edition of the *Lloyds Yacht Register* showed her to be a gaff-rigged schooner of some thirty-nine and a half feet in length with a cut-away transom plus a seven-foot bowsprit, the broker's plans showed that she had since been extended with the addition of a canoe stern and a three-foot boomkin, making her hull length forty-three feet, or fifty-three feet overall. She had also been re-engined and re-rigged with Bermudan sails, giving her extra speed and increased manoeuvrability. She had a twelve-and-a-half-foot beam and a six-and-a-half-foot draught, and her arrangement consisted of six berths in three cabins.

Suspect hull planking was renewed and the surveyor's recommendations carried out in full. Anne and I flew to Valetta and with the help of two friends we sailed *Lucette* back to Britain through some rough autumnal weather. We arrived in Falmouth full of confidence in the seaworthiness of our craft, and Lyn, Douglas and the twins, together with their treasured teddies, joined us.

Slowly we became accustomed to shipboard life. Access below from the ample deck area was via a midships deck saloon which was used as a navigation area, from which a ladder-like companionway led downwards into the main saloon. The saloon itself was the epitome of tradition, with wide settees on either side divided by an offset dining area surrounded by book cases and lit by gimballed brass lamps. A clock and barometer set on the forward bulkhead stood out brightly against the heavily varnished decor. The trunk-like foremast lead through from the deck into the keel and there was a quarter berth on the port side suitable for Douglas. A door at the forward end of the saloon lead into a small V-shaped cabin with two single berths and a hatch leading up on deck, which we felt would comfortably house the twins. Immediately abaft of the saloon was located an open galley and bathroom with a doorway through to the owner's cabin. This was equipped with a double berth to port, suitable for Lyn and me, and a screened-off single berth to starboard, separated by the massive mainmast trunk which was also set into the keel. This would be the only compromise for Anne, who, at an age when her personal privacy was important, would have to share her sleeping accommodation with her parents. The owner's cabin led through to the engine room, with an access hatch to the deck via the cockpit.

Before we could set off on our voyage, however, *Lucette* would need to be fitted with a newly manufactured boom and have additional planking fitted and caulking replaced, whilst her sails were either renewed or re-stitched by machine at the local professional sail loft.

We took up residence in our new home in Falmouth in October 1970. Falmouth was a small, almost quaint town with a population of less than 10,000, surrounded by green fields and located on the estuary of the river Fal in the southwest corner of England. The only industry of note was the thriving shipyard situated near the town centre. Farming and fisheries, together with the seasonal holiday trade, were the only other industries left, after the closure of the copper and tin mines further upriver near Truro. With the decline of the sailing-ship trade, in which Falmouth was the principal deep-water port offering the safest anchorage in the western approaches, Falmouth had become heavily reliant on the shipyard as a source of income, and life seemed to revolve around it and its work programme.

After parting with the family pets and a farmer's lifestyle, which had once seemed it would last forever, life in Falmouth, though pleasant, became a testing time for us all. *Lucette* had won our respect after surviving the trials of heavy seas and strong gales en route from Gibraltar but now, for the first time together as a family away from the farming community which had been our life, we tried to come to terms with our new world.

In innocence, the children had accepted their new way of life without question. Having been used to acres of space, they had adapted to their damp and confined quarters, offering scant comfort or privacy, almost as quickly as they had come to terms with the numerous cleats, stoppers and blocks on which they stubbed their toes, banged their heads or bruised their limbs. Their world had changed beyond their wildest expectations, the call of the curlew over moorland hills now replaced by the incessant wheel of the gulls, soaring in squawking melees behind the salt-encrusted fishing boats that punched their way through the whitecaps on their way to and from the rich offshore fishing grounds. Accustomed to the quiet of the countryside, they were now surrounded by the incessant commotion and bustle of ships and heavy industry in full swing, continuing non-stop through the day and night.

Whilst our offspring had adjusted to the complete change in their environment even better than either Lyn or I had dared hope, we as parents were for the first time beginning to question exactly what we had embarked upon. It had been all too easy to tell our friends and relations that we were selling up in order to sail around the world. From the beginning, we had convinced ourselves that we were not fleeing our economic plight, or escaping from reality, but were doing what was best for our children. Now the world seemed a massive and uncertain place and our proposed circumnavigation, a hugely complex project by any standards, seemed pitted with obstacles and risks. Lyn had become worried about the adverse effects of a possible four-year break, not only on our children's education but also on our own economic circumstances. I began to have doubts myself and even after selling the farm it seemed that money, or lack of it, was still going to be a problem. Indeed, thinking about it only served to deepen my feelings of depression and self-doubt, which in turn affected my conduct and demeanour towards my family, and especially towards Lyn. Our discussions became arguments, the arguments became rows, and within the confines of the *Lucette*, now also occupied daily by repair workers from the local boatyard, life at times became unbearable.

On arriving from Gibraltar, we had anchored in the middle of Falmouth Bay, a hundred yards off the end of the Prince of Wales Pier. The anchorage was traversed several times a day by the Flushing and Saint Mawes ferryboats, from which we often hitched lifts ashore by catching a willing skipper's attention. On one such trip I had a chance meeting with a man who introduced himself as the owner of the nearby Travisome Guesthouse. He was the only other passenger on the ferry that day, a balding middle-aged man with a ruddy complexion, the last vestiges of his jet-black hair receding over his ears and thickly carpeting the back of his head and neck. I envied him his smartly pressed shirt, an unknown luxury in both farming and yachting worlds. He introduced himself as Colin, stating he had moved to Cornwall after leaving the London rat race some years before to live his dream. I remember thinking how simple life would have been if his dream could have been mine too.

While the repairs to *Lucette* were progressing, Colin offered us a room at his guesthouse, free of charge. It was the off-season and he had several unoccupied rooms available. Now at least we could find a bit of private space at the end of each day followed by a decent night's sleep, which in turn made for a better-tempered tomorrow. Our lives quickly developed a new routine and a watch rota was drawn up, with the off-watch five going ashore every evening aboard the aging rubber dinghy, powered by an even more ancient three-and-a-half-horsepower Seagull outboard. Neil and Sandy kept a close and accurate record, reinforced by frequent reminders of who had driven yesterday and whose turn it was today. We kept the room at the guesthouse on even after our free period had expired, and life went by in an easy and established routine.

Later in the month we moved *Lucette* upriver to the Little Falmouth Boat Construction repair yard, where all the underwater works to her hull were completed. Moving back out to the anchorage, we finished the less urgent fitting-out of the accommodation at a more leisurely rate. We also started collecting and stockpiling the many spares and victuals required for the long trip ahead, stowing long-term provisions of the canned and dehydrated variety in varnished containers which we wedged beside the ballast in the bilges. Our money was rapidly running out as we continued preparing for the inevitable day, when having talked the talk we would have to walk the walk and actually set sail, swapping this little haven of security for the great unknown. A day neither Lyn nor I had directly mentioned to each other, since we had first moved to the Travisome Guesthouse, a day when we knew we must shatter this cosy existence and do what we had told the children we were here to do. We both knew that this day, when it arrived, would be the day when it would no longer be possible to change our minds. Slowly and inexorably, the pressure between us began to build.

Then, one day in December, Lyn told me that she was no longer prepared to risk the children's lives or indeed jeopardise our own futures any further. As far as she was concerned the trip was over and the *Lucette* must be sold!

In a single stroke, Lyn had put an end to our new life and an end to our collective dreams of a great adventure. I felt numb and almost paralysed with anger as Lyn delivered her ultimatum and turned my world into a panic-stricken blur. In a daze I reached out, more in frustrated desperation than intending a physical attack, and was snapped back to reality by the sound of a stifled scream, finding to my horror that my hands were tightly gripped around Lyn's neck. Neil, visibly shaking with fright, was watching transfixed from the companionway door. I snatched my hands away and apologised to Lyn, glancing quickly back to the open doorway – but Neil had already disappeared. Like a beaten cornered animal I slumped onto the nearby settee, exhausted by the stress of the situation. I gulped at the air and struggled to control myself, shocked and frightened at the monster I had become. Lyn, now silently pensive, kept her distance and watched me incredulously. I felt uncomfortable under her fitful stare, and without saying another word I made my way up the companionway steps to cool off in the fresh air on *Lucette*'s teak laid decks. Clinging to the shrouds, I gazed across at the busy ship repair yard, filled with aging freighters moored cheek by jowl with large bluff-bowed tankers, resting like sleeping giants, lit by the intermittent glare of welding flashes and the fiery tails of high-speed grinding discs. I watched the cranes and tugboats busy about them in watchful attendance. Lyn was right, it was a foolhardy idea, *Lucette* must be sold and I would return to the sea as a professional seafarer. With the proceeds of the sale, Lyn and the kids could set up home, maybe even here in Falmouth, and I would send money home to support them.

I voiced my thoughts aloud, trying to convince myself that it was the right thing to do, indeed the only sensible option left. I had not enjoyed my previous tour of duty at sea and the prospect of another fifteen years' service seemed daunting. I was suddenly aware of a pair of arms slipping around my waist and, looking down, I saw my eldest son Douglas, tears streaming down his cheeks. 'Please, Dad,' he sobbed, 'please take us with you round the world.' Turning his head, he buried his contorted face into my chest, struggling to muffle his guttural sobs. I hugged him to me in silence, unable to speak about the adventure we had once planned and discussed practically non-stop for the last two years. I stared away to the silvery sea. It seemed to be mocking me, challenging me, calling me, and yet it may as well have been on another planet. With the farm sold and almost all our surplus funds invested in the *Lucette*, calling off the voyage was going to be very damaging indeed, both psychologically and financially.

The shipyard siren interrupted my thoughts, blasting out across the water to signal the end of the afternoon shift. Involuntarily I glanced at my watch, then Anne's voice broke the wretched silence. 'Now come on, you two.' She spoke assertively as she directed the twins onto the Zodiac dinghy moored alongside. 'You too,' she added to Douglas. 'It's Mum and Dad's turn to do the watch on board tonight, and my turn to make the tea.' I failed to register the urgency in her voice or notice the speed with which she organised the boys, chiding them into the boat alongside. Before I could absorb what was going on, I was waving goodnight to them as they pulled away from the side, bound for Flushing Pier. I watched intently as they receded into the distance, Neil bailing the water from the bilge and pouring it over the side, in a manner that particularly irritated me. The dinghy leaked both air and water badly and I couldn't afford to have it repaired. I shook my head in disbelief as I recalled the recent memory of Neil tipping a bailer full of water over the outboard engine, causing it to cut out and leaving us all stranded in the middle of the bay. If I hadn't been so intent on focusing on my children's shortcomings, perhaps I would have realised just how mature Anne had been in that moment. Far wiser than either of her parents, she realised that Lyn and I needed time together alone, to discuss all that had happened and to work things out for the future. Indeed, had I stopped to consider what she had just done, maybe I would have been able to see things more for what they were. Maybe I would have realised that we were embarking on such a trip, not so much for the education of our children, but more because I really wanted to do the trip for myself! With a heavy heart, I turned from the shore and descended the stairway to the saloon below.

Lyn had already wiped the tears from her face, but the finger marks where I had gripped her neck stood out starkly against her smooth white skin. Life with me had not been easy for her. I knew she loved me, even after what I had done to her, but I also had to accept that she had the right to say what she thought, without the fear of bullying or recrimination on my part. I repeated my apology and reached out my arm as if to shake her by the hand. It seemed oddly appropriate and Lyn, showing understanding and forgiveness that only true love can engender, took my hand in hers and, with yet more tears filling her already reddened eyes, pulled herself to me.

'You know, Lyn,' I began, 'I haven't been the best of fathers to the children and they have had it tough.' I stopped for a moment, searching for the words that would best make my point. 'Our farming enterprise was like a long dark night of the soul for me, what with no electricity or hot water on the farm, no television and mostly second-hand clothes for the kids to wear – it was a heartbreaking struggle, to say the least.' I pressed on in quiet desperation. 'The other day Dougie was standing on the pier, cold and wet from the rain, and he asked me if I would buy him a coat. Do you know what I said, Lyn?

Do you? I told him to wait until we got into a warmer climate, then he wouldn't need one.' I continued my unblinking stare in Lyn's direction. She was still listening intently so I continued. 'I was pathetic, Lyn, bloody pathetic. I had no bloody money left so I made my own son shiver in the wet and cold and do without.'

'Life has always been a struggle,' Lyn said quietly, nodding for me to continue.

'Lyn, I've learned that sometimes life gives you a second chance, and with your help I mean to take that chance! I was never able to give our children the trappings of life but I can still give them what most fathers can't.' Lyn said nothing so I pressed my point home in an impassioned all-or-nothing plea that seemed to rise from the very depths of my heart. 'I had a dream, Lyn, a dream that kept me going through those bleak days of farming on Meadows Farm. I had a dream that some day I would pay my children back for all those cold nights and empty dinner tables, the holidays they never had and the days when we sent them to school in shoes that didn't fit. I want to share what is left of their childhood while they still have it, I want to give them my time before it's too late. Lyn, please don't send me back to sea. Perhaps we can still give the children something they will remember forever, something really special, something that even a millionaire couldn't give to his kids – the adventure of a lifetime. Let me have that second chance, Lyn, let us live that dream together. Give us two years, just two ...'

I held my two fingers right in front of her face, pleading desperately whilst searching her eyes for the smallest hint of a U-turn or the slightest glimmer that might give me hope. The future course of our lives depended on the outcome of the very next moment, and as I scrutinised her face her bubble of opposition suddenly burst. 'I'm so sorry,' she choked, 'I've been such a silly woman. I'm just breaking our family apart. Who the hell am I if I don't support you?' She paused and the silence became unbearable. 'I want to go, Dougal. I want to go with you and the children. I want you to take us all with you and sail around the world.' Her voice was thick with emotion and her frame trembled visibly through the murk of the cabin as she fought back her sobs, then it was my turn to break. Rarely given to shows of emotion, I could not stop the tears welling up inside me. Bound in each other's embrace we stood in silence, words no longer necessary, the sounds of the sea interrupted only by the rhythmic creak of *Lucette*'s rigging echoing reassuringly in our ears.

Another hour passed and it had already turned dark before Lyn finally broke the spell, suggesting we have a cup of tea and something to eat. 'I wonder what the children are having for tea,' she mumbled almost beneath her breath as a concerned frown flitted across her face – but that night was to be for Lyn and me alone. We settled down in the shadowy glimmer of the paraffin saloon lamps, talking of our futures together as we prepared and ate a simple meal, during which we made a secret pact. We agreed to put two years aside for the trip. If we had not completed it by then, we would either return to England or settle in New Zealand or Australia and start a new life there. That night we shared an intimacy that had been all too rare in our lives together. Hard labour and lack of money were not the ingredients for romance. As if marking the change in life's course we released ourselves from the prison of emotional confinement and bathed in the glow of a deep and genuine happiness, for the first time in what had been a very long time.

Our slumbers were broken early next morning by the sound of the children's voices hailing us from the dinghy. Lyn rushed up on deck, her face breaking into a broad smile as she took the rope from Sandy's outstretched arm. Douglas cut the motor and manoeuvred the dinghy to the boarding ladder with the expertise of an old seadog. The pensive look on their faces turned to joy as they realised that Lyn and I had made things up between us and that the trip was most definitely on. Anne and Douglas exchanged a knowing look, explaining to us that they had been up all night discussing whether or not we would be going and what the alternatives might be if we weren't. Anne told us that they had decided that if we were smiling as we greeted them in the morning then the trip was on, and if not then no matter how we couched it the trip would be off. In emphatic voices, they both stated that in the latter case there was no way that they would be prepared to return to Staffordshire. The thought of putting our children through such a night left both Lyn and me feeling guiltier than ever. Our offspring were growing up by the day and we couldn't even see it.

Talk quickly turned to exploration and adventure once more as we all worked with a will, getting *Lucette* shipshape and ready for sea. I had already announced that we would sail on the next favourable wind, and an animated urgency gripped us all, as we reconfirmed lists of the ports we wanted to visit and plans of what to do when we got there. Anne, having already found her sea legs on the trip from Malta, recounted her seaborne experiences to the boys, who listened avidly, wishing they too could have been a part of her adventures. I dutifully listened to the weather forecast on the radio every morning and with eager ears waited to see if 'Today was to be the day'. For the next two weeks I could only say, 'Sorry guys, the wind is still southerly, we can't go yet, not till the wind comes out of the north.'

It was at this time that a new boat arrived in the anchorage. *Bonnie* was an Icelandic ex-lifeboat of some 80 feet in length, a substantial motor vessel owned by an Icelandic family. She had already saved over 500 lives in her time at sea – and unbeknown to us all she wasn't finished yet!

The Thorsteinssons, namely Siggi, Etta, their five boys Olaf, Kiddi, Siggi Jnr, Jennie and Battie, and only daughter Bonnie, were already living their dream and doing what Lyn and I were just about to embark upon. Like us, they were planning to sail to the Caribbean, and as Siggi was also a Master Mariner, we had a lot in common from the world of big ships. We spent many a night swapping anecdotes and remedies, finally agreeing to wait for each other from port to port. Initially we planned to sail for the Canary Islands and wait for each other there. 'Las Palmas it is, then,' boomed out Siggi in the middle of the saloon, banging the table with his fist enthusiastically. His words sounded like music to my ears as I repeated them over and over, first to myself and then out loud. Lyn felt a lot happier now the twins had friends to play with, and the days began to fly by. The only thing stopping us now was the age-old constraint that had beset sailors from time immemorial. And so, as they had done before us, we waited for a break in the weather and a fair wind.

The days dragged into weeks and impatience and frustration began to set in. Lyn had renamed various parts of the boat after our old farm in Staffordshire. The engine room was now the garage, the chartroom was the landing, and on deck she simply referred to as upstairs. It filled my heart with joy as she sang 'Blow the wind northerly', a variation on a familiar song, as she hoped to summon up the wind. The twins had set up a puppet-land dynasty in the forecastle, with each of their puppets brought from Meadows Farm – Jimmy, Little Ted, Big Ted, Doggie, Panda and Horsy – fulfilling roles in a micro-society, linking their new and uncertain world with the security of the world they had left behind.

Late one afternoon, as the family were busy about their allotted tasks, a small motorboat approached with two well-dressed men aboard, claiming to have been commissioned by Lyn's sister Mary to take some family photographs before we departed. Unwittingly, we posed as they bade, quite unaware of the deceitful practices of the paparazzi. The next day the national press front-paged the photograph with the headline 'The Robertson's should be made to pay.' The tabloid followed with an article about how we had had our appendices removed on the National Health Service, explaining further in progressively belligerent tones that such operations were too much of a burden on an already overstretched and underfunded service. Given that the photographs and interview were obtained illicitly, we were never given the opportunity to put our side of the story. We had been advised by our doctors that such a precaution was in fact best practice and that the under-utilised Cottage Hospital in Leek welcomed the publicity as it was in danger of being closed, but of course none of that received even a mention.

Christmas and New Year came and went, traditionally a cornerstone of our family's calendar. It was our first since selling Meadows Farm and the first in our new surroundings. The Icelanders brought their cultural angle to the celebrations and I couldn't help but wonder where in the world we might celebrate our next Christmas. The weeks continued to tick by and it was soon the end of January and the end of yet another week of continuous winds blowing out of the south. I was beginning to think we would be stuck in Falmouth for good as I turned the radio on and assumed my usual vigil. We all sat expectantly, waiting to hear what the weather was doing. I had become so used to hearing the weatherman repeating his southerly monologue that I failed to notice at first that he had stopped saying it, indeed the forecast spoke only of northerly winds backing to the west, moderate becoming strong. Our long wait was over and judgement day had finally arrived! Would the wind be too strong for our first trip? Would we have to wait another three weeks or even three months if we let this opportunity go by? Would our money last if we waited any longer? Siggi confirmed he had heard the same news and they planned to leave later that day, as soon as some last-minute spares had arrived, declaring with or without them he would be leaving at the very latest by noon the next day. I felt the first of the old self-doubts return and decided in that moment that if we didn't leave right away then perhaps we never would.

'Come on, you lot,' I declared, 'today's the day.' They knew what I meant and a pent-up bustle of activity released the tension and heightened the excitement as we stowed items of deck equipment and prepared the *Lucette* for sea. The wind was already freshening as we motored alongside the Prince of Wales Pier to top up the water tanks. Twenty minutes later, Douglas let go forward and I gently sprung us off the pier, turning *Lucette*'s bowsprit towards the harbour exit and the open sea. I nodded an instruction to Anne to raise the foresail and she quickly heaved the appropriate halyard on the mainmast, instructing Douglas how to make fast the sheet as she did so. The sail snapped and crackled loudly as it filled with the gusty breeze. *Lucette* gathered speed as she caught the stronger winds blowing across the bay and was soon rushing seaward, rolling steadily in the gathering ocean swells. Wiping tears of joy from my eyes, I gave voice to the fanfares of my mind as my heart filled to the point of bursting. We were finally on our way, and nothing would stop us now. Singing at the top of my voice, I embarrassed my crew still further by stamping on the cockpit floor whooping loud yee-hahs of delight, my face knotted in glee as I waited impatiently for the mainsail to claw its way to the mast top. In a bustle of confused activity, my landlubber crew did their best, pulling on the downhauls and making fast the running backstays whilst turning the air blue with expletives and making a pig's ear of it into the bargain. 'Better rig a preventer,' I confirmed to Anne as my eyes met Lyn's across the coach roof. She was returning my smile as she took it all in. Little did I realise it then but I had forced her to forsake our egalitarian family life for an environment where she was entirely reliant on me for her survival. I had put her in a powerless position, insidiously removing her right to choice in our relationship. Still less did I know that Lyn had already realised that this was so, and had accepted that unless she had been prepared to pay such a terrible price then *Lucette* would already have been sold. I owed her more than anyone for making our voyage possible, and I vowed to make our adventure a time she would never have cause to regret, a time she would recall for the rest of her life with pleasure. Slowly we rounded the harbour buoy and turned for the freedom of the beckoning sea. The cheery smiles and whoops of delight came to an abrupt halt, however, when *Lucette*'s fine hull dipped into the first of the long ocean swells and a lashing of freezing cold spray, blown from the top of our rippling bow wave, whipped across the decks and soaked us all to the skin.

Thus began our trip of a lifetime, an adventure whose final chapter would be recorded in the annals of history, recounted across dinner tables and delivered in fine speeches. An odyssey to be recorded in books and magazines that would touch the very hearts of mankind, and the legacy of which would serve as a source of inspiration to others. A story to be depicted in film and shown in cinemas and on television screens around the world. A chronicle that would be recollected by Lyn and me, and remembered with our children and our grandchildren, to be re-told by them down through the generations, long after we had shuffled off this mortal coil.

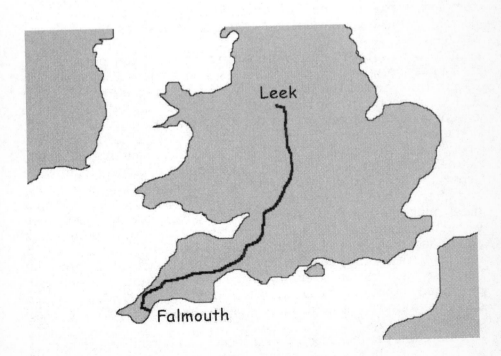

CHAPTER 2

Atlantic crossing

After what had seemed like an eternity, we finally left Falmouth on 27 January 1971, running before a strengthening northerly wind, which by the time we had reached Finisterre had increased to a screaming sixty-mile-an-hour gale. Weeks before our departure I had painstakingly plotted a neat and precise rhumb-line track on the chart, carefully laying off the courses and distances between waypoints, using the time-honoured Mercator sailing tables. It had been my naive intention that we would make good the courses lain. Douglas took the wheel just after we passed the fairway buoy, his trembles of excitement changing rapidly to shakings of fear as the waves steadily grew in size, while *Lucette*'s motion under the severe buffeting of the elements grew less rhythmic and ever more erratic. It quickly became apparent that we had no chance of adhering to the courses I had so meticulously set. In fact the exercise had been a complete waste of time for we could only steer an approximate course, in the general direction of the southwest, as the wind and sea allowed.

It wasn't long before we were shipping green water on deck with every passing wave. By nightfall, seasickness had set in, which left us prostrate across the floor, grimly clinging to whatever we could find for support. In our rush to leave Falmouth I had forgotten to ensure that the dishes and food cupboards were securely stowed, and the floors were now littered with broken glass, smashed crockery and topless storage jars, which had spilt their contents of lentils, oatmeal and freeze-dried chicken supreme in a homogenous mixture across the floor and down into the bilges. Seasickness gripped us all, and after we had finished vomiting up our food we began vomiting a green foul-smelling fluid, followed by bright yellow bile from deep within our stomachs. The strong throat-stinging slime made us retch again, each new bout of retching visibly weakening us as the end of one bout was quickly followed by the start of another. Summoning her last vestiges of strength, Lyn, her voice interspersed with prolonged bouts of heaving, interrupted our individual though collective torment with a desperate plea, 'Dougal – is it time to send up the rockets yet?'

I stared at her in a mixture of disbelief and harsh bemusement as we both clung tightly onto nearby grab handles, flexing our grip as the boat rolled heavily. 'Who in damnation do you think would see them?' I shouted above the roar of the elements, fully aware that only another fool such as I would be out at sea in weather like this. We were ready to call it a day and return home with our tails between our legs, but the weather had become so bad and the winds so strong that we couldn't even turn *Lucette* around to go back, no matter how much we might have wished to. Despite the works carried out in Falmouth, water started to seep in through the heavily worked planks of the hull, and the water levels soon began to rise over the cabin floors. Diesel had leaked from the main fuel tank, giving the entire accommodation an acrid and sickly smell, making a dire situation even worse. All we could do was dig deep on our inner resources whilst running before the mounting seas and hope that *Lucette* and her crew would be strong enough to see it through.

That night we crossed the busy shipping lanes west of Ushant, ploughing into heavy overfalls caused by the strong tidal rip flowing directly against the wind. Passing within sight of its flashing white light, I trembled under my oilskins as the broad beam emitted by the lighthouse picked out the growling whitecaps against the jet-black of the night, and self-doubt began to play on my mind. I stayed on watch until the early hours, finally calling Anne to take over. I went below just after midnight completely exhausted, falling asleep the moment my head touched the pillow.

I was wakened almost immediately by Anne's shrill cry urging me back up on deck. A large fishing boat was closing with us in such a way that she feared a collision was inevitable. *Lucette* was rolling heavily, and I clung on to the cabin handrails tightly so that I could pull myself out of the double bunk. Lyn spread herself into the vacated bed space and braced her legs against the leeboard to prevent herself from being thrown onto the floor. My feet skidded from under me as I tried to keep my balance on the steeply sloped and bucking floor. The icy water, topped with a heavy slick of diesel, swirled across the floor panels and over my feet, coating all the surfaces it came into contact with in a slimy pungent film that left the shifting floors underfoot slippery and dangerous like sheets of ice. The constant metallic whirring of the propeller offered us some small comfort as it signalled our rapid progress through the water, each turn bringing us one step closer to the end of our sea trip from hell.

Hearing the rasp of fear in Anne's cry as she called me a second time, I opted to take the shortcut, and clambered over the engine, popping my head up through the aft hatch. The wind blew the breath from my lungs as I braced my limbs in an effort to face sternwards. Anne was looking over my shoulder, straining to cast her eyes forward, peering desperately through the murky darkness up ahead. She looked like an ancient Egyptian mummy as she stood wrapped in tightly bound oilskins and wrestled with the wheel. The wind screamed in a high-pitched moan as it drove the sea before it, piling the slab-sided ocean into mountainous heaps which tumbled huge barrelling combers into cascading overfalls that lashed us hard with searing sheets of frenzied spray. I struggled to hold my nerve, slowly taking in the sights and sounds around me. It had been bad enough when I was on watch earlier, but now looked truly terrifying. I clung tightly to the hatch coamings on either side of me. A loud and intermittent gurgling, like the breathing of a great whale, repeatedly interrupted my concentration as the cockpit drains sucked away both water and air, clearing the knee-deep seas that accumulated in the cockpit. Involuntarily gybing against her bar-tight preventers, *Lucette* yawed violently, her sails cracking like rifle shots above the raging cacophony around us, as she raced down the mounting forty-foot waves. Only Anne's careful and quick-witted steering prevented us from suffering full and catastrophic broaches, as our old schooner fetched up into successive morasses of swirling white water, each wave heralding the approach of tumbling masses of white angry foam, roaring atop what seemed like watery mountains that charged past us in unstoppable and terrifying succession.

'Where away?' I bellowed at Anne, struggling to be heard above the deafening howl of the wind. She was already stabbing the air towards the port bow with her left hand as I rubbed the sleep from my eyes and tried to focus in the direction of her flailing limb. My head was numb from lack of sleep but what I saw next snapped me wide awake in an instant. A large fishing vessel, deck lights ablaze but not showing fishing lights, was struggling to keep her head up to the wind as a busy cluster of fishermen tried to stow her gear, having just hauled nets on account of the storm. The helmsman must have been either asleep or unable to control his charge in the weather, for she was headed straight for us, less than a hundred yards on the port bow and closing fast. I yelled to Anne that she must hold her course and speed, as under the international rules of the road it was the fishing vessel's duty to give way to us and, conversely, our duty to stand on, maintaining our course and speed. I reached for the air horn and sounded a continuous blast, barking orders in Anne's direction, confirming she should switch on the Morse lamp and direct its beam onto our tightly reefed sails, the pitch of my voice rising from concern to outright alarm. Having become aware of the imminent disaster themselves, men began running aft aboard the other boat, but they were too late to intervene; she was almost on top of us. I closed my eyes as the clippered stem of the fishing boat, clearly visible in the reflected light, hung high above us like a giant dinosaur reared to deliver a devastating and fatal blow. Her two bower anchors protruded from each side of her flared bow like huge menacing tusks. On contact they would pierce *Lucette*'s sides like tissue paper and send her plunging to the depths. Anne and I looked on powerless and dumbstruck, silent witnesses engulfed in a world of hell and damnation; we were in God's hands now!

Even as the fishing boat poised, seemingly frozen on the face of a mushrooming roller, I became aware of another sound. Like a deep rumbling thunder it was clearly discernible even above the noise of the wind and sea. Behind Anne's shoulder, almost directly aft and gaining on us at incredible speed, I spotted a huge vertically sided freak of a wave roaring towards us. It towered over the other waves like a mountain, omnipotent and threatening, its phosphorescent glow shining brightly through the darkness as it raced towards us. A gigantic whirlpool sucked up water from its base, feeding its buttressed sides with streaming torrents of water that tumbled downwards in roaring waterfalls, as the wind whipped its crest into a boiling mass of white gurgling spume. I had been caught in typhoons in the Far East and hurricanes in the Caribbean but I had never seen a wave as big or as awesome as this one. I pointed towards it and tried to shout a warning to Anne but the wind plucked the words from my mouth. In the next moment the fishing boat speared back into my consciousness. The intervening seconds looking aft seemed to have lasted an age but could only have been an instant. In a dazzling glare the vessel descended into the same trough as *Lucette* and I gripped instinctively at the woodwork of the hatch coaming as I waited for the inevitable crash. Frozen to the spot, Anne stood with me. We had no more cards to play and no last ace left to save us. The solid wall of water forming the face of the super-wave loomed high in the darkness for the briefest of moments then, almost immediately, it hit us.

The first torrents of water slammed into *Lucette* high up near her crosstrees at a point where the foresail stay joined the mainmast, bursting the storm staysail into a torn mangle of minute shreds in the same instant. A fraction of a second later the black water engulfed us with such colossal force that *Lucette* was knocked clean onto her beam-ends. Exploding onto the coach roof, an overwhelming barrage of water raced across our decks, ripping the saloon skylight from its housing and smashing it heavily into the leeward railings. Stoutly lashed fenders, lifesaving equipment and sundry deck gear were promptly washed overboard as *Lucette* first shuddered and then jarred, her heavy wooden structure wincing under the impact of the deluge as she lurched sideways through the seaway before rolling horizontally, right over onto her starboard side. Her masts and sails plunged into the foaming waters before completely disappearing from view as they were first buried and then raked through the sea. The wheel spun out of control, leaving Anne dangling on her flimsy lifeline and struggling helplessly to keep her footing against the cockpit sides. The wooden wheel-grips to which she was clinging hammered her hands and fingers as the wheel spun wildly, stopping suddenly as it jammed hard over and locked in position. *Lucette* staggered forward, dropping down the face of the crushing wave before pausing for a moment, trapped on the rim of a dark watery abyss. Then, plunging headlong over the crest, *Lucette* plummeted bodily through the air and smashed into the solid water twenty feet below. Moments later a gushing wall of white water surged aft along the deck, swamping the superstructure on all sides. I ducked instinctively as its pulverised crest hit the hatch coaming and flooded the cockpit, leaving Anne agasp as she held on tight in swirling eddies of waist-deep, bitterly cold water. I was certain it was all over for us, sure that such a knockdown could only be the result of a direct hit from the fishing vessel.

The grim reaper had missed his moment, however, for the other boat swept over us on a different part of the same wave, somehow defying the space–time continuum, only feet away but incredibly above our port quarter. Suddenly we were looking down on the fishing boat's decks, and in another moment she was past and clear, sweeping beneath *Lucette*'s stern in a swirling roar before disappearing into the night's black hell as quickly as she had appeared.

The ice-cold water poured from our battered schooner's sails, cascading onto the decks and in through the wide-open skylight hatch, flooding the saloon below as she struggled to right herself from the devastating knockdown. Anne was trembling beneath her oilskins, visibly shaken as she gripped the wheel with bloodstained hands and heavily bruised fingers, as much for support as in an attempt to steer. A careless fishing crew, no doubt hard-pressed in a full-blown and particularly vicious storm, had almost run us down and in a single moment of neglect could have killed us all. Anne, still deep in shock, her legs weak and her voice timidly quiet, felt fit to faint and was quite unable to continue her watch that night. I dug deep on my energy reserves and told her between breaks in the wind to make her way below and roust Douglas out on deck to take over the wheel. 'Remember, one hand for you and one for the ship,' I repeated to her, shaking a finger of caution through the darkness, waiting and watching for a lull in the waves that would signal her dash from the cockpit coaming to the chartroom door. I had no choice but to get Douglas up on deck. With frazzled nerves I waited for him to arrive, mental traffic choking my mind as I tried to formulate a list of jobs that would require my most urgent attention. The damaged sails needed replacing, the snapped preventers needed repairing, and I needed to get the pumps working, in order to clear the rising water levels below. Once that was done I would need to check around the boat to ensure that all planks and fastenings were still sound and that nothing else had been broken. I also needed to check on Lyn and the twins, who must have been wondering what in the hell had been going on.

I steered to the line of the wind and sea, trying to calm *Lucette*'s heavy and violent rolling. It was then that I noticed tears smarting my eyes and running down my face. I was weeping in uncontrollable silence, my face convulsing in involuntary sobs. I hadn't cried like this since the loss of the *Sagaing* but now, as the delayed shock took hold, touched by my own mortality and humbled by the might of the sea, I found myself crying and trembling like a frightened lamb. I was still weeping when Douglas appeared at the chartroom door, heavily wrapped in layers of oilskins and overcoats, cold, hungry and frightened. He clung desperately onto the rails and handgrips as he worked his way aft, muttering what was to become an all-too-familiar oath and something of a catchphrase for him. 'Bloody typical,' he growled as he banged first his head and then his knee against the unforgiving woodwork.

After what seemed like an age he gained the safety of the cockpit and took the bucking wheel from me. 'Try one-eighty,' I shouted over the wind, forgetting that he actually had no idea how to steer. There was no time to teach him, though, and a quickly barked instruction would have to do. I wedged myself into the cockpit seat, my trembling and tears subsiding as I watched my son wrestle with both the spinning wheel and the corkscrewing motion of *Lucette*. My thoughts returned briefly to my own training when serving as a cadet in the merchant navy. I had been taught to steer by compass on the steady deck of an ocean liner in a dry, warm bridge with the latest electrohydraulic equipment. I had been constantly instructed and corrected by the officer of the watch. I could even recall the red night-light and the cosy secure glow it cast around the steering position, bolstering my feeling of security from the sight of the heavily reinforced structure of the ship. A far cry indeed from young Douglas's induction. After taking only one trick at the wheel as we were leaving Falmouth in considerably less demanding seas than these, he had to learn to steer in these extremely arduous and demanding conditions within the few minutes I had to spare, for I could not delay pumping out the continuing ingress of water accumulating below decks for much longer. Suppressing my impatience, I sat with him and studied his facial features by the glow of the binnacle light. His eyes darted from side to side as he fixed on the rapidly spinning compass card and struggled to keep the southern cardinal mark up to the lubber line. I grimaced repeatedly for him as he tried his best to prevent *Lucette* gybing or getting caught with her sails aback. I felt I did not want to leave him, for as I watched him shouldering the wind he was slowly but surely winning his private struggle, which was reassuring me too in a strange sort of way. By not giving up he was giving me strength and support without even realising it. If my first-trip son could pull himself together and deal with the problems being thrown at him then who the hell was I to sit about crying? I had work to do and he was coping just fine. Taking a leaf out of his book, and feeling strangely inspired, I left him alone and made my way below.

The scene awaiting me in the saloon was one of absolute carnage, the smell of the diesel-scented air, mingled with the stench of vomit, catching the back of my throat as I descended the stairs. I stepped gingerly into the ankle-deep water rushing across the floors, sloshing and snapping at my ankles in time with the random pitching of the hull. Lyn and the twins were desperately clutching each other in open-eyed terror, lying in a shivering huddle on the forward cabin floor. The sail-bins forward, which we had filled with various stores including lentils, potatoes and dehydrated foods, were swinging open and shut with loud clanging reports each time *Lucette* rolled and bounced in the heavy seas. From shortly after we had left Falmouth, the twins, stiff-limbed and cold, had taken to their bunks, vomiting into the sail-bins in time with the roll of the hull in what had looked like a meticulously timed and carefully coordinated double-act. Now their eyes rolled fearfully as they watched the waves from the flooded bilges roll up the insides of their bunk sides, splash on to the deck-heads above them and then soak their bedclothes with incessant drips of foul-smelling water, each roll on one side being rapidly followed by an equal roll in the opposite direction. The submerged floors were covered with a fine film of diesel, which made them treacherously slippery underfoot, and small piles of repulsive smelling vomit littered the furniture and walkways. I quickly discovered that the bilge pumps were defunct and even the hand pump had been punctured by broken glass. I was forced to bail out *Lucette*'s bilges with a bailer and scoop, giving truth indeed to the statement that there is no better bilge pump than an anxious sailor with a bucket. Urging Lyn onto her feet, we worked as a team, passing the loaded buckets up to Douglas on deck as the bilge-polluted wavelets surged inside the accommodation, bitterly cold and loaded with debris, sloshing and growling interminably through the darkness.

It was daylight by the time I had finished bailing out *Lucette*'s bilges, dipping the bailer between the stout oak frames of the hull according to the pitch and roll to clear out the last of the pools that remained there. By the time she was dry Dougie could stand at the wheel no longer and was virtually asleep on his feet, forcing me to take over the watch again as the wind-torn waves became starkly visible in the strengthening light. If I had been scared before I was doubly so now, for I could see the fearful and mountainous seas all too clearly. It was one of the worst storms I had ever seen and it was still getting worse. We were no longer alone, though, for we found ourselves in the company of flocks of seabirds. The only witnesses to our arduous endeavours were themselves completely at ease, masters of both sky and sea and all it could throw at them. I wanted to ask them if we would be all right but they swept on by, seeming to remark, 'This – oh this is nothing, we deal with this sort of thing every day.' I took great strength from the grace and ease with which the gannets, sporting incredibly smooth plumage and long dagger-like beaks, swooped through the air like aerial torpedoes. They patrolled the heavy seas around us like generals in charge, whilst the fragile Mother Carey's chickens dipped and dabbled their feet into our crooked wake. These birds were at home in these elements. They seemed unafraid, which in turn gave us courage and hope, making our own burden so much easier to bear. I called Dougie to resume the watch two hours later. All told, I had been going non-stop for over thirty hours save for the few minutes' sleep, so abruptly interrupted by Anne's call the previous night. I released the wheel to my son and fell asleep right there in the cockpit until my watch came round again.

Over the next three days we slept in cold wet clothes on damp bunks, often too tired to eat. Lyn courageously tied herself to the galley steps, providing those that could eat with as imaginative fare as she could muster. As she struggled to keep her footing she was thrown without warning from one side of the galley to the other. For days, she proudly showed off her purple bruises, stretching down the complete length of her back and legs. When not providing bodily sustenance she was gently reassuring the children that everything would turn out all right. On more than one occasion I heard her coaxing Douglas as he fought to conquer his fear whilst preparing to go back on watch amongst the wild and tumultuous seas that raged ever stronger beyond the confines of *Lucette*'s hull.

Before we had set off we had been advised that babies' potties, having deep plastic bowls and large handles, were perfect for eating from when making passage deep-sea during bad weather, so we had bought some for this very purpose. One day, and for the first time since leaving Falmouth, after literally tying herself to the stove for over an hour, Lyn had managed to cook some re-hydrated chicken supreme and rice. Anticipating a long and arduous trip aft in order to deliver this dubious fare to me in the cockpit, she had put the food into just such a receptacle. Hanging on with hands and feet, she passed the potty up to me through the aft hatch, whereupon, seeing the steaming contents and assuming that one of the twins had been sick again, I quickly tipped it over the side and handed it back to her. 'I've just spent an hour cooking that!' Lyn started with a laugh, and I joined her in an uncontrollable fit of the giggles that lasted over twenty minutes. It had been the first time since leaving Falmouth that laughter had been heard aboard and it was a joy indeed.

We weathered the storm out in mast-high waves under bare poles, with streamed sea anchors trailing from the stern into the gale-force winds, giving my family as rough an initiation to the sea as any pressed crew of bygone days. Anne had been confined to her bunk with flu after that first dreadful night and since we had no self-steering device, Douglas had to fill the gap, working opposite me four hours on, four hours off with a stoicism and resourcefulness which won our respect and admiration. I know of no more satisfying conceit than the discovery of such hidden depths of character in one's own children. As the days slowly ticked by we became used to our harsh surroundings. After the seventh day, though still bitterly cold, the gale had all but blown itself out and I was able to get a navigational fix with my sextant. Securing myself amongst the stays, I concentrated hard through the telescopic sights, eventually bringing the sun's lower limb down to touch the lumpy edge of the visible horizon. It wasn't a clean fix but it would have to do. The position line put us out in the Atlantic well to the west of our course and the noon fix later that same day confirmed it. Our position lay over four days' passage from where we should have been and we were quickly approaching the point of exhaustion. After a brief conference with Lyn we decided to alter course from Las Palmas and head for Lisbon, deciding that when we eventually got there we would turn back for England, for we were both shattered and worn out. We were into the second week after leaving Falmouth before we spotted the first lenticular clouds, grey and sausage-like in appearance, that were a reliable indicator of the proximity of land. Although still unsure of our exact position, we then knew that the coast could not be far away.

The morning of 5 February found us wrapped in bright yellow oilskins atop layers of wet coats and jumpers, studiously enjoying the appearance on the southeast horizon of an inviting grey smudge which was the Portuguese shoreline. When we eventually came close enough to pick out the detail, our first landfall was indeed a beautiful sight to behold, the picturesque houses looking for the entire world as if they had been painted rather than built upon the hillsides. The sun came out and the wind, shifting to blow from right aft, decreased in strength to a mere force six! The coastline remained in view throughout the day and as dusk approached we drew ever closer to the lights of Lisbon itself. We dropped anchor later that night in the harbour roads, joining company with many ocean-going ships already anchored there, beneath the Salazar suspension bridge. The next day, as we docked in the quiet waters of the River Tagus, I couldn't help wondering why I hadn't considered stopping in this wonderful port in the first place. As we entered the marina we felt at one with the brave men whose statues adorned the Monument to the Discoveries, a towering ship-shaped monument dedicated to Henry the Navigator and other early Portuguese adventurers, located at the entrance. Going ashore for coffee and cakes procured from a small family bakery, we were happy to be alive and happy to be together as a family. Young Sandy drank a proud toast, asserting that *Lucette* was not only our home but also part of the family, having earned her stripes in that Biscay storm. Suddenly all thoughts of returning to England disappeared like fog.

It took days of drying out in the marina sunshine before we could resume normal life aboard once more. *Lucette* lay festooned with airing sails, pegged-out sheets and blankets, together with our entire wardrobe of clothes and a bunch of motley teddy bears. Foodstuffs, tools and equipment were spread haphazardly over the coach roof, occupying every last inch of available space under the drying sun. Still following our fortunes, the paparazzi reappeared from behind various street corners, badgering us for more on the English newspaper story. We didn't need to understand Portuguese to see that the articles in the following day's papers had picked up the theme of the British press. We were horrified to discover that they were also alleging we were possibly fleeing from the settlement of outstanding medical bills.

Pushing this new pressure aside, we spent the next week exploring the narrow medieval streets in the labyrinthine Alfama district near the centre of the old city, enjoying our boys' first experience of a foreign land and culture. Our middle ears had been so unbalanced by the passage from Falmouth that we felt the buildings were actually moving, but we enjoyed exploring the stepped and cobbled lanes of the old quarter, climbing up to the moat-encircled battlements of St George's Castle, the one-time fortress of the Moorish governor. On other days we visited the Coach Museum, displaying probably the finest collection of horse-drawn carriages in Europe, and between return visits to the Maritime Museum, filled with comprehensive memorabilia dating from the great days of sail, we even found time to squeeze in the Museum of Ancient Art. When not overdosing on culture, we indulged in a new pleasure, that of simply walking on dry land and enjoying the sights of the city. During our family walks Anne attracted the unwanted attention and hissed cat-calls from groups of working men, gathered in the siesta time sunshine drinking cups of bitterly strong coffee from the numerous cafes and bars situated in Lisbon's wonderfully preserved medieval section. Many days passed before our enthusiasm for sightseeing began to wane, our attention gradually returning to the completion of numerous minor repairs, including re-stitching almost every individual sail, in order to prepare us for our second leg, planned to take us east of Madeira and on to Las Palmas, some 600 miles to the south.

On the day of departure the winds were fair and the sun shone fiercely, enabling us to bask in fine weather for the first time since we had set off from Falmouth – which seemed a lifetime ago. In fine and more predictable weather, we were able to make good the rhumb-line courses plotted and for the first time plot accurate celestial observations, on a relatively stable chart table. Using the Marc St Hilaire method with altitude readings obtained from my ancient vernier sextant, I was able to achieve regular sights of the sun in the mornings and determine our longitude, run up to a latitude fix every noon. I also took the opportunity on clear nights and even on the occasional morning to brush up on my stellar observations, taking stars at twilight, fully aware that I would need to perfect such a method of determining our position, once we started to cross the ocean in the not-too-distant future. Lyn's wedding present to me had been a Rolex Oyster wristwatch and it was with this timepiece that I kept an accurate record of the time, checked against the daily time signal of the World Service from the BBC, the station's booming tones clearly audible from the large single-sideband valve radio fitted above the chart table.

Anne was able to stand her watches now and the twins, assisted by their teddies and an array of other puppets, were able to take lessons from Lyn and myself on how to keep the sails full and steer a course by compass, the strengthening sun slowly tanning our bodies to a rich golden hue. Dolphins and marlin splashed around us in the sparkling waters and the bright sun, shining day after glorious day, made it a joy to be alive. We made doughy bread and cakes in the none-too-hot oven, developed our sailing techniques and practised seamanship skills, sailing steadily southwards in calm seas that yachtsmen dream about. *Lucette* logged a day's run of over 170 miles on the third day out, dispelling any thoughts that she might always be something of a slouch.

On 23 February a German freighter called the *Pentelikon* passed us close to starboard. With seamanlike courtesy she raised her West German ensign and dipped it in a traditional salute as she drew abeam, sounding three loud blasts on her whistle. The twins fairly leapt with excitement as she forged her way past, and the rest of us lined the decks waving enthusiastically. Here was certain evidence that merchant ships had human beings aboard them after all. Neil was sufficiently impressed to remark that he thought sailors must have been very brave on both sides during the war, a salutary lesson to all those of my own generation still scarred by the after-effects of the last world war. Douglas looked on enviously; finally turning to me he said one day he too would go to sea in a ship like that. Slapping him on the back, I felt prouder than ever to be my son's father. I could not have been happier, not that he wanted to go to sea but that at last he knew that he wanted to do something at all. It was for this very reason that I had brought him on this adventure in the first place.

As the evening drew near I rigged the cockpit table for the first time and we ate tea outside on deck, enjoying the spectacular magic of a golden sunset cabaret. The sun's incandescent glow radiated upwards into the western sky, tingeing the celestial quadrant overhead in a thick bar of gold which mingled upwards with orange, red and green in a sequence of constantly shifting and merging patterns. We sat in silence and enjoyed the flowing colours, mixing into each other like suspended liquid, creating multifarious shapes and radiant, ever-changing hues in a spectacular montage that gradually yielded to the encroaching night sky. Dusk brought with it a glorious tapestry of stars and planets, curiously intensifying the darkness before they in turn dimmed into the background, heralding the arrival of the star of the night's show, the glittering and stupendous moon. Appearing inordinately large, its full and luminous globe appeared on cue, first materialising as a streaky reddened-brown disc then climbing quickly above the horizon and into the clear of the night, changing through green to blue then silver, before lighting up the darkness as if it were day. The wind had dropped and we lay completely becalmed, the sails hanging limp and lifeless as we drifted in stillness, and complete silence amongst dancing moonbeams reflecting from the surface of the sea, now flat like a millpond. As I stood the midnight watch, *Lucette*'s image loomed back at me from the surface of the gently undulating ocean, even the stars reflected back amongst a mosaic of irregular phosphorescent flashes. Quietly a school of sailfish, seldom seen in these latitudes, broke the surface of the still water with their sword-like bills and flexed their dorsal sails amid showers of green luminescence, sharing and indeed completing the wonder of the night. Eagerly I called the others up on deck, and the sheer beauty of our surroundings held us spellbound for hours. Awestruck by so much surreal yet natural beauty, we bathed in the ethereal quality of human existence in such absolute peace. It was hard to believe that the mass of still and quiet water beneath us was the exact same water that had produced those super-waves in the Bay of Biscay, only a few weeks before.

Gradually the weather grew warmer as we wafted south past the latitude of Gibraltar and on to the tropic of Cancer. It was still cool enough to require heavy coats on the night watches, though, and even during the day woollen pullovers were never far from hand. As we approached the African shipping lanes converging on Las Palmas, shipping became more numerous and our navigation lights shone brightly through the clear bright nights.

On 1 March we spotted the mountain peaks of the Canary Islands, and finally dropped anchor in the busy harbour of Las Palmas at eleven o'clock that same night, to await the arrival of *Bonnie*. *Lucette* seemed a veritable minnow surrounded by flotillas of large clondykes and Japanese stern-trawlers, whose powerful deck lights merged into the gleam of the city illuminations shining brightly from the shore behind them. The many smells combined disenchantingly with that of a thick layer of heavy black oil on the surface of the water, a stark reminder that we were back in civilisation once more.

We met many other yachtsmen seeking refuge in the Club Nautico anchorage, waiting for the trade winds to stabilise before starting out on the Atlantic crossing. We waited with them, enjoying the Spanish culture in one of the busiest ports in the world. Amongst the comings and goings in the maritime traffic, I saw many of the ships I had known when I was at sea after the war. They stopped to refuel or take on broken stowage cargoes in passing. Las Palmas had become not only a way port but a major marine gas station located on an ocean crossroads, thronging with people of many international backgrounds, working or vacationing amongst the native Spanish population. We made numerous friends, typically intense and emotionally rewarding, and quite usual in the seafarer's way of life. We were indulged in tours of the island and many excursions to ancient and historic museums, including the cathedral, whose foundations had been lain down as early as 1478, and a house visited by Christopher Columbus in 1492. One day we hired a taxi and took off into the mountains, where we toured vast banana plantations and tomato farms as well as fields of cacti being harvested for their food dyes. Douglas experienced his first attempt at picking prickly pears, only to discover the right way to pick them after his hands had been repeatedly spiked by the sharp needle thorns protecting the soft fruit. Whilst driving through the rich green valleys, blooming with red blazes of wild geraniums and many other plants we could only grow indoors back home in England, we were treated to a view inside the deep extinct crater marking Gran Canaria's summit. Towards nightfall, we stopped to help a farmer plough a field of potatoes behind two oxen with a wooden plough, our reward being a bag of potatoes to take back to the boat with us.

Later that same week we sailed around the coast to Mas Palomas, a deserted beach to the south of the island fringed by large white sand dunes, where we swam amongst huge basking sharks, some of which were almost as long as the *Lucette* herself. For mere plankton eaters they certainly scared the living daylights out of us, approaching out of the misty water with wide gaping mouths. They showed no fear or malice but exhibited a clear intent and certainty in their movement that we dared not impede or excite, for contact with one swish of their mighty tails would have broken our backs in the same instant.

Upon our return the next day we were delighted to find a new arrival had anchored in the harbour: *Bonnie* and her Icelandic crew had made it at last. The reunion was as joyful as any greeting of long-lost friends can be and we swapped tales of adventure long into the night. They had been caught in the same Biscay storm as us. It forced them to put in at Gibraltar, from where they had proceeded to Morocco, eventually finding work aboard the Scientology flagship *Apollo*. There they had saved enough money for fuel to get them to Las Palmas. For us the main source of power was the wind, which was free; *Bonnie* on the other hand had an extremely thirsty, long-stroke diesel engine that had to be kept running with a continuous supply of expensive fuel.

The spirit of adventure seemed to be contagious, for later in the week we received a letter from Lyn's sisters Edna and Mary, informing us that they were flying out to Las Palmas in order to bid us a last farewell. On the afternoon of their arrival, Lyn went to the nearby airport to meet her sisters and guide them safely to our anchorage, whence I teased our worn-out Zodiac to the old stone jetty to pick them up. Worn smooth by the constant action of wind and sea over the years, the steps were slimy and slippery underfoot. The ladies stood dutifully, hanging onto the rusted mooring rings affixed into the stonework just above their shoulders, waiting patiently for me to get alongside. During the embarkation and completely out of the blue we were swamped by a rogue swell. Instinctively I managed to hang on but Lyn, Mary and Edna were dumped unceremoniously into the sea. Fully dressed in their best shore-going clothes, they all three floundered in the oily waters, before eager hands hauled them to safety. We set about laughing and didn't stop for days.

From that moment onwards we spent a super few days together. A definite shift in perspective had occurred in our relationship with Lyn's sisters. What had hitherto been merely family familiarity changed into a deep and understanding friendship borne out of respect, which arose from the mutual recognition of our accomplishment in getting this far. Edna, who had been dead set against our trip from the start, enjoyed herself the most of all, declaring between successive bottles of banana liquor that at last she could see why we had embarked on such an adventure. This accolade meant a great deal to Lyn and me, and on the day they departed Edna placed a thick brown envelope in my hand. 'Towards a new dinghy,' she winked with an approving smile. I had always regarded Edna as Lyn's wisest and closest sister, for she had always supported us through our efforts at Meadows Farm and hadn't stopped now. This gift, together with our chance meeting with the Icelanders, would eventually save all of our lives, in the far-off days to come. Lyn and I decided that the new dinghy when procured would be called *Ednamair*, after Edna and Mary.

It was late March before the trade winds had moved sufficiently northwards to enable a trip across the Atlantic to be undertaken. Yachts were beginning to leave the anchorage daily and my own mind, too, was never far away from mulling over the plans and procedures necessary for such a long passage. Food would be limited and water would have to be rationed, with no fresh water allowed for washing or cooking. We loaded victuals sufficient only for passage to Gomera, where we intended to provision *Lucette* with the balance of food and water required for the long Atlantic trip. This was not only the most cost-effective option, it was two days closer to our distant transatlantic destination and would also allow us time to explore the island.

We prepared to depart from Las Palmas with heavy hearts, saying goodbye to the many cherished routines that had become part of our day-to-day lives. Having suffered the emotional trauma of saying too many goodbyes when leaving both Falmouth and Lisbon, we suffered as one the lonely emptiness in our hearts which we had come to dread in the days leading up to departure. We knew that we would have to face similar emotional crises each and every time we set sail, and despite the easy promises of writing letters or of a distant reunion some day, all we were left with was a string of pleasant and ever-dimming memories. We wished our friends goodbye with a hearty pumping of hands and last-minute hugs, accompanied by un-restrainable tears, in the full knowledge that we would be unlikely to see them again.

Slipping the mooring buoy and exiting the port was executed like a well-practised military procedure. My able crew had all four sails hoisted and trimmed in double-quick time as we sailed in the wake of Columbus towards the Old Man of Tenerife, bucketing along in a fresh northerly gale which created steep short swells and made sailing extremely uncomfortable. *Lucette* began to take water again and seasickness beset the entire crew for a second time. I was aware that if the low-pressure system in which we were sailing moved to the east, causing the wind to back into the west, we would be caught in the lee of Tenerife or Gomera and have to beat against it. Conversely, if the cyclone's route caused the wind to veer to the east then we would be trapped, with the Gran Canaria coast dangerously close to leeward. Grimly I recalled the advice given to sailors torpedoed in this area during the war, stating that it was easier to sail across the ocean to the Indies than to attempt the beat back to Africa or the Canaries. Our only escape route if we overshot our destination would be to continue right out into the Atlantic. The northeast trade winds, normally the sailor's ally, would effectively block our return and force us to make our next stop in Barbados, over 2,000 miles to the west. As we were insufficiently provisioned for such a long trip, our only hope was to hope against probability that the wind would stay as it was, until we reached our intended landfall on Gomera, still some two days away.

Later in the afternoon watch, with Anne at the helm, *Lucette*'s speed began to increase markedly, provoking me to get Douglas up on deck to help reef the sails. *Lucette* thundered along at well over 10 knots, vibrating strongly as she pounded through the waves, her wooden decks shuddering violently under our feet. The wind's strength continued to increase, contrary to the information broadcast on the weather forecast, and unless we reduced the excessive leeway we were making we risked entrapment against the lee shore of Gran Canaria. My brain worked overtime, trying to decide what to do and exactly how it must be done, when an event occurred that crystallised matters absolutely. *Lucette*, heeled down to her gunwales and groaning under the press of a greatly reduced sail plan, began to accelerate markedly. The main boom, manufactured from a solid piece of six-inch-diameter Douglas-fir timber, began bending like a bow under the press of the wind, which screamed through the rigging in powerful and ever more prolonged gusts. Without warning we hit a combination of swell and sea that lifted *Lucette* bodily out of the water, whence unbelievably she started to plane across the waves, her speed rising alarmingly as the speed log hit first 15 and then 20 knots. The steering became light and unresponsive, and the bow-wave started to accumulate excessively under the bowsprit net, as we jetted through the water at a speed in excess of our waterline length.

Had the hull been designed with a hard chine or chamfered hull, *Lucette* would have been able to ride over the bow-wave like a speedboat, but our hull was constructed with a deep long keel, designed for straight-line stability when cruising through the large waves of the ocean. As the rapidly rising bow-wave ascended to the height of the deck *Lucette* would simply sail beneath it, sinking within a few seconds at best, literally driving herself under the sea and taking us all down with her. *Lucette* began trimming visibly by the head in mind-numbing confirmation that my suspicions were about to be realised. With only seconds to spare, I wrenched the heavy knife from its sheath under the chart-table shelf and ducking under the main boom, which was now bellied out like a banana, I hacked through the mainsail halyard with two well-placed blows. The rope parted with a ripping crack and in the next instant the pressurised belly of the mainsail tore the luff from its track and carried the mass of white Dacron out over the side. With the main power source gone, *Lucette* slumped into the water, swamping fore and aft as her speed dropped to a crawl. Realising the danger was over, Anne whooped out loud, in a combination of euphoric delight and grateful relief, acutely aware of how narrow our escape had been. As for Gomera, enough was enough – and as we hauled the remnants of the mainsail back on board, I gave Anne a new course to steer, straight back to the safety of Las Palmas. The Atlantic would have to wait for another day.

We were welcomed back amid droll greetings and wry grins, by the group of friends we had been so painfully parted from the previous day. On our second attempt at departure, a week later, we took on board extra crew in the form of two young American graduates, Barbara and Steve, who were seeking to hitch a lift across the Atlantic. As far back as Meadows Farm, Lyn and I had decided that where possible we would carry students from different countries and walks of life, to give our own family a diversion from boring old Mum and Dad. Our departure the second time around had the added bonus of a fee, paid by the Stern Newspaper Group, for permitting them to take pictures of us leaving under full sail.

Unbelievably, not long after our departure the same northerly winds sprung up again, almost as if they had been waiting to complete their unfinished business. Stephen took on a green tinge as he succumbed to seasickness and whilst we successfully rounded the southern point of Los Cristianos, making good progress under the lee of the mountains of Tenerife, the strong northerly gales severely impeded our progress, preventing us from closing the gap with our intended destination of San Sebastian. On the second night out the wind veered to the northeast, allowing us to tack slowly towards the coast. We were only ten miles off Gomera when, during a prolonged gust, the port stay of the bowsprit sheared its securing bolt with a sickening crack, causing the number one jib to rip out its leech, which made the sail totally unusable and more critically forced us to head another point to the south. This was a crucial blow, for it set us on a course that would take us clear of the island altogether. We hove to until daylight in order to effect repairs but no sooner had I finished tightening a new bolt in place than, in defiance of all logic, the wind backed to the north and increased with redoubled fury. *Lucette* began taking water again, the sloshing waves underfoot in the saloon rekindling dark memories of our recent passage through the Bay of Biscay. We took turns pumping the bilges dry, using the manual pump I had repaired in Las Palmas. The routine of this familiar task helped me settle my nerves, and as the repetitive pumping action became automatic I realised it would soon be time to abandon plans for Gomera altogether. The following day was 30 March, and with sea anchors streamed we were driven south again under bare poles, losing all the ground we had made the previous night. I had to admit defeat a second time, but on this occasion we were fully provisioned and the gale-force winds, whilst robbing us of the opportunity to make our landfall at Gomera, whisked us into the waiting trade winds and dispatched us on our way with a quick-fire start into the mighty Atlantic. I had been told that Gomera was a beautiful island; alas, I was never to find out!

The blustery northerly winds and unsettled skies soon gave way to the fluffy clouds and near-constant sea states epitomising the Atlantic trade winds, the sun shining warmly after the storm. We were set on a great circle track that would take us to the northern limits of the trade-wind belt, so called because that same wind had been exploited by mariners in the great days of sail as a reliable and near-constant source of power to cross the great oceans. Blowing all day and most of the night from the same direction at about force four, the dependability of the trade winds became the principal routing factor used by the sailing ships of yesteryear, as they ventured to new frontiers in the name of commerce. Sailing in their wake, *Lucette*'s lively action soon settled to an easy roll; with the wind behind her, life became infinitely more tolerable.

As day succeeded day, the finer weather and steady breezes drove us on through the clear blue waters, eating up the miles at a steady pace. Only Stephen continued to languish on deck in undiminished misery, quite unable to shake off his devastating sickness. Neil and Sandy took over the four-to-six and six-to-eight dogwatches in the afternoon and Barbara joined in the twins' puppet games, even turning her hand to teaching them some extra-curricular reading and writing, during her time off watch. Douglas took to his trigonometry books in earnest and under my rather more brusque tutelage came to grips with chart work and the fundamentals of celestial navigation.

The weather steadily improved as the trade winds lightened, and *Lucette* ran westwards at something less than 100 miles a day. In the mornings, after fixing our latitude and longitude by observing stars in the morning twilight, often with perfect crosses, we made close inspection of the decks and scuppers in order to locate any flying fish that had landed on deck during the night, taking extra care to extract the ones that had wriggled themselves into inaccessible corners. Fried in oatmeal and butter, they made a delicious breakfast and on occasion the haul would be sizable, with some of the catch measuring over a foot in length. When the haul was large our fare after flying fish for breakfast would be flying fish for lunch. Not wishing to be wasteful, we would then have flying fish for tea and flying fish thereafter until they were all gone. After several days of hauling in this bounty it was Douglas who, vocalising the wishes of us all, stated his sincere hope that they would be a little more careful in future; that way at least we would be able to restore some variety to our diets with a clear conscience.

Far out in the placid ocean, we encountered huge carpets of brown and orange kelp growing on the surface, reminding us of crop fields in the countryside back home. *Lucette* gently carved her way through them, leaving a watery track behind her. Barbara discovered a way of cooking carrot cake of the non-doughy sort by first baking the ingredients in a pan before finishing the loaves off in the paraffin oven, which was a real coup as from then on we were treated to fresh baking and the aromatic fragrance of cinnamon wafting through the cabins on a daily basis. On 12 April we celebrated the approach of our halfway point by opening our last can of smoked ham, brought with us from England.

Stephen had been unable to stand a watch thus far into the trip. Catching my mood of impatience, Lyn finally challenged him that this day was to be a day of resurrection or burial at sea for him, maintaining that God helps those who help themselves. Later that afternoon, as we passed into the second half of our ocean crossing, the trade winds freshened and we picked up speed, enabling me to rig trolling lines astern. With the aid of a spinner made from the foil tops of our empty food cans, we caught several large dorado and bonito, which Stephen cooked in olive oil topped with sliced tomato. A better meal could not have been had, even in the best of the better restaurants, anywhere in the world! We all worked as a team after that, sharing the galley chores as well as standing watches at the wheel. We stopped in periods when the boat was becalmed in order to swim and enjoy the deep blue waters that surrounded us. Sailing under gull-winged genoas into beautiful sunsets and dazzling mosaics of shimmering moonbeams, the days ran into weeks and weeks merged into a timeless blur. In our periods off watch, we lay along the decks in listless relaxation, listening to the gurgle of the water as it skimmed the outside of the hull. The long twisting log line, etched in silver by day and in a brilliant phosphorescent green by night, trailed out behind us, faithfully recording every mile as it was completed.

We enjoyed long discussions with the children, Barbara and on occasion even Steve, who had finally beaten his seasickness into submission. We debated long into the warm tropical nights as we touched on every subject under the sun and even some that were not. I was frankly surprised that my kids could hold such strong and informed opinions at such young ages, as talk switched from adventures we had already had to the adventures we were planning, and to what we might do at our journey's end. At last I was beginning to share in my children's lives and more importantly I was enjoying it too. Barbara read the stories of Winnie the Pooh to Neil and Sandy – and to an orderly line of puppets – as the twins enjoyed being little kids again. Their imaginations worked overtime, inventing a fantasy island called Puppet Land for which they drafted several maps, each one different, which mysteriously appeared on the chart table at various times throughout the voyage together with course alterations and lists of harbour facilities. I enjoyed playing along with them, and one night, as we lay quietly in bed, Lyn and I took great pleasure in eavesdropping on one of their off-watch conversations, listening intently as Neil and Sandy, now regularly sleeping up on deck, discussed 'abandon ship' procedures. In the event of such a catastrophe, Neil elected that he would ensure the safety of the teddy bears provided Sandy promised to rescue the others. Their agreement was sealed by a childhood oath. 'A list will be drawn up and their names are to be ticked off as they cross the rail,' asserted Neil in a confident tone, banging his fist on the deck above us. My mind drifted back to the *Sagaing* for a fleeting moment. 'God forbid that they should ever endure the harsh realities and anguish of abandoning any ship large or small,' I whispered in Lyn's ear as I rolled towards her and held her in my arms, banishing those memories to the back of my mind once more, not wishing to lose the feeling that I was getting to know my family as individuals, instead of as a collective unit, as I revelled in the rewards of my corporeal investment.

In the latter phases of the crossing we began to tire of the rationing, the lack of fresh vegetables and fruit, and the taste of stale water, compounded by the lack of variety in our stores. Our lives became more mundane than easy and the routine became increasingly tedious, as day by day we inched our way across the chart, slowly closing with our destination. It was a welcome intrusion indeed when Neil shouted from his watch position in the cockpit, hailing the loom of Barbados rising into view over the starboard bow. It was the end of the thirty-second day out from Las Palmas. It had taken us the same amount of time to cross the Atlantic as it had taken Columbus, almost 500 years before us – but, unlike him, at least we knew what we would find when our long voyage finally came to an end.

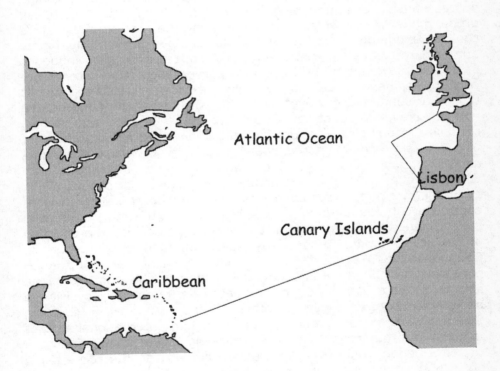

CHAPTER 3

The Windward Islands

The following morning, our landfall stood out starkly against the distant horizon, and the low hills, initially nothing more than dark purple silhouettes, slowly transformed into a blue–green patchwork, gradually revealing more detail as we edged closer to the beckoning shores of Barbados. Rounding the most southerly point, we finally dropped anchor in a wide, open bay forming the roads to the island's capital, Bridgetown. In the days following our arrival, the happy atmosphere of this sun-drenched island exerted its healing influence on the stern monotony of our long ocean passage. The waters were crystal clear beneath us and we could see *Lucette*'s anchor, dug into the white sandy bottom over 40 feet down. Across the harbour, the unmistakeable bouquet of Etta's baking delighted our senses, revealing to our pleasant surprise that *Bonnie* had arrived ahead of us and was already anchored awaiting our arrival. We spent the next couple of days reacquainting ourselves with the Icelanders, with whom we explored this time-trapped, ex-colonial sugar port.

Bridgetown had always been the island's chief port and commercial centre since its foundation in the early seventeenth century, exporting vast tonnages of brown sugar, as well as being home to the production of the world-famous 'Mount Gay' rum. Our favourite landmark in Bridgetown was Trafalgar Square, with its dominant statue of Admiral Lord Nelson, though we also enjoyed visiting the historic Careenage ship repair yard as well. On cloudy days, we found time to visit the eighteenth-century Anglican cathedral and the nearby Garrison Savannah, a former parade ground hosting international cricket matches and other sports events. Following independence from the United Kingdom, only five years before our arrival, the cornerstone policy of the government had been to develop the island's considerable potential for tourism, and they had already taken the first tentative steps to redevelop the port, catering specifically for large ocean liners and thereby reinforcing Barbados's position as economic king pin in the south Caribbean. The island's lofty palms and soft sandy beaches had just enough of the trappings of civilisation, without being ostentatious, to make a prolonged visit comfortable whilst still providing the illusion of escape. We all enjoyed the wide silver beaches, lined with coconut palms, as well as the crystal-clear waters, under which the seabed and marine life were clearly visible. The entire population seemed of a cheerful disposition, frequently stopping us in the street and showing genuine concern for our wellbeing, and often asking us directly if we were enjoying our stay on their island.

The sunlit days passed swiftly as the children swam, snorkelled and explored in what for them had become an adventure without end. The Icelanders procured a Sunfish sailing dinghy and Douglas and the twins quickly transferred their new-found sailing skills to the principles of small-boat handling, teaching the young Icelanders how to tack and gybe as well as how to re-float after a capsize or three. The tender to *Bonnie* had a powerful outboard, which provided more than sufficient power to pull our water skis through the water, and it wasn't long before every last one of us had experienced the thrill of skimming across the bay's quiet waters at great speed. Etta, a past champion, proved she had forgotten little, by demonstrating how to ski on bare feet and perform complex manoeuvres with ease.

Barbara and Steve finally bade us farewell. Being pressed for time, they both had to return home to America. Soft starlit nights framed the dim lights of Bridgetown, with the more distant glare of the burning sugar-cane fields flaring beyond the night horizon in a dramatic backdrop. Once burnt off by the plantation owners, the cane fields would be ready for the teams of machete-wielding cane cutters to start work with the dawn. The night temperatures became so mild that even Lyn and I forsook the stuffy heat of the cabin and moved up on deck to sleep at night, for we were now only 13 degrees north of the equator.

After visiting a sugar factory situated in the heartlands of the cane fields, we soon discovered why heaps of sand gathered at the bottom of our teacups every time we drank tea. The refining process was indeed a crude one, producing only untreated brown sugar, without extracting particles of sand and earth brought in with the cane from the fields. The sugar was in effect a mere by-product of the rum production industry. Amazing though it seemed, the white sugar obtainable in the island townships had first been to England for refining before being shipped all the way back, eventually to find its way onto the shelves of the local shops.

Anne and Douglas, together with three of the older members of *Bonnie*'s crew, set off backpacking around the island. Sleeping in the open fields at night, they trekked from village to village, living amongst the Barbadian people, who we found to be the most pleasant in the entire Caribbean. By the time Douglas returned from his adventures inland, he was suffering from the effects of being virtually eaten alive by teams of fire ants, and his feet were scarred, blistered and sore after night-time attacks by land crabs. On the plus side, he had learned how to shin a coconut palm and how to knock back a glass of the velvety smooth Mount Gay rum in a single gulp. Both dubious qualifications, maybe, but his life was filled with new experiences in which he positively revelled. The twins had taken to swimming ashore, even as far as the Bridgetown yacht club over a mile away, and I was proud of their rapidly gaining confidence as they talked with the people they met. They too were at last making this trip their own.

It was the middle of May before the gentle tugs of more distant islands began to grip at our minds. As the children enjoyed each others' company a great deal, Siggi and I decided to sail not only in convoy but also, for the sake of variety, with an exchange of crews. Leaving Barbados, we headed west, bound for Port Elizabeth on the western coast of Bequia, a small island just 120 miles to the west, due south of St Vincent in the Grenadines. The entire leg was less than a 24-hour sail, and our destination turned out to be a dazzling gem in a bejewelled sea.

With a fair wind, we made rapid progress through the night, passing south of St Vincent and crossing on a southerly course through the inter-island channel known as Great Head. Daybreak saw us standing-to in company with the *Bonnie*, waiting for daylight before we dared enter the narrow channels, leading into Admiralty Bay itself. I put Douglas on watch as I considered he was the only one on board, apart from myself, with the necessary skills to keep our boat stern-on to the confused and tumbling overfalls which rose steeply to form a heavy chop in the lively following sea. I had just got into bed for an hour's rest, when I heard an almighty crash on deck followed by a startled 'Bloody typical,' rapidly followed by a loud bellow of alarm. 'Look out below ...' Douglas's voice was cut off mid-sentence by the muffled sound of gushing water. A wave, landing on the stern and pooping *Lucette*, had filled the cockpit and then flooded the engine room. By virtue of the angle of heel, the swirling water landed on our bed, unceremoniously flushing first Lyn, then me, out of our bed and onto the floor. I was literally shaking with fury as I sprang up to the deck.

'I couldn't stop it,' yelled Douglas, his statement stifled mid-stream as I first shoulder-barged and then pushed him away in a fit of uncontrollable anger. His reaction was swift. 'Take the bloody wheel yourself,' he growled, leaving the cockpit with a mighty leap over the coaming and disappearing forward. Had I stopped to think for a moment I would have realised I was being extremely unfair to him. I should have realised that he would not have purposely let such a wave come on board – and yet accidents arising from just such lapses of concentration, were a danger to us all. Not knowing what to say, but realising that the least now said the better, I took the wheel until we were safely inside the bay, trying my best to be friendly. Douglas showed no reciprocity, however, refusing to look me in the eye as he let go the anchor, close to the point where *Bonnie* was lying. Downhearted and sad, I cursed my arrogance for not knowing how to say I was sorry.

The time we spent in these islands was truly glorious, and remained one of Lyn's favourite memories. The bay in which we had anchored was shaped out of the huge crater of an extinct volcano. Long expanses of wide crescent-shaped beaches with beautiful palm-fringed hillsides girdled the dark blue waters of the anchorage. English sailing ships, from chapters in history long since closed, had sought the bay's refuge in adverse weather. Others had also used the quiet harbour to beach their vessels in order to clear the growth of barnacles and weed accumulated below their waterlines. This practice, known as careening, was completed by building a fire beneath the beached hull, which if not carefully monitored could set fire to and destroy a wooden ship, effectively marooning her crew in paradise until rescue chanced by in the form of a passing vessel. History records that many a blind eye was turned, when the fires were over-stoked in order to ensure some weary crew deliverance from a doomed mission or overzealous captain.

We picnicked on the shore amongst the ghosts of our forebears, sunbathing amid the wavering coconut palms bordering the tropical rainforest, where we drank rum punch from a large bowl that never seemed to get empty. At night, we slept on the decks and recounted experiences and adventures long into the early hours. In the days that followed, we played baseball on the beach amongst the tall breadfruit and lush green mango trees, taking on passers-by to make up the teams. One such team member was a young lady named DeeDee, a vacationing air hostess who somehow ended up aboard the *Bonnie* as part of her crew. The late afternoons were spent sitting around *Bonnie*'s stern table under the shade of her large white awning, drinking coffee laced with copious amounts of rum whilst the children swam in the cool blue waters of the lagoon. Pleasant evenings were spent at the Whaleboners pub, where the garden arches were fashioned from the huge jawbones of humpback whales.

Time flew by and it wasn't long before we felt the collective urge to move on again, driven not only by the need to pace our economic resources but also by the thirst for new adventure and experiences. The urge was contagious, and a feeling of impatience seemed to prevail once we had completed our excursions ashore. As we prepared to leave this paradise, Siggi approached me with an offer I could not refuse. He and Etta had discussed and both now insisted that, as they had two ten-man life rafts on board *Bonnie*, which was more than they needed for themselves, we were to take their spare one as a gift. He explained that they did not wish to hear of a disaster in the future that could have been averted by something they already had more of than they needed. On the same scale as Edna's selfless gift of the dinghy fund back in Las Palmas, Siggi had gifted us an expensive piece of equipment, which would turn out to be pivotal to our survival in the distant days ahead. Eternally grateful for his generosity, Douglas and I lashed the green canvas valise onto the coach roof forward of the saloon skylight, feeling it was far better to have it and not need it, than to need it and not have it!

Heading north, we enjoyed light winds and cruised the 160 miles from Bequia at a leisurely pace. Coasting past the Windward Islands of St Vincent, St Lucia and Martinique to the east, we eventually made landfall on the beautiful island of Dominica, the occasional sinister triangular fin indicating the presence of sharks as we motored into the northern anchorage of Portsmouth. Dominica was most certainly one of the most beautiful of all the West Indian islands, not only for its scenic terrain but also for the wealth of flora in the rich volcanic soil. Our disappointment hitherto at the scarcity of fruit was reversed in these ideal citrus-growing conditions. In Barbados, we had been astonished to discover some of the fruit more expensive than it was in England. Here in Dominica there was an abundance of everything growing, in plantations large and small, bordering the long black volcanic beaches. Ramshackle smallholdings lay cheek by jowl with well-run enterprises operated by international conglomerates. Bananas, pineapples, mangoes, grapefruits and limes grew in scattered profusion. Further inland, we discovered fields of coconuts, cocoa, cinnamon and vanilla beans. Indeed the list seemed endless, and if you could think of a tropical fruit, spice or vegetable it seemed to be growing here amid the virgin tracts of primeval rainforest. Massive trunks of ancient mahogany trees towered upwards, into the dense canopy together with kapok, white cedar and many other rare woods. Being of volcanic origins, pumice stone was also being quarried and exported.

Paradoxically, Dominica, the most able to satisfy the tourists' idea of lush Caribbean beauty, lay relatively neglected, with a very poor standard of living. On our first trip ashore we acquiesced to a request from the twins to visit the local cinema, where we watched the James Bond film *Thunderball*. The cinema was a rickety wooden shed, furnished with wooden pews, which doubled as the church as well as the local courthouse. Sitting at the back in order to remain inconspicuous, we soon discovered that the back was in fact the place to be. Anyone who was anyone sat at the back, and the last three rows were packed. We were prodded and poked throughout the film, whilst the locals swapped seats to stroke Anne's long soft hair, to feel our white skins or simply to get a better look at us. It soon became clear that we had become the main attraction, with the film relegated to a mere sideshow. I have no doubt that our lives were not in danger, but the experience became more and more unnerving as the film progressed, with rapturous applause whenever a black actor appeared and a steady flood of racist jibes levelled with escalating menace in our direction. We left the cinema early and raced back to the anchorage, feeling like escaping refugees, before the small crowd that had followed us outside grew any larger or more menacing.

More than ninety per cent of the inhabitants of Dominica were the descendants of slaves brought from Africa in the eighteenth century, but a small number of the indigenous Carib people still survived in a reservation on the eastern side of the northern foothills. Having heard so much about them both here and in Bequia, our curiosity was sufficiently aroused to attempt a visit. Christopher Columbus, having sighted and named Dominica in the fifteenth century, found the Caribs too powerful and ferocious for colonisation. In the modern world, they represented one of the last remnants of a native tribe whose origins remained lost in the mists of time.

Beyond the immediate outskirts of the township of Portsmouth the terrain was mountainous and wild, with several peaks rising in height to more than 4,000 feet. There were very few metalled roads, making travel both slow and dangerous. Early the next morning we joined forces with the crew of the *Bonnie*, hired a brightly patterned canvas-topped Bedford mami-wagon fitted with rows of wooden bench seats, and set off on the 30-mile journey to the eastern seaboard, where the Indian reservation was located high in the foothills of the interior, overlooking the Atlantic Ocean. The reservation consisted of widely scattered huts in varying stages of disrepair, with a fair number well beyond any sort of repair at all. There seemed to be no central village as such, just a spread-eagled collection of homesteads on either side of the road as it wended its way up the mountainside. Typically, a group of interested sightseers, consisting mainly of young children, gathered to meet us. Some ran behind us clutching the sides of our wagon from the moment we entered the reservation, whilst others gathered round only once we had drawn to a halt, all eager to catch their first ever glimpse of white-skinned strangers. The scantily clad youngsters directed us to the chief's wooden roundhouse, and though he was not there himself, his mother met us with a warm welcome. Despite her advancing years, she was a lady in fine fettle and she took great pleasure in showing us a collection of remarkably intricate baskets, woven by her people. To our surprise, when we asked how much they cost she became affronted, stating that they were not for sale.

On our return along the steep mountain paths back to the waiting truck, we bumped into the chief himself. He rapidly dispelled any stereotype images we may have fostered, for he appeared wearing a T-shirt and knee-length shorts topped with a brightly coloured baseball cap, and he sported a king-sized ghetto blaster on his shoulder. The Chief of the Caribs spoke to us at some length, without inhibition and with certain rancour, about the history of his tribe. He told us of the annihilation of his people throughout the Caribbean by the Spanish and the subsequent enslavement first by the French and then by the British until those remaining were transported from the neighbouring islands and forcibly settled on these less fertile slopes in Dominica. Through an interpreter, he explained that his council was making an application to the Colonial Administration, to grant him the lands to the west that were more fertile and better protected. I was in the middle of wishing him luck when he stepped up to Douglas and gripped his arm. Admiring his well-built muscular form, he addressed him as 'a mulatto bastard'. His embarrassed interpreter interjected swiftly, explaining how the chief thought him well developed, considering his condition! The chief then asked if we could pass our secret on to him, as they had many such mulatto bastards on their reservation, who unlike young Dougie were sickly and inevitably died young.

The short twilight brought the tropical darkness upon us even before we had returned to find *Bonnie* and *Lucette* lying snugly where we had left them. They were swinging to their anchors in the quiet bay, together with a new arrival in the form of large white English freighter called the *Geest Bay*. The ship had stopped to pick up a consignment of bananas, to be ferried out from the shore aboard lighters. Lyn and I smiled again upon hearing Douglas mutter that he wasn't really a bastard, as he and the older boys pushed the dinghies back down the smooth black beaches into the quiet waters of the Caribbean night.

The next day the town of Portsmouth roused from its usual lethargy to a convoy of trucks roaring in from the hills, laden down with stems of bananas. In gridlocked mayhem they were coaxed and manoeuvred into lines and unloaded into a gloomy warehouse, in readiness to load aboard the waiting *Geest Bay*, now anchored close inshore. It was getting late in the day by the time the banana ship started loading operations through large cargo doors in the ship's side. The *Geest Bay* towered above the flotilla of barges that attended her, forming a near-unbroken chain of traffic from the depot ashore. Some of the barges were tied several layers deep from the ship's side, awaiting their allocated slot, to move into position beneath the cargo doors and unload.

Aboard *Bonnie*'s motor launch we spent the morning exploring the forest alongside the Indian River and collected all manner of coconuts and fruits. On our return we approached the ship, to see if we could get aboard and watch the loading in progress. The 8,000-ton *Geest Bay*, lights blazing in the approaching twilight, was a hive of activity as we clambered the sturdy aluminium gangway up onto the broad expanses of her steel deck. Peering down into the cavernous holds, we could see the green stems of bananas being carefully stowed, such that they would ripen over the eight-day journey back to the United Kingdom. I marvelled at the thought that this vessel made a day's run in excess of 450 miles. And we were intrigued to think that some of these bananas were destined to find their way onto the local market stalls back in our home town of Leek in middle England. Having been shown around the vessel by her scrupulously polite officers, we said our goodbyes to the *Geest Bay* and departed. We were already halfway through our return trip back towards the *Lucette*, when we collided with the first of the submerged hands of bananas which had fallen from the barges as they ferried their cargoes from shore to ship. We hauled them on board, pleased at the unexpected windfall, only to collide with a second hand followed by yet another. Surprised and excited at the sheer numbers of bananas floating in the water, we decided to return after dropping Lyn and the twins back on board, in order to collect some more. What a harvest the night yielded up. Joining forces, we used the Icelanders' faster speedboat for the pickups and our buoyant rubberised craft as a storage platform, and collected load after load, well into the late hours of the night.

On what was to be our last run, a long speeding canoe manned by angry machete-wielding natives burst upon us from out of the night. It only took a second for me to realise that they had the clear intention of boarding. Thinking on my feet, I jammed the tiller hard over and rammed the approaching canoe with my starboard quarter in a heavy broadside, which rocked them back into the night. Turning the throttle to full speed, I headed for the *Lucette*, my knees weak and my chest palpitating at the ferocity of this sudden attack. Upon my arrival alongside, I groaned as I discovered the boys had been just as busy as I had. Pile upon pile of bananas were stacked on board, to say nothing of the coconuts and other fruits heaped about the deck. *Lucette* was listing markedly under this unexpected bounty, and in hindsight I find it incredible that it took my children to explain to me what was really going on.

Douglas and Olaf retold what they had heard ashore when they had tried to collect hands of the bananas from the beach. The system was well practised and usually very successful, but we had inadvertently upset the plans of a gang of would-be looters by intercepting the carefully 'spilled' hands of bananas. They had been stowed aboard the barges in such a way that a sharp turn by the helmsman would result in the loss of several boxes, which floated ashore to be collected by waiting accomplices. Once collected, they were spirited away for onward sale within the villages of the Dominican hinterland. I now felt distinctly uneasy. Our windfall was in fact contraband, and with so much loot festooning the decks I was determined to set sail before the local mafia returned with reinforcements. Blissfully unaware that bananas ripen simultaneously and last only a few days before they are too ripe to eat, we heaved anchor and set a course into the night, bound for English Harbour in Antigua. I found myself constantly looking over my shoulder, feeling not unlike a buccaneer smuggler of yesteryear, hurriedly taking flight before a steady breeze under full sail. On reflection I daresay that the likes of Henry Morgan or Captain Blackbeard would have turned in their watery graves at the thought of anyone demeaning themselves by making off with a few hands of a bananas! In the rising sun of the following morning, we surveyed *Lucette*'s decks, loaded with stems of bananas and dozens of coconuts, together with ripening mangoes and bags of oranges, feeling for the first time that our ideas of the West Indies had been fulfilled.

By the following day, the wind had shifted, allowing us to set a course directly for Antigua. Due to our hasty departure the previous night, Douglas and Anne had remained aboard *Bonnie* and three of *Bonnie*'s crew had stayed with the *Lucette*. The morning's light airs permitted only the slowest of progress as we ghosted along past the islands of Les Saintes, until we eventually hailed the coast of Guadeloupe. True to form, the bananas suddenly started turning ripe and it became a race against time to eat them before they became rotten. Banana sandwiches, banana bread, fried bananas, banana cake, large bananas, small bananas, straight bananas or curved, it seemed that no matter how many we ate, there were always more in need of eating. It wasn't long before we were totally sick of bananas.

That evening the weather changed, bringing a freshening wind from the east, and at midnight I calculated that our speedier progress would bring us to English Harbour before the advent of daylight, leaving me no choice but to reduce sail. A few hours later, just before three o'clock in the morning, the rudderpost snapped without warning, leaving *Lucette* out of control before the wind and sea with her rudder helplessly swinging on its pintles. The billowing sails collapsed and *Lucette* turned up into the wind and stopped dead in the water. In an effort to minimise the effects of leeway I hauled the sails down and furled them untidily onto their booms, unable to avoid ripping my finger ends as the blustery wind snatched the folds of heavy Dacron out of my ineffectual grip. How I rued the loss of Douglas's strong arms and Anne's experienced hands as I racked my brains for a solution to this new dilemma. *Lucette* rolled heavily without the steadying effect of her sails, which made life aboard very uncomfortable indeed. Trawling the depths of my memory I recalled that the *Ra*, a papyrus reed vessel built for Thor Heyerdahl's expedition to cross the Atlantic, had been steered by an oar. I figured that if I could make an oar large enough then I might be able to get us under way again. Fearing an accident in the darkness, I decided to wait until daylight. Even with an experienced crew, the project would be difficult, but with my present crew of novices the task would be slow, risky and dangerous. Daybreak seemed to take forever to arrive, with everyone on board kept awake by the heavy random movements of the vessel. A glum silence descended upon us, rent with the occasional shout or curse, as one after the other of our new crew members fell victim to a slip or a knock.

When the morning finally came I was already on deck. It took over an hour to assemble a collection of items from around the vessel, which we then laid out on the deck in order to visualise some sort of end product. 'It's a pity we can't use some of those bananas,' remarked Lyn wryly, helping me reposition the two hatch covers on the deck. I managed a smile as we tied the large wooden hatch covers to both the dinghy oars and the foresail boom with a surfeit of rope lashing, to make a contraption that resembled a giant wooden spade some 10 feet in length. We secured this to the deck with multiple figure-of-eight lashings, and carefully lowered the spade end into the sea. Affixed to *Lucette*'s port quarter, the lower part was submerged beneath the water, whilst the upper part formed a lever from which the helmsman could gain sufficient purchase to steer. With the gear finally in place, the moment of truth was realised as soon as the rig came under pressure. If we lost the contrivance overboard, or if the lashings parted or the boom snapped, there would be no substitute material from which to construct a replacement, and what was a difficult situation would become dire, as we drifted coastward at the mercy of wind and tide. Luckily for all on board, though, it worked and worked well.

With the helm back in operation, I was able to hoist the number two jib and a fully reefed main, and *Lucette*'s heavy rolling abated at a stroke. Thereafter we made slow but steady progress, carefully monitoring the gear for signs of wear, eventually rolling into English Harbour over a day late. We tied up alongside the *Bonnie*, already snugly anchored in front of the huge oak capstans along the harbour wall. The massive black-and-white capstans were still fitted with the bitter ends of huge coir springs, which had not been used in anger since the great days of sail, when in the eighteenth century English Harbour had been the headquarters of the Royal Navy. Great ships of the line had been winched into the landlocked lagoon by teams of slaves, in order to obtain what meagre protection they could from ensuing tropical storms, for English Harbour had been – and still was – one of the safest 'hurricane holes' in the Caribbean.

Having finally got *Lucette* to port, the next problem was to figure out how to repair the rudderpost. The remnants of the upper pintle fitting were all but worn away, leaving the rudder hanging precariously on its skeg. We had to deliver the rudder and its post to the shore-side workshop for welding back together. But the fittings were made of bronze and the necessary skills would not be available for another month, as the only bronze welder hereabouts had in a cruel twist of irony gone to England on holiday. I figured no matter what transpired it would be best to get the rudder out of the water whilst considering our longer-term strategy. Hiring the only diver available, we set about detaching the rudder plate, and all went without a hitch. I personally checked the lashings before we undid the last bronze fastening that would release the crescent-shaped rudder plate from the hull. I had no one to blame therefore but myself as the streamlined slippery shape, defying knots of a 300-year pedigree, simply slipped out of its securing loops and, like a waving, mocking hand, sliced its way to and fro into the murky depths below.

I was forced to re-hire the diver, paying him our monthly budget per day, to find the missing piece. It took two days of worry and frustration, to say nothing of hard work, with one fruitless dive following another, before we had covered the whole area twice over. The kids even built a raft out of coconut palms to use as a snorkel base, insisting that they would assist in the search operations. After they had virtually lived aboard it for the whole two days, I enquired as to their progress and they informed me blithely that they were having so much fun they hadn't actually started looking! Exasperated, I pressed on. By the beginning of the third day without success, I admitted defeat and asked the diver to stop his search. In a deep mood of despair, I watched as he returned ashore, slowly making his way back towards the dive centre. He had travelled a good hundred yards or so when he suddenly stopped in his tracks, seeming almost to jump out of the water before beating a hasty retreat back in our direction, clearly excited by what he had seen. Quite by chance he had come across the errant fitting lying on the bottom in clear water. Having grown tired of its game of hide and seek, it seemed to give itself up as meekly as a kitten, having cost us a small fortune in the process.

Unwilling to risk a subsequent waterborne repair, I asked Siggi if he would be prepared to tow us to the US Virgin Islands, where there were professional shipyards. He agreed without question or hesitation. Later that day we departed in company, the *Bonnie* first pushing *Lucette* as a quarter tug through the narrows before moving ahead and sending out a wire cable, which we secured around the cat head and foremast. *Bonnie* slowly took up the slack, pulling us through the water on a short lead, until we reached the safety of the open waters that lay immediately beyond the channel. Thereafter she extended the long wire hawser to its full length in order to prevent her tow snatching in the seaway. We set course for St Thomas with little faith and a lot of hope.

Two days later we arrived at the large protected bay of St Thomas just after ten o'clock at night, exhausted but satisfied at a job well done. We had completed a complex marine salvage operation with no damage and in record time. *Bonnie* could record an additional notch on her rescue list. Perhaps in exuberant relief at our success, or maybe just because we were all hot and dirty after such hard and dangerous toil, we impulsively stripped off in the darkness and dived into the cool waters of the harbour. Recoiling at the acerbic taste, we didn't swim for long. The next morning we discovered the cause of our displeasure, for the harbour was filled with raw sewage, dumped without treatment at an alleged rate of 10,000 gallons per day. The waters were heavily polluted, with brown sewage and toilet tissue strewn over the surface like ragged confetti. Without wasting a moment, Lyn marshalled us all into the dinghy and shepherded us to the local hospital for hepatitis jabs, our first visit ashore costing another small fortune in medical bills. The next day we planned to track down likely shipyards, where we might obtain affordable estimates, prior to carrying out the necessary repairs.

In the 1670s, the Danes founded the first permanent settlement on the Virgin Islands, naming it Amalienborg or Charlotte Amalie, after their queen. The town, better known as St Thomas, had become a major US tourist resort in recent times. The Danes long rued the day in 1902 when their government, in desperate need of foreign currency, sold the islands to the USA for a pittance. Having come with the sole intention of carrying out repairs, we moored up alongside the West India Company's wharf, instead of anchoring out in the bay and getting ashore by boat, as was our usual practice. Our berth was overshadowed by two large brown freight containers and was fenced off from the adjacent mercantile wharfs, which made access to the dockyard gate a little difficult, but provided us with a quiet berth where we were seldom disturbed.

Everything seemed to be in a hurry here; aeroplanes roared overhead whilst automobiles whizzed back and forth. Flying boats arrived and departed amidst spectacular furrows of white spray, and overpowered speedboats buzzed up and down the harbour at high speed, leaping loudly from wave crest to wave crest. Loud-hailers bawled instructions aboard coastguard cutters loud enough for every boat in the harbour to hear them. Blistering hot days, hamburgers and iced cola proliferated everywhere, expensively of course.

The next day we were to part company with our Icelandic friends, for friends they had truly become. They were off to find work in the Dominican Republic whilst we had decided to proceed to the USA by way of the Bahamas. It was a beautiful sun-drenched morning as we made our goodbyes. 'Miami it is, then,' I choked to Siggi, pumping his hand, as tears stung my eyes. 'Miami it is,' he confirmed quietly. We waved the *Bonnie* on her way as she threaded past the large passenger liners which were arriving en masse out of the pink-and-orange sunrise. *Bonnie*, dwarfed in comparison, looked strangely vulnerable as she chugged her way past the edge of the commercial docks and gained the deeper waters beyond. We ran to the very end of the land, waving our goodbyes, and when we could go no further we stopped and watched her fade into the distance. I hoped, more than anything I had ever hoped for in my life, that we would meet them again in Miami. A mood of despair hung over *Lucette* that day. Lyn, Anne, Douglas and the twins huddled in the saloon, crying with sheer heartache at their loss. Turning to the work in hand, I made an effort to avoid reflecting on our despondency by busying myself dismantling the steering mechanism.

With the assistance of a professional French diver we extracted the rudderpost and placed it on the quay, in readiness for a yet-to-be-found welding team who could effect the repair. We spent a lot of time each day trying to find a yard with the necessary skills, at a reasonable cost, but without success. In order to maintain morale we made the most of our first glimpse of American life, and our close proximity to the Yacht Haven Marina allowed us the luxury of dancing away the warm tropical nights to the melodious chimes of the steel bands whilst enjoying the occasional pleasantly addictive rum punch.

It wasn't long before we discovered the morbid truth about the two containers abandoned on our dock and the purpose of the fence around them. Made of corrugated steel plate, each container measured some 20 feet in length. Their twisted doors lay askew on their hinges, after having been wrenched open to leave their interiors exposed to the outside world. We learnt from the harbour master that they had been used to smuggle children from the out islands to the sin bins of Freeport and Miami, and that the kidnapped children had been discovered only when the putrid contents, stinking in the hot sun, had alarmed the authorities to such a degree that they had opened them up for health and safety reasons, to reveal some twenty young occupants already dead inside. Picked from the streets of the shantytowns in Guadeloupe and Dominica as they walked home from school, the children had been shipped as tractor parts, to fuel the growth of drugs and prostitution in the 'civilised' world. Delays in the docks had led to the containers missing their forwarding connection, after which they had lain in the hot sun for over six weeks, waiting for their owners to claim them, which of course they never did. We shook our heads in disbelief as we were told of the fate that had befallen not only these children but also the others that had gone before them. Lyn and I clutched our little ones to us, empathising with the loss suffered by parents in far-off lands we didn't even know.

Splitting our days into halves, we used the relative cool of the mornings to visit Bluebeard's castle and Fort Christian, and spent many happy hours either on the beaches or in the popular market place. The afternoons we reserved for chasing down leads for suitably qualified engineers, returning to the marina by the early evening in time for the seemingly non-stop festivities laid on at the club house. It was here that we bumped into Zoe, the wife of my best man when Lyn and I had married in Hong Kong. With a new husband, Zoe was sailing on a sedate fair-weather cruise from Fort Lauderdale in the USA. She introduced me to a couple of fitters she knew who were experienced bronze welders. Unable to believe our luck, we hired their services and they went to work with a will, anticipating that it would be a straightforward and well-paid number. The job became complicated, however, first by brittle metal and then by rotting wood and corroded fastenings, eventually taking two whole days to complete and requiring them to work non-stop through the national holiday.

We had agreed 200 dollars for the job, and it was all I could afford, but they refused to take even that money, stating that they had heard the children talking about how we may not have enough money to get us to America. They had therefore decided that this was to be their gift to us. I was truly humbled by these two, for they were poor enough themselves and yet they had taught me a valuable lesson about charity. Giving without counting the cost, their ounce of help was truly worth more than any pound of sorrow.

On the day we sailed, Lyn, breaking into our last hundred-dollar bill, hastily dashed ashore to re-supply our little ship from the local chandlery. Thanks to the modest charges of the Danish dock operators and the wonderful charity of the welders, not forgetting the help from our Icelandic friends who had got us to St Thomas in the first place, we had completed the repairs for a fraction of what it would have cost us had we stayed in English Harbour. On the morning of 17 June we cruised under full sail through the sparkling and turquoise seas before a fresh westerly breeze, bound for Great Inagua over 500 miles to the west in the distant Bahamas. *Lucette* felt buoyant and lively, answering her helm with customary obedience once more. A day later, we technically left the reaches of the Caribbean as we sailed over the coral bank on which the Bahamas stood. As the days passed, things began to feel better once more, and life settled down to a routine of sublime and heartfelt joy. I was together with my family, whom I had rediscovered and grown to love and cherish more deeply than ever. It was on this small leg that Lyn and I decided that if we did nothing else before our children left us, what we had done in bringing them on this trip had been the best decision we had made in our lives.

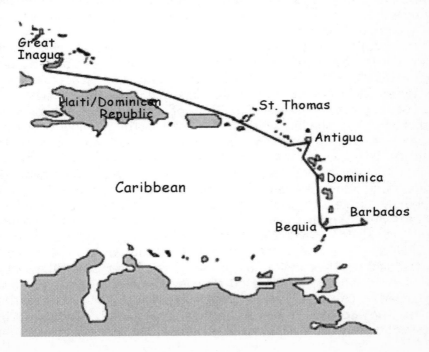

CHAPTER 4
The Bahamas

Unlike the Windward Islands, which were largely independent nations of volcanic origin with high foliaged peaks, the Bahamian archipelago was still a British Colony but with its own flag and currency. Lying spread-eagled over some 5,000 square miles, the island chain consisted entirely of low-lying coral reefs with a few rounded hills, totalling about 700 islands in all with an additional 2,500 cays and rocks. The population was made up of some 150,000 mainly black, Christian folk who were dispersed across less than three percent of the islands. The vast majority of the islands had never been populated; others had been abandoned after becoming economically unsustainable. The warm seas and reefs were filled with every imaginable form of aquatic life, and whilst the water of the Caribbean could not be described as anything other than clear, the waters surrounding the Bahamas were even clearer. So clear, in fact, that it was easy to see a shiny coin on the seabed, in over 100 feet of water. Our first port of call was the island of Great Inagua, so called because it was the largest in its group and as the name suggested, it was a land 'without water'.

We arrived at the open roads of Matthew Town, which offered little in the way of protection from the ocean swells and no safe anchorage. Once cleared in through the casual immigration process, we upped anchor and motored around the point a short distance, to the more protected waters of Man of War Bay. On arrival we anchored in the shallow waters of a cove in the shadow of a huge white salt mountain, sparkling and glinting in the fierce sunshine, the result of non-stop harvesting from the vast salt flats which lay just inland. We hadn't been anchored long when we were approached by three young American lads, out fishing in the bay. They had been extremely successful too, as the bottom of their boat testified, littered with a small shark, several jack fish and a large king fish, together with four silver-blue torpedo-shaped barracuda. Two of the boys were the sons of the managing partner of the salt factory located ashore. They invited us to meet their parents and the rest of their family, who had emigrated from New York City and settled on the island a couple of years previously, risking it all to live their dream. The Jacobson family treated us to a guided jeep tour of the installation, travelling past the huge processing plant and deep into the salt flats, which were set out in fields of some 40 acres apiece. The white salt plains stretched as far as our eyes could see and the vast soda lakes, filled with highly caustic water, were sanctuary to a host of bird life including one of the largest flocks of flamingos in the world, several thousand in number. Taking flight in a cacophony of sound as we approached, the air pulsed to the beat of their wings and the clatter of their beaks, the deafening dyspeptic din forcing us to cover our ears and bury our heads as each bird vied for airspace immediately above us. The salt was deposited by evaporation following the controlled flooding of the plain and harvested by massive grain-harvesting machinery, before being dumped into 20-ton trucks for stockpiling into spectacular heaps. The heaps had steadily increased in size until they had become joined in a single mound assuming the size of a small mountain, clearly visible for miles around. The multi-peaked salt mountain contained hundreds of thousands of tons of glistening white crystals, awaiting shipment by bulk carrier to the distant ports of the civilised world. We all noticed with nostalgic pleasure the blue-and-white logo adorning the factory gates, a logo we had often studied when passing the saltcellar across the dinner table, back in the faraway days at Meadows Farm.

In return for their hospitality we offered to take the Jacobsons' teenage son Alvin and his friend Tom for a sail round the bay. Their reply was to make our visit a truly memorable one, for they suggested instead a trip to the rich fishing grounds some twenty miles to the north on another island called Little Inagua. The island was reputed to be a deserted paradise, and though they had always longed to visit it, they had never been able to do so, for the waters were largely uncharted and the channel too treacherous an undertaking in a small boat such as theirs. Alvin offered his local knowledge to pilot us through the reefs and coral heads leading to the only anchorage on the island, a symbiotic offer that we were only to happy to accept.

After a pleasant afternoon's sail, the next evening found us securely if somewhat conspicuously anchored close inshore in crystal-clear waters at the head of a wide deserted bay. Shaped like a great horseshoe, the shoreline's wide expanses of fine white sand receded northwards in long and gently sloping beaches for as far as the eye could see. To the south, the beach progressively curled southwards in a wide arc which merged into the distant southwest point of Little Inagua.

The following morning, after assembling an excited exploration party, we landed on the broad crescent of sandy beach and constructed a rudimentary base camp, just inside the coral foreshore. Beyond the sand line, where tall fingers of coral reached into the sea, we collected driftwood and lit a large bonfire. 'We're not expecting tigers,' Douglas reassured the boys, heaving another knurled log onto the flames, 'but I have heard there are pumas hereabouts.' He glanced furtively over his shoulder and grinned to the twins, enjoying their fearful grimace as they nervously scoured the whispering palms in the direction of the deserted interior. We lived on this 'island without water' for almost a week. We shared it with the herds of undomesticated donkeys and feral hogs, still living wild and untamed hundreds of years after their ancestors had been marooned here by the Spanish buccaneers and English explorers as insurance to ancient mariners against starvation in the event of shipwreck. The overwhelming peace and silence inland was broken only by the occasional screech of hunting ospreys, ruthlessly patrolling their nesting sites in the sand dunes.

Our first discovery was an ancient 30-foot-wide debris field deposited on the beach by the ocean tides. A great swath of flotsam and jetsam, the rubble and rubbish lay bound together in decades of accumulated driftwood, and had never been seen or touched by humankind since it had become stranded here, some of it before I had been born. Lyn could not believe her luck as she set about beachcombing this hitherto unexplored treasure trove. From pieces of an *Apollo* spaceship to a set of tables and chairs, we also found harbour buoys, wrecked boats, fishermen's floats, bolts of rope, unopened packing cases and a host of other treasures. Lying *in situ* on this rarely seen and virtually untouched land, the collection of paraphernalia about us seemed to have a life force of its own, as if it had been enduring the elements whilst waiting to be found, which in turn evoked a deep sense of discovery in each and every one of us. As we ventured further inshore, we were all touched with a feeling of wonder and anticipation, undoubtedly experienced by early explorers and pioneers since the dawn of time.

Once Lyn realised that nobody was going to remove her stash of booty before we returned, we set off on our pre-planned hike. Douglas, Alvin and Tom had already set off on their circumnavigation of the island in the opposite direction earlier that morning. They had estimated to be away overnight, so the others had volunteered to remain aboard *Lucette* on a diving adventure, effectively standing anchor watch over our home. Exploring further into the flat and easy-going terrain forming the interior of the island, we followed the animal trails as watchful ospreys circled overhead and great flocks of pelican swept past at low altitude. Stunted copses of palm trees, their trunks crisscrossed in haphazard profusion, receded into distant forests inland. Small chirping birds accompanied us, flitting from bush to bush, to get a better look at their strange two-legged visitors. Several types of crane and pelican flocked alongside us, as we rested in the beds of dried-out salt lakes, where all traces of water had long since evaporated. Long-tailed tropical birds and terns abounded nearer the seashore, where many kinds of lizard and land crab flourished amongst the cacti and thorn bushes, whilst other areas were heavily scented with the sweet smell of wild jasmine growing in profusion amongst the diminutive palm groves. Try as we might, though, we found no trace of the fresh water to which we felt the four-legged animals must have had access.

By late afternoon we came upon a clearing leading down to a broad expanse of flat sandy dunes, where Lyn was soon in her element once more, rummaging through the debris and driftwood deposited above the low-water mark. Suddenly she let out a shriek of delight, having discovered an unopened bottle of Marsala wine, lying half-buried in the sand. Carefully Lyn tipped a little of the amber fluid onto her hand, sniffing it cautiously before tasting it. Slowly a mischievous smile broke out across her face and after taking a long gulp she passed me the bottle. It tasted like the nectar of the gods to two weary beachcombers and before we knew it the bottle was empty. Feeling quite heady in the brilliant sunshine, we cast aside our inhibitions and stripped off, sharing wicked enjoyment, skinny-dipping in the crystalline waters of a large inshore lagoon. Formed between rocky outcrops and hidden amongst the sand hills of a beautiful and deserted pink coral beach, the still blue waters were fringed by the undulating fronds of taller palms which swayed in the gentle breeze as their trunks danced rhythmically out over the clear water. We were shielded from the glare of the tropical sun by the gently drifting trade-wind clouds and felt we had truly become part of the new-age generation, when after frolicking in the warmer shallow waters, we lay on the beach and made passionate love like a couple of teenage hippies. Caressing with uncaring abandonment I squeezed Lyn to me in a hot-blooded embrace. I was soon blissfully unaware of the world about me. Suddenly she started laughing, so much so that I couldn't help joining in too. I laughed long and loud, quite unaware of exactly what I was laughing at, until I became aware of the cause of Lyn's merriment. What I saw made my jaw drop and stay dropped. We were centre stage to a crowd of voyeur donkeys that had gathered round to see what all the commotion was about. Completely unafraid, as they had not seen humans before, they suddenly started braying, which set us off in a second bout of gut-wrenching laughter, making the perplexed donkeys bray more urgently and even louder than before. This memory was to harbour a smile within our hearts for the rest of our lives. Indeed, being temporarily lost in this forgotten and deserted paradise became etched in our minds as the best few days of our lives, or, as Lyn was to phrase it, 'It was worth putting up with the first 45 years of my life just to have had this week on God's Earth.'

It was already the edge of dusk by the time we had retraced our steps back to the beach camp. Heavily laden and completely exhausted, we dropped our booty on the sand and plunged into the sea to await the arrival of the dinghy from *Lucette*. Shortly, Douglas and the others returned with exciting news. They had discovered an ancient Spanish galleon, locked into the coral with seventeen cannon and two large anchors, lying where it had been dashed onto the shore just beneath the waters of the inner reef near the western point. As if that wasn't enough, they had also brought home a dinghy complete with outboard motor. They had discovered it washed up on the shore and, even more incredibly, had already started the engine and run it until the remaining supply of fuel had run out.

Tom was minus his right shoe after losing it in a shark attack, his splashing feet proving an irresistible lure to a five-foot bull shark as he pulled the boat through the shallow water along the beach. The shark had bitten his shoe off whilst attacking his foot. It was fortunate that the shallow water had prevented the shark from turning to devour Tom's entire limb, but it had left him feeling not only severely shaken but also distinctly lucky. 'You didn't see any donkeys,' Lyn suddenly interjected, flashing me a knowing grin, whilst fixing a makeshift dressing to his bleeding foot. In the gathering twilight we went back ashore to try our hands at line-fishing. Sandy soon caught a four-pound jack followed almost immediately by a seventeen-pound grouper. Neil found himself in a tug of war with a fearsome barracuda, and only Alvin's expert coaching enabled him to land the monster. We cooked the fish amongst the dying glow of the fireside embers and wood ends which was all that remained of our campfire on the beach.

The galleon was a once-in-a-lifetime find, and the following day I decided to follow the boys back along the donkey trails to witness the wreck site for myself. Momentary thoughts of untold wealth quickly melted as I realised the hotchpotch of cannons and anchors, mixed with a host of other relics, were not fashioned from bronze but were in fact cast iron. The hull appeared completely unsalvageable without specialist gear, as it was lodged under the breaking rollers of the reef. Nevertheless the sight was a wonder to behold. The seabed all around, littered with cannon balls and encrusted artefacts topped by the large anchors and scattered cannon, was all that remained of a time when many must have lost their lives, as their once proud ship had been driven ashore. I decided the least I must do was to register our find with the Receiver of Wrecks.

It was late in the afternoon by the time we had finished our explorations, requiring us to rest before we embarked on the return journey. With renewed energy, we first trotted and then walked the long trip back to *Lucette*, stopping to pick up interesting pieces of flotsam and other sea bounty that caught our eye in the debris field. I was astonished at one point to see a row of suitcases, lined up as if on a station platform, waiting for a train that would never arrive. I discovered later that they had been there for over a decade, abandoned when a Haitian passenger sloop had wrecked on the island during a hurricane storm.

Finally, after a few more days of exploring, fishing and snorkelling, we took our leave of Little Inagua, feeling very privileged to have seen this wonderful island for ourselves. Returning to Great Inagua, I sailed *Lucette* alongside after being unable to start the engine. The loading dock, located adjacent to our own berth, was now occupied by a large bulk carrier flying the red duster. A giant of a man approached the dockside and offered to take our ropes, introducing himself as the boatswain from the nearby British ship. He invited us aboard for bacon, egg and chips the following morning. We all broke into a raucous laugh, as Sandy's little voice piped up from the depths of the forecastle, enquiring if we could go aboard and eat some right away. Thus began a very memorable few days as the cook served up 'English breakfast' times six. The twins' eyes positively beamed and the aroma set our mouths watering to the point of indecency at the delicious feast he set before us.

In response, we invited them all back for a party aboard, on the condition they brought the beer. By eight o'clock we had nine visitors, and by ten we had nine very drunken sailors yarning in the saloon, spread-eagled across the deck, lying over the chart table, and some even passed out in the cockpit. At one point, Paddy the assistant bosun was waxing lyrically when *Lucette*'s side rail, on which he was leaning heavily for support, suddenly gave way and tipped him overboard with a loud splash. 'He can't swim,' someone piped, though nobody was perturbed enough to go in after him, and the conversation quickly returned to normal. I realised, however, that he really was in trouble, his hobnail boots dragging him under as he tried desperately to paddle for the shore with his thumb jammed over the opening of his beer can. 'No good spoiling his beer just because he's drowning,' asserted his shipmate the carpenter, quite oblivious to the danger he was in. Diving over the side, I was able to put my lifesaving skills to good use as I hauled him back on board. I left him lying on the deck and rejoined the party, which had now reached the sing-song state, reciting old favourites from 'Pia-pia-piano' to 'Michael row your boat ashore', finally linking hands for several renditions of 'Auld lang syne'. I was too drunk myself to remember the words to Lyn's final request, 'Little donkey'.

The hot streaming sunshine of the morning arrived all too early, as did the cranium-splitting headaches. Paddy's slumped frame faded in and out of focus as I tried to clear my blurred vision, gripping tightly onto the galley worktops in a vain effort to stop myself spinning out of control. It seemed he was the only visitor left from our band of hardened maritime professionals of the previous night. The thought crossed my mind that if I didn't get Paddy back to the *Bulk Eagle* before she sailed we might be stuck with him for the rest of our trip. I pricked the nozzle of the paraffin stove and lit it in a dowdy hit-and-miss performance. Sliding the coffee pot onto a spitting bright blue ring of flame, I noticed a second pair of legs protruding through the toilet door, and then another set hanging from the chart table. 'I must have drunk more than I thought,' I confessed to nobody in particular, propping myself up against the companionway steps as my head went into another dizzy spin. It was to be another hour before I could gather the strength to summon up the stragglers and take them back to their ship. By the time we disembarked, Paddy's hobnails had dried completely in the dazzling hot sunshine and the reflected glare from the white salt hills and wide expanses of sand stabbed the backs of our eyes, making our heads throb as we turned to enter the dock. The fast-moving conveyor belt laden with salt was already trimming the ship at the other end of the long jetty, which in our compromised state appeared to be several miles away. Paddy, bare-foot and unable to carry his boots any further, decided to put them on the conveyer belt and pick them up at the other end. He had failed to observe that the belt was humming by at some 30 miles per hour and no sooner had he let them drop than they were whisked off into the distance, last seen disappearing into the cavernous recesses of number three hold. Now this cargo was bound for the grinding wheels of salt processing plants in the UK and from there to the fine dining tables of England. 'I wonder which unlucky souls will end up with Paddy's boots sprinkled over their dinner,' remarked Lyn with a twinkle in her eye.

For two more days we enjoyed the hospitality of our fellow seafarers. They looked after us like royalty, then all too soon it was over. The *Bulk Eagle* was to sail at three o'clock that afternoon. Again we lined up to wave our friends goodbye, and again that despairing feeling of loneliness descended upon us. It was getting more than we could bear as the ship slowly departed, her grey hull topped with its white superstructure and giant gantry cranes receding to the size of a small dot on the horizon, before we turned back from the dockside towards *Lucette*. 'At least old Lucy is still here,' offered Sandy, voicing the feelings of us all. Our sadness at the loss of our English friends was tinged for the first time with a little bit of homesickness, for their mannerisms and accents had awakened distant memories of home.

Alvin and Tom were waiting for us back aboard *Lucette*. Alvin flourished a piece of paper in his hand, which was a letter from the Receiver of Wrecks in Nassau. 'Guess what,' he enthused, 'I got the papers back and it's official, we can register the wreck we found on Little Inagua. I thought perhaps Jacob's Wreck,' he continued, his eyes sparkling with the untamed energy of youth. Well, that was cause for a celebration and our collective mood lifted as we remembered our recent adventures together.

The following day dawn broke like a great bar of silver suspended in the eastern sky, revealing my meditative form sitting cross-legged on the coach roof deep in thought. I had been awake most of the night, struggling to balance the need to press on with the voyage against the despair of more goodbyes and rapidly diminishing cash reserves. This goodbye was going to be especially hard, as our stay in Inagua ranked as the most beautiful experience we had enjoyed, not only on the trip so far but also in our whole lives.

Like swallowing medicine, I decided that the sooner we departed the sooner we might start feeling better again. The sun was rising rapidly, and the heat of the day was already beginning to feel uncomfortable, as I announced to the family that we would be setting sail straight away. 'Yes, even before breakfast,' I confirmed to the children, their disconsolate faces caught in the shafts of the dust-laden sunbeams that swirled through the saloon portholes, flushing out the last vestiges of early-morning gloom still below decks. I could not shake my edgy mood, however, and as I turned to go back up on deck I ordered my crew to stow the galley and saloon for sea. At the same time, I instructed Anne and Douglas to let go fore and aft and man the halyards and sheets ready for departure, jobs that required them being in two places at once. An added complication was that *Lucette*'s main engine had been giving trouble starting and the batteries were flat. With the help of one of *Bulk Eagle*'s engineers, I had removed the starter motor in case it had been the cause of a power leak. Whilst my investigations were still in progress, I decided to leave it disconnected as a precaution against any further possible drain, the immediate consequence of which was that we had to leave the jetty under sail.

We had barely cleared the harbour when the first of the ocean swells welcomed us with menacing height for such a comparatively light wind, then without warning I heard an almighty crash down below, followed by loud screams. Leaving the wheel unmanned, I leapt down the companionway staircase in a single bound to see all the breakfast dishes smashed in a pile on the floor, swimming in boiling water from the upturned kettle. The spillage of dishes from the unlocked cupboards had caused Neil to spill a full cup of scalding coffee down the front of his chest, and Lyn was trying desperately to put a cold compress on it. My first thought was how serious the consequences of this apparent carelessness could have been. Neil could well be scarred for life and the dishes would need replacing with money we could ill afford. I snapped, blaming Anne and Douglas for not stowing the boat properly before we had left. Both started to answer back, stating as one that with all the jobs I had set them they had been too busy to tend to the below-deck stowage as well, and in any case I had ordered them to be on deck whilst we departed.

The implication that it might have been my fault made me see red. 'Pick it all up,' I demanded, pointing to the smashed pile of crockery whilst glaring at Douglas. 'Pick it up yourself,' he retorted with a flash of defiance in his eyes. I bellowed the order to him again and punched out at him, striking him full on the side of the jaw. Fearing I was about to strike again, Anne jumped on my back in an attempt to restrain me. In the grip of a violent temper, I brushed her aside, knocking her into the companionway stairs, and then on into the recesses of the toilet. She slammed the door shut and locked it with a loud click. I shoulder-barged the door in an effort to get it open. Without warning, and for the first time in his life, Douglas suddenly attacked me. The worm had finally turned and I felt his strong arms grip me like a vice. My head cracked hard against the galley bulkhead as he shoved me back through the door into the aft cabin, where he pinned me against the locker door. Gripping the front of my shirt, he pressed me savagely into the varnished woodwork with his elbow. His free hand, held high, was clenched into a fist ready to strike, his eyes bulging as his face flushed bright red with fury. Pushing his forehead hard against mine he started to shout, 'Do that again and so help me I'll kill you.' He filled the doorway like a trembling gorilla. Douglas had grown up, he was bigger and heavier than me, and I felt not only severely disadvantaged but also for the first time a little scared. Lyn quickly stepped between us and told me to get out on deck and cool off. 'I will,' I shouted, more like a spoilt child than a responsible parent. 'In fact you lot needn't bother coming up on deck ... for the rest of the darn trip. In fact I don't want any of you touching my boat again,' I continued in a shameful show of arrogance and pride. 'And I will not allow any of you to steer my boat ever again ... ever! And one more thing,' I turned, wagging my finger straight at Douglas, 'don't let me hear you ever say "bloody typical" again or I'll crucify you!'

I turned on my heel before he could reply, feeling smug that I'd found an ace to play as I stamped my way aft, not unlike an arrogant turkey cock. Taking hold of the spinning wheel, the absurdity of what I had just said and done suddenly hit me, harder than even Douglas had. I finally had to admit I had been nothing more than a foolish chump, and no amount of self-chastising would redress the damage inflicted upon my family, still licking their wounds down below. It would take masses of humble-pie suppers to set things straight again.

Lucette had stalled in the eye of the wind during the time I had left the wheel unattended and was drifting aimlessly before the wind. I brought her slowly round and set a course northward towards Crooked Island, past the dangerous Hogsty reefs, some twelve to fourteen hours away. There was no reason to choose that particular destination, but unless I gave myself time to sort out the situation below and make my peace with the others, then it might take days or even weeks of stony silence before things returned to normal. In an overwrought moment of hot-headed stupidity I had virtually destroyed all the bonds of trust and friendship I had established with my family during the trip so far.

After four solitary hours at the wheel I began to flag, my angry words reverberating loud and clear inside my head. *Lucette* was racing along under a reefed main, foresail and number two jib with the log recording over 8 knots at times, and she was becoming a handful to manage. I had to hope there would be some sympathetic understanding from below in the form of a watch relief, especially as

I would need to be alert when we passed the Hogsty reef during the night. No such sympathy or understanding was forthcoming, however; my family took me at my word, leaving me to take the wheel without a break. Just before dawn, feeling completely exhausted, I spotted the loom of a lighthouse over the horizon, with which I confirmed *Lucette's* position on the chart. Struggling to stay awake, I fought the mother of battles to keep my eyelids from closing. When I could fight no longer, I made the decision to anchor up and get some sleep. I counted the lighthouse flashes again, one and two then one and two and three without flashes; no doubt about it, group flash two every five seconds was the designated phase of the lighthouse marking the entrance to the protected bay I had identified on the chart. A quick confirmatory glance at the chart confirmed that a safe deep-water anchorage lay beyond the coral knolls located on what was evidently the southwest coast of Crooked Island.

With my crew still on strike, I decided to try and drop the anchor myself. Leaving the wheel for only a moment, I quickly dashed forward to unlash the heavy fisherman anchor and swing it out over the side, leaving it to hang vertically on the end of its chain ready for instant release. Just as I started the return trip to the cockpit, *Lucette* seemed to snag in the water and then stopped abruptly, listing dramatically to starboard as she did so. We had hit something under the water and were stuck hard aground. Forgetting the anchor for a moment, I raced back to the cockpit hatch and leapt below to start the engine. To my utter dismay I found it still in pieces; I had clean forgotten that I hadn't reassembled the starter-motor unit. I had to think quickly as the falling tide would soon leave us completely stranded. Gripping the starter-motor casing, I pushed it into the crankcase, pressing it hard into its locating aperture. With my free hand I turned the starter switch; the batteries had rejuvenated just enough to slowly crank the engine over with a reluctant whine. The energised starter motor delivered a kick like a mule, jamming my grasping fingers between the hard metal casings of the engine, but at least it started, draining the last morsels of power from the batteries before killing them off completely.

I returned to the helm and slid the engine control to full astern, gently gliding *Lucette* off the reef before turning her back the way we had come, creeping slow ahead until I was back in deeper water once more. I looked back at the lighthouse, pretty sure that whatever we had hit was not on the chart, then I noticed three distinct and separate flashes to each phase of the lighthouse, not two as I had first counted. I must have been dreaming when we had entered the cove, for it appeared I had miscounted the light's sequence and inadvertently sailed into the wrong bay. Instead of finding a safe deep-water channel leading to a secluded anchorage, *Lucette* was surrounded by extensive coral reefs deep within the Bight of Acklins, and standing into mortal danger. Tentatively maintaining a reciprocal course until I was clear of the headland, I rounded the peninsula sighting a second light, flashing twice every five seconds. It marked the location of an open-water anchorage in Crooked Island immediately to the north. Observing for a second time, I fought back powerful urges to close my eyes, for I was virtually asleep on my feet, and rechecked the sequence of the light phase. Only after I had recounted it on three separate occasions, so that I was sure beyond any shadow of doubt, did I proceed in to what seemed like a secluded inlet, taking some comfort from the presence of a large trimaran already anchored there. Feeling I had served my penance, after over seventeen hours non-stop at the wheel, I felt just cause in waking Lyn and asking her to drop the second kedge anchor for me, for thick banks of dark low cloud were beginning to make the weather look ominous.

By the time we were clewed up it was daylight and the sky had the appearance of being unsettled and troubled. Ragged clouds formed distinct bands in the sky above us, superimposed in ever-darkening layers of purple, grey and black as they receded towards the distant horizon. A blustery breeze had sprung up, which persuaded me not to launch the dinghy, at least until the sea had calmed down a little. Craving sleep but remembering the main engine batteries, I decided to break out the portable generator and connect it up. We really couldn't afford to be without the aid of the engine, especially if we might have to negotiate any more coral reefs. Having set the batteries charging, I was able to get to my bed at last, leaving the starter-motor repair for later when I felt more alert. Lyn had finally had enough of Anne and Douglas's work-to-rule and had got them scrubbing the decks. In a poor attempt at re-establishing an accord, I wished them both good night and was dead to the world even as my head hit the pillow. Seconds later, Lyn was shaking me from the deepest of sleeps, 'Dougal ... Dougal ...' The timbre of her voice, distorted by nervous guttural choking, made me realise that she was waking me because the direst of emergencies was about to descend upon us.

In fact, I could clearly hear the distinct buzzing drone even as I hauled myself out of the bunk. Catching Lyn's sense of urgency, I literally sprang up the stairway, barely contacting the stair treads, and reached the main deck just as the rain started to fall. Entering the bay about a mile away and closing fast was an awesome cumulonimbus squall cloud, its massive bulk billowing upwards into the stratosphere, some 40,000 feet above us. A loud thunderclap rent the air as if to announce the arrival of a super-heavyweight wrestler into the arena, then my heart sank to my feet as my eyes followed Lyn's outstretched arm and caught sight of a dark spinning tornado, connecting the cloud to the sea. A thick vertical column of water, some fifty feet in width at its base, ascended hundreds of feet into the cloud base like a giant obelisk. The twister had sucked up the water from the surface of the sea to form a huge waterspout, which towered above us, bristling and wavering its dark spinning pilaster like a child's top. The funnel-shaped pillar drilled a deep furrow into the surface of the sea, throwing up huge waves concealed by clouds of spume and spray, as the main spout spawned smaller spouts and despatched them like evil menacing children from its epicentre. Stampeding on into the bay, the air quivered and trembled as the waterspout swept all before it, bisecting the very route we ourselves had traversed less than an hour before.

The colour of the sea had turned a jet black and the air was still and clammy. Suddenly a bright flash of lightning struck the surface of the water with a loud crackling fizz, followed instantaneously by another deafening thunderclap which sent booming waves of pressure pulsating in our ears. Terrified and dumbstruck, I was rooted to the spot and forced to support myself against the hatch runners by my arms, because my legs had turned to jelly beneath me. I felt an involuntary squirt of urine dampen my trousers, and tried desperately to catch my breath, my mouth drying instantly as the claw of fear gripped tightly at the pit of my stomach. The prospect of losing *Lucette* now stared us full in the face. At best the waterspout might miss us by a hundred yards; at worst it would whisk us up in a direct hit, boat and all being consumed by its awesome omnipotence. It was getting nearer by the second. Then the wind hit us. Mesmerised, I looked on impotently as Lyn and the children clung tightly onto the rigging in order to prevent themselves being blown overboard. *Lucette* snatched angrily at her anchor chain and warp in the short steep waves and the rain began to fall in drops the size of small apples. The surface of the sea quickly assumed the image of a war-torn battlefield under the constant barrage of incoming shells as the huge drops made the water dance in deep-rimmed pockmarks all around us. As the minutes ticked by the raindrops merged to fall out of the sky in huge contiguous sheets, forming torrential runnels of cascading water which raced along our decks like a river in flood. Just then *Lucette* hit the bottom with a sickening shudder. We had started to drag our anchor and were being driven hard ashore. There were only seconds to spare. With or without a plan of action, if I was going to save us I had to do it now.

Driven before the full force of the hurricane-strength winds we cowered in a huddled mass in the lee of the coach roof. 'Get to the anchors and start hauling, Doug,' I screamed, competing with the roar of the wind and rain. 'Get the anchors in and get the foresail up as quick as you can – if we don't get out of this bay within the next few minutes we are finished.'

'Bloody typical,' he screeched in confirmation, his lower lip twitching involuntarily as his eyes rolled wide with fright. Dismissing his fear, he turned sharply without waiting for me to finish and braced himself against the driving wind and rain in an effort to start his journey forward, only too aware of what he must do. Gripping the handrail, I watched as he edged his way forward. Moments later he arrived at the anchor winch; his chest muscles rippled and his biceps bulged as he crouched over the winding handle and took up the strain on the bar-tight anchor chain, which led right forward at a long stay into the angry sea. I looked on as the hounds-band in the centre of the winch began to inch its way round, the rusted links of chain clicking loudly as they hammered their way through the hawse pipe. Not allowing the momentum to diminish, Douglas continued hauling with demonic power and the brute strength of an ox, his torso lashed by the rain and wind. His legs bent in unison with each turn of the winch handle. The wind force suddenly multiplied exponentially in power, making it hard to keep my eyes open or retain the breath in my lungs. I beckoned the twins forward to assist with hauling in the lighter kedge anchor as the slack came onto its warp. Just then, *Lucette* hit the bottom a second time, her hull shuddering and jarring, and her decks shivered violently beneath our feet. A couple more strikes like that and *Lucette* would pop a plank, spelling not only the end of our trip but also the end of us all. The generator was still running and I figured there should be sufficient charge in the batteries to get the main engine started. In any event, the anchor would be up in a few minutes and by then the engine would have to be running or we would be dashed onto the rocks that extended seawards from the shore immediately behind us. Without wasting another second I raced below, setting the main-board master switch to on as I passed through the engine-room door, then my blood froze as I remembered the disconnected starter motor! If I were to get the engine going, I would have to hold the errant component onto the engine casing, and suffer the mule kick once more. *Lucette* hit the bottom again, with even greater force than before, water spurting from between the engine-room planks as she struck. One more strike like that and it would be her last; time had finally run out.

Gritting my teeth, I gripped the starter motor by its case and jammed it into the locating hole in the crankcase, holding it in place as tightly as I could. Oh for Doug's prehensile grip now! 'Bloody typical,' I heard myself yell as I hit the starter button. The casing flew round in my ineffectual grip, jamming my knuckles against the main engine block and sending sharp bolts of pain through my arm as my hand became trapped between the vicelike press of steel on steel. I was prepared to lose my hand, though, in order to ensure success, for this was the only way we could escape the path of the marauding giant outside. In a wondrous moment, the engine turned over with a slow disjointed groan, but my exuberance was short-lived as the motor failed to start. There was enough power in the batteries for one more try and no more. The flesh on my fingers, already split down to the fresh yellow bone, was bleeding profusely, but my hand would have to take another such blow if we were to stand any chance of success. I hit the button again but instead of turning the armature began to smoke and a moment later the flameproof insulation burst into flames, filling the engine room with clouds of acrid white smoke. I had a few seconds to figure out a solution to this new dilemma or my entire family was doomed.

Lucette held up to her anchor cable, heeled and lurched heavily, forcing me to crouch and hand off all manner of tools and utensils that were thrown through the air. A screwdriver dislodged from the toolbox and rolled to and fro across the shelf space, finally coming to rest by catching itself in the electrical crossover-switching unit. I fumbled frantically with the switchgear in an attempt to release the defiant tool, inadvertently switching the twelve-volt system over to twenty-four volts for a few moments. Incredibly, the armature began to turn once more and then, in a flash of inspiration, the solution hit me like the blow of a sledgehammer from heaven. Picking up the screwdriver, I turned the switch back to twenty-four volts and prodded the red-hot armature with a few well-timed flicks of the screwdriver – and the motor suddenly sprang into life, spinning like a lighted Catherine wheel. With bated breath, I rammed the spinning motor into the crankcase aperture. My hand, numbed by the first attempt and unable to feel any more pain, fetched up against the casing for a second time, splitting my wound still wider as the engine begrudgingly turned over, faster than the first time, before suddenly and miraculously bursting into life with an almighty roar.

For a fleeting moment, I knew we were going to make it. Leaping over the engine, I arrived on deck just in time to see Douglas fighting to control the whipping sheet of the foresail as he struggled to get it turned down onto its cleat. Neil was clutching his head tightly in his hands. The heavy steel eye in the clew had caught him full on the face, breaking his nose and bursting it into a bloody profusion. Catching the wind as Douglas made the sheet fast, *Lucette* instantaneously heeled over to port at an extreme angle, which probably prevented her hitting the bottom for a fourth and fatal time. The angle of heel became so acute, however, that the generator, still running and weighing in at over 200 pounds, was catapulted across the deck like an empty cardboard box.

The waterspout suddenly seemed much closer. Shielded by the wind and rain it rushed towards us, mighty and unstoppable, roaring and rasping ever louder as it boiled the darkened waters of the bay into a whirlpool of misty spray, less than a hundred yards to our right. We looked on in awe as inexplicably it altered course and bore down on the large trimaran nearby. A few seconds later, the fragile craft was whisked up by the twister and mercilessly impaled on the rocky beachhead, where she rapidly began to break up, less than 150 yards away on our starboard quarter.

With renewed urgency, I rammed the engine controls into forward gear and, without waiting to see the anchors aboard, jerked the throttle over to full ahead. The generator started rolling, end over end down the deck, heading straight over the side. Anne instinctively reached out and grasped its lifting handle, hanging on like her life depended on it. The momentum squared her up before jerking her clean off her feet and slamming her heavily onto the deck. She plummeted along the slippery planking and smashed into the rail with a heavy thud. Grimacing in pain and barely conscious, she refused to let go, thereby preventing the generator from slipping away. The next moment we had the lee rail under with only the foresail hoisted and swiftly made good our escape. Looking aft, the other boat had completely vanished within the centre of the spout. If there were souls on board then they must have surely perished.

Twenty minutes later it was all over. The funnel cloud had gone ashore and without the required warm-water feed supplied by the sea it had collapsed into a heap of innocuous looking tattered grey clouds, strewn across the eastern horizon. The wind had dropped significantly and the rain had all but stopped, lending an air of unreal calm and serenity to the situation. The sea, now royal blue and streaked by white horses, looked like the scene from a picture postcard as we were driven before a stiff and steady breeze, blowing us quickly out from the harbour entrance into the bay. In sombre and reflective mood, we looked back at the place where the trimaran should have been, a place from where we had escaped by the skin of our teeth. 'If there was anybody on board it would have been quick,' I tried to comfort Douglas, who continued to glare aft as he struggled to restrain the tears streaming down his face. There was not a single trace of the other boat or of anything in the water where she had been.

'I guess you're right,' I caught his barely audible reply, as he tried to suppress another involuntary sob. I mused on the possibility of returning but we were wind-locked from the bay and would not be able to return until the wind had shifted. Without another word, he turned and went forward, where he secured the anchors and trimmed the sails.

'Where are we going?' shouted Lyn from the galley. 'I don't know,' I replied, 'We can have a look on the chart later but I don't want to stay anywhere near here.' There was a unanimous nod of approval as Lyn brought some hot coffee up to the cockpit. Lyn had already bandaged Anne's wrenched shoulder in an improvised sling and all but stopped Neil's bleeding nose. Whilst still waiting my turn for medical attention, I shielded my throbbing and bloody hand. Of all the scrapes we had got into so far, this had been the closest we had come to losing not only *Lucette* but also our lives. It was a sobering moment indeed as we regrouped and stood in silence, contemplating how things might have been. Douglas broke the silence. 'Get Mum to fix your hand and then get some sleep, Dad,' he mumbled, his head bowed as he took the wheel from me. This was his way of forgiving what had happened over the last few days and I was only too pleased to release the helm to him. After Lyn had put her excellent nursing skills to use a third time that morning, I switched on our single-sideband radio and listened to the emergency long-range distress frequency on 2182 kHz, hoping to glean some news of the storm we had just been through. There was plenty of radio traffic, evidencing much damage and destruction inland, and we soon learnt that the owners and crew of the trimaran had been ashore whilst their yacht had been destroyed. Thankfully, they were all alive and sheltering in the local township. Relieved, I dropped into my bed, but sleep did not come easily as I lay in a restless half-sleep, infiltrated with disturbing dreams and bouts of hot sweats. Eventually I gave up trying to get to sleep, and contemplated the events of the last half-hour, which were going to take some getting over for each and every one of us on board.

We visited a number of islands after our encounter with the waterspout, including the white cliffs of San Salvador, where Christopher Columbus had made his first landfall and which the crew of the *Santa Maria* first mistook for the more distant shores of Cathay. With the weather freshening again, and still licking our wounds, we decided against landing and continued to Conception Island, which we found bleak and inhospitable and whose barren reefs we discovered were shallow and lifeless and covered in starfish. Remaining only for a night, we hurried on to Cat Island, where we anchored in the shallows of the Old Bight. The next morning we landed on a wide expanse of golden beach, which had the consistency of the finest of fine talcum powders. There was not a single trace of life in evidence. We explored as far as a tiny hermitage, which we found inhabited only by scorpions and stacked high with bottles of fresh water, intended for the salvation of stranded fishermen. We rested awhile out of the midday sun before contemplating the return journey. On our return trip, we discovered an abandoned plantation and a deserted village. Tying off our shirt sleeves and neck openings to make crude sacks, we filled them with the golden apple-like fruits picked from the bountiful sapodilla trees, still bearing their rich harvest in the ramshackle and overgrown orchards. We felt it strange indeed to have landed, gone ashore and trekked into the interior, visited the hermitage and stopped at the deserted village to pick bags of fruit, then re-boarded the *Lucette* and sailed away again, all without having seen a living soul.

From Cat Island, we made a short hop under full sail through quiet seas to the north, where we discovered the splendour of Little San Salvador's pink coral beaches and dropped anchor less than a boat length from the powdery pink sands. The foreshore was littered with the cartilage remains of hundreds of sharks, the area being the breeding ground for vast schools of bull sharks, which had come to this place to mate year after year since time immemorial.

While at anchor, mindful of our approach to the busy shipping lanes in the Gulf Stream, I decided to overhaul the rogue starter motor and electrical system, so that starting the engine would not be such a risky ordeal in the future. Removing the battery terminals, I placed them on deck in readiness for cleaning. Douglas, wandering about the deck in one of his absent-minded moments, accidentally knocked them over the side with his foot. We both watched in dismay as they sank fifty feet into the crystal-clear water. Realising what he had done, he glanced in my direction, muttered his usual expletive, and then shrugged his shoulders and dived over the side to retrieve them. In personal development terms he had certainly come a long way, considering he couldn't even swim properly before we left England, and I felt a great surge of pride as he returned enthusiastically holding his prize aloft, together with a huge conch tightly interned in its beautiful brown and pink shell. He shouted from the water that he had seen many more on the bottom and was returning to the depths to catch us dinner. His antics were being watched with interest by a middle-aged couple enjoying a romantic weekend break aboard their red bimini-topped speedboat. I waved automatically in their direction, acknowledging their interest, quite unaware as they sped away into the distance that they would change the entire course of our lives in the weeks ahead.

Lying adjacent to us in the anchorage was an aging 35-foot Bahamian fishing boat, painted a dirty brown and smelling out the entire area with the vile concentrated stench of rotting fish, typical of these working vessels. Witnessing Douglas's declaration from the water and admiring his success, one of the crew beckoned him over and was soon showing him exactly how to trap and clean the conch, explaining the technique for breaking the shell in order to extract the meat un-bruised. We quickly learned that the fishing boat, skippered by Fred, a tall thin native man wearing a cloth cap over a wizened face with an ever-cheerful demeanour, was actually anchored in distress. They had been driven before wind and tide for three days with a failed engine before finally, by the grace of good fortune, drifting into the anchorage. They had sent a distress message to the coastguard only to be told that they were a low priority. As their lives were not in immediate danger, and because of a public holiday followed by the weekend and then the Queen's birthday, a rescue boat could not be sent out for a further five days. Even then, they would only rescue the men, and the boat would fall to salvage. Fred was facing financial ruin unless I could figure a way to save him. Fred's problem was aggravated further by the construction of his boat, for like many of the Bahamian fishing boats it was equipped with a wet hold. The fish, initially caught in creels, were kept alive and fresh in a large tank-like pen open to the sea, so that the fish stock would arrive back at the markets of Nassau alive and fresh. Not wasting the extra time they had been adrift, Fred had continued to fish, and the hold was now full to the brim, with several prize species. Kept in captivity in such a fashion the fish refused to eat, and the entire catch would die and be rendered unfit for sale if they were not back to a fish dock within the next few days. I volunteered my somewhat limited mechanic's skills and quickly discovered the fuel pump impeller had disintegrated inside the pump casing. There was no hope of repair other than by fitting a replacement part. Fred was crestfallen and the spectre of ruin settled across his face once more.

That evening we enjoyed the finest of clam chowder entrées followed by freshly filleted grouper steaks, grilled to a turn and basted in an onion and pepper sauce spiked with red chillies, courtesy of Douglas's diving skills and Fred's philanthropic mood, combined with Lyn's expertise at the paraffin stove. My mind flitted back to the two welders in St Thomas and how they had worked on *Lucette*'s rudder without payment. After talking it through with Lyn the following day, I offered to save Fred's fish by towing his boat to Nassau, under sail! Fred was clearly taken aback at even the thought of such a ridiculous proposition. I watched him with uncertainty as he worked it through, his face contorting and creasing in a succession of perplexing stages, his weather-beaten features making it difficult to tell if he was smiling or grimacing. Finally, he chuckled. 'Well, mon, when your boat sinks and your lifejacket busts you grab onto a jellyfish.'

Unsure if *Lucette* would appreciate the innuendo, I could tell he expected me to charge him, but my reply to his unasked question made him whoop in delight. I had agreed with Lyn the night before that we wanted to pay back something of what the Caribbean society had already given to us, the sort of thing that money could not buy. I wanted to repay some of the help, kindness and generosity we had been shown, not just in St Thomas but also at many stages along the way. Help without which we simply would not have made it even this far. In any event, I continued to Fred, there was simply no other option on the table. Signalling his acceptance, Fred, unable to believe his luck, pumped my hand and broadcast the news to the other crew members on board. He enthusiastically offered to pilot us through the shallows of Ship Channel, in order to cut the passage time down to a minimum. The Ship Channel transit was only possible with the help of specialist local knowledge and was a daring and much talked-about route amongst yachtsmen the Caribbean over. It was our turn to be delighted, and we all buzzed with anticipation and excitement, revelling at the remarkable payback transpiring from the good turn we had proffered – for we could not have dared venture through the channel without the help of someone like Fred.

So started another remarkable trip, an event that was to make the front page of the newspapers in Nassau and more. Making the tow fast, we pulled out of the bay, *Lucette* leading the way and taking up the strain at the sedate pace, of 2 to 3 knots. We tugged somewhat ineffectually at the much larger fishing vessel, following close behind us like a large dog straining on its leash, all the time enveloping us in the pungent odours of drying fish. We meandered slowly out of the anchorage and into the confines of Ship Channel, which at times narrowed to the width of a mere cut, with rapidly shelving floors forming the bottom. Beset by strong currents flowing in excess of our speed in both directions, it proved difficult to navigate even with Fred's pilotage skills, living up to its promise of a difficult and hazardous trip right from the off. After two nights we motored the final few miles to our destination, welcomed by a small flotilla of interested onlookers and press boats. It seemed that we had achieved our fifteen minutes of fame.

We sailed under the bridge linking Nassau to Paradise Island late in the afternoon of the third day out from the beach of San Salvador. The tidal rip was in full flow inside the harbour, so Fred insisted that we let him go upstream from the fish dock, in order that his boat could drift into the other amply fendered fishing boats already moored there. Even he had underestimated the strength of the tidal rip, however, and after failing to make contact with the moored up fishing boats by the narrowest of margins he closed with the jetty further downstream out of control and at great speed. His boat loomed large and unstoppable over the concrete jetty and interested onlookers took flight as the screech of a car locking its brakes coincided with the moment of impact. Fred's boat hit the jetty hard, sending a welter of splinters flying into the air before juddering to a stop, where he eventually made fast alongside. Much to our relief the rescue was finally over and his catch saved.

Feeling well satisfied with our accomplishment, we stemmed into the powerful current, mooring up to one of the buoys reserved for visitors just off Mosquito Island near to the downtown area of the city. Modern-day Nassau was a playground for the rich and famous and a cornerstone for the thriving cruise-ship industry. In times gone by, though, Nassau had been the legendary home of Edward Teach, otherwise known as Captain Blackbeard, who had governed a commune of over 2,000 pirates in a thieves' den of iniquity, back in the early eighteenth century during a golden age for piracy. From this very place he had launched many a mission of terror, the natural harbour being well suited for hiding his massive flagship and a fleet of smaller ships until they were ready to put to sea and wield their mischief. 'If only the walls could talk,' said Douglas wistfully as he scanned the old town waterfront, half expecting to see pirates still skulking in the shadows. We had hit civilisation again, and with hardly any money left we were going to find our stay here a tough one, in more ways than one.

The old town of Nassau on New Providence Island lay adjacent to Paradise Island, where new luxury hotels intermingled with health resorts and secluded eastern-cult guesthouses above the picturesque harbour. Cruise ships and private yachts, as well as sailboats of all descriptions, crammed in a hubbub of comings and goings as they plied the channels alongside the out-island ferries and local sightseeing pleasure boats. Marinas, clubs and small boatyards proliferated in great abundance, located in a variety of exclusive and expensive venues, though the passage of the occasional Haitian sloop, like a ghost from a past era, roused more agitation from the camera shutters than the chrome and glass brilliance of the fleets of modern power cruisers. If we thought St Thomas in the Virgin Islands had been expensive, we soon found that Nassau overcharged at a breathtaking rate, not only for tourist attractions and souvenirs but also for staple foods and fruits, which ought to have been abundant and cheap.

The next morning a blond-haired man of towering proportions, looking in the prime of his life and dressed only in shorts and flip-flops, hailed us from the shore and introduced himself as Bill. I recognised him from the anchorage in San Salvador, where I had last seen him aboard the red bimini-topped speedboat. He explained how he had witnessed our rescue of the fishing boat first-hand and went on to say that he owned the local dive shop and tropical fish emporium, based in Nassau. Having made his money back home in the USA, he had sold up and was living his dream – not the first or indeed the second time we had come across such a lifestyle remedy. The Nassau newspapers had covered the story of Fred's deliverance under tow by our old schooner in every imaginable detail, and Bill was sufficiently impressed that he generously insisted on supplying us with diving equipment from his shop free of charge. 'A gift on behalf of the Nassau community,' he enthused. Unable to refuse such a generous offer, Douglas excitedly rowed the twins and Anne ashore, where they selected some quality underwater gear from the best dive shop in town. Remembering not to be overindulgent, the kids selected only flippers and snorkels, but it was enough to enhance their diving trips amongst the beautiful reefs and cays beyond all expectation.

Bill took an interest in us, and took Douglas fishing for crayfish on several occasions. He also taught him how to harpoon larger fish and how to dive for deep-water tropical fish, which Bill and his fish-catching company exported live to many cities in the western hemisphere. One day Douglas returned late, to recount with great excitement how he and the others had gone on an underwater hunt for nurse sharks with a harpoon shotgun. He had almost ended up as the bait himself, however, when a ten-foot blue shark suddenly appeared out of the murk and snapped at his legs as it brushed past him and escaped towards the open sea. Had the sleek killer of men chosen to, it could have taken his arm or leg in a single bite.

The very next day, having caught a huge number of crayfish with the help of his stepson and Douglas, Bill invited us all over to his place to help consume their bountiful catch. Feeling a little out of our depth in such esteemed company, Lyn and I dug deep into the storage chests and found some clothes that would pass for formal dress. We borrowed Fred's wooden dinghy and Douglas sculled us down the bay into a glorious sunset, towards Bill and Enid's waterfront mansion, which was located in one of Nassau's most salubrious waterfront suburbs.

Bill met us at his private jetty and took our bowline. His house was constructed of white block stone with cool marble floors. It overlooked the bay in a prime location, its large wooden verandas shaded by deep overhanging eaves. He directed us to a large open-plan room where a large pile of crayfish tails were marinating in a bowl of garlic sauce. They had laid on a veritable banquet for us and the gastronomic anticipation, triggered by the rich aroma of such fine food cooking, made our mouths water to excess. During aperitifs, talk turned to the wrecked galleon that we had discovered on Little Inagua, and Bill became very interested in launching a salvage party to explore it. I couldn't have agreed more and furnished him with as much information as I could recall, the opportunity cost being several thousands of dollars, and the investment of time so demanding, that I could not attempt such a project in any event. Bill's wife Enid had her son from Canada staying over, who was spending his university summer break with his mother. He was older than Anne, with a sportsman's physique, long dark hair and a finely trimmed beard. His name was Jeff; he was a son from Enid's former marriage, and his father was a wealthy businessman in Canada. We stayed late into the night and got on like the proverbial house on fire. Anne and Jeff seemed to like each other too. I must confess I ate so many of the expertly cooked crayfish that I became sick to the stomach, my body reacting adversely to so much good food after such a long period of shoestring diets and spartan shipboard fare. Our evening out ended with a quiet trip back up the bay under oars, beneath a bright moonlit tropical sky.

The following day, like a bolt out of the blue, Anne announced that she had fallen in love and would not be coming with us any further on the trip. The bottom dropped out of our world. I tried desperately to pacify Lyn, in the knowledge that we only borrow our children from the future, but this turn of events was news of a heartbreaking and devastating kind. If Anne left us we could not simply visit her or even call her, for we would be sailing thousands of miles away, unable to help or show our care for her in any way. In many ways, for me, I felt that our trip around the world had ended.

The next few days were spent trying to persuade Anne to change her mind. Discussions became heated debates and the heated debates became arguments, with many of the arguments becoming full-blown rows. The same old issues kept arising, and in the end it was clear there was no solution.

The situation was further complicated by the arrival of a catamaran that had followed us from St Thomas, on the pretext that her owner was terminating his trip in Nassau, where he planned to put his boat up for sale. He handed his entire ship's stores over to me – which, given our depleted circumstances, I was only too happy to accept. Later he invited me over to the Pilot House Hotel, where he proceeded to ply me with drink. Retiring to his boat, we drank on into the night recounting sailing adventures and telling tall stories. It was well past midnight before he confessed that he had followed us to Nassau, not to sell his boat but in pursuit of Anne. He continued in a drunken slur that on account of the considerable goodwill he had extended to me I was not to stand in his way. It was all I could do to hold my temper as I rose to leave, stating somewhat hypocritically that Anne was already involved, that I for one did not wish to see him again, and that he was banned from boarding the *Lucette*.

On returning to our boat I found Anne, already back from an evening out with Jeff, helping Lyn make some coffee in the galley. In my drunken state I recounted the night's events and conversations with the catamaran owner, and to my astonishment Lyn suddenly flew off the handle. In a fury I had not seen on her since leaving Meadows Farm, she turned on Anne, shouting and gesticulating wildly. The argument quickly became abusive and escalated into a physical attack, Lyn laying into Anne with fists flying like an angry boxer. 'I hope it was worth it,' she screamed, punching Anne hard in the stomach with a blow that winded her and caused her to buckle at the knees. Lyn, putting two and two together to get sixty-nine, had mistakenly perceived the food as some sort of payment in kind. Regaining her balance, Anne slapped Lyn across the face, which checked her advance. Lyn gathered her composure and retorted, 'That's right, hit your old mother!' I buried my head in my hands and groaned.

The following day I tried to persuade Lyn to agree on a consistent and coordinated approach to what had become a multifaceted, difficult and inflamed situation. I made the point that we had given our daughter life and brought her on this trip to encourage her to live that life to the full, and it was hardly fair therefore to blame her for doing exactly that. Lyn slowly nodded her head in agreement and promised not to strike out in anger again.

Things got better after that and Lyn began discussing her feelings with Anne, even recounting her own experiences of young love and explaining how she had dealt with similar situations in her youth. If Anne could not be dissuaded, then the least we could do was to ensure that her heart was not being set up to be broken. Eventually we had a meeting with Bill and Enid who, like us, were set against Jeff giving up his university place to be with Anne. Finally, on bended knee I begged Anne to come with us to Miami, even agreeing to take Jeff with us if she wanted. After days of argument and debate a tentative compromise was reached. After coming with us to Miami, Jeff was to return to Canada and after a suitable moratorium, if Anne still felt the same way towards him and he was prepared to look after her, Lyn and I would accede to our daughter's wishes and allow her to go to him with our blessings. Jeff's parents agreed and it seemed at last we would be able to work things out. It was a calculated risk, and I hoped things would fizzle into nothing when Jeff returned to Canada and resumed his university life in the not-too-distant future.

Such compromises did not mollify Lyn, however, who was not prepared to lose her daughter at any price. 'Anne was an innocent child,' she wailed at us from the saloon. In the belief that he was helping Anne's cause, Douglas, exhibiting the tact of a runaway bulldozer, exclaimed that Anne was far from innocent. In a shocked silence, Douglas revealed some of the secrets that teenagers share. Lyn was horrified at his outpouring and confronted Anne the moment she returned aboard, and when Anne reluctantly confirmed Douglas's revelations, Lyn assailed her with another vicious verbal assault. Anne was terrified, and if we had any hopes of her staying with us for much longer, they disappeared that day. I knew it would only be a matter of time now, Jeff or no, before we lost her.

Almost another week had slipped by before the arguments stopped, and Bill and Enid became regular visitors. News on the wreck turned out to be not so promising, for whilst it was now registered to us, it had been 'gone over' some twenty years previously and considered too precarious an operation to guarantee a return. Amid great feelings of regret, we decided to abandon the idea. Finding our fortunes would have to wait for another day.

Lucette set sail from Nassau before light westerly flurries and the mellowest of waves, gently gliding westwards over a small and insignificant swell. Conversely, her crew were enchained in a fraught and listless mood. We had accepted Jeff as our guest with open arms but he remained curiously muted as we left the low-lying northwest coast of New Providence. I offered to prepare lunch but there was no interest from the others so I went below in order to rustle up something for myself. Opening the stores cupboard I knew immediately something was amiss, for the cupboards were bare; the food that I had seen on board and had planned on getting us as far as America had mysteriously vanished. 'Well, I hope you didn't think we were going to eat his food, did you?' came Lyn's indignant reply to my startled enquiry. She explained that the food I had accepted from the owner of the catamaran had been the equivalent of immoral earnings, and that under such circumstances we could not have eaten it. Resisting the temptation to ask her exactly what we should eat instead, I stared vacantly into the empty cupboards, realising that with no fresh food and only a few tins of chicken supreme left in the stores, we had not nearly enough to get us to Miami. Preferring to starve rather than suffer Lyn's wrath at a suggestion of returning to replace the provisions she had dumped, I studied the chart in quiet misery, seeking an interim destination where we might obtain some provisions with our last few dollars. My attention focused on a distant US base located on Great Stirrup Cay, one of the northern cays of the Berry Islands. It was situated almost on the halfway point of our leg, so I decided to drop anchor there and ask the US Air Force if they could help.

Once anchored, Anne elected to remain aboard whilst Jeff donned his flippers and mask and took up his harpoon, promising us fresh fish for tea. In the meantime, feeling something akin to a subway busker, I decided to see if my begging skills were up to par and gathered my family together for the run ashore. Our Zodiac dinghy, already on its last legs, was badly torn on the inhospitable coral cliffs as we attempted a dangerous landfall on the eroded rocky shore. It was all we could do to prevent our craft flipping over as we surfed ashore and, heavily swamped, ground to an abrupt and ignominious halt. Having disembarked, it was clear that we would have to ride our luck in getting back to the *Lucette*, as the dinghy was nothing short of a total constructive loss.

The Communications Officer received us at the base with a combination of bemusement and suspicion. Finally he took pity on our plight and supplied us with a small bag of donuts, together with a lecture of admonishment regarding the responsibilities of parenthood, and the potentially drastic consequences of failing to plan with sufficient foresight. His rebuke finished with the assertion that he had no time for project leaders who could not plan. I searched for a topic on which I might strike a chord, or even one we might share in common. I concluded I was probably not alone in being unable to find one. Finally, he confessed that in any case the base had little food to spare as communications with the other islands had been severely disrupted since they had lost their inter-island motor launch when it was wrecked on the coral after he had forgotten to secure it with extra ropes in the face of an approaching hurricane. Resisting the urge to comment on the need for good planning, we made a hasty getaway, clinging tightly to what we had been so kindly given lest he ask for it back.

The full extent of the damage we sustained whilst landing was realised as soon as we set off on our return journey, for we were leaking so much air that it was impossible to keep the dinghy's flotation chambers inflated, even with the continuous operation of the pump. Our excursion entered the realms of a humiliating debacle when upon entering deeper water I was forced to abandon our waterlogged craft and swim behind it pushing, whilst Douglas balanced precariously in the bows valiantly sculling what was rapidly assuming the semblance of a giant marshmallow rather than a boat. Eventually reaching the safety of *Lucette*'s side, we hauled anchor and set sail. Ironically it was only Jeff's endeavours with his harpoon gun that provided us with sufficient food to get us the rest of the way to our journey's end.

The second night following our departure from Great Stirrup Cay, we perceived a luminous glow in the western sky. Reaching from the horizon, it stretched right over our heads and blotted out the stars across the entire firmament before us. It was the vibrant loom of Miami, beckoning us onward like a giant magnet, enticing and welcoming us like a hypnotic homing beacon. As dawn flushed the eastern sky, the glow paled into daylight and the whole western horizon took on the irregular shapes of tall concrete skyscrapers, rising out of the ocean on each side of us for as far as the eye could see, until the whole coastline lay before us. We had finally arrived in the United States of America!

CHAPTER 5

American affairs

Later that July afternoon, we stumbled upon, rather than sailed into, the rambling port of Miami, and quite by accident tied up alongside the customs and immigration berth in Biscayne Bay, adjacent to the mouth of the Miami River. On our way inbound we had instructed our children about the close friendship which ties our own country to the USA, with common ideals of democracy and freedom for the individual, and about our shared insistence on the protection of the weak from the strong and of the oppressed from the oppressor.

We were dismayed, therefore, to be subjected to the most protracted and inefficient, insulting and indeed threatening port entry we had made on our trip so far. We were threatened with large fines for breaking landing regulations, small fines for breaking docking regulations, expulsion for breaking immigration laws and impounding for breaking clearance regulations, as well as long and bitter recriminations for not having obtained certain papers, which should have been given to us by the US consul in Nassau in the first place. I finally had to help the elderly official interpret his own documents, fill out his multitude of forms and bring to his attention the fact that we had done nothing the signs did not tell us to do. This last observation resulted in a further admonishment for introducing the concept of taxation without representation, back in the eighteenth century. After seven hours bogged down in a quagmire of red tape and unmitigated bumbledom, he finally stamped our visas, stating that now we had done things his way, we were welcome to enter the United States of America. After such an unpleasant experience, we were not at all sure that we still wanted to. Leaving the customs and immigration berth, we sailed into the city marina. After enquiring about the cost of mooring and discovering that we had only sufficient funds left to tie up for about twenty minutes, we motored back out into the bay and dropped anchor in front of an expansive park located in the heart of the city. We had at long last landed in America, which was to be our home for the next six months.

Florida was originally settled by the Spanish in the early sixteenth century. It enjoyed a subtropical climate, with mostly flat terrain and over 30,000 lakes, offering ideal conditions for the mass production of citrus fruit and vegetables, which was Florida's largest industry and primary export. Even so, by the early 1970s, faster and more modern jet liners were making tourism an increasingly significant cornerstone of the Floridian economy. It was a far cry indeed from the lands and cultures we had visited thus far. For the Robertsons, life was going to be very different for the foreseeable future. Seeking adventures of a different kind, we had to re-learn to incorporate the daily pursuit of gain back into our lives – and quickly, as we had only three dollars left to our name.

In 1971, Florida and Miami in particular were still dealing with the exodus of the Cubans fleeing from the communist regime in Cuba, which lay just 80 miles to the south. Having been brought to the brink of nuclear annihilation by the Kennedy-led missile crisis less than a decade before, the advent of low airfares had brought about a dramatic new prosperity to Florida. Tourists flocked not only to Disney World in the virtually unknown city of Orlando further to the north but also to a host of similar, less glitzy entertainment establishments that had sprung up all over the state. Richard Nixon was President and young American men were assiduously questioning, ever more remonstratively, their role in Vietnam. Further north along the eastern seaboard, the Kennedy Space Center had already placed a man on the moon and all about us in this progressive and mighty nation was hustle and bustle. Miami, already a gargantuan city by any standards, was on the brink of explosive economic growth and a massive expansion in its population.

Most important for us, though, was that work was available to all who wanted it. Indeed, we found Miami more than a little intimidating as we stepped gingerly ashore to explore our new surroundings, looking for a slice of the fabled American pie. We slowly took stock of the biggest and most powerful economy in the world, where the proverbial 'better mousetrap' had made millionaires of its creators overnight. 'Over four million sold!' screamed the McDonalds signs, and Burger King had just opened their first outlet in Flagler Street. Howard Johnsons were eateries and milk-shake bars, offering a staggering 29 varieties of ice cream, and the city had just completed building its first official skyscraper. Just walking in Miami was an education in itself. The downtown section comprised many tall buildings, which were not actually classified as skyscrapers but looked every bit as though they ought to have been. The office space they provided climbed over forty storeys in height, towering above the scree of business motels and department stores, eateries and car parks.

The city was bordered on the eastern side by the fabulous Biscayne Boulevard, which in turn fronted the extensive Bay Front Park lying next to the marina and sheltering the river estuary, in which *Lucette* lay quietly at anchor. On the western side, the city quickly degenerated into a dreary vista of sleazy boarding houses, second-hand goods shops, bars, strip joints and liquor stores, where the sidewalks, littered with the squalid stains of humanity, finally gave way to the Overton area, a place where white men increasingly feared to tread. Near the centre of this area, which was served by a complex series of freeway intersections and broad interlinking avenues, lay the city hall and administrative offices. Further to the west lay the futuristic jet-a-minute international airport, beyond which the city finally surrendered its suburbs to the flat bush country and mosquito-ridden swamps of the Everglades.

Miami was home to vast entertainment complexes that were merely sideshows compared to what the state visionaries were planning. Killer whales in a giant sea aquarium, and monkey jungles where the visitors walked around the park in cages and the wildlife ran free, were already being supplanted by vast theme parks that were to become world-famous attractions. Miami's allure brought all manner of humanity together, from the wealthiest of America's citizens, who spent their retirement in the comfort of a warm climate enjoying air-conditioned luxury and numerous gimmicks of the machine age, to the drug addicts and street sleepers who had drifted into this sunshine state. Life in the city was a wake-up call indeed for an innocent family abroad.

Later that first night, as we lay quietly at anchor, we were delighted by the most pleasant surprise we could have hoped for. The twins were the first to recognise the familiar melodic chug of *Bonnie*'s distinctive Atlas Imperial engine, as she sailed past us in the darkness. The Icelanders had been in Miami for some time and were making their way back to their river berth after the completion of a long day's charter. Seeing us anchored in the bay, they quickly altered course and came alongside, the children jumping across the closing gap as the two vessels gently nudged each other in the watery shadows. Once alongside we exchanged hugs and kisses, reunited again at last. Indeed, the reunion lifted our hearts with feelings more readily associated with the safe return home of long-lost family members.

The familiar high-pitched drone of mosquitoes whining in our ears severely disrupted our attempts at sleep. The insects forced us to retreat below decks, where we caught up with each others' adventures long into the early hours. Siggi and Etta had obtained full-time work visas before arriving in the USA, and Siggi was already working as a sea captain on one of the inter-island coasters, an ancient relic of a ship, converted from a wartime landing craft, named *Out Islander*. Our Icelandic friends looked after us like true friends, helping us in our hours and weeks of need without ever counting the cost.

Lucette had built up a substantial amount of weed under her waterline, requiring us to dry-dock her before we moved on. In order to pay for this essential overhaul we planned to get work and save as much money as we could. Our endeavours were impeded, however, by the seemingly endless myriad of visitors that waited by the shore steps to be invited on board, ostensibly just to talk to us and hear our tales of adventure. From vice-presidents of banks to cinema owners, bowling alley operators and even retired bank robbers, we met all kinds of folk who in one way or another charmed us all, each in their own inimitable style. Amongst the lost causes there were a few genuine people, and some of the friendships forged in Bayfront Park were both enduring and significant.

One such friend was a male nurse called Oz. He advised Lyn on how to weave her way through the maze of red tape to obtain employment back in nursing. After getting her visa altered to allow her to work, it wasn't long before she struck lucky and landed a job at the Cedars Hospital, her generous wage enabling us to enjoy the full hospitalities of civilised America and repay our Icelandic friends. Douglas was the next to get work, gardening in downtown residential areas and working for a local yacht broker, polishing gin-palace motor yachts. He gave every penny he earned to the family and was proud to do so.

Anne had become a very shapely young lady and Douglas had developed into the fine stature of a man, and both attracted constant streams of men, of different orientations, vying for their attentions. Indeed, they were both in serious jeopardy, but Lyn and I were unaware of what was happening and did not have the experience to notice. Later in the month Siggi was due to return to sea for a few weeks, and he suggested that while he was away we should moor our boats alongside each other for mutual protection. This allowed the kids to play together, unimpeded by the stretch of water normally separating us when lying at anchor. Unfortunately, this also started what the *Miami Herald* newspaper was to call the 'Downtown Commune', in a weekly column in which they referred to us as the 'Biscayne Gypsies'. Soon after Siggi's departure, Olaf and Douglas were almost kidnapped off Miami Beach by two wealthy Cubans, and Anne and Douglas had other 'friends' calling at all times of the day and night. The twins, however, settled down to some intensive 'catch-up' schoolwork aboard, and took advantage of the magnificent public library located close by, from which I was able to structure a daily learning programme for them.

Anne and Jeff were becoming more and more of an item, and just when our lives seemed to be settling down to some sort of order, Anne raked the ashes of tranquillity by asking if she and Jeff could move into the forecastle and share a cabin together. Lyn fretted over the issue for days, then she polarised matters absolutely, managing to make a complete crisis out of the issue, by declaring that Jeff could not 'move in' with our daughter unless they first got married! She had inadvertently given her approval to such a union, infuriating Jeff's parents in Nassau, as they believed that we had now gone back on the moratorium agreement we had made before we left Nassau. Lyn's ultimatum also gave Anne and Jeff licence to spend their time running around getting blood tests and making marriage arrangements. They soon discovered that being under twenty-one they needed to get parental consent, and when they found that such consent was not forthcoming, either from our side or from Nassau, they decided to flee to Georgia, where consent was not required. Typical of their years, they took Lyn at her word and asked her for the return airfares. When Lyn said no, she effectively scuttled their plans, leaving Anne deeply hurt by a perceived change of heart. By then, however, their time was up and Jeff had to return home to Toronto or face being thrown out of college.

When Siggi returned from his stint at sea, it was clear that he had been thinking long and hard about the future. In an impassioned plea, he asked me to sell *Lucette* and put the money into the *Bonnie*, to finance a joint trip to Australia and New Zealand. I was faced with a very hard decision indeed. I had previous dealings with a legal partnership when I first started farming, and it was the bankruptcy of my partner that had depleted the farm's reserves to such an extent that when hard times came there was no cash cushion left to enable recovery. *Lucette* was my family's only remaining asset, and Siggi's proposal required that her sale proceeds be converted to a share in the *Bonnie*. I felt I simply could not afford to risk the last of our family's wealth in such a venture. There was another issue too. Such a joint venture would rule out any flexibility if Anne was going to leave us in the future, and I felt that I had to be free to respond to her needs. I could not really do that if we were all together aboard *Bonnie*. I had to say no. My decision was both painful and final and it represented a crushing and pivotal moment for us all. Lacking the necessary funds to go on, it marked the end of the road for the Icelanders' voyage. The following day my dear friend Siggi put precious *Bonnie* up for sale. When he returned from the yacht brokers we all shed a tear together, mourning the loss we knew we must all soon face.

Less than a week later, new owners purchased the *Bonnie*, intending to incorporate her into their business interests in Haiti. The sale, being subject to survey, meant that we finally had to untie these two old friends. As it turned out it was no easy task, as their anchor chains had become intertwined in a barnacle-encrusted rats' nest. After several hours of turning *Lucette* and *Bonnie* with the aid of the dinghies, without success, I took a hacksaw and cut through a steel joining shackle, severing *Lucette*'s chain and unwrapping it from around *Bonnie*'s stouter links before shackling it together again. In melancholy mood, *Bonnie* pulled away towards the mouth of the river and faded into the distance, chugging her way towards the dock where she was to be surveyed. She did come back to the anchorage afterwards, but she seemed different now that she was in new hands. Neither Lyn nor I was to set foot on her decks again. But Anne and Douglas soon got to know the new owners, and our children began spending a lot of their free time with them, both ashore and afloat. Again, I was uneasy with their choice of friends but felt powerless to intervene. The only saving grace was that at least Jeff would be well and truly out of Anne's mind. How wrong I was.

As the income flowed in from the weeks of paid employment, our cash flow turned positive, enabling us to make good the dinghy fund that Edna and Mary had so kindly gifted to us in Las Palmas. We decided to purchase a brand-new fibreglass dinghy from a Mr Stuart of Fort Lauderdale. Admiring its stout lines and the good quality of its workmanship, Lyn even remarked how our lives might depend on it one day. True to our word given in Las Palmas, we named the little boat *Ednamair* after Lyn's sisters. It had been built as a class project by the pupils of the Miramar High School in 1970, and Douglas immediately took to it in an almost obsessive way. In his travels he had acquired a couple of stout oars, the shafts of which he had lined with metal and then assembled with rowlocks, to produce a one-piece contraption that he attached to the gunwales for extra purchase as he rowed. And how he could row! It wasn't long before he had the dinghy planing under oars alone. Onlookers stood and applauded as he sped by, and still he rowed. Hour after hour the evenings would pass to the rhythmic beat of his rowing, as he perfected his technique and extended his routine. It was as though something deep inside him already knew that one day our lives were really going to depend on it.

The most influential and indeed helpful friend we met in Miami was a man named Albert. He was also a male nurse, and he had watched us from the shore for many days before eventually introducing himself by baking a Cay Lime Pie in anticipation of our meeting. He was to play a significant part in our lives, for he attached himself to Douglas and usurped my role as his father right from the start. I must have been truly blind not to see his intentions for what they really were.

We never really got over the departure of our Icelandic friends. On the day they left the anchorage for the last time, a part of us went with them. Our loss was compounded even further by the sad departure of the *Bonnie* herself, later in the month of September. Several other sailboats joined us in the anchorage and the *Miami Herald* soon extended its column, rallying its readership against the Biscayne Gypsies. It was about then that Baxter Still, one of America's foremost yachtsmen and a yacht broker of considerable repute, approached us in the bay. He had an offer of work for us. Douglas and I were to accompany him to Panama and deliver back to Miami a classic Alden schooner called the *Puritan*. She was gaff-rigged and over 125 feet in length, in effect a little sailing ship. It would take a month to complete the voyage but I figured that with the money from this project, and with Lyn's wage still coming in, then by the time we returned we would have saved enough money to dry-dock the *Lucette* and still have enough to get us across the Pacific.

The trip aboard the *Puritan* was as entertaining and eventful as it had promised it might be. After hiring a crew from the Colon brothels, we sailed into Miami five weeks later, under full sail and in a blaze of glory. True to his word, Baxter paid us well for the job. While we had been away, Lyn and Anne had suffered a few adventures of their own and the anchorage was filled with boats of all shapes and sizes, the commune having expanded significantly in our absence. Anne recounted how a would-be suitor had even tried to swim out to the boat to try to speak to her. Another man claimed he had been sent by God and could not swim for much longer in the fast-flowing current. Lyn threw him a rope, which he rapidly hauled in hand over hand. As he got closer, Lyn saw that he was armed. Wondering just how she could have been so gullible, she steeled the children for the worst. Then the end of the rope she had thrown him disappeared over the side and into the water. The would-be mugger was quickly whisked downstream in the ebbing tide. Thankfully, she had forgotten to tie the other end of the rope onto a cleat, her carelessness actually saving their lives.

Before the month had ended, the riot squad attended the anchorage in fast patrol boats, armed with machine guns and shields, and served the flotilla of yachts gathered there with orders to leave. The *Miami Herald* had made its point and the anchorage was cleared of the 'Biscayne Gypsies' by order of the courts. Baxter found us a berth upriver that was effectively free of charge and very close to the hospital where Lyn worked. From here, we continued to work and save. I delivered several more luxury yachts for Baxter, and the twins made new friends in the form of two little girls about their age called Hope and Mary, who lived nearby. A few weeks later, after we had successfully dry-docked *Lucette*, overhauling and repainting her as well as re-checking the rudderpost, we had saved enough money to leave. Douglas was back working full-time on the *Puritan*, until she was finally arrested for non-payment of bills.

We had now been in the USA for longer than our three-month visas and several extensions permitted, and we were informed by immigration control that no further extensions would be allowed. The only way we could stay longer was to sail to a foreign port in order to get our passports date-stamped and then re-enter the USA with new three-month visas. A Bahamian island called Bimini lay a mere 45 miles away to the east and was the easiest foreign port to get to. I was busily explaining to the family why we needed to make the trip and when we would be sailing, when Anne dropped another bombshell, announcing to us all that Jeff had dropped out of university, and she would be leaving us within the next few days, to join him in Nassau. We had set them every possible hurdle to jump and still we returned to the same spot. It was clear that the issue of Anne and Jeff would not be settled by keeping them apart. Indeed, our best option, Lyn concluded, was to allow them sufficient time together in the hope that they would soon get sick of each other. I asked Anne to stay until we left for Bimini, and after much remonstrating she agreed. The short interval of time remaining would at least give Lyn and me time to think.

Fighting the vagaries of the powerful Gulf Stream currents, it took us two whole days to complete what should have been a six-hour passage. Albert accompanied us on the voyage and we were all happy to be back in the Bahamas again, but things had changed. Douglas was going to nightclubs now and Albert seemed to be constantly at his side. Anne became wistful and preoccupied, whilst the twins became ever more deeply immersed with Hope and Mary on the one hand and their puppet-land fantasy world on the other. I was certain that Neil fully expected us to call there one day. Taking a marina berth, we made our stay in Bimini into a family holiday. On the sixth day Anne packed her things and told us she was taking the small open ferry boat across the sea to the inter-island seaplane base. After all the talk and tribulations, this time there would be no turning back. When the moment for departure finally arrived Lyn and I walked her to the dockside in silence, each step an agony like the last walk of the condemned. All too soon, we reached the edge of the small wooden jetty, where the brightly coloured ferryboat lay bobbing to and fro in the easy swells, patiently waiting for the appointed time of departure. We had only a little time left. Anne rejected Lyn's last-minute pleas to reconsider, saying that she was in love and that nothing else mattered. We each struggled to hold back our tears as we faced our last goodbye.

My mind flitted back to the times when she had been our little girl, times when she had dozed in front of the open fire at Meadows Farm, times when I had carried her up the stairs to her room and read her bedtime stories that had sent her into innocent sleep. Together we recalled her school concerts and the times spent heaping houses in the summer hay, of her wrapping up warm on winter's nights, and of the little spring daisies she had brought home from the front meadow. Smiling through the stubborn and misconceiving years of her adolescence, in a more serious tone we then remembered the stoic and heroic strength she had unselfishly provided, to get us all this far. Anne did not want to leave us and most certainly not like this, for she too could not stop the stream of tears running down her high cheekbones so profusely that, even her blouse was stained with large damp patches. She knew she had to go, though, instinctively she knew her happiness depended upon it. Like the loving family she was leaving behind, she too had a price to pay. No longer our little girl, she had become a beautiful woman, and the decision she had made was that of a woman beyond her years.

We sobbed our last farewells, and, unable to suppress my weeping, I squeezed her in my arms for one last and precious time. We were still her parents and would always be, we still loved her dearly and we always would. Now the only way to show her how much we loved her was to let her go with our blessing. Turning back as she stepped away, she waved last kisses to us across the lengthening divide. We watched intently as she hesitantly climbed the little boat's boarding ladder, at the head of the gangway. We watched in silence as she visibly steeled her nerves before us then with a show of renewed determination stepped forward onto the solid bulwarks of the craft before disappearing from sight into the hull of the boat. Our eyes smiled relief though our hearts were torn asunder when she reappeared from under the canopy, still waving and still sobbing. All too quickly the ferryboat, its flimsy sun canopy flapping noisily in the breeze, pulled away from the jetty and out into the bright blue waters of the channel. Our little Anne seemed so fragile and helpless as she waved from the side of the canopy. We returned her wave and didn't stop until long after the boat had disappeared, unwilling to leave while there was still a chance that she might return. It was not to be. With hearts of lead, we turned back for the long walk home, our glum silence interrupted only by our sobbing. We had almost reached the *Lucette* before Lyn managed to speak. 'Take me back to our island, Dougal, take us all back to Little Inagua where we were happy.' I hugged her to me, unable to comfort her, for we had lost our little girl to an uncertain world, and though I could not show it, I too was torn apart in anguish. 'Well, we still have our boys,' I said, trying my best to sound upbeat.

'We have that,' she replied, a new resolve settling on her face. She was going to make the most of them while she could, for they too had their own way to make in the world, and the autumn chills of our time with Douglas were already making themselves felt more strongly with each passing month. He would be eighteen on his next birthday and our time together would surely not last for too much longer.

We waited two more days in Bimini before we felt certain that Anne would not return. With heavy hearts, we slipped our moorings and started the short trip back. On returning to Miami we were handled by the same sanctimonious immigration officer who had cleared us in originally. This time, however, he was more concerned with the fact that Albert's American passport did not have a visa in it and in accordance with the law he stated that the *Lucette* would have to be detained. After umpteen explanations that Albert, as a US citizen, did not need a visa to enter America, I saw a faint glimmer of understanding flash across his eyes. Eventually he cleared us inwards, and we returned to our river berth. It felt like home. In light of Anne's return to Nassau, Lyn and I decided that we would wait until after Christmas in Miami and then return to Nassau before heading for the Panama Canal. It was a deliberate ploy to coax her back, after the initial blush of romance and the novelty of her first true relationship had subsided. Albert was now teaching Douglas to drive and treated the whole family to many outings, meals and evenings in front of the television at his downtown home. He invited us along to celebrate the Christmas festivities, which were topped with a long telephone call to Anne, making our first Christmas and New Year away from the wintry climes of England not only happy but also complete.

It was almost a year to the day since we had left Falmouth in that Biscay storm, when I met Douglas and Albert returning from yet another driving lesson, late one January afternoon. As they walked aboard, I overheard their conversation, and it made my blood run cold. Douglas was clearly involved with the gay scene in Miami Beach, and it seemed he had inadvertently become mixed up with the newly emerging drug set there. It was also clear from the whispered exchange that his relationship with Albert had what I considered inappropriate sexual connotations. I simply had to tell Lyn that I believed Albert was conducting a homosexual affair with our son, right under our noses. Lyn insisted that I ask Douglas outright, and when I did, he just blanked me, scared of admitting that he knew he had lost control of his situation.

We could not risk losing Douglas as well as Anne, so Lyn and I made secret plans to sail for Nassau before the month was out. The following day Lyn suggested that only she needed to remain till the end of her notice period, and one of her colleagues had a small apartment for rent. She insisted we sail before the end of the week. She would then work out the rest of her contract and join us in Nassau by seaplane. I agreed, and the following day I waited until Albert stopped by on his morning jaunt, ostensibly to take Douglas for a drive, which they almost always followed with a prolonged mid-morning breakfast. As Douglas and Albert made their way ashore, I informed them both that breakfast would be taken on board this morning, as we would be sailing on the tide straight afterwards.

'Sailing where?' interjected Douglas, clearly taken aback at the news, the thought of leaving Miami quite alien to his thoughts. Albert appealed to me to reconsider, but on seeing the determination in my eyes he turned to Douglas and offered him a new life in America with him. When the chips were down, my eldest son had the habit of making the right decision, nevertheless my heart raced as he considered the offer before him. There was an ominous, overbearing silence. Whilst I never expected him to leave us, I sighed in grateful relief as he turned to Albert with tears in his eyes and kissed him on the cheek, hugging him tightly in a farewell embrace right in front of us all. He clutched Albert's hands and clasped them tightly between his own, not wanting to let go but knowing he must. His mind made up, Douglas slowly stepped away, turning as he did so to dismiss, with a wave of his upraised arm, each of Albert's urgent and ever more fervent appeals for him to stay behind. We were rooted to the spot as we witnessed another painful goodbye. Douglas sobbed openly as he strode back towards the *Lucette*, then he stopped and we watched as he turned back towards Albert, who was now on his knees pleading and begging young Dougie to reconsider.

'I'm sorry, Al,' he continued in a quiet but determined voice, 'my family cannot go on without me and I will not forsake them now.' I wiped an irksome tear from the corner of my eye. Before my very eyes, my son seemed to have blossomed into manhood. Then, in a bizarre outturn of events, I could not believe my ears as I heard Douglas ask his mother to stay with Albert for the rest of her stay in Miami. At the same time, he secured from Albert a promise that he would not only look after his mother but also deliver her to Chalks seaplane base downtown, in order to ensure her safe arrival in Nassau. It was testimony indeed that I felt a lot safer leaving my wife with Albert than I did my son.

Leaving Miami in such haste was an unpopular move with everyone on board. An air of disbelief hung over our little craft as we made hasty preparations to depart, for in many ways we had come to regard Miami as our home. The twins went immediately to retrieve their puppets from the homes of Hope and Mary and after hurried goodbyes returned to the boat clearly upset that they must leave their dear friends behind them. That was the good thing about living on a boat, however, for when circumstances went pear-shaped and were no longer tolerable, as at the end of the day Lyn and I believed they were, then by simply weighing anchor it was possible to flee. And that was exactly what we did, just over six months after our perplexing arrival and not quite twelve months after leaving the shores of England.

Miami had been good to us and would forever remain deeply embedded in our hearts. From exciting airboat rides amongst the natural beauty of the Everglades to running the gauntlet of the downtown fleshpots, we had experienced the good the bad and the excessive of all that was humanity. The American people had been both generous and kind to us and we had made many friends and enjoyed many adventures. However, we had not only lost our daughter and almost our son but also our Icelandic friends. Furthermore, both Lyn and I felt that as a family we had also lost our innocence.

Our time in Miami had come to an end, and with heavy hearts we cleared outwards from the environs of the mercenary city and headed out to the deep blue water of the waiting ocean. Huge barrelling rollers blocked the confined harbour entrance as *Lucette* stood on her beam-ends, rolling and pitching her way into the Gulf Stream offshore. It seemed that even *Lucette* did not want to leave. As we cleared the harbour walls with only inches to spare, my eye fixed momentarily on the large green valise secured on the forward coach roof, containing the ten-man inflatable life raft, a final but enduring reminder of our friends the Icelanders and of the *Bonnie*, who we were also leaving behind. With all sails set, we picked up speed, and it wasn't long before the skyscrapers of Miami Beach faded into the sunset, leaving us alone in a gently heaving sea, which quickly imposed its cleansing effect on our spirits and refocused our minds. Moonless, the velvety night sky hung suspended above us and a plethora of phosphorescence flashed gleaming bright flares of lucent green amid the luminescence stirred up in our turbulent wake.

Crossing the Florida Strait the next morning, we bypassed the island of Bimini, our painful memories of Anne's departure flaring only briefly, for we were bolstered by the certainty of seeing her again soon. With only the boys and me aboard the *Lucette*, we arrived at Cat Cay and cleared inwards with the Bahamian authorities, a fifteen-minute formality with a most courteous official. We politely declined a berth in the marina, at a price double that of the already exorbitant prices back in Miami, choosing instead to anchor for the night in the familiar and crystal-clear waters. Next morning we traversed the Grand Bahama Bank, a leg of just over 100 miles through shoal water, where depths of little more than seven feet in places left us with only inches beneath our keel. The dazzling blues and greens of the ocean shone like sparkling emeralds against the white sandy seabed, whilst the rich hue of the shimmering waters varied markedly according to the depth of the water. The sea bottom gently undulated in long capricious sand banks, hiding innumerable shoals of barracuda, king fish, sailfish and marlin as they pursued smaller fry beneath us. Our trailing line astern was soon snatching to the violent throes of a giant king fish, the excellent large-radius gaff given to me by the boys for Christmas proving most effective as I hauled the monster on board. Its bright blue and silver scales quickly dimmed to grey as we landed it on to *Lucette*'s sun-baked decks. Slowly but surely the simple family values and egalitarian mores of our shipboard existence re-established themselves and an air of contented fulfilment pervaded on board. Arriving at Plantation Cay under a magnificent sunset, we spent that night at anchor in a small, protected cove.

The following morning we set sail, and after a pleasant day cruising through calm seas before a mild breeze we sighted the low coral hills surrounding Nassau, New Providence. Anne was waiting on the jetty to meet us and her eyes lit up as we embraced in a gleeful and happy reunion. In accordance with the grand plan, we met Lyn off the seaplane three weeks later and for a glorious couple of weeks after that we enjoyed our days like a family again, for what was to be the last time. It was clear that Anne had every intention of stopping where she was. Her interest in round-the-world voyaging had waned as she had been taken by her new lifestyle in the playgrounds of Nassau. Lyn and I finally accepted Anne's decision to stay in Nassau and pursue her own destiny. Leaving her with sufficient funds so that she could rejoin us should she change her mind, we said our goodbyes with typical English restraint, fully aware that we might never see her again. On the day of our appointed departure goodbyes were made with smiling embraces for once, and we waved heartily to Anne as she walked back down the jetty, her arm interlinked with Jeff's, his face fixed with a grin as he folded the hard-earned dollars I had given to Anne into his pocket. Reaching the far end of the jetty, she got into his car and, without even so much as a look back, drove away.

CHAPTER 6

To Jamaica

The children's mood was surprisingly upbeat following Anne's departure, as *Lucette* slowly meandered southwards towards the Exuma Cays. For Lyn and myself, however, leaving Nassau was one of the hardest thing we had ever done in our entire lives, and our only hope was that in the days and weeks ahead we would come to terms with our loss, which now seemed so full and final. Sailing by day and anchoring by night, we visited small tropical cays, some consisting of nothing more than a few coral heads and a palm tree or two surrounded by a smooth bed of sand. Douglas and the twins revelled in the warm waters, surfing the soft beach breaks under clear skies and the warm sunshine typical of these small and extremely beautiful Bahamian islands. Diving to gather sponge corals and to explore underwater caves, the boys harpooned barracuda and crayfish and collected conch by the bucketful. Our skills as hunter–gatherers had improved beyond measure, which delighted us all, for the more we could catch, the more varied and healthy our diets and the less we had to buy. We spent a further two days exploring a vast pink beach on Stocking Island, formed entirely from the finely crushed remains of shells and corals polished to a crystalline pulp by thousands of years of exposure to the tide and waves. Burnished under the rise and fall of countless suns, the texture of the sand resembled the finest pink dust, which puffed in clouds around our feet as we galloped in joy across its unspoilt tracts.

On the day we left Great Exuma, our mood was heightened by excited anticipation, as we cruised through the crisp morning sunshine. We were bound for Kingston in Jamaica, home to the famous pirate town of Port Royal, the origins of which were steeped in history that dated back to the UK's Elizabethan era. The northerly wind was fresh, backing gradually to the west, to produce a smooth sea in which *Lucette* rolled easily under full sail, trundling east on the first leg of our route. We were headed on a course that would take us clear of the northern tip of Long Island, after which we intended to head south, towards the aptly named Windward Passage, a channel of tempestuous waters formed by a tongue of the ocean dividing the politically troubled Cuba from the austere regime that governed an equally troubled Haiti. I had calculated that it would take us a week to complete the 500-mile sea passage to Kingston. I hoped that from there we would be able to call Anne, to give her one last chance to rejoin us if she wanted to.

We maintained a steady 6-knot average speed under genoa and mainsail, later rigging the fisherman flying headsail for the first time since leaving England. Racing on in an easterly direction, it was my plan to clear the hazardous reefs and rock fields lying offshore from Long Island's northern point before nightfall. The calm seas and fair winds allowed us to press on under full sail, slicing through the water at a good speed, the sun shining brightly and the mood balmy as we fell into our familiar watch-keeping routines. During the mid-afternoon watch a curious and potentially deadly weather phenomenon crept insidiously down upon us. To the north of us, a front banked dark clouds on the distant horizon and rapidly spread cold fingers of wind across the calm sea. In hindsight any number of courses of action would have been appropriate to meet this hitherto unquantified challenge, but the course of action we chose was most definitely not. Lulled into a false sense of security by the mildness of the weather and the calmness of the sea around us, we did absolutely nothing.

Sandy remained at the wheel, soaking up the sunshine, as a long line of disturbed spume and spray came into view, steadily overhauling us from the direction in which we had come. It was a clear and distinct demarcation line whipped up by the juxtaposed wind and current, marking the point at which the frontal boundary had descended to sea level, where its leading edge had formed a disturbed and angry confluence on the surface of the sea. As destructive a natural phenomenon as a tornado or a hurricane, it stretched towards the horizon as far as the eye could see on either side, slowly descending upon us from the north. Without warning, the wind shifted to become variable from the south and dropped to the strength of a light breeze.

The sails collapsed from lack of wind and we wallowed in the seaway like a stranded whale. The sea state in our proximity was calm and serene, giving the impression that there was nothing to worry about. Deceptively, the sea appeared flat and smooth even beyond the frontal edge, belying the force of the elements at work within it.

'So what could it be?' enquired Douglas in a perplexed tone, as puzzled as myself by such a conundrum, his voice raised in anxiety but lacking the necessary conviction to trigger any alarms. 'I really don't know,' I replied, gazing through the binoculars before passing them on to him so he could get a better view of the burgeoning line of white horses. As the front edged closer we could see the water was pockmarked by swirling eddies and shrouded in clouds of spray, as steadily and silently it closed upon us in what was to be a deadly embrace. 'Maybe it's the edge of the Gulf Stream playing tricks,' I continued, my voice wavering as I struggled to be convincing. The pervading air of serenity lulled me into neglecting a cornerstone of good shipmaster's practice, however, for I should already have had all hands on deck, to reduce sail until the hazardous phenomenon had passed. Instead, blissfully unaware of the approaching danger, I watched practically mesmerised, as the doglegged line of bustling white water got closer and closer until finally it hit us.

Too late, the immortal words of Joseph Conrad flashed across my mind: 'Any fool could carry on but only a wise man knew to shorten sail in time.' On this occasion, I had been the fool and my window of opportunity had been lost. *Lucette* reeled onto her beam-ends as though struck by a broadside of cannon, the hurricane-force wind striking her with a sudden and violent blast of immense force from the northwest, which shook her viciously in its mighty grip. The sudden ferocity of the gust, coupled with a near-180-degree change in the wind direction, brought all the sails aback with an ear-splitting report, and in a single perilous moment the genoa and fisherman sails were ripped to shreds, long ribbons of canvas whipping and cracking in the wind like flailing tentacles. Caught with full sail up, *Lucette* remained heeled over at an alarming angle and picked up a dramatic turn of speed, as she bludgeoned her way through the water, her decks awash and her coach roof and sails drenched from heavy deluges of stinging spray. The horse having well and truly bolted, I scrambled all hands onto what had become a perilous and steeply angled deck, to haul in the remnants of the tattered sails. The mainsail, under the severe press of the wind, had jammed and was impossible to reef or take down. My only option was to feather it under a long sheet, before securing it with a hastily rigged preventer, doubled back for safety.

The jib sails were not robust enough to remain hoisted in such conditions for long, and in the manner of a well-practised team we fought furiously against the elements to replace them with stronger storm sails. This reduction enabled us to maintain an approximate course by bringing the wind onto the port beam. Reaching through the rough and uncomfortable sea, however, we were generating an inordinate amount of leeway and being driven directly towards a group of dangerous jagged reefs, partially submerged in the rock field off the northern peninsula of Long Island lying up ahead. As darkness approached, the wind shifted without warning once again, veering to blow out of the north, though thankfully abating as it did so. Even so, from time to time erratic gusts blasted us for prolonged periods at a very uncomfortable force eight or more, compelling us to remain on a broad reach in what had become a treacherous cross-sea with a heavy chop. With the un-reefed main we were forced to carry, I was all too aware that even with the assistance of the engine our leeway would be so excessive that *Lucette*'s course made good would be several points to the south of our original course and straight towards the land, reducing our safety margin to zero.

As darkness closed in it was with certain relief that on depressing the starter button I heard the diesel engine burst into life beneath my feet, the jinxed starter motor having been completely overhauled during our Miami dry-docking. The additional action of the propeller race on the rudder enabled *Lucette*'s head to be brought closer to the eye of the wind, but still headed too close to the point for comfort. Directing Douglas to keep his eyes peeled in case he should sight the lighthouse I had predicted should appear on the starboard bow, I descended the companionway and tried to determine our position. My eyes were sore from prolonged concentration and lack of sleep and my eyelids felt like they were scraping over crushed glass, inducing me to remain below in order to try and get some sleep. If I was to take the midnight watch past the rock-strewn foreshore up ahead I would need to have all my wits about me. The rest of the family lay in their bunks in a gloomy and determined silence, enduring the rough ride whilst trying to snatch what rest they could before their own watch periods came round. Having been unable to obtain a navigational fix in the afternoon, and having missed stars in the brief evening twilight, I was unsure of our position. As darkness fell, I had not sighted the low-lying peninsula towards which we were headed and I became terribly uneasy about our situation, feeling obliged to voice my fears to Lyn. I was worried that in such weather we might not make it around the point ahead, as the strength and direction of the wind was effectively pinning us against the lee shore.

I unfolded the admiralty chart I had procured from a returning yachtsman during our stay in Miami. On the scuffed and grubby surface of the dog-eared parchment I had plotted our estimated position, together with an extrapolation of our probable course. I had already adjusted the course line several times over, not only for set and drift but also for the increasing leeway brought about by the onset of the weather and the changing winds. Looking at the chart with me, Lyn squinted her eyes in the loom of the bulkhead light, her gaze following the succession of irregular crosses with which I had tracked our course made good. Her gaze followed my finger as it traced along the faint pencil line, at times barely discernible through a mixture of water stains and oily fingerprints. The projected course line needed no explaining. Extending from our current dead reckoning, it bisected the shaded area at the lower corner of the chart used to denote land. The northerly point of the Long Island peninsula lay not more than five miles downwind and we were headed straight for it.

'What can we do?' enquired Lyn, her incredulous stare fixed right on me in the semi-darkness of the cabin. The tension was palpable, so much so that I could actually hear her heart beating as I placed my arms around her, as much to calm myself as to offer her comfort. The piercing drone of the wind and the roaring of the waves merged with the violent flapping of the sails and halyards aloft. This, combined with the sliding contents of the lockers slamming against the stoutly locked cupboard doors and the violent swinging of the gimballed galley stove, required me to shout in order to be heard above a shrill and compelling cacophony of sound.

'We … We can't run before the wind,' I competed, unable to suppress my nervous stammer. 'With so little sea room we would run aground on the coast only a few miles downwind. It would be nigh-on impossible to turn *Lucette* around in a sea like this. Even if we could, our route to the south would be at the cost of so much leeway that we'd be borne down onto the coast well before daybreak.' I stopped for breath and to formulate my next sentence more clearly in my mind before continuing. 'Our only hope must be to continue beating northwards against wind and sea with the help of the engine, whilst hoping and praying that we round the point before we hit it.' I paused as she took in what I had said. 'Once round the point, we will have to attempt to turn and run before the wind, away from the land and through the straits into the safety of the open sea.' I turned my attention back to the chart, desperately willing for the wind to drop. We stood side by side in gloomy silence, holding onto the leeboard in front of us for support, our worried faces etched in the gloom as we rechecked my workings with nervous preoccupation. I was unable to stop myself blurting into the darkness, 'Lyn, I just can't help feeling that we aren't going to make it!' My words trailed to a whisper and I reached for her arm again as I realised the full implications of what I had said.

'What is the name of the point?' Lyn demanded, fine beads of sweat turning her skin clammy to my touch. 'Santa Maria,' I replied, uncertain of her purpose. 'That's Saint Mary.' Lyn said, her mood suddenly uplifted. 'Don't you see, my sister Mary will look after us, we will get around the point, Dougal, just wait and see.' It was my turn to speak, but I could only manage a stunned silence as I searched desperately for something more tangible to say, a definitive or quantifiable last straw of hope that we could both cling to. The seconds turned to minutes but nothing came that would substitute for Lyn's mulish reliance on help from above. My shoulders slumped in defeat, leaving me in the full knowledge that even if we cleared the point we still had to avoid the rock field and submerged reefs that surrounded the shoreline of the peninsula. I trembled in the darkness as I tried to take stock of our situation, realising that if the wind did not abate significantly, and soon, our machinations would have all been in vain, for given our present course and speed we were unlikely to clear the land, let alone the reefs. To attempt the dubious 'safer option' of grounding on the shore rather than stranding on the reef would require the successful negotiation of the rocks in the proximity of the point, which remained hidden from view in the atrocious weather and the darkness of the night. Even if we did manage to get through the hazardous seaway somehow, then grounding in this weather would almost certainly be fatal. With rocks to the right of us and reefs to the left, with land blocking our way ahead and our return route cut off by the wind, my throat became dry and my breath shallow as I returned to the same conclusion as the one I had started with: we were all as good as dead!

My worried ruminations were suddenly interrupted by a shout from the cockpit. Douglas had spotted the lighthouse. I dashed up the saloon companionway and gripped the main boom to hold myself upright on the steep windswept deck. Within a few seconds, my worst fears were realised, for Douglas was pointing over the port bow. The light should have been on the starboard bow if we were to have any chance of clearing the point. Then I saw it too, the loom of the Cape Santa Maria lighthouse, peeping intermittently above the horizon ahead and to the left of us. From its position, it was clear that we had already entered the rock field which extended seawards in all directions from the point. We were already trapped amongst the rock towers and submerged obstructions that littered the area for the next few miles. My heart missed a beat as I stared over the leeward rail, my eyes fixed on a swirling morass of breaking waves that pounded the nearby shore in a merciless onslaught of destructive power. The bleak and hostile coast was cloaked in the half-light of the waning moon as it peeked from behind the ragged wind-torn clouds scudding across the night sky. The boiling expanse of sea had been beaten to a milky white, covering the entire foreshore in a blanket of foam, blotched with dark protrusions of rock and exposed areas of submerged reef. Plumes of exploding water, lofted high into the air under the near-constant barrage of barrelling rollers, merged to form cliff-sided white-capped buttresses of solid water that tore with thunderous energy into the rocks, propelling mast-high clouds of spume and spray over the sharp rocky pillars on the nearby coast. Bereft of power, the spent water was channelled by the rocky gullies into cascading rivers, pouring back into the sea only to be swamped in the watery onslaught of the next approaching wave.

A silent witness to the deafening roar of these unbridled elements, I felt sick to my stomach as I desperately racked my brain for a plan. The wind hummed a shrill drone in my ears and the mainmast was bent forward under the excessive strain of the mainsail, the rigging groaning ever louder under the weight of the excessive canvas we were forced to carry. The waves were losing their deep-water pattern and beginning to pile up in steep toppling pyramids, a further indication of the close proximity of the sea bottom. *Lucette*'s motion became sluggish, as she beat against the wind and plummeted bodily into the rough head-seas. Only the regular pounding of the engine helped me to think, as I tried to focus on the abject alternatives still left open to us. If we continued on our present course we would definitely be stranded on the nearby shore. If we survived the stranding and got the life raft away, we would be marooned. If we were lucky we might just get away with our lives; if not then like the vast majority of shipwrecked sailors we would be dashed against the rocks and drowned. If we slashed the mainsail in an attempt to halt our progress we would have insufficient power to get clear of the area, eventually grounding in any event. If we altered course to put the lighthouse on the starboard bow, we would almost certainly collide with one of the uncharted rock pillars littering our exit route. On the other hand, if we made a lesser alteration and ran for the lighthouse direct whilst we tried to locate our position, then we would soon be overwhelmed and swamped by the towering white rollers as they drove us hard aground on the jagged rocks of the foreshore. Suddenly the booming surf of the shoreline seemed much closer, and fear gripped my soul as large rollers overhauled us in quick succession, exposing large areas of reef both ahead and astern, incontrovertible evidence that time was running out and quickly. In truth, I concluded, only the devil's alternative remained open to us, a broad alteration of course to port, away from the coast, which would require us to change tack through the eye of the wind. If we could pull that off, then provided we kept a sharp look out for the telltale glow of the white-water reef breaks around the bases of the rock stacks, we might be able to thread our way through the lethal maze of protruding hazards and submerged reefs that surrounded us on all sides.

The decision made, I cleared my throat, understanding full well the irreversibility of my orders once put into action, and acutely aware that the lives of us all depended on what I was about to say. Confronting my fears, I gulped fiercely at the air. Fighting the wind, I shouted my first instruction into the blustery storm, a manoeuvre designed to prepare us for a subsequent alteration of course across the eye of the wind that would put the lighthouse on the starboard bow. In response, Douglas pushed the wheel down slowly, putting the helm to port, but *Lucette* failed to respond. If I was to get our schooner back out to the safety of deep water, then I needed a substantial and instantaneous alteration of course without delay. I repeated the command with another shout in his direction but he simply stood there mesmerised, rooted to the spot, whilst gripping the wheel with a look of resigned determination etched upon his face.

I dared not wait any longer, so throwing caution to the wind I dashed across the slippery open deck towards the cockpit and pushed him aside brusquely. 'If you can't do it properly then get out of my way, you great oaf,' I barked at him, failing to make allowance either for his tender years or for the fact that he had already been at the wheel for hours under very testing conditions, which must have rendered him close to exhaustion. Enraged by my actions, Douglas regained his balance and shoulder-barged me back in an attempt to regain the wheel. I shoved him backwards again and punched at him with all my might. My clenched fist caught him full on the side of his head. His eyes glared wide and a threatening scowl set across his face.

At that very moment, without warning but as a direct result of the violent corkscrewing motion of *Lucette*'s hull combined with the lapse in steering, the mainsail suddenly gybed, snapping the preventers like a piece of cotton. The main boom swung over with a splintering crash, striking me full on the head with a blow like a steam hammer. My senses reeled and I temporarily blanked into unconsciousness. Catapulted across the deck, I flew through the air from the sheer force of the blow. Douglas, still shaking in fear and anger and high from an intense rush of adrenalin, subconsciously threw his arms into the darkness. His lightning reactions checked me mid-flight as he gripped my oilskin jacket, bringing me down hard on my back, transfixed across the scuppers. Douglas adjusted his grasp and held on tight, preventing me from being washed overboard. Seizing my lower legs, he left me precariously balanced out over the side, the speeding water from *Lucette*'s wake growling and snapping at the back of my head. He stared down on me like thunder, neither pulling me back inboard nor releasing me from his stifling grip. My forehead was streaming blood from a deep gash above my temple, which mixed with the salt water as it splattered into my face. My eyes stung as I hung perilously outboard. My senses slowly returning, I became aware that Douglas, having pulled me back a little, was shouting into my face less than an inch away, 'Promise you'll never hit me again, ever, or so help me I'll dump you over the side right now,' he screamed into my face. I looked back at him blankly, totally helpless and completely at his mercy. 'Promise, you miserable schmuck,' he roared in a fearsome scream, shrill and intense and far louder than anything I had ever heard from him before. His warm spittle spattered across my face, his muscles bulging and rippling in the half-light of the moon as his index finger stabbed my face, sending repeated bursts of pain into the recesses of my brain.

'Pull him back on board, pull him back.' Lyn had appeared at the chartroom door and was shouting at Douglas, her eyes rolling in genuine fear. I met my son's eyes through the darkness and I knew I would never strike him again, as I first mumbled and then screamed the promise that ensured my deliverance back aboard. Hauling me clear of the water, he dumped me unceremoniously into the scuppers and returned to the wheel, before motioning his mother to come and tend to my head. *Lucette* meanwhile raced onwards into the darkness, driven before wind and sea.

Our bitter furore was suddenly interrupted by a bright light casting a luminous dazzling glare across the open span of sea around us. A large tanker had mysteriously appeared and slowed almost to a stop, its probing searchlight revealing the full extent of the terrifying sea, whipped up into a frenzy of unrestrained and ferocious power by the gale-force winds. The blazing finger of light glinted like diamonds in a suspended blanket of spindrift tossed up by the wind, defusing the beam in a series of overlaid translucent layers that settled into a thick dense fog. We were trapped in a veritable cauldron of churning water that boiled in the darkness and threw up great clouds of spray. Perhaps it would have been better not to have seen such a terrifying sight, as we looked on in awe, totally spellbound. I wedged my legs into the wire railings to maintain a secure foothold in the scuppers, instinctively gripping a nearby stanchion, in order to brace myself against the violent rolling motion of the deck beneath me. Douglas scanned the ship through binoculars. Shining ethereally and shrouded in misty spray, she seemed almost on top of us. 'Bloody typical – I can't see anybody on the bridge wings, it's like a darn ghost ship,' muttered my son with teenage certainty, directing the binoculars from side to side, scanning the ship's shadowy length for signs of life. *Lucette*, no longer alone, seemed joined in the company of a guiding presence.

The main beam of the searchlight danced across the water as it pierced the darkness, penetrating the shadows created by the scattered turrets of rock protruding skywards from the foamy water like an army of sentinels. In a fleeting moment, I could see our route out, the stabbing beam of light showing us the way with continuous sweeps across the rock field. I concentrated with every ounce of energy I could muster, furiously memorising the locations of the rock formations, whilst estimating the courses and distances required to make good our escape. I fixed in my mind the routes that would take us clear of the rock field and then beyond to the Santa Maria lighthouse, whose inviting loom still beckoned us from over the horizon. I pulled myself back onto my feet, still shaking but able to drag myself forward with the support of Lyn's guiding hand to get a clearer view of our immediate surroundings. I was fearfully aware that each yard of *Lucette*'s progress through the water was a yard closer to the point of no return; each minute now seemed to last an eternity as we sped unchecked into the night.

Lodging my torso into the shrouds at a suitable vantage point, I began barking directions aft, still muted from the knock on my head. Lyn relayed my words back to Douglas, as she tried desperately to bond us back into a team. In accordance with my instructions, Douglas put the wheel hard to port, forcing *Lucette*'s head up into the wind. With the heavy chop, however, *Lucette*, did not have enough momentum to bring her on through the eye of the wind and simply luffed up with all her sails aback. Before I could voice the order again, Douglas was already paying off the helm, with the throttle set to maximum and the engine churning loudly, preparing for a second attempt. If we were to get through the eye of wind, onto the starboard tack, we needed more speed and we needed it right away.

'More power,' I screamed aft, leaving my position in the shrouds to help Lyn weather the jury-rigged jib. The bow steadied, ready to come up into the wind for a second attempt as the engine began shuddering violently under the extreme load. We were unable to hold the jib to windward in the strong wind, and the yacht's head fell to leeward a second time. *Lucette*, having lost her momentum, rolled and wallowed heavily as Douglas paid off the helm ready for a third attempt. He cupped his hands before his mouth and proclaimed that he was preparing to try one last time. Casting aside my immediate desire to hug him, I made to lift my hand in an effort to delay the manoeuvre so *Lucette* could gather more speed. He had already stopped looking in my direction, however, as he lifted his foot and kicked down on the throttle lever, jamming it over the upper limit stop in a final all-or-nothing attempt.

The engine screamed an octave higher and revved still faster, literally shaking itself to pieces as it juddered the deck beneath our feet. The high-temperature alarm whistled loudly, the gauge needle standing hard over into the red. The engine would only last a few minutes more before the red-hot rocker heads seized into a solid lump of overheated fuming metal. We rapidly gained speed again and with split-second timing Douglas put the wheel hard over between waves, as Lyn and I struggled once again to weather the jib to windward. We slowed perceptively as we came up into the eye of the wind, *Lucette* shuddering on her beam-ends as she ploughed headlong into the vertical face of an oncoming mountain of roaring white water. Her rigging shook and rattled as the wind held her momentarily in irons. Just as I thought she was about to stall and all would be lost, she swept on through onto the starboard tack, the press of the jib sail lifting Lyn and me clean off our feet before dumping us into the scuppers in a wet bedraggled heap. We were still regaining our senses, carefully untangling our intertwined limbs and trying to reorient ourselves in the semi-darkness, when a raging mass of cold water crashed onto the deck and struck us full square on our backs and midriffs. The cold water hit us hard, sweeping us arm-in-arm a full twenty feet along the deck, finally discarding us in a dishevelled heap of interlocked arms and legs. Lyn held onto me while I gripped tightly onto the coach-roof grab rails in order to prevent us both being swept over the side. A few moments later, the wind filled the sails and *Lucette*, pushing an exaggerated bow wave before her, carved her way through the sea in a desperate dash for freedom. Unable to adjust the throttle of the engine, its lever still jammed in the double-full-ahead position, I had no choice but to shut it down before the labouring diesel blew itself to smithereens. From now on *Lucette* would have to cope under sail alone. Anxiously I scanned the breaking seas on the receding coast to leeward as the mainsail flogged in the high winds. The tough Dacron fabric took heavy punishment, the double-stitched seams ripping further and further down the length of the sail head as more and more stitching gave way. From the very cusp of annihilation we slowly clawed our way offshore, maximising sea room as the seconds gradually turned to minutes and *Lucette* inched her way to safety.

My head continued to pound with mind-numbing throbs of debilitating pain, as the blood poured once more from the reopened wound on my head. There was no time to reapply the bandage, however, so I held what was left of the dressing Lyn had applied earlier in place, pressing it hard against my head. Stemming the flow of blood, I relocated myself in the shrouds, once more. Lyn came to me and slid her arms around my waist. 'Hold me, Dougal,' she breathed softly, half sobbing and half laughing as she held me in a tight embrace. Touched with the respite of the moment, we marvelled at each other in euphoric appreciation, our faces contorted with a heady mixture of joy and relief. The minutes ticked by in a timeless haze, but we were still not out of danger, so I ordered Lyn to lash me to the rigging and then to go aft and take up station over the coach roof, in order to continue relaying my commands back to Douglas. The passing minutes seemed interminable as we edged our way out of the shoals, until at length I was able to give the command that would bring *Lucette* onto a course putting the lighthouse broad on the starboard bow. Pushing on through the darkness, we had only a few more miles to go and the light would then be abeam, thereby making our getaway all but complete. We felt we had witnessed the work of the Almighty in all his glory that night. With the immediate point of pressure passed, Lyn's face became fixed with a broad grin as she replayed our fracas in the scuppers repeatedly in her mind's eye. The mighty sea had punished us all for daring to challenge its supremacy, and in particular, it had shown me a distinct lack of deference. My crew had seen *Lucette*'s fearsome dare-all skipper treated with utter disdain by the might of the sea, which had tossed him aside like a rag doll with its immense power.

The sudden release of tension brought with it a contagious change of mood, for even Douglas had a broad grin fixed across his face. He called to his mother, pointing an outstretched arm in my direction, 'Old Captain Bligh's had a rough night of it,' his terminal chuckle echoed by Lyn as they both struggled to suppress their rising mirth at my expense. Feeling distinctly thin-skinned, I tried to ignore their mockery and made exaggerated importance of scanning the murk ahead. I refocused my binoculars on the sweeping searchlight of the ship that had been our saviour, until I too had to shield my face in order to conceal an equally wide and silly grin that had become stubbornly fixed across my face. Much to my chagrin the name of 'Bligh' was to stick, for my reputation as a bucko seaman had taken a severe bashing indeed.

For another agonising hour, minute followed desperate minute as we piloted our way on a wavering zigzag course, following the sweep of the searchlight from the bridge of the ship of our salvation. We looked on in disbelief as we passed only a few yards to windward of the last cluster of rocks that towered above us into the darkness like the foreboding gate-tower of some ancient ruin. The wind backed once more to the northwest as the surge of the rolling breakers swept us over the extreme rim of spume-ridden reef, catapulting *Lucette* over the shallows and into the deeper waters beyond. A second alteration of course downwind brought us out of the rock field and into the more rhythmic waves of the ocean, enabling us to set course for the lighthouse itself. It was with a great sigh of relief that some forty minutes later we slipped safely under the loom of the light tower, less than a cable length from its rocky base. Against what had seemed like impossible odds we had finally made it.

Rounding the point, I allowed the bow to fall away, setting course downwind for Crooked Island Passage and the eastern point of Cuba. The ship that had saved us had vanished, disappearing into the night as mysteriously as it had come. I strained my eyes and ears into the darkness in an attempt to catch a glimpse of its navigation lights, or even the trace of a give-away sound, but there was only the black empty sea. Lyn smiled one of her beaming all-knowing grins, 'I told you my sister Mary would help us.' I decided to keep my mouth shut in order not to encourage her untenable zeal, quite unable all the same to offer any better explanation for the appearance of the vessel, or the part it had played in helping us to avoid certain catastrophe.

The ship had saved all our lives that night by showing us the passage out between the rocks, but why it came to us and where it went to I would never know. *Lucette* had survived a ferocious storm as well as any she had fought in her fifty-year life, demonstrating her soundness of design and stoutness of build with flying colours, her grown-oak frames and pitch-pine timbers remaining completely unscathed.

Sensing the change in mood, a small voice piped up from below, 'Can we take our lifejackets off now?' Forgotten in the turmoil, the twins had donned their life preservers and had been cowering below decks, awaiting the order to abandon ship. Alone with their fear, they had been listening intently to all that had been said and had assembled the puppets ready to jump when the command was given. We smiled contritely at each other as Lyn led them below and put them back to bed. The sheer terror of that tempestuous night would remain as a vivid and surreal memory, sending shivers down our spines, on every occasion it was discussed or recalled.

The wind blew fiercely for the rest of the night, the waning moon revealing black heaving seas steaming in the cold north wind as they reared balefully about us, racing ahead to the south. As watch followed watch, daybreak saw the wind abating perceptively beneath a grey overcast sky. Under the ease of the following wind and sea, *Lucette*'s motion settled considerably and by mid-morning we were able to glimpse occasional shafts of sunlight beaming onto the decks.

We surveyed the full extent of the damage sustained during the previous night and spent the whole morning carrying out running repairs to the rigging, halyards and sheets as well as re-securing the loose fastenings on the shackles and blocks. I freed up the main engine throttle and refilled the sump with oil, for it was bone dry. With great daring, Douglas climbed aloft into the rigging as *Lucette* rolled fiercely from side to side. We watched pensively as he struggled to free the buckled track above the crosstrees on the mainmast, which allowed us to hand the mainsail down and rig a smaller replacement.

Ruefully inspecting the damage, it was clear that the sails would need two to three days' stitching with a palm and needle at the very least. Our off-watch periods, when not spent sleeping, were spent on a round-the-clock sewing bonanza, as we stitched and patched what was left of the sails back together, only stopping when we had worn the very skin off our hands. One by one we managed to get more sail back up as we surfed, sometimes at 12 knots or more, down the long faces of the deep-blue Atlantic rollers, which steadily built in height before the blustery north wind. That afternoon saw us cleaving our way past the Mira Por Vos Cays, fighting our way through the slab-sided ocean. The dangerous pillars of rock stood implacably like sombre giants as huge rollers buried them in white plumes of pulverised spray and foam. Like massive geysers, the oncoming waves checked for a moment before being blasted skywards with loud thunderclaps which reverberated across the intervening seaway like firing howitzers. With each blast, great columns of white water and spindrift were hoisted aloft, to hang in mid-air over the exposed reef before plummeting earthwards in great swirling showers of foam and spray. I was thankful to be passing them during daylight as the evening saw us herded into the confines of the Windward Passage itself. It was Lyn who pointed out that we were less than 100 miles from the place where the waterspout had ravaged us, nine months earlier. I made a mental note to give this area a miss should I ever find myself sailing around the world again.

In the early hours of the following morning, the high escarpment of Cuba appeared through the haze. Skirting the coast in choppy waters at the respectful distance of some eight miles, we re-entered the Caribbean Sea, the large bulk of the island of Haiti affording us shelter from the east. Before the end of the forenoon, we were able to alter course for the western point of Jamaica. The seaway softened markedly under the lee of the Cuban peninsula, allowing *Lucette* to settle down to a slow but awkward corkscrewing motion as she was driven before a quartering swell, racing on through a still-turbulent sea but at good speed in the direction of the quieter waters offshore. The following day, dawn's greeting was resplendent with red and purple bands of interlocking colour, and the wind dropped considerably by the time the sun had ascended into the early-morning sky. Soon we were completely becalmed our sails hanging like washday linen on a lazy summer's day. We used the engine once more to keep moving until the trade winds returned in the evening. Trimming our sails, we continued to make excellent progress through the night. The following daybreak turned into a bright sunny morning, to find us coasting gently along under the shadow of Jamaica's Blue Mountain Range. It was the stroke of noon on a wonderfully hot February day by the time we dropped anchor in the roads of Kingston harbour, in the shadow of the ancient portals of the brick-built fort called Port Royal. Arriving two days ahead of schedule, we were weary and fragile after our recent brush with mortality. For this reason we opted for the relative luxury of berthing alongside in the famous Morgan's Harbour marina, which was to become a wonderful stopover, once we had completed repairs and had a well-deserved rest.

Jamaica's emerald seas bordered white sandy beaches, which in turn gave way to green rolling hills, rich in vegetation and carpeted with thick rainforest, rising over 7,000 feet into the high rugged peaks of the Blue Mountains. Jamaica had gained independence from England in the early 1960s; centuries before, in the days of the buccaneers, it had been a famous outpost of the British Empire and a principal naval base, flexing its military muscle to exert England's influence over the entire Caribbean. In its day the base at Port Royal had been frequented by intrepid explorers such as Sir Francis Drake and naval commanders like Admiral Vernon, as well as by notorious buccaneers and pirates, including the infamous Welsh pirate Henry Morgan.

The rapidly ascending roadways, skirted with lush tropical flora, gradually gave way to banana plantations and tropical pine forests, eventually merging into the Blue Mountain coffee plantations, home to the famous brand of the same name, known and relished the world over. Sir Anthony Jenkinson's Morgan's Harbour was a quintessential haven of British solidarity after the razzle and dazzle of Miami. For several days we lay alongside, mending sails and overhauling gear, chatting to visitors from Britain and Canada, Australia and New Zealand, as well as from a host of other nations around the world.

Jamaica had suffered much in the way of economic mismanagement and fiscal ineptitude, in which thievery and crime had flourished. Governing an island such as Jamaica with its sectarian history and faltering economy had always been a poisoned chalice. The vast majority of the population were uneducated and largely destitute, while most of the wealth and power was still in the hands of their former colonial masters. Jamaica needed something of a revolution to shake itself into the twentieth century. It was our joint opinion, however, that this wonderful island had a magic air of tranquillity and expectation, in exactly the right measure, that promised to make our visit not only truly memorable but also an absolute delight.

The ruined town of Port Royal, lying adjacent to Morgan's Harbour, was a historic site, with much of the fort and ancillary buildings still standing. The highlight of the tourist's visit was the museum located in the old army hospital, which contained many artefacts including gold doubloons, pieces of eight, ancient cannon and ornate woodcarvings. These items had been carefully restored and preserved to form a tantalising display, which as part of our English heritage fired our imaginations and rekindled nostalgic memories of home in equal measure. After suffering a severe earthquake in the late seventeenth century, which laid much of the town to waste, the present-day fort had been rebuilt on the site of the old one. It had counted amongst its most famous defenders a young officer, then only twenty-one years of age, by the name of Horatio Nelson. The Royal Navy had been forced to vacate the base after a second earthquake, moving much of their operations to other parts of the Caribbean. Port Royal was finally debilitated as an operational centre by an even more powerful earthquake at the beginning of the twentieth century, and the modern-day site remained deserted, save for the exploring forays of the more discerning tourists and film-makers. Indeed, the film *Thunderball*, which we had watched in Dominica, had been filmed on location here.

One of the principal reasons we stopped in Jamaica was to pay our respects to the chief of our clan, who bore the name 'Robertson of Struan'. It was with both delight and trepidation that I called him on the telephone and arranged a meeting. The twins fully expected to see a sporran-wearing, kilt-bedecked, wild-eyed highlander, and did not betray their disappointment when the chief, a gentle white-haired man advanced in years and wearing a smart suit, alighted from the taxi which had brought him out from Kingston. Robertson of Struan's ancestors had migrated to Jamaica over one hundred and fifty years before and the chief soon had us agog with ancient clan legends and vivid tales of heroic endeavour. Sunrise was already upon us before he took his leave, bidding us convey his greetings and good wishes to other clan members in the far-off lands of the Pacific when we got there.

Our mooring, located next to the Captain Morgan's bar, brought many interesting folk our way and we took full advantage of the surroundings, enjoying many short trips outside the harbour to swim and explore the reefs. We met numerous yacht-club members and kind residents who took us on excursions around the island's tourist spots, including the Blue Lagoon and the Enfield army barracks, the many English voices adding a nostalgic and refreshing air to our surroundings. Douglas was still causing us problems, however, this time in the form of an older woman called Natasha. 'At least she's a woman,' muttered Lyn in some relief as we watched them cavorting in the sand. Eager Saturday-afternoon sailors, in need of able crew, poached the boys to take part in the spring offshore yacht race trails. Douglas was nowhere to be seen, however, for when he was not improving his rowing technique aboard *Ednamair*, he was away improving his technique with Natasha. The twins, rediscovering past form, improved daily in their ability to dive and swim amongst the blue depths, retrieving pieces of eight from the golden beaches of Lime Cay, a small islet lying just offshore. Lyn and I just tried to relax and enjoy what was finally becoming what it had always promised to be, the adventure of our lives.

Treating ourselves to a happy-hour rum punch at the bar one day, Lyn and I met a well-to-do businessman ordering drinks in an all-too-familiar accent. His name was Chris Birch and he was a former resident of our home town of Leek. He was also a committee member of the Royal Jamaican Yacht Club, located nearer to Kingston in the area known as Palisadoes. He offered us free moorings for a week, which tempted us to move *Lucette* further into the bay, where we tied up opposite the clubhouse. Once inside, we were extremely pleased to receive a copy of the *Leek Post and Times* newspaper, to which I had been sending regular progress reports on our voyage. The following day we were all asked by various skippers to assist as crew in the finals of the local yacht regatta. Recalling that there was no such thing as a free lunch, I had little choice but to agree, allocating the twins to one boat, Douglas to a second and myself to Chris's 32-foot glass-fibre racing cruiser. The race was a closely fought contest around the buoys, within the confines of the harbour basin, and after exercising great skill and daring I managed to get Chris's boat home in second place, only to discover to my horror that Douglas had got home before me, by a country mile. A fact I was not allowed to forget!

On the eastern side of Kingston, Jamaica's capital city, the sprawl of slum dwellings located in the district of Spanish Town gave way to more respectable residential areas near the centre, where large parks, surrounding the Governor's and Prime Minister's palatial homes, provided beautiful open spaces. The western fringe of the city contained street upon street of secluded homes and apartments belonging to the middle classes, with business and industrial sectors occupying the entire waterfront. Pushed together like the first, second and third-class waiting rooms still to be found in the nearby railway station, many of the overcrowded and disenfranchised denizens in the middle were forced to resort to crime to make ends meet, and the streets of Kingston had accordingly become increasingly unsafe for travellers, especially after dark. Great care was necessary not to be stranded in the less salubrious areas of the city as evening approached, for darkness redrew the transient city boundaries denoting which areas were safe and which were not. The authorities had made real and sincere attempts to curb the outbreaks of crime, which ranged from outright muggings to elaborate stings and ruses, such as road- accident scenes concocted to engage unwitting passers-by, whose interest was absorbed until they had been robbed at the roadside, often without even knowing. The efforts of the police were greatly hampered by the high unemployment, coupled with the seemingly unstoppable growth in the population, which continually outstripped advances in economic development. The right-wing Jamaican Labour Party had been in power for the previous decade since independence from Britain but most people now hoped that a rising star in the People's National Party by the name of Norman Manly would win through in the upcoming elections. The population were seeking radical change and it was to him that they were turning in order to bring about successful and non-destructive reform.

We stayed a couple of days after the expiry of our free week and were brought brutally back to reality when we received the bill for mooring fees from the marina management. Not wishing a repeat of the money shortages we had experienced in Florida, I decided it was time to move to a quieter part of the island, where we could anchor without charge. This would allow us to maximise our stay in this paradise of tropical paradises. Returning to Morgan's Harbour for the briefest of stopovers, we said our goodbyes and prepared once more to leave. With *Lucette* shipshape and ready for sea, we departed from Kingston with pleasant and indelible memories etched in our minds. We sailed towards the easternmost edge of Jamaica, headed for the north-coast township of Port Antonio, a traditional banana port where the banana hands were still shipped down river from the interior aboard bamboo rafts. Here we felt we would be able to meet more of the native folk than was possible in the pulsating tourist-ridden metropolis of Kingston. Under shortened sail, we made smooth progress through the fine morning air, but met heavy rollers as we approached Morant Point. Caught in the brisk tidal rip, it became clear we would need all our headsails hoisted in order to tack close enough to the wind to round the point. Acutely aware of the promise he had wrung from me that dreadful night off of the Punta Santa Maria, I asked Douglas as politely as I could to shin out onto the bowsprit and rig the number one jib sail. The full implications of the task were not lost on him, as the bowsprit buried itself in the seaway with each wave. 'Bloody typical,' he swore good-naturedly under his breath, bravely venturing out to a soaking in the warm barrelling rollers as *Lucette* repeatedly slammed her bows into the oncoming swells. Once round the point, we endured an uncomfortable day's sail against unusually strong trade winds, which fell calm during the night, leaving *Lucette* wallowing viciously in a heavy cross-swell. The beauty of this wonderful natural harbour rewarded our discomfort well, however, for our stay in Port Antonio was to be something akin to a vacation whilst on holiday, a rest from rest itself.

The election was in full swing ashore and we found the PNP's slogan of 'Power', in conjunction with an upraised clenched fist, somewhat intimidating at first. The grocery stores doubled both as bars and meeting places, making political dialogue inevitable sooner or later. As a farmer I was able to empathise with the local smallholders. Having been a keen debater in my formative years, I added my own two-penny-worth to the hotchpotch of sound bites and political dogma that seemed to be on everyone's mind. A small group of locals, impressed by our interest, invited us to see how the present system was failing them and took us on a tour of their newly built concrete-block homes, some of which were even fitted with glazed windows. The vast majority of their houses, in contrast, were nothing more than converted wooden hen huts or hovels. The agricultural plots upon which they relied for daily sustenance were often miserable scratchings in the fertile soil, interspersed only sporadically with the occasional well-tended plot. Whilst starvation was not a serious threat, natural fruit being abundant, malnutrition from an unbalanced diet was evident on every street corner. The dullness of the average Jamaican diet was in itself a searching criticism of the government's education policy, for much of the population remained starving, in the midst of plenty.

The following day brought victory for the PNP, and Port Antonio had never before witnessed scenes of jubilation like it. We were showered with gifts of fruit and tropical vegetables, an act of impulsive generosity from our new friends. They canoed out to us loaded to the gunwales with papaya, breadfruit, eggplant, cho-cho, kallaloo, limes, plantain, titi apple, green bananas, pumpkin and yams, as well as some fiercely hot cayenne peppers. With a great palaver they insisted on demonstrating how they should be cooked, even instructing us how to boil the water before sitting down to our table and promptly eating almost every last morsel of what they had cooked, following which they promptly announced that they must depart, as their wives would have prepared dinner for them back home!

The next day brought a welcome visitor into the anchorage. She was a cargo ship named the MV *Pentelikon*, the same German freighter which had passed us over a year before on the other side of the Atlantic. She had called at this port to load a cargo of bananas. Many hands of the green and as yet unripe fruit had already been delivered to the docks from the interior aboard the bamboo rafts. I was amazed to see that they really did have a talisman counting the hands of green bananas as they passed the ship's rail. We all smiled at the memory of our 'debacle in Dominica' as we prepared to go aboard and meet the young officers and their captain. Douglas's eyes positively glowed as he cast his eyes across the bridge. 'Dad,' he said, 'I really, really want to go to sea when we get home.' I laughed at the inconsistency of his remarks and simply told him that one day he would do exactly that.

In Port Antonio we met a young Czechoslovakian couple named Gita and Milan, who were visiting the town whist enjoying their vacation. Having escaped with their lives from the Eastern-block tyranny still in power over their homeland, they had eventually set up home in the frozen wastes of Labrador in northern Canada, some three years previously. We decided to treat ourselves to a trip to the head of the broad winding valley of the Rio Grande, in order to see for ourselves the origin of the banana rafts. Skippered by 'captains', they were fitted with seats and available for hire by the more daring of passengers when there was no cargo to ship. The ten-mile expedition from the loading station to the sea down the broad winding river was a refreshing and glorious trip. Passing through desolate village communities, we threw silver coins to young divers, who retrieved them from the fastest of the flowing waters. We then swam in the deep freshwater pools, after which we shot two sets of white-water rapids which held us white-knuckled in excitement.

A few days later it was Douglas's eighteenth birthday, and we arranged a two-day safari adventure with Gita and Milan to mark the occasion. All seven of us piled into Milan's car and set out on a mountain-climbing expedition, driving into the heart of Jamaica over tortuous mud-ridden mountain roads until we arrived at the foothills of the Blue Mountain peak itself. We pushed and pulled the car along the steep inclines of the un-metalled roads, struggling against precipitous gradients and across cool mountain streams. In this remote area we found the villagers quite hostile. Bands of youths attempted to hold back the car, ostensibly offering assistance as we collectively pushed it, skidding and sliding through muddy puddles, in the soft clay tracks. As we passed one small and squalid hamlet, a group of stick-wielding brigands began openly pulling the car back down the slope, demanding payment for the privilege of allowing us through. More joined them and the situation began to look ominous when Milan in a sudden burst of inspiration waved his upraised arm with a clenched fist and shouted 'Power!' The effect was as remarkable as it was effective, for they withdrew in confused alarm.

Twilight was upon us by the time we reached a small hostel located some distance beneath the peak. The seventy-year-old veteran proprietor, a white-haired bespectacled gentleman speaking the finest Oxford English, introduced himself as Mr Algreave, a white Jamaican heralding from a bygone era. He had seen his living standards slowly decline since independence, and as a member of the establishment he had always been against the PNP. He was the last of his line, having no alternative when he retired but to sell his plantation to the new-age blacks, at a fraction of what it had been worth when he had inherited it.

That evening our host joined us in a supper of chicken pilau expertly prepared and cooked by Lyn and Gita. We toasted Douglas's coming of age and retired early for a few hours' sleep, the twins chattering excitedly, as Douglas and Milan teased them with ghost stories long into the night. The alarm clock shrilled at one forty-five the next morning and by two fifteen we had assembled in a rather bedraggled though enthusiastic group under the bright moonlight, our teeth chattering from the unaccustomed chill in the thinning air of the higher altitudes. We struck out along the moonlit trails which led to the summit. Milan, himself an experienced mountaineer, took the lead and I shepherded the tail in order to encourage the stragglers. We climbed upwards along the rough mountain track, first through open hillsides and then steeply upward through the thickening forest where the moon, temporarily lost to view, accentuated the darkness and emphasised the sounds of the night in the thick foliage canopy overhead. We trudged upward through clearings and rocky outcrops, our sea legs aching as they rediscovered muscles that had grown lazy in the confines of *Lucette*. Three hours after setting off, the greying light of dawn saw us clearing the forest and ascending the final pathway to the summit, exactly 7,402 feet above the sea. The still-slumbering island lay below us wreathed in patches of mist, revealing range upon range of mountains rolling gently away to the sea, the distant lights of the coastal villages becoming ever more densely packed as they merged into the urban brightness of Kingston. To the north lay the heavily forested homeland of the legendary Maroon tribesmen, with ridge upon impassable ridge merging into the blue-hazed valleys, eventually blending seamlessly into the distant coast.

For fifteen minutes a glorious sunrise broke the distant horizon and we were treated to an unrestricted view of the beautiful dawn sky. Superimposed bands of yellow, orange, red and violet glittered in deep perspective through the clear morning air, ranging far into the distance to create a truly stunning vista. It was not long before the chill mists rolled up the early-morning mountainside, shrouding our small group in cold, clammy and obliterating cloud. Within minutes every last one of us was shivering, and we turned to the descent with a will, soon emerging into the bright sunlight below cloud level. Loping on down through the forest, we stopped to identify many wild flowers found back home. Stunted trees and tree ferns festooned with long mossy tassels gradually gave way to luxuriant tropical vegetation as we descended to the warmer levels of the hostel where we had spent the previous night. Bacon, eggs and coffee soon revived our flagging spirits and Mr Algreave joined us for breakfast, sweetening his tea with spoonfuls of thick-cut marmalade. Flicking out the orange rinds with his finger, he stopped his ritual midstream and asked us if we would consider picking coffee beans on his plantation, in lieu of the more customary monetary payment for our overnight stay. The late morning therefore found us spending a quiet few hours picking bright-red coffee beans from the orderly rows of large bush-like trees, the sun shining on our backs in typical Jamaican splendour. This high-altitude coffee was much prized for its flavour and could only be picked by hand, as the beans ripen at different times according to their location on the bush.

We had done our work well, for Mr Algreave, looking the image of empire in pith helmet, knee-length stockings and knee-length shorts, rewarded us handsomely with sacks of lemons, oranges and tree tomatoes. With the car fully loaded, we commenced our descent back to Port Antonio. The 30-mile return trip along twisting roads and sharp hairpin bends was frequently interrupted, as we stopped to admire the breathtaking scenery and to buy more produce and supplies from native stores at the roadsides. We stopped at a large river spring and bathed in the fresh, clean and sparkling water, where we washed the Blue Mountain mud from our clothes. In the heat of the day they were dry enough to wear just fifteen minutes later. Our groaning car lurched down the steep slopes, jolting heavily on its suspension as it tottered over deep ruts and hard ridges that blighted the roadway, until we finally rejoined the tarmac road leading back towards civilisation. We arrived back at Port Antonio just before six, as the short tropical twilight brought an end to another magnificent day, and we were delighted to find *Lucette* still swinging gently to her anchor in the bay. With *Ednamair* loaded down to the gunwales, and with the welcome assistance of a couple of Australian brothers from aboard a new arrival in the form of a ketch called the *Metung*, we ferried the sacks of produce across the still waters of the bay. The Blue Mountain peak loomed large and imposing above us, impassively dominating the skyline, its peak shrouded in mist as it melted upwards into the night sky.

The following day we took Milan and Gita sailing aboard *Lucette*. Milan had long harboured the desire to undertake an adventure like ours, but alas, he succumbed to seasickness whilst Gita, much to his chagrin, remained full of beans. Douglas taught Gita the intricacies of steering a yacht under sail and the function of the individual downhauls and halyards. Milan's health returned as we gained the lee of the land, leaving him more determined than ever that such an affliction as seasickness would not quell his desire one day to realise his ambition. We waved goodbye to those two brave young people that same evening, hoping we had helped them enjoy their vacation in the sun as much as they had helped us to enjoy ours. Unlike us, however, they would soon be back in the 30-degrees-below-zero temperatures prevailing back home in their adopted country of Labrador. We had all been touched by this happy couple. Their lives were tinged with sadness in the knowledge that they would never see their families

The *Sagaing* at sea in 1940.

Dougal and comrades abandoning the *Sagaing* in 1942 after she had been hit by Japanese carrier aircraft in Trincomalee.

Dougal and Lyn on a beach in Hong Kong, circa 1950.

Anne and Douglas as small children at Meadows Farm.

A group picture at Meadows Farm, about 1965.

▲
The family in Falmouth before departure.

◀ Dougal at the wheel of *Lucette* in Falmouth.

Lucette leaving Falmouth to sail round the world.
▼

◀ *Lucette* approaching Lisbon after the rough Biscay crossing.

Lucette becalmed at sunset after leaving Lisbon.
▼

◀ The family visiting the Alfama district of Lisbon.

▲
Douglas loading supplies in
Las Palmas, ready for the long
Atlantic crossing.

►
Dougal scanning the
shoreline in Las Palmas.

Douglas preparing to let go the
mooring buoy in Las Palmas.
▼

Lucette leaving Las Palmas for the distant shores of Barbados.

◀ Anne and Douglas bending on sails in Las Palmas.

Lucette entering Admiralty Bay in Bequia.

Going ashore with the Icelanders in Admiralty Bay, Bequia.

Douglas in Dominica, visiting the chief of the Carib Indians.

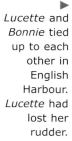

Lucette and *Bonnie* tied up to each other in English Harbour. *Lucette* had lost her rudder.

◀ Under tow after losing the rudder, *Lucette* leaving English Harbour on the way to St Thomas.

Alongside in St Thomas awaiting repairs. The jury-rigged rudder can just be seen.
▼

◄ The broken rudder, repaired by two local fitters in St Thomas.

Bonnie leaving St Thomas. We waved to her until she disappeared over the horizon. ►

◄ Great Stirrup Cay. Douglas rowed ashore to get some food from the US Air Force. The dinghy was on its last legs.

again, for neither could return to their homelands as each faced a long jail sentences should they do so, the penalty for escape from tyranny.

That evening Douglas disappeared aboard another visiting yacht anchored adjacent to us in the bay. A sloop-rigged ketch, her twin masts rose awkwardly skywards in a curious V-shaped fashion. She was the unique brainchild of her owner, a wealthy American who had brought the yacht to this place to visit her designer, one Bill Tritt, who resided in an exclusive, colonial-style house located on Navy Island in the middle of the bay. Lyn and I spent a pleasant evening with our new Australian friends aboard the *Metung*. Their circumnavigation, embarked upon two years previously from Melbourne, was approaching its last leg, for once across the Pacific they would be home. Over a bottle of mellow red wine, we discussed our proposed itinerary with them, making several amendments as we went. They told us how they had shipped their yacht by low-loader across the desert, alongside the closed Suez Canal, thereby taking full advantage of the shortcut from the Indian Ocean to the Mediterranean Sea and avoiding the long passage around Africa. Advising us to avoid a long beat against wind and current to visit Lima in Peru, they recommended instead that we travel from Panama straight to the Galapagos, and then take the trade-wind route across the Pacific to the Marquesas. From there we could sail south to Tahiti and then west via the Cook Islands to Tonga, Fiji and then south to Auckland in New Zealand's North Island.

We talked on into the night, even debating the possibility of settling in New Zealand. Alternatively, after exploring the mud lakes of Rotarua and watching the whales off the west coast of South Island we would depart for Adelaide in Australia. From there, we would sail to Sydney and then to Darwin, where after a short dry-docking we would sail to Bali in Indonesia and then on to Singapore. I couldn't see us getting that far inside eighteen months, however, and the enormity of the project we had embarked upon began to slowly sink in. When our companions suggested we visit the Andaman Islands and then continue through the Bay of Bengal to Sri Lanka, my blood ran cold and all talk of exploration temporarily ceased. The sinking of the *Sagaing* some thirty years previously had occurred in those very waters, and the revival of such dark memories brought a change to our collective mood.

Whatever route we took after Singapore, though, we definitely planned to include a train journey across India from the port of Madras, followed by a visit to the coral islets of the Maldives and the larger island chain of the Seychelles on our leg to Mombasa and the safari-lands of Kenya. Out of Africa, I decided that whatever way ports we visited we would opt for the Suez shortcut, thereby eliminating the long ocean passage around the Cape of Good Hope, and conclude our world tour with a cruise through the Mediterranean. It seemed a hell of a long way to go, though, and our initial two-year plan would need extending to at least four years to allow us time to complete it. I shook my head as the familiar questions and self-doubt crowded back into my mind.

Just on midnight we were ferried back to the *Lucette* by our amiable hosts. Buoyed by all the talk of adventure and the prospect of adding Egypt to our itinerary, Lyn and I tried to get to sleep in the stuffy heat of the night. It was the early hours of the next morning before Douglas returned home from what had been a heavy rum-guzzling session. Continually disturbed by his raucous laughter echoing across the water I eventually went on deck to shout him home. I watched in disbelief as he pulled away under power from alongside the sparkling new yacht, under the watchful eye of the owner, who waved him goodbye with a hooting peel of laughter. Departing at speed, he executed a round turn to starboard, only to cut it too fine and inadvertently ram his host hard amidships with a loud metallic clang. The collision forced the dinghy to dip her lee rail before turning sharply to scrape huge gouges out of the pristine yacht's thick epoxy paintwork – whereupon, without stopping or even slowing, Douglas completed a second full circle and rammed her for a second time. 'Sorry again,' I heard him slur with overzealous mirth as he killed the over-revving outboard, deciding rather more wisely to row back in the general direction of *Lucette*. Fearing a repeat of his calamitous attempts as he came alongside, I hurriedly re-positioned the fenders as he closed with us at too vigorous a pace through the darkness. Reaching down for the painter I made the dinghy fast on the port quarter and hauled him up onto the deck, where he tripped over the mooring bollards before crashing to the deck with a hefty thud. Happy that he was at least safe, I left him to it, his loud snores and intermittent groans echoing across the bay. The following morning, bright and early, he awoke under a blistering sun nursing the most wretched of hangovers, in full view of a visiting passenger liner. I thought it typical of human nature that curious passengers were focusing their pay-to-view deck telescopes on him throwing up over the side, rather than on the scenery or the activities laid on for them ashore. Alas, I sensed it was time to leave these enchanting shores.

The following day we joined the owners of the sloop-rigged ketch to visit Natalie and Bill Tritt on Navy Island. Bill was a distinguished yacht designer who exuded creative spirit even as he walked. He enthused over the leading-edge technological innovations that had led to the building of his extraordinary creation anchored in the bay below. He and his wife had despaired of trying to live peacefully in the rising turbulence of Los Angeles and had moved house to realise their dream on Navy Island in Port Antonio. The Tritts made us all welcome in their beautiful home, where we became regular visitors, fascinated by their substantial library of seafaring literature and model yachts, which absorbed our interest with every visit. Their son Scott befriended Douglas, and the twins struck up a friendship with the younger children on Navy Island, one of whom owned a six-wheel-drive amphibious craft, upon which the kids took off together for whole days at a time. Driving into the river estuary and onwards, over constantly shifting sands and mud banks, they spent many hours travelling deep into the unexplored territory upriver.

At a farewell dinner party thrown by the Tritts just a few days before we were scheduled to depart, we met a friend of Bill's, who was by profession a tax lawyer from Chicago. Upon examining Lyn's wage slips from her work at the Cedars Hospital, he vowed to complete a tax return on her behalf and forward the overpaid tax she had not claimed whilst working in Miami. 'I'll send it to you at the yacht club in Panama,' he promised. 'God bless America,' yelled Lyn joyously when she realised a tax cheque of almost a thousand dollars would be due. Bill recounted his own sailing adventures as a boy to the Mulatas or San Blas archipelago and recommended we visit them too, handing us a set of customised charts he had retained from the days of his youth, which indicated the navigable routes through the barrier reefs. It was too good an opportunity to miss and I resolved there and then that these islands would be our final destination before leaving the Caribbean. During our last few days in Jamaica, Douglas and Scott spent their time sailing the dinghy and exploring the bay, inadvertently spending an entire afternoon stuck on the shoals of the river estuary after being caught by the powerful crosscurrents flowing between the mud banks of the delta. Sensing Bill's desire, I asked if his son would like to join us to the San Blas. Scott considered it a dream come true, whooping with delight when he learned that he would soon be retracing his father's footsteps. So it was that we mustered an extra crewman in the fine March sunshine on our day of departure. We gathered to say our goodbyes after what had been a wonderful and memorable stay. Jamaica had been good to us, and instead of the usual pangs of depression when we left port, we found ourselves revelling in an air of delighted expectancy at the prospect of the adventures to come.

We set sail in the fine Caribbean winds on 15 March 1972, passing the township of Ocho Rios by late afternoon and observing the receding coastline of the western part of Jamaica as it melted into the dusk. Just after sunset, *Lucette* under full sail swung southwards to commence the 600-mile journey to the Isthmus of Panama. The gentle breeze remained steady, and under the night sky the graceful lines of *Lucette*'s rigging murmured gently to the bubbling phosphorescence churning beneath her counter. The lighthouse on Negril Point gleamed fitfully as the tops of the ocean swells obscured its rhythmic flash, until it too finally dipped beneath the horizon, lost behind the curvature of the earth's surface. The spread of sail burgeoned into the night, held aloft by the light breeze as the rhythmic creak of the pulley blocks, faintly audible, worked in sequence with the gentle motion of the hull. The moon had deserted the sky that night, but dawn brought a bright-red and cloudless sunrise as we struck out on a southwesterly course for the distant Central American coast. The kindly weather helped our new crewman to settle in, for although he had sailed small boats and dinghies before, night steering by compass and stars was a new experience for him and *Lucette*'s sail plan something of a mystery. We cruised before near-perfect following winds beneath brilliant white tufts of cotton-candy cloud, with each new day offering even better sailing conditions than the day before. On the third day out, we caught deep-water game fish with our trolling line, including a large dorado and several smaller bonito. Neil insisted that his teddies be on deck to witness the kill and became so wrapped up in his muttered commentary to them that he began to neglect his steering duties. Unnoticed by the rest of us, he allowed *Lucette* to wander so far off course that the wind came around on the lee side of the mainsail, which gybed her with a deafening crash.

I would have given him a lecture right there and then had my attention not been drawn to the trolling line aft, which was dancing vigorously to the death throes of a giant blue fish, jumping clear of the water in its vain attempts to get free. The line cut deep into my hands as I struggled to haul it in whilst Sandy rushed aft to help Neil get us back on course. Like characters in a play, we paused as one, our proceedings halted by the approach of a long dark shadow approaching from astern. Menacing and with an air of certainty, a large shark closed with us, its giant triangular fin parting the water with clear purpose. A moment later, the line I was struggling with became limp as the blue fish dancing on our hook was bitten clean in half by what we soon identified as a great white shark. Turning in our direction, it started to gain on us. Measuring almost a third of the length of *Lucette*'s hull, it seemed almost as wide owing to the refracted distortion caused by our elevated viewing platform. Its large dorsal fin, reaching as high as the planking on our decks, was serrated along its trailing edge and closely followed by a whipping dagger-like tail, thrashing both air and water in a series of powerful thrusts, which propelled the mammoth fish straight towards us. Warning us with a display of its awesome multi-layered teeth, held ready for instant use behind its sharply pointed nose and beneath its rapidly undulating gill slits, the dull black eyes monitored us with a singular and powerful intent.

Feeling like stalked quarry, we were genuinely frightened as we observed this apex predator, for it did not know the meaning of fear. An involuntary chill went down my back as I pensively returned its piercing stare. 'Standing on deck you are safe,' I heard my head reminding me. Looking aft, Sandy was pointing to another dark shadow as a second smaller shark joined the chase. They seemed to be working in tandem, one staying aft and one close by. The shark alongside, only a few feet away in distance, remained firmly imprisoned within his watery domain. The sea's interface with the air seemed like an intergalactic portal keeping us both safe inside our different worlds yet only inches apart. 'Keep in from the side,' I warned the intrigued audience gathering along the side rails, for I was all too aware that a simple slip would result in certain and bloody death. The smaller of the two sharks moved up to join the larger one, keeping pace alongside as it maintained station off the starboard quarter. Sandy remarked how he felt we were communicating in some way, as though some empathic interchange was taking place. The great white sharks followed us for several miles before finally giving up and dropping aft, merging into the dancing shadows of the waves and disappearing. It was strange how silent we had all become in the company of these majestic beasts, their very presence causing a quickening of the heartbeat and a timbre in the voice, palpable to us all. It took the rest of the afternoon before the sound of laughter was to be heard along *Lucette*'s decks once more.

With the added excitement provided by our departed visitors, Scott decided he had been smitten by the bliss of sailing. We were quick to remind him that bliss and sailing were words that were not always united in the seaman's vernacular. By the following day, the friendly trade winds had carried us steadily towards the dangerous shoals off the coast of Honduras and Nicaragua. Rusting freighters, some many decades old, emerged from the haze, starkly etched against the misty horizon. They stood out eerily, like deserted ghost ships stranded on the reefs, their bottoms literally torn out after they had grounded at full speed, victims of errors in judgement or downright bad seamanship. We counted seven wrecks in this maritime graveyard. Unsalvageable, they stood like silent bastions guarding invisible frontiers, their glazed portholes and varnished wooden doors still glinting in the bright afternoon sunshine, their deserted lifeboat-falls swinging in the breeze, silent witness to the final desperate moments their crews must have suffered as they strove to get away. Now relentless waves were slowly breaking their backs in a persistent battle of attrition with the elements. It was late evening, the day after our meeting with the ships, before we found ourselves funnelled into the busy shipping lanes converging upon the twin ports of Colon and Cristobal, on the Atlantic coast of Panama.

Dawn of the seventh day after leaving Port Antonio saw us entering the wide breakwater defending the bay of Colon at the northern end of the Panama Canal. The port of Colon was a busy crossroads of trade and commerce, with ships of every nationality anchored in the harbour, waiting to effect safe transit through to the west coast of the Americas. Colon had little to endear it to the traveller, either in its dull tin-roofed cement buildings or in its flat streets, linking squalid shanty towns and overcrowded apartment buildings via grandiose churches to open-air markets and a flourishing red-light district, situated in the downtown area bordering the Canal Zone. Heavily guarded by the US army, the Canal Zone was of both strategic and commercial importance to the United States, and was in fact classified as US sovereign territory.

In stark contrast to the city, the Club Nautico Yacht Club was well equipped in the provincial style, catering for visiting yachts as well as the middle-class residents of the outer suburbs. Our stopover at Colon was necessary in order to obtain the requisite documents and permits that would allow us to proceed unimpeded to the islands of the San Blas. I anchored *Lucette* in the same spot that Douglas and I had anchored the Alden schooner *Puritan*, when delivering her for Baxter the yacht broker some six months earlier. Douglas and the twins had much to interest them in the continuous stream of shipping using the Panama Canal. After minor frustrations, attendant upon a non-Spanish-speaking foreigner tangling with non-English-speaking officials, the permits were finally acquired. Our plan was to proceed eastward to the ancient fortress town of Portobello prior to venturing still further into the little-known recesses of the San Blas archipelago.

Portobello lay only 20 miles down the coast from Colon and had been a favourite haunt of such notorious buccaneers as Morgan and Hawkins. Drake had sacked the city even at the height of its power over the Spanish Main. Portobello had been the strongest of the South American outposts of empire in the medieval world, being the main port for assembling cargoes of silver plate and other precious materials from El Dorado, ready for transhipment to Spain. The town situated inside the bay was guarded by substantial fortifications; the narrows at the entrance to the bay were watched over from both sides by derelict and deserted castles that once policed not only the maritime traffic in and out of the port but all shipping that sailed to and from the entire region. The curtain walls of the forts, some 20 feet thick, had been impenetrable by any cannon of the day, but it had been well known to the English that the large guns positioned to guard this valuable trade route had an Achilles heel, for ships reaching a waypoint just outside the entrance were then below the guns' lowest elevation. Gaining the narrows allowed ships to sail under the line of fire, straight into the harbour and on into the town. It was easy to see how the privateer Henry Morgan could pause his attack when passing the stalwart towers, and indulge his crew by taunting the Spanish guards with polite promises of vile retribution, knowing full well that though they were standing only feet away in the darkness they were quite powerless to stop him. *Lucette* glided into the beautiful bay, tacking smoothly under genoa and main. As she slipped through the narrows it was not difficult to visualise those tall ships tacking in under the huge fortifications that lay on all sides, firing broadsides at the defenders ashore whilst despatching boat parties to run in and attack at close quarters.

Immediately beyond the town lay the extensive, undiscovered and almost impenetrable jungle of the San Blas Mountains, beyond which lay the large swamps and unspoilt jungles of the Darien Gap. Douglas wanted to mount an exploration party up the river as soon as we landed but could not muster any volunteers; not even Scott, who was recovering from a heavy dose of mosquito bites. Neil offered the puppet-land brigade, but Douglas remained singularly unimpressed as he sat with the sulks, gazing longingly towards the shore. Once in the town we mingled with the friendly Portobello townsfolk, buying fresh produce at the local market and even attending the Roman Catholic church, which was opulent and disproportionately appointed considering the poverty of its congregation. As we had seen in Jamaica, the tombstones recorded the terrible and devastating toll of yellow fever and other diseases that had decimated the early settlers, slave and master alike. The additional bloodletting by the Spanish conquerors and the pirate brotherhood of the Spanish Main had made this coast one of the bloodiest in history. Sir Francis Drake's grave in the bay was still marked by a small islet named 'El Draque', and after paying our respects to this most famous of England's sons, still lying where he had been interred after sustaining fatal injuries during an ambush hundreds of years before, we finally took our leave, setting an easterly course. Even though we had only stayed in this historic place a few days, it left intense and vivid memories imprinted upon our minds.

Departing before nightfall, we anchored the following day to explore the virgin reefs of Isla Grande, where we were amazed to discover huge crabs living encased inside the coral. Their one-time bolt-holes had closed around them with the encroaching coral growth, finally sealing all the exits about them and encasing the crabs' soft-shelled bodies, imprisoning them for life inside their thick coral cells. Entombed, there was no escape as they hung their huge clawed arms from the reef walls, waiting to capture unsuspecting passers-by. When the crabs had died, their arms dropped outside the coral and generation upon generation of their claw bones had formed huge piles at the base of the reef. They looked like children's forearms heaped in piles and picked clean, shining brightly in the glimmering submarine sunshine like skeletal bones piled up in a wartime killing field. Later that afternoon Douglas called me into the water to witness several hundred barracuda churning in a huge barrel as they corralled large numbers of reef fish in a killing orgy of gargantuan proportions, falling victims themselves to attacks from patrolling sharks even as they ate their hard-earned prey.

Heaving anchor later that day, we arrived at Nombre de Dios Bay just as night fell. Like Portobello, this had been another bloody hunting ground for buccaneers and pirates. They had profited immensely from preying upon ships laden with bullion as they waited for favourable winds or sheltered from passing storms. It was from here and other similar strongholds that convoys of square-rigged sailing ships had assembled, prior to returning across the ocean with their looted wealth of South American gold and silver, to bolster the coffers of the European empires. We anchored in the same bay where the *Golden Hind* had anchored centuries before, and journeyed ashore to see if we could find what remained of the 'Royal Road' linking this once pivotal trading centre with the city of Panama on the other side of the isthmus. The town consisted of nothing more than a collection of tin-roofed huts surrounded by the dense jungle. We were soon rewarded for our efforts, however, when one of the townsfolk directed us towards a cobbled mule track leading inland. This track had once been the only link to the west coast and practically all of the gold and silver transported to Europe had passed this way. Douglas and Scott were positively enthralled that they should be walking on the very same cobblestones as Sir Francis Drake, during his ill-fated trek to capture a king's ransom in gold for the English crown some 400 years before. We walked along the path for a little way, discovering, to our utter amazement, ancient cannon still installed in the overgrown battlements.

From Nombre de Dios, another day under fair winds and calm seas took us to Porvenir, the entry port for the San Blas Islands, which looked more akin to the south Pacific than the Caribbean. Tall coconut palms grew in profusion on rocky bases and reached out over the clear blue sea. Skirted by golden beaches and surrounded by tranquil lagoons, they were protected by substantial outer reefs upon which the heavy surf pounded relentlessly day and night. The San Blas archipelago consisted of a group of approximately 350 barrier islands located off the Darien coast of eastern Panama. The inhabitants were exclusively Kuna Indians, who had been resident as a tribe since long before European explorers arrived in the fifteenth century. Unlike many places in Central America, Panama allowed complete autonomy to the Kuna, who governed the San Blas archipelago with little outside interference. The islands were mostly uninhabited, though some were temporarily occupied whilst harvested for their coconuts and fish stocks by passing villagers. Indeed the vast majority of the outer islets were sandy atolls, pristine in appearance, untouched and virgin. Contrastingly, those islands that were inhabited were more reminiscent of mini versions of Manhattan, cleared of trees and populated over their entire surface, with tightly packed grass-hut style houses. These islands the Kuna called 'village islands'; and though friendly and welcoming they guarded their cultural identity with great care, handing down their Chibchan language and Kuna artistry from generation to generation by word of mouth and spirit of community, for there was no written language. For the next month we planned to experience life within their tribal system, an anthropological anachronism that had remained virtually unchanged since the dawn of mankind.

Although the reservation extended inland to the top of the San Blas mountain range the mainland remained quite uninhabited, consisting mostly of dense unexplored jungle. The Indians travelled from their villages daily to the mainland by dugout canoe, in order to cultivate their small fragmented plantations and to bring back fresh water to the islands. Porvenir was the largest of the village islands and home to their tribal chief. The palm huts, some of which were mounted on stilts, were densely packed, with narrow paths and walkways leading from the houses to the main round house at the village centre. The Kuna women displayed their wares for sale along the roadside, including large collections of sponges, coral necklaces and intricately stitched shirts decorated with brightly coloured tapestries they called Molas. At the last census the largest island had a population of about 900 souls and since the entire island was covered by huts it was unlikely to have altered significantly, there being no room for further expansion. The number of children in a family rarely exceeded three or four; it was usually only one or two.

The Indians were small in stature, with copper-coloured skin and regular classic features, invariably topped with straight black hair.

Their homes offered only the most primitive of comforts, consisting mainly of one-room huts fashioned from untreated wooden frames, with woven palm leaves sufficing as thatch for both the walls and roof. For the most part, the Kuna slept on simple coir matting placed on the floor, though some huts had furniture and some were even equipped with a double bed. Many were decorated with brightly embroidered tapestries. The most impressive building by far was the large round building with a central chimney known as Congress Hall, where village functions, tribal gatherings and council meetings were held. Standing above the other buildings in its immediate vicinity, it looked impressive and foreboding. High vertical walls disappeared beneath low sweeping eaves and intricate carvings decorated the protruding beam-ends. The great double doorway at the front of the building continued up to the circular roof, which swept upwards to form a central point like a great inverted cone. Light flooded in from the latticed walls below the line of the eaves and the wide earthen floor was firm underfoot. At the centre stood great supporting pillars of mahogany, carved and painted with pagan symbols showing deference to the seasonal harvests and the animals they hunted. Centrally, a large fire burnt in an open hearth and the smoke, drawn to the roof by the updraught, billowed out into the clear sky above. A long bench seat was situated around the periphery and a raised wooden stage at one end indicated the space reserved for the chief and his entourage.

The womenfolk in most cases wore a heavy gold ring on their upper lip, suspended from the nose. Their heads were covered by scarves and they wore richly patterned Molas and colourful blouses decorated with seeds, fish bones and teeth, embroidered with complex patterns of animals and birds. Mostly barefoot, their lower bodies were clothed with what seemed to be a standard-issue sarong tied at the waist. The men, by contrast, were drably garbed in western-style shorts and T-shirts. While growing up from childhood to puberty, tribal custom required all girls to wear their hair long with heads uncovered, but on attaining marriageable age and a partner found, usually of the girl's choosing, their hair was cropped short and covered with a scarf, after which they were forbidden to uncover their heads again. The boys lived a much less restricted life, carrying out fishing and boat work out of school hours. After marriage they joined the wife's family, working her father's plantations and out-island fish traps. The women formed the line of continuity, their beautiful young brides donning veils and shaving their heads when they married, with the groom having no choice but to subordinate himself to his wife's father, working for him to provide for the nuclear family. Concerning the marriage ceremony we laughed out loud when told, 'When man and woman marry they get in hammock like this.' Our guide clapped his hands loudly and rubbed them together with a knowing grin, 'Then they are married.' He explained that according to the status of the couple concerned there was sometimes a ceremony, held by the whole village and lasting two or even three days. Our guide concluded somewhat wistfully that some men did not always marry for love; some were more interested in finding an easy-going father in law!

Although the women performed most of the domestic chores, they were able to move about the community without let or hindrance, there being no taboos or restrictions. They took turns in baking the village bread and transacted most of the trading in beads and Molas, managing their canoes with skill and strength and paddling many miles, sometimes in convoy, to do the washing in the great rock pools situated on the banks of the swift-flowing Rio Diablo on the mainland. Doing the laundry was both task and ritual and not so straightforward as it first appeared, for once on the mainland a sharp lookout had to be kept for jaguars, pumas and alligators, all of which roamed the riverside jungle.

On a couple of occasions Lyn managed to rope Douglas into joining the washing expedition upriver in the dinghy, now proudly sporting her painted name banner *Ednamair*. Douglas, though strong and fit, found it necessary to pace himself for the long row in order to keep up with the women. The freshwater laundry pools were situated well beyond the mangrove trees that flanked the entire coastal region, and the canoes were beached near a wide bend in a quiet part of the river. Douglas was given the honour of keeping lookout for wild beasts, though his mother claimed he was more interested in looking after the prettier girls who, away from the formal atmosphere of the village, shed all inhibition and set about their duties in various combinations of topless and even bottomless splendour. The elder womenfolk, amidst great chatter and mirth, instructed Lyn on the cleaning methods, using the sap extracted from special soapwort plants as well as laundry stones and cleansing lime soils. As the clothes lay on the hot rocks to dry, Lyn began exploring and quickly became fascinated by the tiny flocks of hummingbirds, suspended by the rapid beat of their wings as they drank from the nectar dishes created by the larger jungle blooms. Brightly coloured kingfishers and wagtails, brilliantly patterned parakeets and ponderous herons also frequented the river, though numerous insect bites and stings, together with the watchful attendance of creepy-crawlies, snakes and lizards lent credence to the wisdom of the island settlements. Lyn's enthusiasm for joining the Indian women on their tours of duty was severely tempered a few days later when, as she ventured into the jungle to gather more soapwort, a giant spitting iguana confronted her. Squaring up in a belligerent demonstration of territorial protection, it flicked its forked tongue and swished its spiked tail, spitting and hissing loudly as it stood its ground, refusing to allow her passage along the path. Lyn retreated watchfully, then turned and fled, still trembling at the knees long after she had regained the relative safety of the river.

The Kuna burial grounds were located on the higher banks of the riverside on the mainland, and were model villages with graves covered by long houses. They had been constructed with meticulous care. Above the richly carved portals of the ornate doorways, flurries of colour erupted to blend perfectly into the upturned eaves and sweeping ornamental gables. We passed through two such villages of the dead during our travels inland. Each palm-woven house contained tables, stools, eating and drinking utensils and other personal belongings of the deceased for use in the afterlife. Certain days of the social calendar were reserved by the Kuna for sharing time with their ancestors and maintaining the grave sites, their respectful remembrance of their forefathers providing not only a record of their past but also a basis for their futures.

Upon hearing Lyn and Douglas's tales of the laundry pools the twins, not to be outdone, insisted that they be taken on a similar adventure of their own. Stowing food, water and a few spare clothes, together with the machetes, the boys and I set off in the *Ednamair*, following the same route up the Rio Diablo past the mangroves, the villages of the dead and the laundry flats, before proceeding on upriver, further than even the remotest of the plantations. Schools of fast-moving archerfish darted in and out of the mangroves, spitting at insects perched on the overhanging branches, which they expertly dislodged and promptly devoured as soon as they hit the water. Large black-and-white catfish hunted prey from the riverbed where the river and sea formed a constantly shifting brackish interface, and we watched with particular interest as large piranha patrolled the deep pools further upriver. Eventually we were forced to disembark and haul *Ednamair* over white-water rapids and rippling shallows by hand, until we found the turbulent waters too fast flowing for safe passage with our boat. We located a suitable ledge upon which to leave the dinghy, and continued on foot. Trekking into the open forest along deserted tracks, we initially made rapid progress, but the trails finally petered out into a series of overgrown pathways, leading us ever deeper into the impenetrable jungle until we were forced to a complete stop, surrounded on all sides by solid walls of varying shades of green. The chatter of spider monkeys and the screech of macaws punctuated the hot morning air and sweat ran down our faces in rivers, the salt stinging our eyes as we rubbed biting insects from our faces. The jungle aroma, a heady concoction of decaying vegetation mingled with the sweet perfumed scents of flowers in constant bloom, was extremely pungent, making our nostrils twitch as new smells materialised and mingled around us. Great vines of blossoming foliage and all manner of flora blazed vibrant shades of purple, orange and yellow from within the green shrubbery and wild orchids hung in large clumps, with long trails of beautiful petals and flowering buds everywhere we looked. We laboured step by step, unsure of what we were looking for, snakes slithered across the tree canopy, and whole families of black spider monkeys watched us intently. Forced back towards the riverbank we kept a sharp lookout for alligators and crocodiles, before stumbling across the fresh footprints of a large cat that had recently been to the water's edge to drink, sending us a chilling reminder of our vulnerability in such a harsh environment.

Insects hummed and buzzed about us, one large black variety biting pieces out of our arms mid-flight, without even stopping or alighting as they did so. Spiders the size of dinner plates patrolled their silvery webs, which they had expertly suspended across clearings in the undergrowth. Hordes of mosquitoes billowed like pulsating clouds over our heads and it seemed that eyes were watching us from behind every tree. It was through exactly this sort of dense jungle that a British expedition had recently carved and hacked its way across the Darien Gap, the nearby tract of unexplored swamp and forest yet to be bridged by the eight-lane Pan-American Highway. Sandy reminded us pointedly that seven members of that expedition were still in hospital with obscure tropical ailments. It wasn't much longer before we decided that the all-too-abundant insect life, which no doubt harboured these and other diseases, was too attentive for us to continue. We had had enough! Having covered less than a mile in the last two hours, we decided we could go no further, quite satisfied that we had earned our stripes as intrepid explorers. After a short rest we turned back the way we had come, our path already indistinct in the thickly packed undergrowth closing in around us. We could easily have been confused into following any number of blank trails until we were hopelessly lost, had we not been able to continually check and recheck our orientation from the constant hum of flowing water afforded by the proximity of the nearby river. We retreated from the green hell, where the machete was a man's best friend, hacking as vigorously at the encroaching ferns and creepers as we had when clearing our inbound route only an hour before.

Rediscovering the *Ednamair* where we had left her, we paddled downriver at incredible speed, carried by the strong currents, and were soon merging with the familiar dugout canoes of the Indians going about their daily business. I was astonished to observe a shaking fist from a burly native aboard one of the nearby canoes. His loud expletives were incomprehensible to us but clear enough to warn us that they meant trouble. We hurried on towards the *Lucette*, snubbing her anchor chain gently in the flat waters of the bay as she slowly swung across the late afternoon breeze. A convoy of canoes gradually formed around us, escorting us towards the boarding ladder, which was still hanging over the side where we had left it. Amidst much chatter and pointing of fingers a smaller group of canoes broke away from the others and sailed close by, inspecting the *Ednamair*. I boarded *Lucette* with trepidation grateful to see Scott, Lyn and Douglas were all in good fettle.

'What's going on?' I enquired in a harsh whisper, my concern unrestrained as some of the Indians were wielding machetes and the situation looked like it might turn nasty at any moment. Douglas looked sheepishly in the direction of a large hand of green bananas lying on the cockpit floor that he and Lyn had brought back from the jungle the previous day. 'They want them back,' Douglas remarked petulantly as he stabbed the air with his hand in the direction of the fruit, 'But we got them from the jungle, and finders keepers.'

If I didn't act decisively we would have a diplomatic incident or even a cold-blooded murder on our hands. I did not want a repeat of the events that had forced us to leave Dominica a year earlier. 'Hand them over,' I commanded without a moment's hesitation, pointing first to the bananas and then to the waiting canoes. Sensing the rift between Douglas and me and smelling victory in their grasp, the Indians began to chant louder and louder, clattering their machete blades on the canoe sides in a menacing beat. The Indian plantations were not simply well-cultivated fields, or for that matter even marked-out plots of land, but a collection of interspersed trees and plants, growing haphazardly where the jungle let them. What Douglas and Lyn had perceived as a wild banana tree growing in the middle of the jungle had in fact been cultivated by one of the villagers. The Indians wanted them back and they wanted them back right there and then. Douglas's face looked resigned as he handed them over the rail to their scornful proprietor, and the chanting turned to high-pitched victory whoops as the flotilla quickly dispersed.

'Food, any food, is valuable but not worth dying for,' I hissed in Doug's direction as Lyn handed me a warm cup of coffee, my limbs atremble and my knees weak with shock, forcing me to lie down before I fainted. Within the hour, a lone canoe with two traditionally dressed Indians on board approached, hailing us from the water. We were commanded to come ashore the following day for an audience with the chief. It seemed that the incident was not over after all.

Returning below, my rest was anything but relaxing. Struggling to control my composure, my thoughts kept returning to the chant of the Indians. It had stuck in my mind because it sounded almost English, then like a bolt out of the blue it came to me. 'Henderson', that was the word they had repeated over and over in threatening and intimidating chants. I leapt out of the bunk, cracking my head on a deck beam with a jolt that made stars flash inside my head. I fell heavily to the floor with a loud crash, causing Lyn, who was preparing tea in the galley, to push open the door to see what the commotion was about.

'Are you alright?' she enquired, helping me to my feet. 'Henderson,' I replied, 'who is Henderson?' It was Douglas who came up with the answer. His name had been mentioned to us back in the yacht club in Colon, for he was a notorious local pirate who specialised in raiding yachts. My immediate desire was to weigh anchor and sail, but Lyn interjected with a reminder of our summons to the chief on the morrow. If we were to finish our cruise of these idyllic islands, and not risk any collateral implications regarding our proposed canal transit or with the Panamanian Authorities, of which the chief was technically the legal representative, then we had to keep our appointment.

'Maybe we haven't actually got an appointment with the chief,' voiced Scott, joining in the debate from on deck, 'It would be a perfect way of ensuring we stayed put overnight if they intended to carry out a raid.' I needed a drink, and a large one. Breaking open the liquor cabinet, I poured large rations of dark rum into a hastily formed line of glasses that Lyn had put out.

It was then that I recalled reading about a similar problem faced by Joshua Slocum during his solo circumnavigation aboard his gaff-rigged sloop *Spray*, back in the 1890s. He had sprinkled his decks with upended tacks, so that a raiding party had punctured their feet, not only disabling the would-be boarders but also forcing them to give away their element of surprise. 'Perfect,' declared Douglas, punching his open palm with his fist before rushing aft to locate the nail box in the engine room. He and Scott withdrew to the deck and sorted out a suitable array of defensive sharps. It was dark by the time the trap had been set, and Douglas and Scott both insisted on sleeping on deck in order to stand by and deal with any trouble. The lightest of sleeps interrupted by vivid full-colour dreams came to Lyn and me in fits and starts, and when we eventually drifted off it seemed we were immediately roused from our slumbers by a loud commotion on deck. I watched in disbelief as Douglas repelled borders, wielding a large machete at the darkness and looking for the entire world like a white rajah in a native uprising. 'Bloody typical,' he cursed, kicking his foot in the direction of the last fleeing attacker as he fled over the side rails. Turning where he stood and shaking in heightened verve, Douglas wiped away the thick runnels of sweat trickling down his brow with a cursory sweep of his hand, his face breaking out into a wide victor's grin to Neil, Sandy and Scott who were standing by his side.

The following morning I dressed early, determined to see the chief and report the phoney summons and subsequent attack. 'Surely there must be a police force ashore, who could deal with the events of last night,' voiced Lyn in a defiant mood. Douglas, still on a high, rowed us to the nearby jetty, where Lyn and I were welcomed by what looked like a VIP welcoming committee. Our anger turned to confusion, however, as well-dressed and cordial walkers waited in formation to escort us to the chief's residence. All our hypotheses the previous night had clearly been wrong; the summons by the chief and the raid orchestrated by Henderson had been an uncanny coincidence. Far from being asked to account for the theft of the bananas, the chief wished to thank us for the diplomacy and tact we had shown in settling the matter! We were ushered into his chamber, an annexe to the great round Congress Hall where his wrinkled visage scrutinised us with great care from the comfort of a well-worn, over-stuffed brass-tacked leather armchair. After confirming his welcome he asked us many questions through a series of interpreters, wanting to know where we had come from, how we had come to visit his island, and how long we intended to stay. Remarking on the difficulties of introducing new blood into his people he also enquired if one or both of my elder sons (he presumed Scott was mine) would like to marry into the tribe!

Lyn and I were taken aback as the chief, dressed in a collarless white cotton shirt and dark serge trousers, enquired of our Queen across the ocean, keenly interested in the line of succession and asking that we convey his greetings to her majesty the next time we saw her. The formalities over, he methodically apprised us of his tribe's history. The Kuna, having no written language, recorded their chronicles in scenes of tapestry, meticulously sewn on ancient cloths by ancestors long since dead. The chief had a huge well-preserved collection carefully catalogued and stored in boxes, with the most salient ones mounted prominently on the walls around us. Those recording specific endeavours that had changed the course of their history through the ages were pinned onto the inner walls of his chamber.

He told us of the ethnic cleansing his grandfather had initiated, when all crossbred tribesmen had been murdered in their beds during a single night in order to purify the tribal blood. Later he himself had ordered the destruction of the pump wells installed by US aid organisations in the 1950s, in an attempt to reverse the adverse effect it was having upon his people. The installation of the pumps had stopped many of the historic practices and rituals that had formed the cornerstone of their successful existence through the ages, inadvertently destroying traditional values in the community and leading to fights and even large-scale riots. The provision of well water had obviated the need for canoe trips to the mainland, which in turn curtailed their practice of worship and the honouring of their ancestors in the villages of the dead. Above all, the wells had dispensed with the ritual of settling arguments and disputes with their neighbours on the mainland, such practice not being permitted by tribal law to take place on the islands themselves. Finally the chief told us of great stone monuments and settlements built by his ancestors at the height of their tribal power over a millennium before, when the tribe lived on the mainland and exerted its influence over a huge region, extending as far as the pre-Inca Chimu people in Peru and the Aztecs in Mexico. Originally carved from the mountain ranges deep in the interior, huge stone blocks had been dragged to the coast by teams of wretched slaves, to fashion huge temples and construct vast cities long since devoured by the jungle. He finished by telling of the fortune in gold and silver plate his ancestors had kept hidden from the Spanish by painting it with black animal dye, only for it to be lost a few years later in a massive earthquake that had destroyed their great cities and removed them as a power in the region.

Tired by all the excitement, the chief eventually began to flag. Our meeting ended with an exchange of hugs and an insistent invitation to a festival arranged for that evening by the village elders. It was clear that he was unaware of the previous night's fracas over the bananas and we saw no need to tell him of it now. In fact, we were honoured guests, with what amounted to the 'freedom of the city' sealed by a chieftain's decree; sufficient guarantee, we felt, to ensure no further attacks would be made upon us.

Hearing our news, Douglas was eager to head off to the Darien Gap in search of his fortune once more. The next we saw of him, he had persuaded Scott to accompany him and had found an Indian to be their guide. Seated in the front of a dugout canoe, paddle in hand and looking for all the world like Livingston, he and his entourage headed off towards the mainland, bound for the interior. The closest they got to any form of gold, however, were the over-ripe and maggot-infested mangoes they were forced to eat after their food was carried away in the rapids of a deep-water river crossing, far upstream. Crestfallen after being forced to beat a hasty retreat under the ferocious attacks of insects that had bitten them from head to toe, Douglas and Scott were back before dusk, still as determined as ever. They did not appear to comprehend that if the Indians hadn't found their lost treasure in over 2,000 years, then it would take more than an impulsive and unplanned excursion with the help of a single guide, to achieve even the remotest chance of success.

After extracting a promise that they would follow us later and join in the festivities ashore, we left Scott and Douglas licking their wounds whilst Lyn prepared our only shore-going clothes, still musty and wrinkled from their long period in storage. We scraped green bands of mildew from them and dressed for the greatly anticipated feast that the Indians had prepared ashore at the Congress Hall. Just before nightfall, a lone canoe ventured out to the anchorage to ferry us ashore. 'Chauffeur-driven limo to boot,' I chuckled to Lyn as we sat in expectant silence and were slowly paddled landward. The narrow streets of sand ran haphazardly between the huts and were thronged with singing, dancing villagers in varying states of sobriety. The menfolk especially were showing adverse effects of intoxication from overindulgence in a homegrown and extremely potent brew they called Inna. Concocted from fermented sugar-cane juice, cocoa and crushed maize, it tasted not unlike oversweet and fortified sherry.

We were led to the Congress Hall, where it took a little time for our eyes to adjust to the dimly lit, smoke-laden room. In the centre a pig, or at least that was what we hoped it was, lay roasting in a stone-clad ground oven and all manner of vegetables were lodged in the glowing embers beside it. Beside the stage a small group of musicians played soulful laments on crude musical instruments, some striking a heavy beat from tall bongo drums whilst others plucked at single-stringed banjo-like instruments. The crude hardwood tables were laden with fruit and flowers and empty gourds were filled to the brim with alcoholic and non-alcoholic versions of the sugar–cane drink. Blossom petals were strewn across the floors and themed tapestries had been draped across the walls. Flowering vines cut from the jungle were woven into the cornices to form long trails of tantalising colour and fragrance from ceiling to floor. Light supplied by blazing torches, fuelled by flammable oils extracted from jungle plants, flickered across the room, forming shadowy patterns on the horde of faces seated on the wall side benches, who peered inquisitively in our direction. A second row had been formed by the younger folk, sitting cross-legged on the floor, leaving a large open space in the middle of the room. Together with the children we were ushered to chairs immediately to the right of the chief, who sat resplendent in a white doeskin suit and black patent-leather pointed hat. He looked noble and enigmatic, as he sat surrounded by his tribal elders, indeed he would have looked truly regal had it not been for his protruding bare feet. I guess the three of us looked as ridiculous as each other in such 'nearly but not quite' garb. Wrinkled and smelling of mildew, Lyn and I found it quite bizarre that in order to impress we had all three adopted such formal attire – that in truth belonged to a world we had each decided to be no longer a part of.

In the midst of all manner of natural tools and utensils, the Indians to our horror had rooted out a couple of darkly stained plastic tumblers and filled them to the brim with the sugar-cane liquor, which they placed directly in our hands. 'In honour of your western origins,' we were informed by our translator approvingly. The music suddenly stopped and two singers appeared on the floor before us, their stamping rhythm quickly taken up by the onlookers, abruptly changing the collective mood. The duet, now barely visible through the smoky gloom, began to warble a high-pitched and continuous drone. Teams of dancers took to the floor, forming a double line and taking turns to hurtle the full length of the hut, missing the supporting uprights by inches as they skimmed past, before circling to perform intricate and graceful imitations of bird dances. Turning to rejoin the line at breakneck speed as the next dancer took up his turn, each new dancer tried their best to outperform the one who had gone before. All the time the warbling drone was sustained, with the rhythmic beat of the bongos supplanted by the increasing tempo of stamping feet, which in turn maintained the delicate rhythm of the dance. I was amazed that the singers, with only the beat of the drums to aid them, could orchestrate such a melody. Our translator explained that only as a result of many generations of dedication to their art was such ability possible, with each younger developing the skills passed onto him by his elders.

Our conversation with the chief continued through a succession of interpreters, each being replaced as their degree of intoxication rendered them incapable. The committee of elders was marshalled to formally greet us and they approached in turn, offering us a warm welcome and showing sincere deference and genuine reverence to their hereditary chieftain. In broken English they recounted various histrionic versions of 'The chief he say', reminding me of playground jokes from my own childhood as they searched for the right words, often stopping to slap either myself or Lyn heartily on the back to impart emphasis. As the alcohol flowed, they repeatedly fell over our feet as well as their own, much to the chief's frowning disapproval. Once the effusive welcome had subsided, we were able to sit back and watch the dancers perform with seemingly inexhaustible vigour, to say nothing of outstanding athletic prowess, as they repeated their routines over and again in a seemingly never-ending rhapsody.

Finally the drum beats and the dancing stopped, but the singers continued their routine, gazing into the middle distance and looking for all the world like old-time concert-hall comedians as they rendered their now tuneless ballad with tunnelled determination. What we were witnessing was not just entertainment, but also the formal handing down of tribal stories and the real-time creation of folklore. This recounting of ancient tales and recording of epic battles and brave deeds by lamented heroes was a very necessary process, for without a written language there was no other way of preserving such details of their tribal history for the benefit of future generations. The people could accept such tales as the truth, since they were recounted before their chief, whose presence kept the speakers honest and ruled out any doubts as to their authenticity. He was effectively ratifying the stories of the traditional tale-tellers, much as our own civilisation must have done in the Middle Ages and before.

Understanding the change of purpose in the proceedings we decided to take our leave, and thanked the chief for his hospitality. He invited us to cruise the rest of the islands with his blessing, and finished off by asking if we could send him some new spectacles when we returned to the civilised world. We promised we would and returned to the *Lucette*, gratefully gulping the frangipani-scented air, after enjoying a unique and memorable experience in the acrid smoke-laden atmosphere of the Congress Hall.

We did not see the Kuna chief again but he, more than any, cemented in our minds the value of this trip to our children. Once on board, Lyn and I sat hand in hand on deck long into the night, looking up at the sparkling multitude of stars above us. 'If only Anne could have shared this with us,' whispered Lyn quietly, caught in the iniquitous trap of sadness and guilt that never seems far away from parents whose children are no longer with them and who are denied the pleasure of sharing with them something which they know that child would have loved. I hugged her to me, trying to reassure her that Anne at least was happy and would be doing just fine, my face contorting in the darkness as I struggled to suppress my own tears of regret.

We left our anchorage the next day and headed out towards the more remote islands of the San Blas. Strong currents ran out of the lagoons, making navigation extremely tricky. Even with the help of Bill's modified charts with their scribbled rune-like notes, a keen watch for coral heads was still required. Gingerly but positively, we nosed our way through the tireless surf, where swirling tiderips presented a difficult and dangerous obstacle, before reaching the safety of the anchorages within. Whenever we could we moored stern-to, tied to overhanging palm trees, and caught breakfast fresh from the clear, tepid lagoon waters with our harpoons. The silvery underside of the sea's surface reflected overhead, trailing inverted curls of sparkling air bubbles left by gentle wavelets and mellow beach breaks that lapped against the sun-bleached sands further inshore. We rested our bodies on powerful thermals of rising hot water, bubbling upwards through the lagoon-locked waters amid schools of brightly coloured and glittering tropical fish. Ascending these underwater clouds we rolled off their tops like acrobatic skydivers, peeling off on cue as if to an unspoken command, as the cold down-currents bore us back towards the hotter epicentre and the start of another exciting loop. Fissures in the coral formed hydraulic conduits from the ocean into the lagoon, pressurising the seawater with each approaching wave to form mighty submarine geysers, spurting powerful horizontal jets of aerated water. Observing the fish, we trod water in front of the yawning nozzles, waiting to be scudded across the seabed like balls from a cannon, as the surge of water powered in from the waves crashing on the reef's outer wall. Colder water, flowing over the reef top, cascaded down pink coral terraces formed along the insides of the outer reef, feeding great sponges and shaking vast arrays of multicoloured fans that waved incandescent shades of blue, yellow and purple from amongst gigantic domes of wrinkled brain coral that towered upwards amid submarine gardens of unspoilt beauty and splendour. Occasional patrols of darting grouper and brightly patterned parrot fish, hunted by posses of larger stingray and barracuda, had to dodge the attention of individual marauding shapes. Dark and indistinguishable, such solitary predators were unwelcome visitors, temporarily trapped within the confines of the lagoon but nevertheless part of the cycle of life wheeling inexorably onwards. We explored the unspoilt reef by day and sometimes even by night, moving from island to island as the mood took us. The small hamlets on the out islands, populated by one or maybe two families, were less sophisticated than the villages, with simple huts that were crude and bare. Some hamlets were completely deserted and used only by villagers who came to tend their coconuts, to harvest sponges, or simply to burn debris and clear the undergrowth.

The next afternoon, as we approached an uncharted anchorage inside a remote lagoon, I posted Douglas and Scott as far forward as possible over the bowsprit, to warn of our approach to any uncharted coral heads. Manoeuvring *Lucette* through the reef gap with a few full turns of the wheel and well timed thrusts of the propeller, I headed for a long spit of sand reaching seawards with pincer-shaped fingers which met in the middle of the lagoon to form a beautiful heart-shaped bay. Without warning, we struck a miscreant rock with a hard grating lurch, which caused our old schooner to heel at an acute angle to starboard. We ground to a complete and shuddering halt perched atop a large purple coral head.

Reminding Douglas with a few curse-laden phrases that he was stationed at his vantage point in order to avoid just such an occurrence, I decided on a whim to let *Lucette* rest where she was, secure on the rocks until we were ready to leave. I was beginning to wonder what was happening to me. Usually so conscientious regarding my navigational probity, I found it difficult to be concerned that we were fast on the rocks. A situation that would have caused alarm and anxiety just a short month before, with a call for all hands on deck, seemed to pass without a care here in the quiet lagoons of the San Blas. I wondered if I was finally succumbing to the laid-back style of island life. Lyn brought me back to earth with a few well-chosen words, stating that she was of the opinion I had turned completely native. I gazed at her across the coach roof and my eyes caught hers as they had on the day we left Falmouth in the teeth of that storm. She returned my gaze and our eyes locked for a moment. I felt rich beyond measure to have her at my side and wished our days together could last for a thousand years. Later in the day, the mood of enchantment undiminished, I powered *Lucette* off the reef as the intruding darkness dimmed the glowing sunset in the western skies. We remained for many more days exploring palm-topped islets with wide deserted beaches and long expanses of fine white sand. We all agreed that our time in these beautiful and unique islands topped the league in the long list of top experiences we had enjoyed to date.

As each day passed, however, Neil became more and more obsessed with the adventures of his puppets, often refusing to join Sandy and myself fishing or sailing around the lagoons aboard *Ednamair*, upon which I had now rigged a mast and sails. Proving his superior skill with the fishing line one early evening, Sandy caught a huge bonito, which made a wonderful barbeque on the beach. We cooked it on an open campfire and washed it down with an ample supply of coconut milk and the last of our Mount Gay rum, brought all the way from Barbados.

'Do you know what day it is?' enquired Lyn as we sat around the embers of our beach fire. I had to confess that I didn't – nor, much to my vexation, could I recall even the month. With some backtracking and repeated counting on fingers, we decided it must already be May. We had not only lost all track of time, but it seemed that our concept of time itself had gone awry.

Douglas and Scott interrupted our deliberations later the following morning when they returned with the dinghy in pieces, having been caught in the heavy surf, which had literally ripped out the thwarts as they had been driven ashore. I took this as a sign, deciding it was time to make plans for our return to civilisation once more. After effecting temporary repairs to the dinghy, we decided to spend our last afternoon on one of the deserted atoll islands. By chance, we caught a huge thirty-pound tuna fish just before tea that afternoon and filleted it on *Lucette*'s deck. Incredibly, it still shivered in the pan even as we fried it. That evening the approaching sunset was truly glorious; myriads of high pink clouds shone golden sunbeams through turreted tufts and a green hue adorned the tropical sky, as the large red disc of the sun, distorted and shimmering, hung in silent splendour on the distant horizon and surrendered gently to the sea. It was to be our last amongst these islands, and we really believed that if we sailed for another twenty years we would not top this day for the sheer pleasure of simply being alive.

I decided to ask the family if now was not the time to return to England. 'I want to go back home, Lyn,' I lamented. 'We have all but spent the money I had budgeted to get us to New Zealand, and if we turn back now there will be sufficient funds to see us home. In any case we would have been at sea for two years by the time we get back.' I reminded my wife somewhat overzealously of the two years I had agreed to set aside, back in those far-off days in Falmouth. My prepared speech went down like a lead balloon, however. Not even Lyn would consider the offer to return home. Douglas stated flatly that travelling was now his life and that he hoped it would never end, and in any case he wanted to sail on at least as far as Adelaide to meet his childhood sweetheart Robyn. 'I just hope it never stops,' he finished, his eyes pleading with me to carry on. Neil proclaimed that neither big Ted nor indeed little Ted would be happy with a return to England, if we had not first visited their puppet-land realm!

I repeated that we did not have the finances to carry on, but eventually compromised, agreeing to return to Colon. If the tax claim promised by our lawyer friend from Jamaica actually materialised, then we would proceed across the Pacific. I felt strangely sad yet curiously elated in my perception that the money would not turn up – after all, holiday promises rarely came good. Secretly I began planning our return trip home.

We weighed anchor the following morning and *Lucette* glided across surreal crystal-clear waters as we approached the reef. All about us was dead still, the lagoon bathed in a ghostly and stunning silence. Indeed, it appeared that we were sailing on air, the water so flat and clear that we could not discern its existence above the ocean floor. Side-stepping the growling coral heads flanking the outer reef and feeling more than a little downhearted to be leaving this wonderful paradise, we hauled the main and genoa sails before finally killing the engine and setting a course back towards Colon in Panama. Early in May we entered Colon for the second time, the gateway to the west and the Pacific Ocean. At the Club Nautico we were greeted by a thick wad of crumpled letters that had finally caught up with us. Forwarded from England, Las Palmas, Miami, Nassau and Jamaica, they were from our friends and relations, the kids' school friends and my own and Lyn's family members, together with a number of cables from Scott's worried parents. Edna and Mary, following their foray to Las Palmas, had talked their respective spouses into letting them visit us again when we got to Australia. Siggi and Etta from the *Bonnie* had got residents' visas and settled in Fort Lauderdale, whilst Albert in an effort to get over us had sought treatment from his analyst. Our adventures seemed incomplete until we had read and reread the welcome mail from home, the most treasured letter of all being a one-page note etched in a hasty scribble from our daughter Anne, informing us that she and Jeff had moved to Canada.

Cristobal was the Atlantic terminus for the canal and consisted mainly of commercial warehouses and docks. The city had grown considerably since 1914, when the canal had finally opened after several failed attempts and at the cost of hundreds of lives, lost not only to the perils of construction but also to the ravages of yellow fever and malaria. Anchored once again in the Colon Yacht Club anchorage, we waited and slowly prepared for another long voyage. Armouring myself lest it be the Pacific whilst surreptitiously hoping it would be the Atlantic, I reworked the conversion I had started in the San Blas, to make the dinghy into a sailing boat. Bolting the mast shoe and leeboard housings permanently in place, we continued with our normal shipboard routine and waited with increasing impatience to see if the promised tax rebate would actually turn up.

When not practising his rowing, Douglas would be ashore with Scott, learning how to have a good time in the numerous bars and dens of iniquity that bordered the city and served the thousands of troops stationed to guard the ten-mile wide strip known as the Canal Zone. Just as we were ready to give up and start planning the long trip homeward an official-looking letter was delivered to the yacht club for Lyn. I was surprised to find steak on the dinner table that night, and when I enquired as to the cost of steak these days I was informed that our friend in America, true to his word, had sent the money through. I was shell-shocked. With the required finances in place, my bluff was called. My family reiterated my obligation to make good our agreement and continue on to New Zealand and Australia by way of the South Pacific islands. Once we were through the canal there would be no turning back. Arrival at our initial way port in the Galapagos Islands, downwind and down current from the continental land mass of the Americas, would commit us to the ocean transit, which would in turn commit us to our journey to the Antipodes. Homeward-bound back to England by way of Indonesia and Africa and Suez would complete our circumnavigation. Our decision to continue west from here would be irrevocable. Our plan to sail around the world had finally moved from the realms of hope and possibility to that of reality. I couldn't help but smile as the thrill of excitement charged my body. After all my hopes of returning home, I found myself looking forward with certain eagerness to our Pacific adventure.

We bade sad farewells to young Scott, who had grown into a man in the seven weeks he had been our guest, returning home to Jamaica and to his anxious parents, his life changed indelibly by his experiences aboard. The very next day we purchased a selection of spectacles and sent them by post to the Kuna chief.

On our return from the main post office in Colon, we met another young adventurer in the Club Nautico foyer in the form of Robin Williams, a twenty-two-year-old Welsh graduate in economics and statistics, whom we welcomed aboard for the voyage to New Zealand. His cheerful smiling visage and adventurous spirit made him stand out amongst his bored, unhappy and introspective contemporaries and as eager parents we hoped that a little of his arithmetical prowess and acumen would rub off on our twins.

Our passage through the Panama Canal, for a very modest fee, was fascinating to the boys and the morning was full of expectation as we motored through Limon Bay to pick up our canal pilot. Completely absorbed, we watched in wonder as huge track-borne mechanical mules whirred and chugged, carefully manoeuvring great ships with ease as they shepherded their charges through the locks. Thick grease-coated wires snaked across the water, where busy mooring gangs hauled them on board to the age-old chant of ancient sea shanties, and well-dressed ships' officers relayed instructions to and from the bridge. Squeezing in after the ships, enormous gates closed silently behind us. Crammed together inside the vertical walls of the cavernous locks, we were all slowly lifted some eighty feet into the Gatun lakes. Once clear, we motored southeasterly alongside the pioneer single-track railroad which spanned the isthmus, forming the only land link through the dense tropical jungle that separated one ocean from the other. Having descended the giant maritime staircase of Miraflores, we arrived to hearty cheers at the final set of locks, which lowered us to the Pacific tidewater level. From here we motored on through the quiet night airs until we gained the bright lights of Balboa.

We were at the gateway to the world's largest geographical feature, for the Pacific Ocean, some 64 million square miles in area and 35,000 feet deep, was home to over 30,000 islands spread across almost a third of the earth's surface.

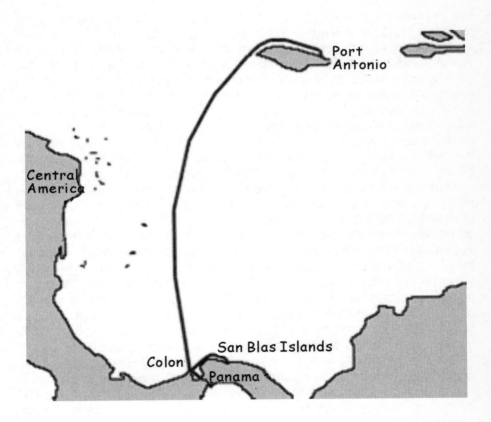

CHAPTER 8

Pacific blues

We anchored off the US quarantine zone that night and the following morning, feeling strangely reluctant to quit the land, we weighed anchor and sailed southwest into the Bay of Panama where we passed under the lofty span of the Pan-American bridge, the offshore breeze making for easy sailing in pleasant conditions. Bright golden sea snakes undulated their three-foot length in the blue seas and looked far too pretty to be as highly poisonous as we had been told they were. Myriads of seabirds ranging from stately frigatebirds and gulls to terns and tiny petrels held our interest as we cruised past the coastal farmlands of Panama and out into the long rolling swells of the Pacific Ocean, en route to the Galapagos Islands.

With practised ease, we settled into the necessary watch-keeping routines and enjoyed several days of fine sunny weather. Our sturdy craft cut a fine wake as she dashed through the water at a sprightly gait under full sail. The ocean beneath us had taken on a deep blue appearance and the waves were much longer from peak to peak, lending the water a unique characteristic that the French had failed to appreciate fully when they gave the name *Pacifique*, meaning tranquil, to this ocean. Unlike our Atlantic crossing, where sea life had been remarkably sparse, this section of the Pacific was populated with many forms of aquatic life and we were visited daily by large sea turtles, dazzling sea snakes and leaping dolphins.

On the ninth day out we were deserted by the northeast trade winds and drifted, becalmed in hapless mood. A change in the wind had brought a change in the weather as we edged our way into the doldrums, encountering towering squall clouds and variable winds. The ensuing days consisted of uneasy calms interspersed with squalls and thunderclouds, which left us stranded in prolonged showers of heavy rain, making the days tedious and our spirits listless. We made our way south and west as the wind and sea allowed, using the engine for prolonged periods for the first time since we had left the UK. The turtles we encountered in this section of the ocean were even bigger, some over six feet in length, and new species joined the parade every day, including giant manta rays, sharks and schools of pilot whales, which swam in company with us for many hours in impressive and acrobatic arrays.

Early one morning we were all summoned up on deck by excited shouting from the cockpit. 'A whale,' shouted Douglas, unable to contain his excitement at the proximity of a great leviathan that rolled onto its side, blowing powerful blasts of putrid air through its blowhole and covering us in foul-smelling concentrate expelled from the depths of its lungs. It kept station alongside us before suddenly and quite deliberately merging its course with that of *Lucette*, making the gentlest of contact before drawing away to approach for a second time. It was evident that the beast was eying *Lucette* with more than a passing interest. We quickly identified it as a female sei whale.

Some fifty feet in length, longer than *Lucette*, she was grey-brown in colour and followed us in parallel formation until without warning she rolled over onto her side to reveal her large expanse of yellowish-white underbelly. Unbelievably, she was trying to mate with *Lucette*'s hull. 'We must look like a whale from beneath the water,' I mumbled half to myself as we watched in awe, waiting to see what the great whale would do next. She tracked us for some ten minutes longer, rolling onto her back repeatedly before turning to drench us with more smelly breath and soaking us with torrents of cold water, splashed up by her flailing tail flukes and pelagic fins. She constantly manoeuvred her huge bulk alongside, adjusting her relative position whilst waiting for the right moment to close us, in what would be a crushing and destructive contact. 'Ease her downwind,' I urged to Neil, who stood transfixed at the helm as I tried desperately to increase the rapidly narrowing space between us. The spray from her air vent intensified the evil-smelling mist surrounding us until Lyn, trying to lighten proceedings held a handkerchief to her nose and demanded 'Get to leeward – your breath smells.' As if to heed her bidding, the whale dived a little deeper and popped up on the starboard side, repeating its spectacular rolls in an impressive courtship ritual. The whale tried twice more to contact us beneath the water, before she finally took her leave, disappearing into the deeper waters below as mysteriously as she had arrived. Robin, his seasickness forgotten for a moment, talked excitedly with the twins, whilst Douglas shook his upraised fist after the disappearing giant, emphasising the fears and uncertainties we had all felt. We had had a lucky escape from a most unlikely source of danger. Yet I realised then that to be wrecked in such a freak incident as a collision with a whale would be as catastrophic as sinking from any of the more usually perceived risks that litter the minds of all who venture out to sea in boats and ships.

The day after our encounter with the whale, *Lucette* was still reeking from the stagnant odour, which clung persistently to the sails and fabrics in the saloon and cabin. During Lyn's watch later that day a loud crack, like that of a flensing bullwhip, pierced the air as the boomkin stay aft, which in turn supported the mainmast backstay, parted at the hull fastening, requiring immediate and perilous over-side repairs. Had such an event occurred in anything but the calmest of weather, we would have been dismasted in the blinking of an eye. With Douglas tending the safety line on deck, I swung outboard and hung inverted beneath the pointed canoe stern. Examining the damage as the Pacific waters sped by, just inches away from my head, I could see the eye fastening had worn completely through, allowing the mainmast to rock excessively to and fro as we pitched in the seaway. The motion afforded by the missing stay was rapidly loosening the other fastenings, which as soon as they had worked free would bring the sails, masts and the entire rig crashing down onto the deck. Exercising nothing less than inspired technical brilliance and a significant amount of acrobatic skill, I managed to rig a replacement stay, relieving the strain and reducing the mast's motion to tolerable limits. *Lucette*'s standing rigging looked tired, her stainless steel stays though free of burrs had become permanently stretched, the peeling mast varnish had lost its gleam and the porthole brasses were green over in a thick crumbly tarnish. Several of the side-rail stanchions were loose and the galvanised rail wires were rusting through under their plastic coating. The paint on *Lucette*'s hull was flaking off in several places and her hull sides were streaked with dark rust stains. Unsightly blemishes had formed down the hull planking from the base of the chain plates to the waterline and the coach-roof paint had become dull and insipid. Though I knew *Lucette* was sound of hull I also recognised that she was desperately in need of some planned maintenance and a thorough cosmetic overhaul. Incredibly, it had already been some nine months since the last works had been completed in Miami.

Robin settled in commendably with the children as well as the adults on board. A well-qualified young man, he was brimming with facts and figures acquired from an excellent education, but he lacked both application and experience upon which to focus his new-found knowledge, making him overemphasise detail at the cost of overview. Nevertheless, he tried his level best to learn the necessary skills for sailing the *Lucette* without assistance.

We drifted along in the doldrums in changeable weather and prolonged thunderstorms for five full days before we picked up the first zephyrs that heralded the clearer skies and cooler southeasterly trade winds that would bear us to our landfall in the Galapagos, also known as the Archipelago de Colon. The dark isolated and remote volcanic peaks of the Galapagos Islands slowly materialised over the southwest horizon. A fresh breeze blew steadily from the south and close-hauled we beat southwestwards in an increasingly uncomfortable sea. It was the eleventh day out from Panama before we sighted Marchena Island and coasted round the strangely barren coastline of black lava. We continued to tack southwards against wind and current, passing the islands of San Salvador and Santa Cruz on our way to Wreck Bay, situated on the western tip of Chatham Island.

The monotony of the last week had made us all feel happy that the first leg of our ocean crossing was almost at an end. The seas cooled significantly as the Humboldt Current created a great confluence in the vicinity of the archipelago, teeming with all manner of aquatic and bird life. We caught several succulent tuna fish on the eve of our arrival that made a substantial meal, amongst the best food we had ever tasted. Neil caught, cleaned and prepared some eight or so of the silver-blue darlings and treated us all to a rare example of his culinary skills. 'It's amazing that a simple meal of bread and fish could taste so good,' Lyn enthused as she congratulated Neil on his offering.

In view of the delicate state of the jury-rigged backstay and the proximity of land, I decided to reduce sail before nightfall, in order to delay our arrival at Wreck Bay until daylight the following morning. The wind was blustery and large overfalls, formed by the assimilation of the equatorial drift and the upwelling of the fresher cooler waters, made the sea rough and the hull motion quite uncomfortable. Having completed the sail reduction with the help of Neil I went below, leaving him at the wheel, with instructions to call me if he sighted any lights. The dishes from the evening meal were strewn about the cabin and Douglas, Robin, Sandy and Lyn were sitting jammed into each corner of the saloon, forlorn and sullen and totally unmoved by the sliding crockery slamming back and forth in the open cupboards. The loose chattels needed some urgent re-stowing before something got broken. More than a little vexed, I voiced my disquiet and immediately tempers began to flare and they turned on me as one. They were tired and disconsolate at the end of a long passage, impatient at the perceived delays I had brought about by reducing sail, which forced them to suffer another uncomfortable night at sea, instead of enjoying the quiet sanctity of a still-water anchorage. The row was in full swing, when following a sudden lurch the cutlery drawer slipped from its housing and landed with a loud crash on the floor immediately below the cooker. Increasingly exasperated by the inactivity of my crew, I pointed my finger at them and chronicled their deficiencies in explicit detail.

'Oh shut up, Captain Bligh,' came back Lyn's incredible retort, reflecting how they all felt. I saw red and with a loud slap of my hand on the galley counter I demanded they shape up and get the boat stowed for the night, my temper rising by the second. They stared at me in fear and trepidation, for they knew from bitter experience I was about to blow my top in an uncontrollable bout of rage and fury. Just then, *Lucette* dipped suddenly into a deep sequence of overfalls, rolling jerkily to starboard before checking for a moment, then hit a solid wall of water up ahead. Rocked off balance, I gripped the overhead handrail and held on tight as a large wave landed on the deck above us. We waited in silent dread as the water swamped the decks above us before swirling aft to burst through the open porthole above me, the cascading seawater landing full-square on top of my head, soaking me right down to my toes and leaving me drenched to the skin. As suddenly as it had come, the wave was gone and *Lucette* settled back to a steady rolling motion, as if nothing had happened. My surprised crew began chuckling. 'That showed yer,' came a suppressed mutter from the dark recesses of the port-hand sofa. My ardour severely dampened, the stunned silence was suddenly broken as Neil burst in through the door, looking for the entire world like a drowned rat. 'I think I just hit the bloody equator,' he quipped breathlessly. Unable to prevent myself smiling I joined the others in an unrestrained bout of mirth. It was as if the Almighty himself had intervened, shutting me up before I could do any real damage to my overstressed, overworked and unappreciated crew.

The Galapagos Islands, straddling the equator, were the sovereign territory of Ecuador, which lay over 650 miles away on the South American mainland. Divided into specific National Parks, movement from one island to another was only possible under licence. The islands were a naturalist's paradise. Inhabited by varied and unique fauna, they had attracted the attention of scientists and researchers since before Charles Darwin published *The Origin of Species* in 1859. This great scientist collected much of his data about evolution and natural

Marine iguana

selection on these islands during his famous expedition aboard the HMS *Beagle*. Six species of giant tortoise were unique to the archipelago and other reptiles on the islands included two species of large lizards in the iguana family, a burrowing land lizard and an unusual marine iguana, the largest of which reached over six feet in length. The islands were home to some eighty different species of birds including flamingos, flightless cormorants, penguins and finches, now known as Darwin's finches in honour of the key role they played in his research. Large pods of dolphins and sea lions, together with vast shoals of black-tailed barracuda and immense schools of tuna, swam side by side with rare fur seals and mammoth sperm whales and numerous other species of fish and mammals more commonly found in the deep oceans. The archipelago consisted of fifteen large islands and several hundred small islands covering some 3,000 square miles in area. Distributed over almost 23,000 square miles of ocean, they could only be effectively explored by sea. It was my intention to clear inwards at Wreck Bay on Chatham Island and then tour these remarkable islands at our leisure.

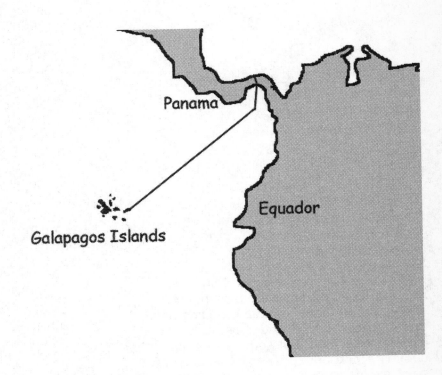

CHAPTER 9

Under attack

Our arrival at Wreck Bay the following morning was accompanied by throngs of seabirds, soaring into the light fluffy clouds as they waited for the exact moment to plunge upon their intended victims in the fast-moving waters below. The coldness of the water, despite the tropical temperatures, was caused by the proximity of the Humboldt Current, routing westwards across the northern reaches of the south Pacific. The opalled plumage of the frigatebirds, with their forked tails and puffed red throats, made them clearly distinguishable from the blue-footed boobies and patrolling albatross that flocked around us in

Waved albatross

great numbers. Hundreds of dolphins swam alongside in tight formation, literally turning the seas black as they plunged and dived in pursuit of huge schools of tuna and dorado. On arriving at the anchorage, we were dismayed to learn that the high amoebic content of the fresh water rendered it unfit for consumption other than by the indigenous population, who had developed sufficient immunity. This meant we could only explore this unique island ecology for a short time, as the limited water supply we already had on board could not be replenished until we arrived at the Marquesas after a trip of forty days or more across the Pacific.

Although the town was completely without electricity, we soon found the immigration centre, which doubled as the post office and fuel stop for the limited number of tractors and Land Rovers on the island. It was also the general store for food, clothes, hardware and supplies of every possible description. Lyn and I could not help but smile as the official cuffed a brooding hen off the top of a thick pile of dusty record books and loose-leaf forms, for even in this lonely outpost it seemed that some sort of paperwork was necessary before obtaining pratique. Having cleared inwards we spent the next few days exploring our new surroundings, and started on the essential repair work aboard, renewing the backstay eyebolt as well as replacing the worn backstay fastenings, before re-seating the worst of the loose handrail stanchions. With Douglas and the twins assisting,

I was able to organise a maintenance plan to get *Lucette* ready for the long ocean trip ahead. We managed to tighten the slack rigging shrouds, serve and parcel the turnbuckles, renew the wire in the upper side rails and replace a number of worn shackles, sheets and ropes. Later we all turned to, washing and painting *Lucette*'s hull as well as applying several coats of varnish to the coach roof and deckhouse bulwarks, this last restoring some glamour back to the old girl. Later in that same week an inter-island mail coaster arrived at the anchorage and we were able to send some letters home.

The mail coaster had also come to collect cattle from the island in order to transport them to mainland Ecuador, where they were to be sold. We were treated to the unusual site of seeing the cattle herded down dirt tracks and into holding pens temporarily assembled on the beach. Some of the more fiery bullocks were hobbled with stout ropes fastening their feet to their horns, before being crammed into the backs of small Land Rovers, where their drovers sat unceremoniously on top of them. When the coaster was ready, the black-and-white cattle were ushered into the water and tied alongside canoes by tail and head, where with the help of a stick they were persuaded to swim out to the waiting ship. Once beneath the pitch of the loading crane they were hauled with the aid of a stout canvas sling out of the water and onto the deck, where they were confined in purpose-built pens. I couldn't help but wonder what the local farming community back home would have made of it all.

Later that week an Ecuadorian Navy supply tug came to the rescue of the townsfolk with an emergency shipment of diesel fuel, with which it proceeded to refuel the local electricity generating plant, pumping the fuel through a half-mile-long four-inch rubber hose. They estimated that the operation would take over a month to complete provided the weather held out! The pace of life had certainly slipped down a few gears since leaving Panama. Once our repairs were completed and fresh provisions, including four sacks of oranges, a sack of lemons and another of avocados, as well as several bags of onions plus a variety of local vegetables and fruits, had been securely loaded on board, we picked up a few dry goods from the local store and were ready to depart. Eight days after we had anchored in the bay, we bade farewell to our friends, Señor and Señora Garcia and their daughter Elizabeth, with whom we had spent many hours learning about their island homelands. After clearing outwards at the immigration station, Lyn and I opted for a final walk back via the waterfront, through the gardens of the Naval Academy, where we stopped for lunch under an imposing statue of Charles Darwin. Even as we arrived back at the exposed stone jetty, Douglas was manoeuvring the dinghy alongside the steps with great caution, for embarkation was going to be far from easy in the heavy six-foot surge. With us safely aboard young Dougie flexed his powerful muscles and took us skimming across the harbour with rhythmic strokes of the oars. Aboard *Lucette*, a hive of activity ensued before chaos gradually gave way to order and the shipshape appearance of a yacht ready for sea. Our departure was finally delayed by a neighbouring yachtsman asking advice on the best route to Hawaii, making it late afternoon before we finally weighed anchor and sailed for the seal colonies of Barrington Island, some thirty miles distant.

Lyn and I decided, in the limited time we had available, to make our adventure a visit not only to the protected national parks of the islands but also to the more remote areas lying off the beaten track. It was to be a non-stop tour of sightseeing and discovery and the treat of a lifetime for our children. Dusk had fallen by the time the cliffs of Barrington were near enough to distinguish the detail necessary for safe navigation into the tricky entrance leading towards the only anchorage, so we stood off for the hours of darkness, watching in awe the interlocking luminous trails of phosphorescence made by the sea creatures playing around our hull. As daylight revealed the mysteries of the rocky coastline, so it concealed the identity of the living things in the sea and it was not until a dog-like whiskered face popped up nearby that we realised that the inhabitants of one of the Galapagos's largest seal colonies were escorting us into the harbour. With an ease which we had hitherto attributed only to dolphins, the seals dived and cavorted around *Lucette* as we steered carefully through the entrance to the cove and anchored close to a white ketch named *Albatross*. She was the only other yacht in the anchorage. The boys watched with intense interest as the seals lifted their graceful shapes on clumsy flippers and waddled up the rocks of the nearby island, informing their neighbours of our arrival with discordant, cow-like bellows.

Ednamair was soon lowered and Lyn and the boys set off to explore the seal colony, scrambling over the cactus-covered rocks, worn smooth where the seals had dragged their bodies to and from the sea. Large pelicans watched solemnly, unperturbed by the proximity of the boys when they approached to obtain photographs. Robin and Douglas climbed the slopes of the main island to look for land iguanas, whilst Lyn and I chatted to the owners of the ketch, old friends from Antigua who remembered our rudderpost troubles and were enthralled to hear how we had got it fixed. The twins, having completed their essays of our journey to date through the islands, went swimming with tireless energy in the cool Pacific waters. We had intended to look at Charles Island next but our friends persuaded us not to miss Hood Island, so that night we weighed anchor and beat eastwards against wind and current, hoping to make the anchorage before dark on the following evening. En route Douglas and Robin described how they had seen and followed several land iguanas, large lizard-like creatures ranging from about three feet to over six feet in length, endowed with sharp frilly combs down their backs, survivors from a prehistoric world. We were spellbound as they recounted their adventure, describing how they had first cornered and finally photographed them. The slow-moving lizards, like the pelicans, had been quite unafraid at the approach of humans. We arrived in Hood Island's Gardiner Bay with only half an hour to spare before dark, anchoring in the sheltered waters of a beautiful sandy beach, distant honking piercing the resonant boom of the surf and betraying the presence of yet another colony of seals.

We scrambled ashore next morning, picking our way through the herds of seals sunning themselves on the beach and into the scrub-covered hillside beyond. Mocking birds, finches and pigeons watched us curiously, quite unafraid; some even landed on us, picking at our clothing with lively interest. The Garcias from Wreck Bay had told us of blood-drinking vampire birds further to the north and this display left me in no doubt concerning the truth of such reports. Red-throated lava lizards darted around in the rocks whilst keeping a wary eye out for the hawks circling above. Small snakes were quite numerous and made us wary of treading on them. On our return to the beach, we plunged into the sea to cool off. While we could easily outmanoeuvre the seals on land, they were quick to show us who were the masters in the water. In rafts of ten to twenty they swooped close by us, leaping clear of the water at times and banking in circles around us, like playful children. Only on one occasion did they touch us, one of them playfully nipping at Douglas's rubber flipper when he had dived towards it. Ungainly on land, they were as graceful as dancers in the sea and we never tired of watching them at play. Later that day Douglas came across a huge humpback whale and her young calf. The mysterious whale with its large soulful eyes tarried in the bay and touched Douglas's heart in a way that would shape his thinking for the rest of his life.

Visibly moved by his time with the whale, Douglas seemed locked in a daze as we moved *Lucette* to the anchorage at the western point of Hood Island, in order to visit the nesting places of the seabirds there. Before we were to see them, however, we came across the island's sole human inhabitant in the form of Dagmar, a young blonde German postgraduate studying the life and habits of the lava lizard under the auspices of a Swiss university. She explained her work recording the life of the hardy little lizard, and introduced us to her friends the little finches and mocking birds. We crossed the island's rocky plateau, entering a vast rookery of gannet-like birds nesting among the rocks. They were blue-footed boobies, peculiar to the Galapagos, equipped with long sharp beaks and bright blue feet, and spectacular divers when hunting for fish.

As we approached the weather side of the island, the great roar of breaking surf grew in volume and even though we were some 300 feet above sea level the salt spray drifted across the plateau in heavy, soaking downpours. Sandy and Neil raced after Douglas and Robin to the cliff edge and stood in silent wonder, gazing at the breathtaking vista before them. Far below, huge Pacific rollers dashed in white fury against the rocks with a thunderous roar, flinging spray high onto the cliffs above. At frequent intervals, a column of water and spray vented through a blowhole in the lava. We watched in open-mouthed wonder as the watery column blasted hundreds of feet into the air, projected by the incompressible dynamism of repeated and incessant action from the waves. It seemed nonsensical that such enormous resources of natural power and energy lay neglected and untapped, ignored by man's blinkered commercial vision. Curtains of misty spray drifted across us in waves, glistening in the bright sunlight as they settled over the black cliffs, projecting vibrant superimposed rainbows gleaming the complete spectrum of colours across the sombre background formed by the dark backdrop of rock. In the distance, seals flopped lazily beside deep-sea pools where scarlet sally-lightfoot crabs sparkled the black rocks like a primeval rash. Nearer to us, on a tower of rock isolated from the cliff, black marine iguanas lay piled on each other in motionless heaps intertwined like hideous black spaghetti, their dull wrinkled skin and toad-like heads emphasising their heritage from a land before time. Overhead, the gulls, frigatebirds, petrels and boobies kept constant vigil, swooping in graceful flight as they soared over the deep blue ocean. If we had seen a prehistoric monster emerge from a cleft in the rock none of us would have batted an eyelid or been the least bit surprised.

Frigatebirds

The area in the vicinity of the spouting geyser kept us absorbed for the entire morning. As we ascended the hillside, we were treated to the astonishing sight of a huge bird, its beak snapping like a rifle shot and its wings outstretched to a span of some eight to twelve feet. Tottering on uncertain legs to the edge of the cliff, it launched itself into space, gliding in a graceful shallow dive to gain momentum before soaring high into the air to make for the open sea. Hood Island was the only place in the world where the waved albatross bred, and as we meandered back through the scrub we saw many of them brooding their large single white eggs, and were even lucky enough to watch a pair perform their peculiar mating dance. The birds faced each other, wings dipping and beaks snapping, their feet stepping as their heads bobbed close together in unison. We were vividly reminded of the nuptial dances performed by the San Blas Indians some months before. In trepidation, we edged our way carefully between the nesting sites of the waved albatross and wandered amongst huge flocks of blue-footed boobies and jet-black frigatebirds. We watched intrigued as they pecked and called, constantly vying for more of the tightly packed space. The bird life seemed completely unafraid of humans, hissing and clapping their large bills as we encroached upon first one and then another hotly disputed or fiercely defended territory. Dagmar gave us a conducted tour of the wildlife and later we made a campfire on the beach, where we enjoyed her company for tea. Later that night in the dying glow of the fireside embers, we feasted on fresh tuna and charred iguana tails, whilst sharing a bottle of wine with our host under the bright stars and clear moonlight. Dagmar spoke of the huge sperm whales prevalent offshore and we told her of our run-in with the sei whale just a few weeks earlier, but she assured us through the darkness that there was no danger of whales attacking small yachts. I was mighty pleased to hear it too and drank a loud toast to the resourceful young lady, her fine angular features enhanced in the dancing flames, as I stoked the fire with a knurled stick to ward off the cool night air.

The next day we explored the rock shelves below, populated by the crawling masses of red, yellow and purple crabs, which were repeatedly washed from the rock face by each approaching wave. We watched in wonder as they swam furiously back to safety, lest they be devoured by ever-watchful sea lions. We meandered amongst the masses of black, turquoise and pink marine iguanas basking in the sun. They too were fiercely territorial and not afraid to nip at our passing feet. Mainly black with bright green tinges to their flanks, they resembled the fledgling children of fabled dragons, as they piled themselves in massive heaps to preserve body warmth. We swam with whole schools of dolphins and sometimes involuntarily with massive patrolling fur seals who chased us from the water with aggressive barking displays. On such occasions we were quick to leave the water, whence we lay in the sun on wide deserted beaches of yellow sand and black volcanic ash, sited in complex mosaics like pieces of a surreal giant jigsaw.

It was midnight on 10 June by the time we took our leave and headed for the volcano island of Fernandina. Later the following afternoon, we passed Post Office Bay on Charles Island, where the old barrel used by the early whalers as a post box still stood. We cruised around to the southern point of Isabela Island, gradually psyching ourselves up for the long journey across the Pacific. Our penultimate port of call, we all agreed, would be to attempt the summit of the smoking volcano of Fernandina, which was located immediately to the west of Isabela Island.

By the next morning, *Lucette* was reaching before an easterly breeze, along a barren coastline of cinder-like lava. Isabela was the largest of the Galapagos Islands and home to the giant, bright-eyed tortoises, eking out an existence in the craters of its extinct volcanoes. On the bleak highlands forming the backbone of the

Galapagos seal

island, several unwary explorers had met their demise after becoming disorientated, or lost in the thick undergrowth of the arid mountainside. Later in the morning, we were joined spectacularly by a massive sixty-foot sperm whale spouting great jets of spume with loud even blasts from her vent pipe whilst dutifully shepherding her small calf behind. Her giant square head, smooth save for where it was punctuated with a huge watchful eye, nodded evenly as she kept pace alongside, her massive undulating body glistening in the sunshine as it powered through the water with slow deliberate swishes of her tail. Vast schools of pilot whales swarmed in play around us, turning the dark ocean waters white in a bustling profusion of spray and foam. They carpeted the sea in a cavorting mass as they swam purposefully on each side of our hull, sometimes leaping clear of the water, many feet into the air, and belly-flopping back into the sea with loud, resounding body slams. We were surrounded by all manner of marine life, including for the first time flocks of Galapagos penguins, which darted about within the clear waters, altering course at breakneck speed in pursuit of fry. We plodded our way northwards, until finally the cone-shaped peak of a huge volcano loomed out of the haze ahead, silhouetted starkly against the setting sun. It was the black volcanic island of Fernandina. We anchored in an unnamed bay on the southeast point, the call of the seals and birds accentuating the loneliness of the black and untamed wilderness.

Cloaked in the rays of the rising sun, the dawn view of Fernandina was breathtakingly beautiful. A green belt of vegetation around the volcanic peak shone like a bejewelled collar above the forbidding black slopes of lava, thrown in tortured profusion by earth tremors after the molten rock had hardened into petrified rivers. We pulled the dinghy well up from the water's edge into a narrow belt of mangrove trees, and after setting a modest target for our walk to one of the hillside craters we struck out across the wonderland of barren lava. We quickly discovered that where the surface had not been broken up by subterranean upheaval the going was quite good and we made rapid progress across the smooth lava skin. Here and there a lone cactus stalk like an elongated pincushion held precarious root in the arid surface but otherwise there was no vegetation, moss, insects or animals of any kind. As the sun rose in the sky, waves of heat emanated from the black lava surface, which turned to the razor-sharp consistency of cinder as we approached our objective, forcing us to prematurely abandon our hike. In fact we were lucky to get back without injury, as our track took us perilously close to rivers of molten rock enveloped by gas clouds that left us faint and gasping for air. After four hours of hard labour under a hot morning sun, having ascended only a few hundred feet, we felt we could go no further. Climbing volcanoes, we decided, was as difficult as trekking through the San Blas jungles. Our shoes were torn and our feet blistered as we decided to return to the inviting clear blue waters of the bay below. The twins, thankful to reach the sea again, dashed from rock pool to cove, marvelling at the variety of fish life to be found

Flightless cormorant

alongside the brilliantly coloured crabs. We carefully skirted the seal rookeries, where many baby seals were being suckled under the mangrove trees, as we did not wish to invoke the wrath of the feeding cows. When we reached the cove where the dinghy was beached, we plunged headlong into the sea without bothering to disrobe, cooling off before a beady-eyed audience of flightless cormorants, pelicans, gulls and boobies. The black volcanic mountain of Fernandina towered high above the tall masts of *Lucette* as she lay at anchor, rolling gently in the remnants of the long Pacific swell which surged round the rocky headland of Cape Espinosa, sending searching fingers of white surf curling into the sheltered waters of the anchorage.

Galapagos penguin

A fine afternoon's sailing saw us beating into a fresh northerly breeze, which brought us off Tortuga Point by dusk. Rather than risk the tricky approach to Espinosa in the darkness, we decided to stay in the deep-water anchorage of Tagus Cove for the night.

We tacked in towards the high mountains of Isabela, starting the engine as the hills deprived us of the wind, and motored slowly in through the gathering darkness. In starlit silence, the hills closed in around us as Douglas heaved the lead line from the bows of *Lucette* and found no bottom only a few yards from the shore. Our echo sounder was working rather erratically and I preferred not to trust it. The phosphorescence gleamed brightly around *Lucette*'s hull as she eased her way into the cove, the lead line splashing showers of green sparkling fire as it struck the sea and plunged into the depths, until a shout from Douglas informed me that we had at last found bottom. The darkness was intense so we lowered *Ednamair* and I sent Douglas and Sandy ahead to sound out the cove in front of us. Charts, especially of the earth's remoter regions, were known to be disconcertingly wrong at times and could not always be relied upon. Navigating by soundings alone, we dropped anchor a short distance from the almost vertical walls of rock that surrounded us. Being at the point of exhaustion, we quickly fell into a peaceful night's sleep.

We were awoken by Neil early the next morning, excitedly shouting out yachts' names. We all hurried on deck to view this astonishing record of the cove's past visitors. Douglas, accompanied by Neil and Sandy and a tin of yellow paint, carefully scribed *Lucette*'s name and port of registry on the sheer sides of the northern shore, amongst the impressive array of yachts' and fishing vessels' names already written there. The names and dates served as a chronology of the many visitors to the cove over the past century. The name of *Lucette*, emblazoned on the cliff in two feet-high letters, lent the anchorage an atmosphere of gaiety and companionship, which lingered with us long after we had left the sun-sparkled waters of the cove.

After a leisurely breakfast, we spent a pleasant morning sailing across the strait from Tagus Cove. The light-heartedness of the early afternoon was contagious and seemed to be reflected in the antics of the seals and dolphins as they escorted us into the strait. Our mood was soon soured however as gathering clouds obscured the sun, causing us to shiver in the slightly sinister atmosphere of Espinosa, where we made a last trip ashore to see the Galapagos penguins and the flightless cormorants disporting themselves in factual support of Darwin's *Origin of Species*. We landed on a dark sandy beach surrounded by jagged fangs of black rock jutting out from the headland. The rather scruffy appearance of the birds, so sleek and beautiful on the other islands, lent an air of depression to Espinosa that dispelled our usual enthusiasm and wonder, as we witnessed half a dozen penguins grouped at the water's edge, ready to take to the water at our near approach. Robin peered anxiously through his spectacles at the lens of his camera before pausing to take a rather distant photograph, then muttered darkly as he moved closer to get a better vantage point, causing the penguins to plop neatly one by one into the sea and disappear. I walked with him, past the stacked piles of black marine iguanas and the scarlet shells of the sally-lightfoot crabs, to where Lyn searched in the rock pools for additions to her shell collection. A white-crested crane walked with a dignified gait on the nearby rocks, quietly ignoring us as it scanned the small pools, while pelicans flapped their ungainly wings overhead, suddenly changing shape into streamlined projectiles as they homed in on their prey in the cloudy waters of the bay. We had passed the bloated body of a dead seal on our way in and the sinister triangular-shaped fin of an oceanic white-tipped shark still patrolled near by. I had told the lads to keep close inshore if they wanted to swim. Only Douglas ventured into the water and even he, intrepid reef explorer that he was, had made a quick exit when a seal covered with boils poked a belligerent snout at him.

We rowed back to *Lucette* aboard the *Ednamair*, feeling rather disappointed at such an anticlimax to our journey around these wonderful equatorial islands with their strange anachronisms of wildlife. On the eve of our departure for the Marquesas Islands, 3,000 miles to the west, the wind swung to the east under a grey mantle of rain cloud and I felt anxious to be gone, in the knowledge that leaving before dark would put us out from under the lee of the island by morning. Lyn protested vehemently at the thought of starting our journey on June the thirteenth, her fears refusing to be quelled when I pointed out that even the most superstitious of seafarers didn't mind, so long as it wasn't a Friday as well. Both Douglas and Robin joined with my feelings of anxiety to be gone and after a short spell of intense activity we had stowed and lashed the dinghy, and secured all movables on deck and below. By five o'clock in the afternoon we were ready for sea. With mainsail and jibs set, we heaved the anchor home and set course on a broad reach past the headland and out into the strait, en route to the waypoint where we would alter course to the west and run free towards the open Pacific. With a thousand square feet of sail billowing above her, *Lucette* moved easily along the ragged black coastline of Fernandina, towards the largest stretch of ocean in the world.

Lucette with no self-steering device had to be constantly steered by hand, so with night-time watches once again negotiated and agreed and with watch-keepers finally appointed, we sailed quietly on through the darkness. Douglas voiced his discontent, having drawn the graveyard twelve-to-four watch whilst Robin with typical novice's luck had managed to secure the four-to-eight twilight watches. Crossing the sheltered stretch of water in the lee of the massive bulk of the grumbling volcano, we made steady progress until at three-thirty in the morning the booms were swung over and both running backstays and sheets hauled taut and made fast, putting us on a course to cross the Pacific. Our freshly varnished and newly painted schooner heeled, gently at first and then with steeply inclined decks, as she reached across the steadily increasing southeasterly trade winds. We were soon careering positively through the water at a steady 7 knots, and by the morning of 14 June the Galapagos Islands had receded into the distance astern. The distant peaks merged with the clouds of an overcast sky as *Lucette*, rolling and pitching in the heavy swells, struggled in the rougher seas offshore, increasingly untypical of the Pacific trades. Even so, we made rapid though distinctly uncomfortable progress west by south, towards the distant Marquesas Islands.

Despite the fact that we had been sailing for over a year, our stomachs still took a little time to adjust from the quietness of sheltered waters to the more lively movement of the open sea. Throughout the day those of us not actively engaged in steering and sailing rested as best we could in the bunks below, supplied at intervals with hot soup or coffee from Lyn's indomitable labours at the stove.

Talk that morning seemed to be dominated by strange dreams experienced by us all at some time during the night. 'I kept dreaming that the saloon clock and barometer wouldn't work because they were under water,' remarked Douglas in response to his mother's animated recollection of her own troubled dreams, where she had seen us all rowing an empty ham tin across the ocean, having lost *Lucette* to a rough sea. 'Best get some rest,' I interjected, anxious to dispel any notion of superstition at the onset of such a long trip.

The wind moderated a little during the following night and breaks in the cloud enabled us to catch glimpses of stars in the pre-dawn sky. On the morning of the fifteenth we caught our first glimpse of the sun since leaving the Galapagos and, with a slackening in the wind and a commensurate reduction in speed, *Lucette* settled to a more comfortable movement in the diminishing seas. The morning sun shone sporadically through the thinning cloud as I balanced myself against the heave of *Lucette*'s deck, sextant glued to both hand and eye in an effort to obtain a sight, which would enable me to start tracking our ocean passage. I carefully selected and adjusted the shade combination before rechecking the second hand of my Rolex chronometer. The sun's lower limb slowly traversed its celestial arc and as it kissed the visible horizon I noted the exact time. I quickly reset the sextant by five minutes of arc and then checked the second hand of my watch again, waiting for a good sight of both time and sun, no easy combination when deck and horizon bucked and surged in constant motion.

Douglas and Sandy were in the cockpit, one steering and the other tending the fishing line, making an inordinate fuss over a squid that had become entangled on the hook overnight. Robin, finding it difficult to sleep in his own bunk on the port side of the main cabin, had nipped quietly into Sandy's bunk on the starboard side of the fo'c'sle where he was still resting after his spell on the morning watch. Neil was reading a book in his own bunk on the port side of the fo'c'sle whilst Lyn, after getting out of bed herself and cleaning up the usual chaos resulting from a rough stretch of sailing, had retired to the bathroom to dress. At last the sun, the horizon and the deck cooperated to give me an accurate observation and I noted the local time by my watch: it was exactly nine fifty-four and forty-five seconds.

Collecting my logarithm tables and nautical almanac from the chart table, I made my way below, towards the relative comfort of the aft cabin, to work out our longitude. With my sextant carefully replaced in its box, I returned to the companionway. Cupping my chin in my hands, I rested an elbow on the chart table and started to work out a reasonably accurate dead-reckoning position, which I planned to use in my calculations. Books in hand, I descended the companionway once more and made my way through the saloon, where I placed them securely on my bunk. Opting to make a strong cup of coffee to help my brain kick in, I returned to the galley and lit the paraffin stove, which was swinging steadily on its gimbals in time with each lurch of the hull. Sliding the metal cafetiera onto the bright blue flame, I adjusted the fiddle rails to obtain a secure fit and upon hearing Lyn shuffling about inside the bathroom behind me confirmed through the door that I would put on enough water to make coffee for us both. I shook the last of our Blue Mountain coffee grains into the percolating chamber and waited for the water to come to the boil, before turning down the flame and allowing the coffee to gently percolate, slowly filling the saloon with its strong and rich aroma. I had no idea then that not even a drop of that delicious nectar, so carefully and lovingly prepared, was ever to pass my lips. I stumbled through to the aft cabin and dropped onto my bunk, carefully laying out my working papers and log tables, in readiness to begin the lengthy longitude calculation. I checked my watch again: it was nine fifty-seven exactly. Remote from the world though we were, the events of the next few seconds were to change our lives forever.

Far to the north, a pod of some twenty orca, also known as killer whales, were on high alert as they plundered the oceans in their incessant search for food. Their murderous rampage was led by a fully mature bull whose fearless leadership made him warlord commander of all he surveyed. His group, consisting of a few males and several females, had not eaten properly in over a week, and he knew by instinct that unless he found food and quickly his position as leader would be threatened. Wreaking havoc in the whale breeding grounds of the equatorial pacific, they had killed a young baleen whale-calf earlier that morning but the mother, after a spirited and potentially lethal fight back, had escaped into the depths. The killers knew from experience that it was only a matter of time before she must surface for air. All they had to do was wait; a feast on the leviathan mother would more than make up for the previous week with nothing to eat. They hadn't been waiting long when the giant bull orca spotted movement through the murk, at the extreme corner of his eye. With powerful thrusts of his mighty tail flukes, he accelerated to strike speed, sounding the attack signal as he went. Two other males joined him and they charged as one into the soft underbelly of their quarry.

The first of three sledgehammer blows slammed the hull beneath my feet like an exploding torpedo. The incredible force lifted *Lucette* bodily out of the water, as a deafening report was followed almost immediately by a sickening, ear-piercing crack. Along with my navigation books and papers, I was catapulted across the bunk and slammed into the solid oak bulkheads concealing the sturdy framework of *Lucette*'s hull. In rapid succession, two more bone-jarring strikes followed the first, each jolting the hull and noticeably checking our speed, as reverberating ruptures splintered timbers deep within the keel. I knew in my heart that we were finished, even before I dropped to my knees and tore up the floorboards beneath my feet. I tried desperately to think how I could stem the rapid flow of water already flooding into the cabin beneath me. Terror gripped my heart and the pit of my stomach churned in a nauseous panic as I gazed in horror at the blue Pacific through a large splintered hole punched up through the hull planking, between two of the grown oak frames forming *Lucette*'s hull.

Water mushroomed upwards through the gaping hole with torrential force. Lyn called out that water was pouring in through a second rupture beneath her feet as well. The water level inside the cabin began rising with incredible speed. My senses reeled as I stood transfixed, the roar of inrushing water purging all other sounds and thoughts from my mind. A rapidly accelerating surge swiftly swamped the lower drawers in the bunks as it rose over the engine-room sill, flooding the galley and then the saloon beyond. 'Whales, Whales!' I heard a shout from Douglas up on deck, as I jammed my foot over the broken strakes and shouted to Lyn to hand me some large cloths, or anything else she could find that would help stem the flood. Wading through water already up to her calves, she threw me a pillow and I jammed it down on top of the broken planking and rammed the floorboard back in place before standing on it, my weight holding it firmly in place. But the roar of the incoming water continued at an undiminished rate, and the water level, rising above the mezzanine floor in the engine room, was soon beginning to sluice around my knees. I pushed my make-do salvage mat down still harder as the first waves of panic dried my throat and robbed my limbs of their strength.

Lyn gripped my shoulder; it was in this spot that she had asked if it was time to send up the rockets, back in that Biscay gale when our voyage had first started. It was also here that she had asserted through the darkness that Mary would help us get around Long Island point, during that terrible storm in the Caribbean. This time she had no words of comfort to offer, and her jaw trembled as she struggled to speak. 'Its no good, Dougal, we can't save *Lucette* from this.' She paused for a moment as if assessing the situation and then, catching her breath, continued, 'We must go, Dougal ... We must go now while there is still time to save ourselves.' She waited by my side in quiet determination, her voice calm and subdued. I returned her stare and fought back stinging tears of anguish as we both realised our worst nightmare was about to come true.

A cry from Douglas up on deck snapped us both back into action. 'Are we sinking, Dad?' 'Yes! Abandon ship!' My voice felt remote as numbly I watched the water rise up the engine casing. 'Abandon ship? Where in hell do you expect us to abandon ship to?' interjected Douglas, his indignant glare trying to hold my eye. 'Over there,' I pointed in the direction of the ocean outside. 'Over there?' Douglas mocked, pointing towards the open sea, a combination of anger and fear making his words run together in a frightened slur. 'Its not Miami Marina over there,' he retorted sarcastically, shaking his outstretched arm as if he expected me to change my mind. 'Abandon ship – get the life raft over the side,' I stammered, my voice chill and desperate as I waved him forward. The water was already lapping my thighs as I turned to follow Lyn, who was hastily rummaging through the under-bunk drawers in search of our papers and logbook. Her pearl necklace came to hand, my gift to her when we were married in Hong Kong some twenty years before, our eyes met for a fleeting instant and we silently hugged each other in what we both realised could be our last embrace. 'They came from the sea, they can go back,' she sobbed, discarding the necklace and turning to pick up a small bag of onions from the galley counter instead. Scrambling forward, she urged Neil and Robin up on deck. There was not a moment to lose as *Lucette* settled visibly lower in the water with each passing second.

I waded past the galley stove just as the coffee pot, now bubbling with hot coffee, was hurled across the counter by the rising floodwaters sweeping across the galley worktops and snuffing out the paraffin flame as they swirled into every last nook and cranny. The brass clock and barometer which Douglas had so recently dreamt about were already dipping beneath the rising water as my eye glimpsed the sharp vegetable knife. I grabbed it in passing and leapt for the companionway. The water, now over my waist, was already lapping the top of the batteries in the engine room and flooding the bookcases on the starboard side of the saloon. It was my last glimpse of *Lucette*'s interior, our family home for almost two years. Lyn was already on deck by the time I got there, tying the twins' lifejackets on with rapid efficiency. I slashed at the lashings holding the bow of the dinghy to the mainmast. Deep in shock and struggling to come to terms with the world he had come to know and love disappearing so rapidly from under him, Douglas had furled away the number two jib and was inexplicably starting to do the same with the number one. It took a harsh word from me to snap him back to our inescapable reality. Releasing the halyard, he turned his attention to freeing the self-inflating life raft from under the dinghy, whilst I ran forward to cut the remaining lashings that held its stern to the foremast. Lyn shouted for the knife to free the water containers and I threw it towards her. Douglas struggled with the large green life-raft valise, shouting for confirmation that he should throw it overboard, still unable to comprehend or able to bring himself to believe that we were really sinking. 'Yes, get on with it!' I yelled, indicating to Robin, who had successfully donned his lifejacket, to join in and help.

Grasping the handles at the stern of the dinghy, I twisted it over from its inverted position and slid it towards the rail, noting that the wave tops were already lapping at the scuppers and would soon be level with *Lucette*'s deck, as she wallowed sluggishly in the seaway. Water was cascading in waterfalls down through the open doorways and pouring through the portholes from the deck, flooding the companionway steps and access hatches, effectively sealing them shut. The deck lockers winced as spume-covered waves rolled aboard in quick succession. It was at exactly that moment that the awful recollection of the sinking of the *Sagaing* hit me like a thunderbolt, invading my consciousness in a rerun of the events that had irrevocably changed my life some thirty years before. Vivid memories I had locked away for decades came to my front of mind as the implications regarding the loss of the *Lucette* struck home. I had lost my young family that day. Now my blood froze as I contemplated what the sea was about to take from me for a second time. Rooted to the spot in a spellbound trance, I looked on blankly as Douglas put down the life raft and raced to the afterdeck and returned with a pair of oars which he thrust under the dinghy thwarts, before heaving the fragile little boat seawards across the coach roof. I shivered at the thought of us all having to survive in such a cockleshell should the life raft fail to inflate, then he took the stern from my ineffectual grasp and slid the *Ednamair* the rest of the way into the sea. Robin was at his side, clutching the painter tightly in order to keep it from floating away.

I watched in numbed detachment as Douglas made fast the raft's inflation painter and then with the strength of a titan plucked the eighty-pound raft from the deck and tossed it overboard. Lyn, having severed the lashings on the water containers and flares, carried them to the dinghy. Shaking myself out of my daze, I picked up the knife and shouted the order to abandon ship once more, for I feared *Lucette*'s rigging might catch one of us as she went down. Time was running out, and fast, as I slashed desperately at the lashings around another bag of onions and handed them to Sandy, unable to shield from him the tremble in my hands or the look of fear in my eyes. I studied his little face etched with fear and squeezed his deathly-cold hand in mine. I could not help but wonder if I would ever see him alive again as I ordered him to leave. With decks awash, I turned to grab a bag of oranges, which I threw into the dinghy together with a small bag of lemons. Douglas hauled furiously on the inflation painter of the raft in continuous hand-over-hand tugging motions and after what seemed like an interminable age the raft to our relief, our great and lasting relief, went off with a bang and began inflating rapidly, unfolding in a jerky robotic mime. I looked on thankfully as it continued to expand.

Seconds later *Lucette*'s bow dipped and a large rolling breaker buried her bowsprit, before surging across the foredeck in an unchecked fury of foam and spray, swamping the hatch covers before crashing into the coach roof with the full force of the sea. I could only watch in agony as Douglas was plucked off his feet and swept head-over-heels over the side. I reached out involuntarily towards him, my hands gripping desperately at fresh air. My eldest son, whom I loved more than I could ever have told him, had been taken before my very eyes, cruelly swallowed up by the sea directly into the midst of the patrolling killer whales. I shivered at the daunting prospect that we might be forced to witness him being torn limb from limb before our very eyes, before the rest of us were devoured in a similar fate.

Neil had moved aft and was hanging precariously outboard of the starboard rail, dabbing his foot into thin air as he tried his best to locate the dinghy, snatching sharply at its painter in the short aggressive chop that had built up in *Lucette*'s lee. Caught in two minds whether to make for the raft or stay with the *Ednamair*, he carefully timed his leap to find the centre of the dinghy but his limbs, already weakened from fear and shock, lacked the necessary power and he slipped from the bulwarks and tumbled headfirst into the turbulent waters alongside. Fearing the whales would eat him alive, I bellowed for him to get out of the water. He desperately hauled himself onto the central thwart of the little craft and sat head in hands, locked in abject misery. Robin tried to join him in the dinghy only to inadvertently step onto the gunwale, which pushed the side under the waves, leaving *Ednamair* three-quarters full of water and totally ineffective as a means of escape.

I shouted that they should both make for the raft but incredibly Neil, soaked to the skin and with his mind in an absolute dither, jumped back aboard *Lucette* and, in fulfilment of that mid-Atlantic oath to his brother, retrieved his puppets lying where he had left them, discarded on the deck. He hastily stuffed his favourite teddy bears under his lifejacket before plunging back into the sea. Tears welled up in my eyes as I watched him swim strongly for the raft, which was now fully inflated and glowing a bright luminous orange, just a few yards away. The raft drifted slowly away from the protection of our lee where its canopy caught the wind. I looked on in dumbstruck horror as our only means of escape began to speed away from us.

Just as it occurred to me that things could not get any worse, the recently repaired backstay suddenly parted with a crack like a high velocity rifle, followed by a loud reverberating swish as the shiny wire recoiled through the air with a vicious backlash. The increased pressure on the masts and stays produced by the submerged and immobile hull had caused the newly fitted stainless steel fastening to snap. The ridiculous notion that I had a spare in the engine room flashed into my mind as the masts and sails began to sway and creak, creating a real danger that the rig aloft would collapse on top of us at any moment. Whatever fate had in store for us it was too dangerous to stay aboard *Lucette* any longer. Robin and Sandy had already left and Sandy, still in the water, struggled frantically to close with the raft, his energy all but spent. I could only look on helplessly as no matter how hard his little arms thrashed the water he seemed unable to close the gap. The raft continued to gather speed and momentum in the wind as it drew clear of the wreck site, and seemed to maintain a position just beyond his reach. Dark triangular fins appeared ominously for a moment and I grimaced in despair as I watched him dig deep, gritting his teeth to find that crucial extra turn of speed that would save his life. At the tender age of twelve he did not deserve to be required to swim so desperately, but showing tenacity and courage beyond his years he performed the lung-bursting dash through the water and gained the safety of the grab ropes affixed to the raft sides, which he gripped tightly with both hands and hung on. I sighed in grateful relief as he then hauled himself up the boarding ladder and rolled over the inflation tubes that formed the sides of the raft before disappearing from view into the safer confines within.

Lucette's log line was hanging vertically, final testimony that she had stopped dead in the water and was about to commence her final downward plunge, bow first, into the deep. Water poured in torrents over the sills of the open doorways and portholes, as a mounting wall of water enveloped her decks and rolled up the main deck along the full length of the hull. The ocean swells began to roll unchecked across her decks, blasting white flumes of water into the air as unfettered waves slammed into the coach roof, skylights and access hatches. The windows in the deck saloon suddenly shattered under the pressure of the climbing water levels and the wooden decks had finally stopped clearing between successive waves.

In her bid to get away, Lyn had become caught up in the newly tightened wire railings, the tails of her housecoat well and truly tangled in the stanchions. She was stuck fast without a lifejacket and unable to get free as the waves buffeted her mercilessly. Struggling to keep my own footing on the slippery deck, I was unable to help. In horrified disbelief I watched helplessly as she was dragged under the surface, like an animal trapped in a snare. She could not escape as *Lucette* gripped her in an unshakable embrace, pulling her beneath the waves with each roll of her swamped hull. If she didn't get free, she would be unable to avoid joining *Lucette* in her rapid descent to the bottom of the sea. Lyn had waited too long to get off. As ever putting her family before herself she had ensured that both the twins and Robin had got safely away, fastidiously helping them to don their lifejackets and guiding them clear before looking out for herself. Beyond my help, she was powerless to get free and her life hung in the balance.

Time had finally run out. There was no place left to go. Driven from the accommodation below by the encroaching water and forced from the deck by the falling masts and rigging, the water closed in on me on all sides. *Lucette* was literally disappearing from under me as I walked into the sea, throwing the knife into the submerged dinghy as I went. Fearful of a renewed attack from the whales, I urged everyone to stay in the raft, which was still near enough for me to hear it noisily exhausting its supply of surplus gas.

The familiar noises of a working sailing boat at sea fell curiously silent as *Lucette* slowly submitted to her fate and an eerie quiet prevailed. I tarried in the water, locked in confused anguish, to see if Lyn or Dougie would appear. Then my heart stopped as swirling eddies of turbulent water welled up around me. Unseen, the whales were patrolling close by, the loud blasts of their venting blowholes interrupting the unearthly quiet of our new surroundings with menacing regularity. The raft was being driven ever more rapidly before the wind and was getting further away from me by the second. If I was going to get to it, there was no time to delay, as it would already take my best effort to reach the children before the raft drifted out of range, leaving them alone and helpless in the vast wastes of the Pacific. Neil's shrill cry, barely audible, was borne away on the wind as he waited desperately for a response, clear notes of panic sounding in his voice as he shouted out for his mother. The adrenalin boost was now subsiding within me and I found myself beginning to succumb to the effects of shock. The kids and Robin could not survive without me; they were on their own and afraid. I could wait no longer. Lyn and Dougie would have to look out for themselves now.

I took up *Ednamair*'s painter from the water and wrapped it around my left hand. Summoning my last vestiges of strength I struck out for the raft in a desperate front crawl, expecting to feel the fatal embrace of razor-sharp teeth grip my torso with each and every agonising second that passed. Luck was with me, however, as slowly and surely I made good my frantic escape. Gaining the open doorway of the raft, I made the submerged dinghy fast, which acting like a sea anchor halted the raft's progress through the water at a stroke. Hauling myself out of the sea, I sat astride the inflated raft sides and peered inside. Little faces gazed back at me, eyes wide open and rolling in desperate fear, seeking answers to unspoken questions, answers that I could not provide.

Robin was kneeling on the raft floor holding each of the twins tightly to him with soothing words of comfort. His spectacles askew, his lower lip quivered and I realised he was trying to talk, his voice nothing more than a broken stammer. 'Dougal?' he tried again, still trembling with shock, 'Dougal?' The rest of his words simply would not come, choked out of existence as fear gripped his senses. I reached inside the raft, my arms searching for the outstretched hands of my little boys. Freezing cold, they trembled fearfully in my grasp as I clutched them to me. They needed, more than they had ever done before, assurances that I could not fairly give them. Clinging to life by the most perilous of threads and charged with the awesome responsibility of saving the lives of what remained of my family, I gulped at the air in deep gasps, struggling to bring myself under control as successive waves of sickening fear gripped my soul. I waited in a paralysed stupor for the whales to press home their attack in a final frenzy of bloody destructive carnage. Jessie and Duncan appeared in my mind in a bright clear vision and I wondered if I was about to join them. I momentarily lost control of my bladder and was unable to calm my erratic breathing, as I clung onto the flimsy fabric of the raft, waiting in an unrelenting and agonising eternity for my first sight of the tall dorsal fins that would spell our end. I looked again at Robin as he held my young children, their thin little bodies and gawky limbs in a wet dishevelled heap on the raft floor. I pondered for a moment if I should join them inside the raft but I knew instinctively that no matter what the risk, I must return to the wreck site whilst there was still an outside chance of rescuing Lyn, or finding young Dougie alive. At the very least, I needed to salvage whatever flotsam I could, before we were blown clear of the wreck site.

With the aid of the outstretched painter now attaching the raft to the dinghy, I pulled myself gingerly back towards the *Ednamair*, which was completely swamped and surrounded with oranges floating inside and around it. Standing inside the dinghy to protect myself in case of further attack, I threw what remained of the oranges and lemons still within reach into the raft. The water containers had already floated away or had sunk, together with the box of flares. Since the dinghy under my weight was now under the water, I made my way back to the raft, grabbing a floating can of petrol as I went. On leaving the dinghy, I caught a last glimpse of our dearly beloved *Lucette*. She had been like a mother to us and we had considered her part of our family. She had sheltered us from storms and given us many wonderful adventures. In one fleeting moment she had been destroyed by a brutal and massive attack, her stout hull, strong enough to withstand all that the sea had thrown at her thus far, now smashed below the waterline. The sea had overwhelmed her in just a few moments, yet she had remained intact and stayed upright long enough for us to get off alive. On a morning that had started out like so many others, her life had been suddenly and dramatically cut short, forcing us to flee from her sinking decks and leave her to her fate. Gritting my teeth, I sobbed our old schooner a last farewell. 'Goodbye, old girl, and God bless you,' I whispered in a final prayer as she descended into her watery grave. I watched in anguish as she submitted to the inevitable and her last voyage ground finally to an end. My eyes stung as I wiped away the tears with the back of my hand, and when I looked again *Lucette* had curtsied below the waves and gone.

Galapagos Islands

Cape Espinosa

Fernandina

Isabela Island

Part 2

Shipwreck in the Pacific

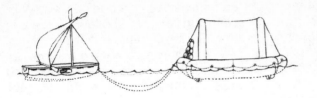

CHAPTER 10

Castaways

Terror stabbed at my heart as I swam towards the hastily launched raft in a robotic trance. My limbs, heavy like lead, steadily weakened with a combination of delayed shock and fatigue as I strove to regain the safety of our tiny craft. With faltering hands and a surge of relief, I finally gripped the rope lifelines attached to the inflated sides and clung on tightly whilst I remained in the water for a few moments to catch my breath, my head still resounding with the ear-splitting crack that had hailed *Lucette*'s end just a few minutes before. My body shook violently as I hauled myself on board and perched myself atop the bright yellow inflation tubes for a few moments before allowing myself to topple forwards into its cave-like structure, where I joined Robin and the twins, still huddled together in a frightened heap near its centre. My heart skipped a beat as the spaces where I expected to see Lyn and Dougie loomed large, my mind recoiling in horror at the sudden depletion in our numbers. Other than shivering with the effects of shock we sat motionless in an open-mouthed, wide-eyed daze, unable to speak as we blankly absorbed the alien sights and sounds about us, waiting in uncertain silent dread to see if we had escaped what had seemed like certain death only a few minutes before. The survival raft forming the boundaries of our new world measured no more than eight feet by six, divided by a central thwart and covered by a bilious yellow canopy, which shook vibrantly in the wind and emitted a foul rubbery stench from within. It felt safe though and it was dry, save for small pools of water that were gathering ominously in the depressions where we sat.

I peered seawards through the small opening in the canopy, trying to dispel the light-headed unreality and stunned disbelief which permeated my entire being. I felt sure that at any moment I would awake to find it had all been some horrible dream. I touched myself to confirm I was actually awake and then involuntarily checked my watch; it seemed real enough, showing the time to be just seventeen minutes past ten. My senses reeled as wretched self-guilt crowded out my initial feelings of despair and hallucinatory uncertainty. Palpitations raced through my leaden heart in an erratic flutter, leaving me to ponder our stark reversal of fortune and the terrible fate which I feared must have befallen Lyn and Dougie. Enchained in my misery I returned the blank stares of the others, who continued to gape at me in quiet desperation.

Rather than help, I could only squirm in helpless impotence as the minutes ticked by, conscious that the chances of seeing my wife and son again were diminishing exponentially as each second passed. With my feeling of loss so absolute, my breathing came in shallow gasps and my guts churned in stinging torment as I tried to block out the brutal anguish of the passing moments. I wallowed in a paralysed trauma, as waves of nausea and self-pity swept over me, dulling my senses and merging my thoughts into a timeless dreamlike tumult. As I fought to bring my emotions under control, stabs of jittery panic took over, leaving me prostrate and trapped in a mindless dither as my thoughts jumped from one meaningless topic to another. Unable to quash the trembling in my knees and hands, I sat ashen faced staring blankly at Robin who was soothing the twins through their own silent torture.

'We're scared, Dad,' sniffled Sandy, reaching out with his little hand in my direction. I cloaked his frail and shivering limb in mine. It was as cold as ice and trembled involuntarily at my touch. I hugged him to me. 'Be strong, my son. Do not be frightened, for we are alive and out of harm's way for now.' I knew such vague rhetoric would do little to succour him, but the security of my soothing words and the warmth of my arms around him seemed to calm his nerve. I held him a little longer before extending my embrace to the other two, quite aware that they had all had to find exceptional courage just to get this far. We hugged each other in silence, an empty desolate and overwhelming silence; a silence of the soul that blanked out all other sounds around us. In that moment, I vowed with a resolve of iron that I would not fail them. I owed my children and Robin their lives and whilst I had breath in my body I would not rest until I had got them on a steamer home.

Slowly I became aware of a voice speaking and suddenly realised it was my own. 'We will make it back to land,' I heard myself promise to the others, more in hope than in belief, for I hadn't the slightest idea how we would achieve such an undertaking. My thoughts continued with a silent vow pledging that I would get my boys back to land no matter what it would take, for I could not let myself live and see them die, no matter what. I looked away, faced with an impossible task, cast adrift thousands of miles from the nearest continental landmass, the prospect of surviving long enough and of ultimately finding terra firma seeming as remote a possibility as had been the attack of the whales in the first place. Getting my boys out of danger and back to safety would be an undertaking that, miracles aside, would push my ingenuity and gumption to its very limits, the loss of our lives being the penalty for failure. Aboard *Lucette*, I had deliberately avoided any talk about even the possibility of shipwreck, always believing it could never happen to us. Now it had happened and I had been both unprepared and ill equipped to deal with it, leaving my options as stark as they were elusive.

Like the sword of Damocles, the expectation of the attacking whales returning to devour us remained unshakable, making everything we said and did feel hollow, pointless and totally futile. Each minute felt like borrowed time as we waited and wondered how and when our torment would end. I returned to the bitter silence, pondering all that had happened whilst trying to comprehend the wider implications, desperately racking my brains for a plan. Where was Lyn? What had happened to young Dougie? Without them to help how was I going to cope? What would be required of me in order to succeed? We had no knowledge of whales attacking small boats at sea, but plenty about yachts that had simply gone missing. Was this the fate that had befallen them, a fate from which there had never been any survivors? I shuddered at the thought and wondered how many of those unfortunate souls had got thus far only to fail later. Was it even possible to survive such an incident or were we simply 'dead men in waiting'? How could I sustain hope in the others, when I didn't even know what must be done myself, or if there was even a possible way out for us? When and if I did discover what to do, would I be able to do it alone? I mulled over the permutations and scope of our dilemma. A myriad of questions bombarded my mind. 'Answers will come,' I decided, knowing for now that I had to be strong for the sake of the others.

I scanned the sea for signs of life in cold desperation as my thoughts leapt back in time, remembering Lyn and our days of courtship back in Hong Kong. She had been a nursing sister and I a navigating officer in the China Navigation Company. We had fallen in love from our very first meeting, but our time together had hardly been a bed of roses. After long periods at sea, I had almost missed our wedding due to the delayed arrival of my ship. On our return to England I had, against her wishes, changed my career and given her a hard life of farming before eventually sending her out to work in all weathers on a motor scooter, in a vain attempt to keep our ailing farm business afloat. Finally, I had coerced her into undertaking this voyage, which had now so suddenly and dramatically come to a full and terrifying stop. Maybe even as I searched for her she was already dead. Would she have forgiven me? Would God forgive me? And what of Dougie? Always made to do without, his hard little life had been rewarded with very few treats and still he had been totally loyal to me, but I could count on one hand how many times I had kissed him. Now they were both gone and it was all too late.

I gripped my head in my hands and shivered as the bitter pill of remorse relentlessly tortured my soul. My gaze drifted in and out of focus as I scanned the desolate sea in an effort to avoid the searching faces of the others, my eyes finally straying to the survival pack located on the floor of the raft. Struggling to bring my head-spinning emotions under control, I asked Robin to pass the container over, which he did without uttering a word. I tussled with the tangled knots that secured the lacing cord of the small orange valise, unable to suppress the shake of my hands as I unfolded the outer polythene lining. Frustrated by my lack of progress, I decided to try again later. Still seated by the boarding access point, I continued to stare balefully out at the restless ocean. Keeping a lookout was not easy from such a low elevation, as I hoped against hope to catch sight or sound of my missing wife or son. I scoured the ocean's horizons, my eyes searching for the slightest irregularity in the wave formations or break in the eye line. I stared outboard, adjusting my focus as I scanned across the broad expanse of the open sea, a thing I had done so many times before from the security of *Lucette*'s teak laid decks; how different it looked from here. The waves seemed much larger and more menacing as they swept swiftly and uncaringly by, the whitecaps growling tacit warnings of danger as if muttering veiled threats of what was to come. We were held in the clutch of the southeasterly trades, which bore us off towards the equator, ever further into the vast recesses of the Pacific, reducing our chances of rescue with each passing minute as we were carried further and further away from the already distant islands of the Galapagos.

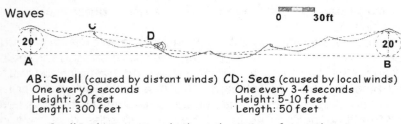

AB: **Swell** (caused by distant winds) CD: **Seas** (caused by local winds)
One every 9 seconds   One every 3-4 seconds
Height: 20 feet   Height: 5-10 feet
Length: 300 feet   Length: 50 feet

Swell in this case travels about three times faster than seas

Finally finding his voice, Robin broke the silence. 'We seem to be leaking, Dougal.' His shaken voice was distorted with high-pitched alarm as he pushed the soft rubber floor downwards, allowing a large puddle of yellow-stained seawater to collect. Small rivulets seeped through from punctures in the crease between the floor and the side tubes, continuing to feed the deepening puddle, allowing more and more cold seawater to gather beneath us. 'It's nothing we can't bail out,' I observed dismissively, trying to remain as positive as I could. I handed him a wire-rimmed container that would double as a bailer, which I had extracted from a sleeve sewn onto the inside of the raft. 'As long as the punctures don't get any bigger,' Robin commented, as he took it from me, his cogent warning a pertinent reminder of the fragile and tenuous thread by which all our lives now hung.

Large swirling air bubbles suddenly disturbed the water in front of us and I instinctively moved back from the edge of the raft in a moment of panic, my only thought being that finally the whales had returned to finish us off. Like a glorious miracle, though, Lyn suddenly burst through the surface of the water, right in front of my eyes, accompanied by loud splashes of spray and bubbles. Unable to believe such good fortune, my grimace turned to a joyful beaming grin as I grabbed her hands in a vice like grip, for I was not going to risk losing her again. Without adjusting my hold, I hauled her on board in a single movement and hugged her to me with glee in what would have to pass for an embrace. I kissed her quickly on the lips, grateful beyond words that she was alive and that I was able once again to hug her, knowing that with her by my side we at least had a chance of getting out of this tragic mess alive.

Stopping for sharp intakes of breath, Lyn chronicled the turn of events that had brought her back to us, her torn clothing testimony to her method of escape from the sinking hull of *Lucette*, her chest heavily contused with burns and bruises from the deck-side rail wires. Whilst under water, she had been forced to rip off the hem of her housecoat in order to free herself from her deadly intertwinement with the railings, only to become entangled in the rigging as she had made for the surface. Trapped inboard of the shrouds, she had held her breath and, with lungs at bursting point, had hauled herself hand over hand up the inside of the spread of wire ropes, until she had finally gained the surface. An accomplished swimmer, she had then given chase after the raft, duck-diving beneath the wave crests in order to maintain her pace.

'Did anybody see any signs of Dougie yet?' she gasped, snatching the sweet air in a series of deep and rapid gulps. 'Not yet,' I murmured, avoiding her gaze. She continued breathing purposefully, her face simultaneously crossed with lines of worry and the grimace of fear; no news was still good news for now. 'I saw him trying to fix a leak in the raft,' she stammered, then trailed off into silence. My heart immediately lifted with Lyn's news. 'When? Where exactly?' I demanded, holding her shoulders and looking directly into her eyes. She pointed outside towards the empty sea and my heart sank again as I observed our current rate of leeway. We were being blown over the water at a considerable rate of knots, snatching the dinghy, in tow behind us. Hoping for the best whilst fearing the worst, we knew that Douglas was not the strongest of surface swimmers, and at our current speed he would never be able to keep up with us, let alone make up so much lost ground in such a heavy sea. Refusing to consider the worst possibility as the only one, I closed my mind to what might have happened to him and returned to my lookout post. When not scouring the seaway I busied myself, examining the inventory strewn inside the raft, mindlessly surveying various items of flotsam, passing them from one hand to the other and then back to the floor of the raft, incapable for the moment to see how any of it might be of possible use.

Unable to locate his two favourite puppets, Neil's sobbing rekindled afresh. The two bears he had so valiantly returned to *Lucette*'s sinking decks to rescue had slipped from under his lifejacket as he swam for the raft. Positively distraught, he sobbed to his mother. Not only had he lost *Lucette* but even after all his preparations and planning his two teddies had been drowned as well. I couldn't help but feel for him. His puppets had been a major part of his life on board and had achieved the status of real-life pals in his mind, and now on top of everything else they too were gone. Lyn did what mums do best and cuddled him to her with gentle words of reassurance. Sandy, also in her arms, recounted the desperate swim he had made from the *Lucette* and how he had very nearly given up on two occasions, as the raft seemed to drift further and further downwind and beyond his reach. 'I suppose it would have been easier if I'd let go of these onions,' he smiled, still gripping the bag I had handed to him during our last moments aboard. We couldn't help but grin at his show of grit and determination, as he continued telling us how *Lucette*'s steering had become very sluggish and he thought we had hit a mid-ocean reef, until a group of whales had surfaced behind him. 'There were many of them in the water swimming right next to us and one looked hurt,' he confirmed as he recalled the events of his last terrifying minutes aboard *Lucette*. The whole family had a story to tell, individual feats of heroism and endurance that had not only saved their own lives but would also contribute to the survival of us all.

After what seemed like an inordinate amount of time, I slowly steeled myself to announce that Douglas might have become a casualty when as large as life he swung into view, appearing at the door like a beaming apparition. 'Bloody typical,' he bellowed, flinging himself inboard and collapsing onto the floor of the raft, hurling down beside us a collection of items he had gathered from the sea. Not knowing whether to laugh or cry, Lyn and I hugged him as one, so happy to once again feel his substance and body warmth and to hear the sound of his dulcet and over-productive tones, for we had never known him to use one word when he could somehow make use of two. With up-cast eyes, we were grateful beyond words to see his form grace our sight once more. I silently vowed that in future I would show him how much I loved him, and never again refer to his profuse vocalisms as verbal diarrhoea. We listened in joy as he explained in his typical enthused manner how he had constantly felt for his legs to check they had not been bitten off, whilst he feverishly cleared the non-return valves in the sides of the raft and then stood by until they had clicked in, preventing any further loss of the pressurised inflation gas. Douglas had stayed in the water to ensure the raft was safe for the rest of us, refusing to desert his post even though he feared he might have been eaten alive at any moment. In my eyes, my son had not only shown exceptional courage but had by this single act saved the lives of us all. How dark those minutes had been when I believed I had lost not only my wife and mother of my children but also my eldest son – and how joyful things seemed now I knew they were alive, regardless of the dire consequences we still faced. Facing our futures together relegated the threat of the unknown challenges that lay ahead, and seemed to diminish the dark cloud of uncertainty that remained hanging over us.

'Killer whales,' continued Douglas, answering our unspoken questions, 'all sizes, about twenty of them I reckon. I saw a group in the distance then Sandy and I saw three of them from the cockpit right after we had been hit, two large ones and a small one and the largest had a V shape cut in its head. They were chasing behind us on the port quarter and there was blood in the water too and after *Lucette* had gone, the whales vanished with her,' he concluded, his face suddenly tired and ashen, his blue lips trembling as his energy seemed to finally desert him. What he had told us sent shivers down my spine as I struggled to take in the implications of the attack. I studied the huge genoa sail, lying on the raft floor where Lyn was sitting with the twins. 'How the hell did that get there?' I asked stupidly. Douglas grinned. 'I saw the fishing line spool floating on the surface rapidly unwinding itself,' he said, 'so I grabbed it and pulled it in and the sail was hooked onto the other end!'

Three killer whales had hit us, I recalled the one named Hugo we had seen in captivity at the Miami Sea Aquarium, which had weighed in at over three tons. Such beasts we had been told swam at about 30 knots into an attack; at least that explained the holes in *Lucette*'s hull. Excited by the blood, the others whales in the pod had probably eaten the injured one, thereby paradoxically saving our own lives in the process; for it must have split open its skull when it had slammed into *Lucette*'s three-ton lead keel. *Lucette* had not abandoned us to our fate as I had first surmised, she had in fact been blameless with regard to design and condition, and had served us well to the bitter end.

Lyn gazed numbly at me, quietly reassuring the twins, who had started crying again. With only the noise of the sea and wind around us, we gazed in silent disbelief at our new and strange surroundings, and at the dishevelled forms of our young castaways. Racked with guilt, Lyn and I beheld their innocence, able only to guess at what manner of suffering and privation we had now brought down on the heads of our little children.

'If we only do one last thing with our lives, Dougal, we must get our little ones back to land.' Lyn's words were emphatic and compelling and I nodded my agreement automatically. The moment passed and as the tension subsided Lyn remorsed in heartfelt sobs, 'It's like we've lost a member of the family,' her sobbing increasing in volume as she slowly came to terms with the loss of the *Lucette*. 'We've lost our home, our dreams, our possessions – everything, I don't think we could lose more; how could God have let this happen?' she implored, her normally bright eyes glazed over as her sobbing rhetoric descended into a ramble. 'We still have each other,' I interjected pointedly, for incredibly all souls were now accounted for, our gaunt faces glowing bizarrely in a bright orange hue as we huddled beneath the translucent canopy of the raft. Lyn for the moment however remained inconsolable as tears of fear, sadness and suspended relief ran down her cheeks in a single torrent. Stopping as suddenly as she had begun, Lyn reached for my hand and in a poignant and heartfelt moment stammered the first line of the Lord's Prayer. Though none of us were of a strongly religious leaning, we all joined hands as she led us through the piece. Faltering at the start, her voice became strong and determined as she regained her composure. Indeed, I was sure the Almighty had already been at work this day, for the fact that we had managed to abandon *Lucette* after sustaining such a catastrophic attack without losing a single life was already nothing short of a miracle. Rarely given to praying, it was with some gusto and unadulterated sincerity that I quietly mouthed the words of prayer along with the others, the thought that perhaps we were not alone after all clearing the blind haze of shock that crowded my mind as the fear and apprehension began to subside. From now on, we would live our lives one day at a time, our goal being simply that of survival, measured in twenty-four hour periods. The reward for our success would be nothing more than to remain alive and witness the morrow's sunrise in the eastern skies, when we would start our daily round again and, if luck stayed with us, be able to endure the torment of another day.

First day

We sat on the salvaged pieces of flotsam scattered across the raft floor, our faces a pale bilious colour under the semi-transparent canopy, and stared at each other, the shock of the last few minutes gradually seeping through to our consciousness. Neil, still mourning the loss of his teddy bears, sobbed in accompaniment to Sandy's hiccup cry, while Lyn repeated the Lord's Prayer again, then in an effort to comfort us sang a heartfelt if misplaced rendition of the hymn 'For those in peril on the sea'. Douglas and Robin watched at the doors of the canopy to retrieve any useful pieces of debris which floated within reach and gazed with dumb longing at a distant five-gallon water container, bobbing its polystyrene lightness ever further away from us, as we were carried in the grip of the steady trade wind. Their eyes travelled over and beyond to the heaving undulations of the horizon, already searching for a rescue ship whilst knowing there was none to be found. Having scanned fruitlessly across the limitless waste of sea and sky, I once more ranged over the dispersing debris field. Our dinghy *Ednamair* was completely swamped and wallowed nearby, the line firmly attached to it from the raft. Of the killer whales which had so recently shattered our very existence, there was no sign. Lyn's sewing basket floated close by and Douglas hauled it aboard followed by a couple of empty boxes, the canvas raft valise and a plastic cup.

I leaned across to Neil and put my arm round him, 'It's alright now, son, we're safe and the whales have gone.' His tears stopped for a moment and he looked at me reproachfully. 'We're not crying 'cos we're frightened,' he sobbed, 'we're crying 'cos Lucy's gone.' Lyn gazed at me over their heads, her eyes filling with tears. 'Me too,' she echoed and after a moment added, 'I suppose we'd better find out how we stand.'

This was the question I had been dreading. Again feelings of guilt flooded through me. Our present predicament was due not only to my unorthodox ideas on educating our children, of which there had been plenty of critics, objecting that I was needlessly jeopardising their lives, but also to the fact that I had failed to foresee this type of disaster occurring in the first place. Damage to *Lucette*'s hull from a single killer whale would have been enough to be fatal. The fact that we had been struck by three now engulfed me and this, added to the fact that we had lost almost everything we possessed as well as the *Lucette*, depressed me to the deepest depths of despair. How could I have been so foolish as to trust our lives to such an old schooner! I recalled in my mind's eye the last minute I had spent aboard and the damage I had witnessed under the floorboards of *Lucette*. Not only had the frames withstood the impact of the blow but also the new garboard strake, fashioned from inch-and-a-half pitch-pine and fitted in Malta at the surveyor's recommendation, had been one of the hull planks that had been smashed inwards. Her hull had taken a full minute to sink below the waves whereas a modern boat, constructed with less regard to substance than *Lucette*, would have sustained much heavier damage and sunk even more quickly, with results that would have certainly been more tragic.

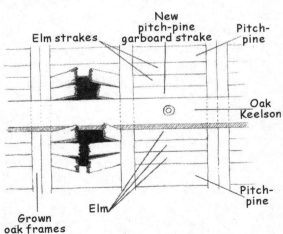

Damage to *Lucette*'s hull from one killer whale, a fatal
blow in itself.
She was struck by three.

I looked at Douglas, who had grown to manhood in our eighteen months at sea together. The twins, previously shy and introspective farm lads, had learned to interact with the different peoples we had met, taking an interest in their various ways of life, and were now keen to learn more. I tried to ease my conscience with the thought that they had derived much benefit from their voyage and that our sinking was as unforeseeable as an earthquake, plane crash or other unlikely catastrophe.

We cleared a space on the floor and spilled out the contents of the pre-stowed survival kit, which was part of the raft's equipment, contained in a three-foot-long polythene cylinder. Slowly we took stock: vitamin-fortified bread and glucose for ten men for two days; eighteen pints of water in individual tin cans; two parachute and six hand flares. I began to call out the names of the pieces as I identified them, holding them aloft for all to see as I counted each item in turn: one bailer, two large and two small fish hooks, one spinner and trace, and a fishing line marked twenty-five pounds breaking strain. I handed a small bulbous-ended knife and unsheathed it. We took turns to examine its specially designed blade, shaped so that it would not puncture the raft, or anything else for that matter. I took out the rest of the inventory from the bag: a signal mirror, a torch without spare batteries, a first-aid box, two sea anchors, an instruction book, a set of bellows, and three bayonet-type paddles. In addition to this there was the bag of a dozen onions which Sandy had so dutifully clung on to, to which Lyn had added a one-pound tin of biscuits and a bottle containing about half a pound of glucose sweets. Finally, there were the ten oranges and six lemons I had scooped out of the *Ednamair*.

How long would this have to last us? As I surveyed and counted our meagre stores for a second time, my heart sank and it must have shown on my face for Lyn placed her hand on mine. 'We must get these boys to land,' she said quietly. 'If we do nothing else with our lives, we must get them back to land!' I looked at her and nodded. 'Of course we will,' I managed, the answer coming from my heart as my head was telling me a different story. We were over 200 miles downwind and downstream from the Galapagos Islands. To try to row the small dinghy into 200 miles of rough ocean weather was an impossible journey, even if tried by only two of us in an attempt to seek help for the others, who would have to remain behind in the raft. The fact that the current was against us as well only put the seal of hopelessness on the idea. The Marquesas Islands, on the other hand, lay 2,800 miles to the west but we had no compass or means of finding our position. If by some miraculous feat of endurance one of us made the distance, the chances of actually striking an island seemed infinitely remote. I concluded there would be no salvation from the direction in which we had come nor in the direction we had been going, and there was nothing to remain where we were for, but death.

New rules for staying alive would have to be devised and rigidly applied; there would be no chance for trial runs and no absolution if we got it wrong. Feeling that God was already shaking his head as we formulated our plans, I watched a small flock of frigatebirds flying in the skies above, safe and aloof in their heavenly kingdom. If we were to succeed, we would have to become like them, masters of all we surveyed. The frigatebirds swept by and held us in their sight. I pondered if we would eat them or they would eat us, and wondered if they were thinking the same thing too, as they soared high into the sky. We would have to adapt and improvise, hunt and not be hunted, prey and not be preyed upon. Like stone-age man we would have to compete with the wildlife for our food and when necessary take it by force or stealth, or we ourselves would become victims of the ruthless cycle of life in which we found ourselves trapped. We would have to learn quickly and effectively to pit our limited skill and resources against that of the natural world. Unlike us, its birds and beasts were equipped with the necessary tools and expertise derived from evolution and adaptation, honed to their specific purpose over millions of years. If and when we had learned what we must do, then even in our darkest hour we would need to find our courage and steel our nerve, refusing to give up or yield to setbacks, whilst remaining constantly on guard to dispel the dark clouds of self-doubt and defeat that would be constantly waiting to engulf us.

Starting from a position that could not have been much worse, I reflected upon our situation. We had the flimsiest of platforms to keep us out of the sea, and we had food and water sufficient only for the next few days. I knew also that we needed more than just shelter and sustenance if we were all to get home alive; we would need the help of old mother luck and in good measure, unable to afford being unlucky even the once. As time went by our chances of staying lucky would become ever more unlikely and our chances of success increasingly more improbable. The odds seemed stacked immeasurably against us as we looked from the sea to the sky and then to each other, lost in what seemed a boundless ocean without the means for sustained survival or of fixing our position, both cornerstone prerequisites if we were to get back to land. Having had no chance to send out a distress message before we sank, we were drifting ever further into the Pacific at the mercy of the elements in a leaky raft with a sunken dinghy, in a race against time. My thoughts returned to the alternatives, my morbid conclusions seeming more incontrovertible than ever as our fragile nest of humanity drifted at the mercy of the sea, lost, alone and without hope.

The coast of Central America, more than a thousand miles to the northeast, lay on the other side of the windless doldrums, a notorious area of calms and squalls which had inspired Coleridge's

Water, water, everywhere,
And all the boards did shrink;
Water, water, everywhere,
Nor any drop to drink.

I was a Master Mariner, I thought ruefully, not an ancient one, and could count on no ghostly crew to get me out of our dilemma. What were our chances if we followed the textbook answer, 'Stay put and wait for rescue'? In the first place, we wouldn't be missed for at least five weeks, at the very best estimate, and if a search was by some miracle initiated where would a search party start looking, in 3,000 miles of ocean? In the second place, the chance of seeing a passing vessel in this area was sufficiently remote that it could be discounted completely for, of the two possible shipping routes from Panama to Tahiti or New Zealand, one lay 400 miles to the south and the other 300 miles to the north. Looking at the food, I estimated that six of us might live for ten days on what we had and since we could expect no rain in this area for at least six months other than from an odd shower, our chances of survival beyond a couple of weeks would be doubtful indeed. The more I thought about it the more it seemed that we were destined to become one of Robin's statistics.

My struggle to reach a decision, gloomy whichever way I looked at it, showed on my face, and Lyn leaned forward. 'Tell us how we stand,' she challenged, looking round to the others for support, 'we want to know the truth.' They all nodded. 'What chance have we?' they chorused, fully expecting to hear the worst. I pondered on the ethics of stating a lie that would offer them comfort against a truth that would confirm their worst fears. If they were soon to depart this life then I had no right to withhold such information from them; even so, I could not bring myself to tell them I thought they were going to die, so I slowly spelled out the alternatives and gradually formulated the elements of a plan.

The books all stated that we should stay put and wait for rescue, but were we to stay in the south Pacific trades we would soon run out of water, and the Humboldt Current was preventing any possibility of a return to the Galapagos Islands. In the doldrums to the north there would be rain enough, but what then? Would the counter-current carry us eastwards far enough to reach land, or would the squally rain clouds whip up the sea so much that it would swamp us?

With the certainty of a child, Douglas voiced his opinion for all to hear. 'We can survive three days without water and thirty without food. In thirty days, surely we would be picked up? Water is what we need first and water lies to the north.' I had to admit all the signs pointed north; north to the doldrums, north to the rain and north to the counter-current, which in turn would lead us back to land. Robin, exercising his statistical brain, agreed the chances of being picked up would only increase as we neared the distant shipping lanes off the

American coast and that thirty days was probably the maximum time it would take to get there. We would all be dead from thirst long before then if we didn't find water, so that had to be our first priority.

As our lives depended upon this decision, it had to be a unanimous one. I looked from one face to another as each nodded their agreement in turn. In that moment, the decision was made and things began to look brighter. We had a plan and if we were to die then we would die fighting for our lives rather than just sitting and waiting for the end. We all agreed there was just one course open to us: we must sail with the trade winds to the doldrums 400 miles to the north. We stood a thin chance of reaching land, and our chances of being picked up were higher on the busier shipping lanes lying in that direction; further, our only possible chance of rainwater in any quantity also lay along that route, even if it was hundreds of miles away. The first leg of our voyage back to land, however improbable or remote, also lay on that course. We would work and fight for our lives, at least a better option than dying in idle apathy!

'We must get these boys to land,' Lyn's words echoed through my mind. I felt the reality of the decision lifting the hopelessness from my shoulders and looked around. Five pairs of eyes watched with unblinking stares as I spoke, Lyn once again clutched her arms around the twins, and the moment was heavy with expectation as Douglas and Robin each at their lookout posts waited for me to speak. 'We have no alternative,' I proclaimed, 'we'll stay here for twenty-four hours to see if any other wreckage appears, then we will head north and hope to find rain in the doldrums.' I looked round, 'We might also find an easterly current there which may help us reach the coast of Central America, if we've not been picked up before then.' The lifting of my depression communicated to the others and as I talked of the problems and privations confronting us I saw the resolve harden on Douglas's face as he finally accepted the grim reality of our sorry state of affairs. In the moments that had changed our world, his life had altered from one of discovery and adventure to one of hunger and unknown suffering with the prospect of almost certain death. Robin nodded before firing a question about shipping lanes. Lyn smiled at me, not caring that I was offering her torture from thirst and starvation that would probably result in the loss of her life, for all she now wanted was a working chance. The twins dried their tears and eyed the sweets. Suddenly we were back in business.

With one of the sea anchors streamed we set to work, clearing the raft floor of the debris we had collected: the huge genoa sail, 200 feet of nylon fishing line with a breaking strain of 100 pounds, three gallons of petrol, two oars and two empty boxes. Lyn was examining her sewing basket, which turned out to be a treasure beyond wealth and a veritable Aladdin's cave. Not only did it contain the usual threads and needles but also in the top section were fish hooks, two scalpel blades, four knitting needles, a blanket pin, a hatpin, three plastic bags, a ball of string, buttons, tinfoil, a shoehorn and two small plastic cups. In the bottom section Lyn discovered two plastic boxes, two small envelopes of dried yeast, a piece of copper wire one foot long, some elastic, a bottle of soluble aspirin, a pencil and a biro pen. We also had a half tin of copal varnish and a very sodden edition of a West Indies pilot book, and one cracked and waterlogged smoke-flare. My watch would give us the time of day and the first-aid box contained artery forceps and scissors, but otherwise we had no compass, no charts, and no instruments of any kind. There was nothing in fact that would aid our navigation or measure our distance run.

We stowed our utensils and other items of equipment as best we could, then set to work, our first task being to strip out the long luff wire from the genoa sail so that it could be used to join the dinghy to the raft. It was at this point that we met our first real drawback, for Robin and Neil were beset with seasickness. They found the undulating motion of the raft in the high swell and breaking seas impossible to get accustomed to and were unable to settle to the constantly erratic movement. Lyn administered anti-seasickness pills from the first-aid box as soon as she thought the boys were able to retain them, but they had already lost precious quantities of body fluid. Lyn and I continued to work on the sail while Douglas checked and re-stowed the rations and equipment. In one of the raft pockets, he found two sponges and an assortment of puncture repair plugs and patches together with a repair kit, but the glue had completely dried out, rendering it useless. In another pocket he found the instruction book which gave little intelligent information on how to preserve one's life in mid-ocean, but gave a lot of superfluous jargon about morale, leadership and dependence on rescue, finishing up with the two most un-sensible words in the whole book: GOOD LUCK!!

Expletives aside, Douglas's strong arms eventually managed to separate the genoa luff wire from the sail. Some delicate cuts with the safety knife, supplemented with some tearing by our bare hands, left us with a large expanse of cloth and a wire rope covered with white plastic, about forty feet in length. We then set about cutting a sail for the dinghy. We set aside the remaining Dacron sailcloth to use as sheeting and for clothes and covers for additional warmth at night, since we were clad only in swimming shorts and shirts with the exception of Lyn, who was wearing only her torn nylon housecoat. 'I suppose it was an appointment none of us had to dress for,' Lyn grinned as she excused her scanty clothing. The wire would make an excellent towrope for the dinghy, and I fastened it outside the raft to give us a little more space in which to settle down for the night. As evening drew in, we feasted on a biscuit and one glucose sweet apiece, followed by a sip of water each and an orange between the six of us; meagre enough rations at the time but a sumptuous banquet in the light of things to come.

In the dying light Lyn sang 'The Lord is my shepherd', and then prayed most earnestly for our safety. Slowly the sun began to set and the wind grew suddenly colder, making us shiver in the chill air as we drew our Dacron sailcloth sheets about us. Lyn suddenly laughed out loud. 'Well, tell us,' we urged. 'When I was swimming to the raft,' she said still chuckling 'and it was making that funny noise with the excess gas, Douglas thought the raft was still leaking and blocked the pipes with his fingers. Then he shouted to me to give him a patch; in the middle of the Pacific!' The source of her merriment was finally revealed. 'He kept on, so I gave him an orange and said, will this do?' We all laughed with her as Dougie protested that it hadn't happened quite like his mother had told it, but I was happy to see his embarrassed grimace turn to a smile as he managed a chuckle of laughter along with the rest of us.

The raft's flotation chambers had gone soft with the cooling of the night air, so while Douglas pumped them firm with the bellows, Lyn tended to Neil and Robin, both still retching from the effects of their seasickness. I closed the windward door of the canopy, leaving a peephole for both lookout and ventilation purposes. Robin insisted that he take his share of the adults' two-hour lookout watches in spite of his sickness and as darkness fell we curled round the collection of boxes and tins, with legs and bodies overlapping, and tried to rest. The raft was still plunging and lifting in the long fifteen-foot-high swells, while the shorter crested waves built up under the force of the local winds surged heavily around us, causing the raft to jerk into the troughs as it brought up sharply on its sea anchor. As we turned and twisted around, seeking ease for our aching limbs, we began to experience curious bumps and sharp nudges through the inflated floor of the raft. At first I thought something sharp had wedged under our craft and became concerned lest it should puncture the flotation chambers, then I heard Lyn give a faint shriek as she too was nudged from below. Douglas, on lookout, said that he could see large fish swimming under the raft. Dorado, he thought, and they seemed to be after some smaller fish, swimming close by under the raft floor. The bumps and nudges occurred at frequent intervals, as the dorado performed endless gyrations under the wobbly raft floor, often several times in the space of a minute. The severity of the bumps depended on the speed and angle of the dorado's impact but generally speaking they were mild compared with the blows from the sharks that soon joined the dorado, and quite distinct from the hard bump of a turtle's shell, which we identified later.

The bites and bumps were never hard enough to penetrate the double skin beneath us, although they were probably responsible for many of the leaks which developed in the air chambers that formed the raft floor, thereby destroying the buffer effect of the air chambers against the assaults of the fish as well as their protection from the cold. With so many fish around I thought hopefully that perhaps we wouldn't find it so difficult to supplement our rations after all. Nevertheless, the experience of being poked sharply in the posterior when drowsing or, worse, having it bitten whilst asleep was quite startling and on each and every occurrence it woke us with a start.

Having discovered the source of our discomfort, we settled down once more and my mind ranged over the events of the previous week. I tried to remember the distance between the islands in an attempt to arrive at the coordinates for the position in which we had been sunk. I knew that our latitude was 1 degree 15 minutes south of the equator, from the course line on the chart, but I could not remember the longitude of Cape Espinosa although I did recall that Wreck Bay on Chatham Island had a longitude of about 89 degrees and 30 minutes west. If only I'd worked out that dead-reckoning position a little sooner. I lay on the damp floor and listened to the breaking waves outside. My attention transferred to the shaking canopy as it flapped noisily in the wind, gripped first by one gust and then by another. I returned to my ruminations and tried to plot our route backwards in my mind, so that I could arrive at a starting position, regretting also that I had not paid more attention to the terrestrial coordinates when the land had still been in sight.

Hood Island, I remembered, had been roughly on the same longitude as Chatham Island and we had sailed from there at midnight, travelling west by north to Charles Island at about 4 knots. We had arrived off Post Office Bay around three in the afternoon, say 60 miles, and had then turned west-northwest to round the south point of Isabela Island the following morning. Allowing for calms and currents, I reckoned on a distance run of about 120 miles before we had turned north for Fernandina Island. My mind jolted back to the present as the raft floor shuddered under the assault of several large dorado, and hearing the mumble of voices turned on my side to assure myself that Robin, taking over the watch from Douglas, was fit enough to keep a good lookout. He fumbled around on the floor of the raft, looking for his glasses. After finding them, he leaned out of the raft and wretched emptily into the sea. 'You alright, Robin?' I asked. He muttered something about being as right as you can be when you're stranded on a raft in the middle of the Pacific with no food or water and feeling very seasick, then put his glasses back on. 'But if there's a ship out there, Dougal, I'll find it!' He added owlishly in the faint light afforded by the night. 'Let me know if you're in doubt about anything, and don't hesitate to wake me,' I returned. I turned on to my back again, watching Robin's silhouette moving against the doorway of the canopy as he scanned the horizon; his six-foot frame was thin, but he was both determined and tough and completely unflappable. If anybody would survive this, I thought he might.

I listened anxiously as his spluttering cough became a gasping wretch before petering into silence once more. My mind switched back to the longitude calculation. We had stopped at the south end of Fernandina where after that exhausting exploration of the lava beds

Neil had been so glad to get back to the *Lucette*. 'Good old Lucy', wherever she was now, she had been a true home to him. I glanced over to where Neil lay asleep, his limbs entangled under Sandy's and on top of Lyn's; he was a very loving child, with unorthodox views and a stubborn streak of determination, which would stand him in good stead in the days to come. Lyn was worried about his seasickness, for his young body would not stand up to the loss of fluid as well as Robin's.

Douglas grunted as a dorado collided with the raft beneath him. 'We'll have to do something about these fish, Dad,' he mumbled, half asleep, 'like catching them for a start.' Doggedly I returned to the problem of longitude. We had made a little easting; say fifteen miles as we had travelled to the northern side of Fernandina Island then about half that distance in a westerly direction to arrive at Cape Espinosa. With a distance of 112 miles from Wreck Bay that would mean the longitude of Espinosa would be roughly 91 degrees and 20 minutes west.

'Two o'clock!' I jerked awake from my doze to see Robin bending towards me in the darkness. 'Aye-aye! Everything alright?' I crawled across to the doorway to take over the watch; the stars twinkled brightly in the arch of darkness beyond the sweep of the sea. Robin nodded towards the water. 'No ships,' he muttered and crawled into his place beside Douglas. I peeped round the canopy of the raft at the dinghy; the *Ednamair* lay disconsolately awash at the end of her painter, her white gunwale just visible above the surface of the water. She was helping the sea anchor, I surmised, but we'd have to bail her out first thing in the morning, for the wooden thwarts, which contained the polystyrene flotation reserve, would loosen and come adrift if they became waterlogged. Suddenly the water exploded as a thirty-pound dorado leapt high in the air in hot pursuit of a flying fish, landing with a loud slap on its side in a shower of green luminescence. I glanced down to where several large fish swam beneath us, constantly rising to skim the underside of the raft's edge and sometimes striking it a heavy blow with their high jutting foreheads. Douglas was right: we would have to do something about these fish!

Flying fish

Second day

The long night paled into a beautiful dawn sky typical of the south Pacific, as we slowly collected our scattered wits. Already our dreams of being elsewhere other than on the raft had taken on the vivid reality of vibrantly coloured apparitions that seemed real enough to reach out and touch. Douglas had dreamt he was aboard a gleaming gin-palace motor yacht we had seen moored alongside in St Thomas and Lyn had been back at Meadows Farm in the Sunday bed. For myself, wretched with cramp and discomfort, I had simply walked next door and found my childhood bed, so clear in every forgotten detail, waiting there for me. As we stirred from our sleep, reality flooded back to us in all its brutality.

The pressure in the raft's flotation chambers had dropped drastically during the night so our first task was to top them up with air. Douglas connected the bellows pipe to the non-return valve in the inflation chambers and started pumping. We took turns to keep the bellows going; after fifteen minutes we could see no improvement in the pressure so we disconnected the bellows and tested them for leaks; there weren't any bad ones, but the intake valve didn't close properly and most of the air escaped the way it went in. Douglas and I exchanged glances; we knew the answer to this one, for the bellows we had used for our old inflatable dinghy had served us in a similar fashion. Douglas cut the pipe from the bellows, not without difficulty as the curve of the knife prevented any proper sawing action, then placed the pipe in his mouth and blew mightily. We took it turn about for a few minutes and the raft was soon fully inflated and back to normal, but we knew even then that we had not seen the last of this particular trouble.

I looked across at Lyn, rubbing the cramp out of the twins' legs. 'We'll see to the *Ednamair* after breakfast,' I stated emphatically, looking at the water jar, which was nearly empty. Lyn had emptied the glucose sweets out of their glass jar so that it could be used to hold the drinking water, which we decanted from the tins. We discussed the issue of equal rations of water, even though there wasn't enough to do that, and then decided to simply pass the jar round, each person limiting him or herself to the minimum needed to carry on; at the same time the visible water level in the jar enabled everyone to see that there would be no excesses. 'Take as much as you need but as little as you can,' I echoed as the jar was passed from one to the other, for the rapidly dwindling supply was far too valuable to be used for any other purpose. Breakfast consisted of one quarter-ounce biscuit, a piece of onion and a sip of water, except for Robin and Neil who could not eat and were with difficulty persuaded to take some extra water with an anti-seasickness pill. We had used two pints of water in one day between six, hardly a maintenance ration under a tropical sun, which I remembered the merchant navy had placed as high as two pints per person per day. We ate slowly, savouring each taste of raw onion and biscuit with a new appreciation. Although we hardly felt as if we had breakfasted on bacon and eggs, we were still sufficiently shocked at our altered circumstances not to feel any hunger.

Our repast over, Lyn and Sandy sorted the various pieces of sail, which we planned to use for bedding. Douglas and I took up positions either side of the raft door and pulled the dinghy alongside. Initially we attempted to bail it out as it lay swamped, but the waves filled it as fast as we bailed. We turned the stern towards the raft and lifting slowly tried to tip out the water, only to look on in dismay as the bow submerged in equal and opposite measure. Slumping back into the recesses of the raft in perplexed frustration, I tried in vain to find a solution to this brainteaser as the dinghy remained awash, with no more freeboard than it had before. We tried bailing at speed with the small raft bailers but it rapidly became clear that re-floating the dinghy was going to take nothing short of a minor miracle.

In a sudden moment of inspiration, Douglas plucked the box-shaped gas-bottle holder he had salvaged at the wreck site and with a gleam in his eye stated 'It's time to let brute force and ignorance have a go.' Gripping the wooden box, its base riddled with drain holes, he stretched out horizontally from the raft whilst I pinned his legs down, enabling him to bail in a rapid and repeated scooping action. He had to be quick as the water drained rapidly from the box, but with a rapid succession of massive scoops he had soon bailed out enough water to allow him to board the dinghy and bail it dry with the smaller bailer. The sight of little *Ednamair* afloat once more cheered us all, then with a cry of delight Douglas held up his Timex watch, which had been lying in the bottom of the dinghy since the shipwreck and was still going. He also found what was to prove our most valuable possession, the stainless-steel kitchen knife which I had thrown aboard from *Lucette*'s sinking decks.

After we had each had a segment of orange for elevenses we discussed various options as to how we could best use the dinghy, with ideas ranging from a storage unit to a tugboat. With a new sense of purpose, we set to work as a team and transferred the piled-up flotsam from the raft. The oars and paddles were first to go, followed by the empty boxes, the can of petrol, the hundred-foot raft painter and the piece of the genoa designated for the dinghy sail. Climbing into the dinghy, Douglas and I started work on the jury rig which would convert the *Ednamair* into our chosen option of a tugboat, to take us on the first stage of our journey north. The others in the meantime helped Lyn to reorganise the inside of the raft now that there was more room and then topped up the flotation chambers. Douglas rigged one of the oars into the mast step, which I secured with improvised fore- and backstays; the leeboards, mast and sails had been stowed below decks aboard *Lucette*, and had of course gone down with her. I had already taken the precaution of shackling the luff wire we had extracted from the genoa between the towing straps of the raft and the ringbolt in the bow of the dinghy, in case the nylon painter were to fray.

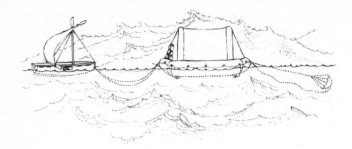

I had decided the dinghy would have to perform her towing function by proceeding stern first, otherwise her cutaway aft end would be too exposed to the overtaking waves, creating a real danger of swamping. With the aid of Douglas's powerful muscles, we cut notches in one of the raft paddles and bent the head of the sail onto it, forming a square sail. With extra rigging to secure the mast in place, we then fastened the paddle to the top of the mast to act as a spar, and a second oar lower down across the stern, which served as a boom. We then rigged the makeshift sail between them. It was an unorthodox rig and it looked somewhat ridiculous as it pulled away from us, taking up the slack on the line, but it was the best we could manage. A violent jerk sent me sprawling into the bottom of the boat and I realised that after two and a half hours without a break our plan was suddenly operational. I climbed back aboard the raft for lunch, which consisted of a small piece of fortified bread taken from the pound and a half we had stored in the emergency rations, followed by a mouthful of water. I felt very thirsty after my exertions in the raft and *Ednamair* was now straining at her leash, so I instructed Douglas to trip the sea anchor and haul it aboard. The time was two o'clock in the afternoon and we had started our voyage to the doldrums. I estimated our position at latitude 1 degree south and longitude 94 degrees and 40 minutes west – or, more accurately, 200 miles west of Cape Espinosa.

The white plastic-covered luff wire snapped taut with a considerable jerk as *Ednamair* yawed at the end of her towrope. Having little use for the petrol, I lashed the can to the centre of the towing wire to act as a tension buffer, which it did quite effectively. We now turned our attention to the flotation chambers of the raft to see if we could locate some of the leaks. The raft was an old model, a gift from our good friend Captain Siggi Thorsteinsson of the Icelandic rescue craft *Bonnie*. We remembered with deep gratitude his concern when he had presented us with the raft in Bequia and how I had expressed my hope that we would never need to use it.

We had cursed its unwieldy bulk many a time as it lay on *Lucette*'s cramped coach roof, even as it had afforded us comfort by its presence there. Now we owed our lives to it. The double canopy alone was worth a gallon of water a day as it shielded us from the heat of the sun, and its emergency rations were available to us now only because they had already been stowed inside the raft. We examined the raft's flotation chambers as well as we could, pouring water over all the exposed surfaces, but could find no leaks, although there were one or two old repair patches. Finally, we called a halt to our search, putting down the loss of air to seepage through the treated fabric of the raft. We arranged a regular routine of topping up on each watch to keep the raft as rigid as possible, for the continuous flexing of the softened chambers by the waves was already showing signs of wear. The double floor in the after section of the raft, which was divided by a central flotation piece, had been holed from below and a tiny hole in the upper skin was allowing seawater to seep through to our bedding, requiring us to perform mopping-up operations at frequent intervals. Later we tried to repair the leak with sticking plaster, but without success.

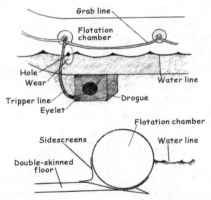

Areas of wear on inflatable: at water level (above)
and at floor level (below)

The sun dipped towards the horizon and our attention turned to the things which had to be checked before it got dark and thereby ensure our safe passage through the night. These included the lashings on the towing wire and the sail as well as the rigging on the dinghy, which were each inspected individually and made secure where they looked in need of attention. I tripped the two small drogues at the forward end of the raft to increase our speed, which I estimated to be about 1 knot. Adding this to the north-northwesterly current of 1 knot, I estimated we would be making 2 knots or 50 miles per day towards our mid-ocean waypoint and interim goal.

This was news indeed and became the major point for discussion as we gathered round for 'tea'. Our meal consisted of a one-and-a-half-square-inch biscuit, a small piece of glucose and a mouthful of water, and was positively relished by each and every one of us. Neil and Robin had regained their sea legs with the help of the pills, and as dusk drew in Lyn settled the twins to sleep by playing 'I spy' and singing them a lullaby, recalling their happier days at Meadows Farm. Robin was more cheerful and chatted about his travels across the continent of America by bus, working casually for his keep. As we listened, we wondered if we would ever see land again. During the day, Lyn had cut pieces of sail for the twins and Douglas to write letters, telling their friends in England and America what had happened. Lyn wrote a loving farewell letter to Anne, to which I added a paragraph telling her how sorry I was for what had happened, and how much we both loved her. Robin wrote to his mother, and I added a footnote apologising for having been instrumental in ending his young life. These farewell notes were written on a 'just in case' basis and placed in a waterproof wrapping, tucked in one of the pockets of the raft, for we knew that when the time came to write such letters our minds and bodies would be unable to cope with the effort.

Our collective mood became sad, gloomy and depressed as we each considered the prospect of our demise, and especially little Neil, who I felt could visualise more clearly the privations which lay ahead of us without knowing the possibilities or the ways in which they could be avoided. Earlier in the day he had looked a very sad and forlorn little boy, lying in his mother's arms gazing unblinking into space and seeing heaven knows what terrors in his mind's eye, but now, tucked in beside Sandy under sheets of sail cloth, he was chatting quietly with his brother about their friends in Miami and Colon.

Neil's logbook, written on a piece of raft canopy

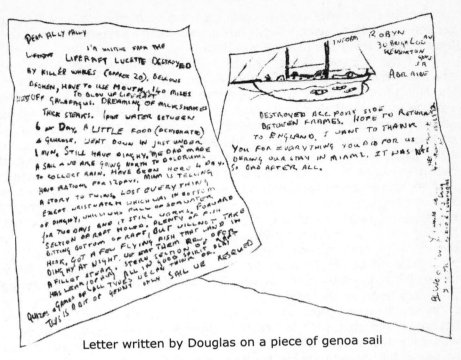

Letter written by Douglas on a piece of genoa sail

Robin had first watch of the night and I reiterated the points that needed scrutinising on the dinghy, which in the increasing wind was now pulling hard on the towrope and yawing widely, as the pull on her sail swung the stern around. The concept of sailing her stern first to permit her to ride the seas without swamping seemed to be working well. As I settled down beside Lyn she leaned across and whispered, close to tears, 'If Neil goes, I shall not allow him to go alone.' I was shocked that she could even be thinking in terms of giving up her life and felt it could be as much a result of writing the farewell letters as the effects of the incessant guilt we both endured, each time we caught the eyes of our children. I clasped her hand in mine. 'Neil's a lot tougher than you think and I don't think it will come to that,' I soothed, adding 'but if it did, you could help more by staying.'

Lyn was one of the most competent people in an emergency and my deep respect for her capabilities as a nurse, wife and mother had grown steadily over our twenty years of married life. I feared that she could be holding back on something in Neil's medical condition that I was unaware of, which made her feel so despondent, but as she talked it became clear to me that the shock of the last thirty-six hours was finally catching up on her, as indeed it was with us all. I switched the conversation to our chances of being picked up and, if we weren't rescued in that way, then the possibility of reaching the coast of Central America. I continued speaking into the darkness, aware that all ears were now listening intently. 'We will feed ourselves on fish,' which I felt certain we would soon learn to catch, 'and by collecting the rain we will drink.'

'And the rain our drink,' murmured Lyn in reply. Han Suyin, the author of the book *And the Rain My Drink*, had worked as a doctor in the Hong Kong hospital where Lyn had been a sister, and I knew she was no longer thinking of death but of the happy days we had spent sailing together in Hong Kong. 'I'll draw you a map tomorrow,' I concluded, wriggling around to find a comfortable place for my head, even though there wasn't one. Neil's and Sandy's legs were crossed over the top of my body and I could feel the pool of seawater, which had seeped through the hole in the floor, gathering under my bottom and chilling my kidneys. 'Pass me the sponge and the bailer,' I muttered to Lyn, as she got ready to go on watch. Silently she passed them to me, our hands touching in understanding through the cloak of darkness that shielded our eyes from our children's as we struggled to come to terms with our desperate plight. Dry once more, I lay down to think in the slow hours of the night, calculating just how long it would take us to reach the doldrums, and our chances of finding rain once we got there; an exercise that was to occupy my nights with increasing urgency as our meagre store of water cans gradually dwindled. Robin had puffed rather ineffectually at the inflation tube before he went off watch, but the raft was still soft, so I stuck the end of the tube in my mouth and gave it a good blow, inflating first one end of the raft and then the other. Robin, I decided, would get better with a bit more practice.

Third day

My watch period in the dawn hours started with a clear sky, but as the sunrise tinted the clouds in surreal beauty the wind freshened from the south and the tall pink-tipped clouds with greying bases became heavy enough to give rain. As soon as it was light, I pulled in the dinghy and climbed aboard to inspect the sail fastenings and stays, one of which had worked loose in the night. While I was securing the stay, I caught sight of a small black shape under the wooden box by the thwart. I crouched down and lifted our first fruits from the sea, a flying fish about eight inches in length. I gutted and de-scaled it then passed it over to Lyn, who was now awake. She promptly marinated it in a squeeze of lemon juice, which acted as a cooking agent. We breakfasted an hour later at seven, each savouring our tiny piece of fish, done to a turn in the lemon juice, followed by a crunchy piece of onion and a mouthful of water. The raft had begun pitching heavily again, surging on the crests of the breaking seas and dropping steeply into the troughs. To our disappointment, both Neil and Robin started being seasick again, and though Lyn offered them more pills they decided to do without and try to get used to the motion of the raft instead.

The waves began to break over the stern of the raft, and with the swell running at some twenty feet in height it looked as if we were in for a bad day. *Ednamair* yawed violently as the wind gusted in her sail and she snatched hard on the towrope, jolting it clear of the water at times, forcing me to take a reef in the sail to ease the strain on the towing straps of the raft. Douglas hauled the dinghy alongside the raft and held her while I balanced precariously on the seat. To reef her, I simply tied a rope around the belly of the sail, giving it an hourglass effect and reducing its effective pulling power by half. I had just completed the operation and was standing upright again to return to the raft when a large breaker surged round the raft and slammed into the dinghy with a mighty broadside. As she tilted, I gripped wildly for anything that would help me maintain my footing, and finding the mast I held fast in order to prevent myself falling into the sea. *Ednamair* heeled sharply with the increased leverage, causing the sea to flood in over the gunwale. Before I could let go and drop to the floor, the boat was swamped, retaining a mere three inches of freeboard. I dived through the door of the canopy into the raft and the dinghy, relieved of my weight, floated a little higher for a moment before being completely overwhelmed by the very next wave. Douglas's bailing skills were called upon a second time, as he reached over from the raft with the box and bailed frantically for several minutes, steadily gaining on the influx of water slopping over the gunwale as the waves surged and growled at us from all sides. After an effort that was nothing short of superhuman, he eventually got enough freeboard to allow me to return to the *Ednamair*, and as Douglas recovered from his labours I removed the last dregs of seawater from the bottom of the boat.

I breathed a huge sigh of relief to see *Ednamair* dry once more. During the previous night I had considered the possibility of us taking to the dinghy altogether and leaving the raft, but this incident served to highlight the difficulty of such a move. With a very small freeboard, trim would be of paramount importance, and with what had just happened I sincerely doubted if the dinghy could take the six of us and remain afloat in the open sea.

After what had been a demanding morning we rested for a while, lunching on a mouthful of water and a few crumbs of fortified bread from the ration box, which although made up in tablet form disintegrated at the first touch. This made the conveyance of the crumbs from container to mouth an operation that required great care to avoid spillage and resulted in some waste crumbling onto our garments. Even so every stray crumb was hunted down from wherever it had landed and mercilessly consumed. With the main course over, we indulged ourselves in a piece of orange.

The clouds thickened as the day advanced and high cumulus began to drop rain in isolated showers some distance away. The wind freshened still further, and with the breaking waves slopping through the canopy door at the rear of the raft we were forced to close the drawstrings on the flaps, as much as was possible without cutting off the ventilation altogether. With the large blanket pin I punched bigger holes in the empty water cans and made plugs from the puncture repair kit to fit them, just in case a shower should provide us with water. Douglas blew lustily into the pipe to make the raft as rigid as possible in the heavy seas, whilst *Ednamair* bounced around at the end of her towrope like a pup on a leash.

I was considering taking the sail down altogether when the patter of raindrops on the canopy warned us that we were about to get our very first rain. A pipe led down from the centre of a purpose-built rain catchment funnel sewn into the top of the canopy. By pulling this down to form a depression in the roof, we prepared to gather what had become the most valuable commodity of our new world – rainwater. With eyes agog, we gazed at the end of the pipe. The liquid that dribbled from the tube was a bright yellow in colour, repugnant to smell and tasted bitterly of rubber; it was even saltier than the sea. As soon as the salt had been washed off the roof, however, we managed to collect half a pint of the yellowish rubbery-tasting liquid before the shower passed over. I looked at the jar of fluid – one could hardly call it water – and surmised sadly that we would need to do a lot better than that if we were to survive. The raft, now pitching heavily, required Dougie's blowing attentions every hour to keep it rigid, and the jerky undulations did nothing to ease the spasms of seasickness which Neil and Robin were suffering. They both looked drawn and pale and refused water in spite of Lyn's pleading.

As the raft slid up the twenty-foot swells to the breaking whitecaps at their crests, Lyn prayed desperately for calm weather and for more rain. She urged the rest of us to join her in prayer with such insistence that I had to remind her that freedom of thought and religion remained a matter of individual choice, and no one should be coerced. Lyn looked at me, startled, and continued praying aloud while Robin, on the verge of expressing an opinion himself, thought better of it and stilled his tongue with some half-said words. Although he described himself as a non-practising Christian, the religious fervour with which Lyn had appealed to us clearly embarrassed him. Silence, interrupted only by the hiss and roar of the breaking waves, followed Lyn's praying, then quietly she sang 'The Lord is my shepherd' to the twins as I put away the unfilled cans and the jar containing the foul-tasting yellow stuff. At least it was better than seawater. Late in the afternoon, I passed the water jar around for 'sippers' before we partook in our meagre ration of biscuit, reminding everyone that our water supplies were now very low and that only minimal amounts should be taken. 'We must try to drink less than two pints per day between us,' I stated. 'We have only twelve tins left and we still have over 300 miles to go.' A quart of water each for the next 300 miles. It didn't sound much, and indeed it wasn't.

As darkness closed in, Douglas settled down to his two-hour watch-keeping vigil. Our rest was continuously interrupted by incessant bumps and bites from the dorado fish through the bottom of the raft and I resolved to try to catch one in the morning. Neil and Sandy were sleeping soundly after helping to blow up the raft and mop up the water, which was now coming through the floor at a greater rate than before. They looked so vulnerable that my heart turned over at the prospect of what lay ahead for them: death by thirst or starvation, or just a slow deterioration into a long sleep from the effects of dehydration or exhaustion. Lyn's words echoed many times through my mind that night. 'We must get these boys to land.' Try as I might, sleep would not come to ease the burden of my conscience.

Fourth day

During the night, the wind fell to a gentle breeze and the sea calmed to a tolerable condition, allowing the raft to move more easily in the lumpy seaway. Dawn brought a clear sky and the promise of a hot day, during which I hoped the calmer weather would allow Neil and Robin to make a full recovery from their seasickness. To avoid undue disturbance in the raft, we used one of the bailers as a toilet, and named it 'the pissoir'. The call for the pissoir was heard less often now and our urine had taken on a very dark colour, emitting a strong pungent smell. I had contemplated tasting some to find out if it was palatable but Lyn said that she had already tried hers. 'It was very salty,' she said rather sadly. 'I understand from an article I once read by some professor that we might derive some benefit from drinking each others', though.' 'Would you like to try some of mine?' I offered. We both burst out laughing to Lyn's reply of 'Not yet, thanks.' Douglas looked at us disgustedly from the doorway. 'For God's sake!' he grimaced, 'what's for breakfast?'

Our mirth was suddenly interrupted as we experienced our first sighting of a turtle. Its purple–brown shell was covered in moss-like algae and sported the odd small barnacle as, seemingly unafraid, it trundled into view in an ungainly but effective motion that carried it through the water at a deceptive speed. In a spontaneous impulse, Douglas reached into the water and lifted it from the sea with an almighty two-handed grab. On contact, the turtle burst into frenzied action, chopping the air with its fore-flippers in a fit of fury as it fought desperately to escape. Douglas held it away from his body but his forearms were chopped with a succession of hefty blows from the sharp bony trailing edges of the turtle's flippers, which were also armed with stubby claws along their leading edges. Screaming in a combination of pain and anguish, he was forced to release the beak-snapping reptile inside the raft. Like hens in a henhouse disturbed by the sudden appearance of a fox, we scrambled for safety, shouting and cursing in Douglas's direction. Lyn and I jumped onto the central thwart as the twins hopped over into the forward compartment with

Robin. I had sudden visions of the raft being torn asunder by the flailing flippers and, pushing my fears aside, reached for the frightened animal and lifted it bodily from the soft rubber floor, to eject it though the forward hatch and back into the sea, not too sure which one of us had had the lucky escape.

'Douglas, the next time you try something like that at least warn us first,' I admonished. 'I just thought we might eat it somehow,' he replied with a grin across his face. 'Well,' I retorted rather stupidly, 'I can tell you one thing, young man, I have no intention of resorting to eating turtle at this stage of the game!' I held his eye but he was unrepentant and I think he knew I would be eating not only turtle meat but also my words in the very near future.

I climbed over to the *Ednamair* to shake the reef out of the sail, and to my delight found a large and a small flying fish in the bottom of the boat. Quickly gutted and dressed, they were then divided with much ceremony, the heads being put aside to be used as bait later on. Robin and Neil were looking better and were able to eat their share with a little extra water. I watched Lyn carefully to see that she took her sip of water, and when she didn't I insisted that she should do so, for we could not afford to have her sick, and especially not by self-infliction. If we were going to die from thirst and dehydration then we'd do it together. We each chewed our piece of onion and segment of orange slowly, opting to go without any biscuit, as the dry food was going too quickly. 'We shall have to try to catch some fish,' I proclaimed. 'We tried the line out yesterday morning,' said Lyn, 'when you were working with the dinghy, but when we pulled it in the hook had gone.' She looked across at Sandy. 'Did you try again?' Sandy shook his head. 'No bait, we only had the one fish head.' He looked questioningly at me and I wondered what could have taken the hook, guessing that it might have been a shark, in view of the absence of any struggle. Not wishing to dwell on the matter, I announced, 'I'll try the spinner from the dinghy and if that doesn't work then I'll try again later when we got more bait.'

I climbed back into *Ednamair* to try my hand at catching a dorado. Since they were game fish which fed mostly on flying fish I would have to use either live bait or a spinner, and since I had a spinner to hand I decided to try that. I looked doubtfully at the wire trace, wondering if it would be strong enough, as I fixed some weights to it and de-spooled a length of line. Before casting I took a couple of turns around the mast with the line and then swung the spinner and cast it thirty feet to the lee side, pulling it in smartly to make the spinner rotate. To my surprise three dorado dashed for the spinner, but turned away before striking. They were big fish and would surely break the line if I hooked one. I looked around to see if I could perhaps cast at a smaller one. I stretched out more line and made a few tentative casts in the direction of some smaller fish which resembled small jack, but they ignored the flash of the spinner, though once again the big dorado followed without being tempted to strike. Three small female dorado suddenly swam nearby and renewed hope rose within my breast as I cast the spinner well out ahead of them. To my utter dismay, I watched the spool of line curve outwards in a gentle arc after the spinner, to land in the water and sink quietly into the depths. The line had gone. I was tempted to go after it but a lively deterrent in the shape of a large triangular fin belonging to an oceanic white-tipped shark appeared on the other side of the raft, leaving me to curse my stupidity in frustrated anguish. How could I have been so careless as to leave the line unfastened? Our only spinner and its valuable wire trace, thrown over the side like so much garbage. I beat my brow with my knuckles and cursed. If I was going to make stupid mistakes like this now, what would it be like later? This was the sort of carelessness that cost lives at sea, and if I was already making such errors, what could I reasonably expect from newcomers to the sea like Robin, or youngsters like Neil and Sandy? I resolved to examine my every move before execution, and check every decision before it was acted upon, for sooner or later, because I had overlooked something, one of us would die.

I made my apologies to the others for losing the line and set to work immediately fashioning a second spinner from the tinfoil on the lid of the 'crumbs box'. Attaching a hook and weight to the nylon line, I was ready to cast again by midday. Returning to the raft for a mouthful of water, I was astonished to see that the twins had spruced themselves up and with Mum's help had actually combed their hair. They looked like they had just got ready to go ashore! Returning to the dinghy, I cast in all directions for nearly an hour, trolling at different speeds, trying variations of red and white bunting on the spinner and flying-fish heads on the hook, but all to no avail: the dorado would follow the line with interest but would not strike. I gave up exhausted, my mouth dry with thirst under the noonday sun, and tumbled back into the raft, depressed but glad to be in the cool again. Douglas, on watch for ships, motioned me to the door of the raft and pointed to a sinister triangular fin approaching; we gazed in dumb awe as the ten-foot-long torpedo-shaped silvertip shark glided quietly under the raft, its attendant bevy of pilot fish keeping station in perfect arrowhead formation across its back. We looked at each other and made a silent pact not to tell the twins of our unwelcome visitor.

Lunch consisted of a piece of orange with the peel, which we had decided we should not waste, together with a piece of biscuit followed by a small mouthful of water. Our meal was over all too soon and we settled down in the afternoon to rest during the heat of the day. The twins were finishing a sketch of 'Lucette and the whales' with pencil on sailcloth and Lyn was embroidering a message on some blue cloth in case our written letters were obliterated by immersion in seawater.

Fearing a mood of depression similar to that experienced after we had written our farewell letters, I decided it would be a good time to draw my chart. I fetched a piece of wood from the dinghy to use as a table, and laid out a dried-out reference map which we had saved from the now pulped West Indies Pilot. With a pencil I had found in Lyn's sewing basket I marked in the coordinates from the Panama Canal to the Marquesas Islands, with the Galapagos and as many of the islands as I could remember to the north. I then drew in the rhumb-line route from the Marquesas to the Panama Canal and our own position with our projected route to the doldrums.

'We should start crossing our next possible shipping route in a couple of days' time,' I remarked to my collective audience. Robin leaned over and studied my tiny scribbles. 'How far to land?' he queried. 'I'll have to draw that on a different scale,' I said, 'but you can see from my map that if we don't see a ship en route from the Canal westwards, our next chance won't come until we cross the shipping lanes from North America to Peru or Chile, and we'll have to get well to the east of the Galapagos before we reach them.'

I marked out a larger scale and from memory drew in the square from the American coast through the Galapagos to the position where we had been sunk, then northwards to take in the whole of the doldrums area, which at this time of the year stretched from about 5 degrees to 15 degrees north. I enlarged each boundary line to cover about 20 degrees of latitude as my chart neared the Central American coast. With the chart constructed, I lightly pencilled in the route which I thought we might take to get to land, northwest to the doldrums, then east-by-north or northeasterly to the coast. I had difficulty remembering which country started where on that stretch of coastline, but I knew it ran in a northwesterly direction all the way to Mexico. Robin had travelled down the isthmus by bus but was unable to provide much material assistance. He took the view that we would land several hundred miles north of Panama. 'Perhaps around Nicaragua,' he thought. I drew in our position, which I now estimated to be about 1 degree and 30 minutes north and 220 miles west of Espinosa (about 95 degrees west), and measured our distance from the limit of the doldrums. 'About 250 miles to go before we get rain,' I murmured, 'two hundred and fifty miles at fifty miles a day, five days, and we have' – I looked over to where the cans of water lay on the raft floor – 'ten tins of water left.' I paused with my head hung in my hands, and biting my tongue was unable to stop myself saying, 'We should make it – just!'

I tried to sound cheerful. While we could see that we had already grown thinner, we weren't exactly emaciated; indeed although Neil and Robin could ill afford to lose any weight from their already thin frames, I had been putting on weight before the attack. Sandy and Douglas were well fleshed, and Lyn had a pound or two of fat which she could afford to lose. We had good body reserves to live on, and if the wind held I felt we could reach the rain area in time, even though I knew the winds would die away before we reached the doldrums, as would the northwesterly current. Our margin for error was lamentably small, and the length of time we would have to drift between the trade winds before we reached the rain area was anybody's guess.

Robin looked at my little map and pointed questioningly to some squiggly arrows I had drawn on it. 'Those represent the counter-current which runs through the doldrums,' I replied to his unspoken question, 'and when we get there we should get a lift in the right direction. I don't think I've seen an estimate for the rate of the counter-current, but it should be at least half a knot,' I guessed out loud. I hoped it would be more but feared that an overzealous estimate would be a bad blow to our morale, if at the end of many weeks of arduous struggle we did not find land when we expected to see it. I measured up the distance covered by the dogleg course line with the can opener. 'About a thousand miles, fifty days at twenty miles a day; it doesn't sound bad if you say it quickly.' If we already looked thin after four days, I couldn't help but wonder what sort of condition we might be in after fifty. It was a grim prospect. 'Of course, we could reasonably expect to be picked up before then,' I said confidently. 'If nowhere else then most certainly on the busy coastal shipping routes leading to the Panama Canal.' Robin now looked a bit more cheerful, and he chatted happily to Lyn about his experiences as a porter in various hotels in Wales and Ireland during his university holidays. I had purposely said nothing of two tiny islands called Culpepper and Wolf, part of the Galapagos archipelago, which lay between us and the mainland. How nice it would be if we could land on one of them, but that would be a matter of luck as well as good navigation.

The raft now required topping up with air at much shorter intervals, three or four times a watch, and though we looked again for the leak it wasn't until Lyn went on watch in the evening that she spotted the telltale bubbles rising from under the towing straps. We spread out the puncture repair outfit to see if we could use any of the patches with the rather old rubber solution, which had deteriorated to the consistency of chewing gum. The patches were old ones too, and didn't have the sealing compound on them which one finds in a modern kit. We had four rubber plugs, some patches of ordinary rubberised fabric, and a bit of emery paper. We would have to try something in the morning. Maybe that tin of varnish would come in useful after all.

As the evening drew in and we had supped our morsels of food and water, we discussed ways in which we might catch the dorado. I thought that if we plunged our hands downwards as they skimmed under the edge of the raft, there was bound to come a time when we could grip them where the body of the fish narrows to the tail, the only place where it is possible to grasp and hold on to its slippery, streamlined body. We might have to try hundreds of times but since we had only sporadic duties to do at night, like looking for ships and blowing up the raft, we could try such a method in our spare time. Sandy's voice piped up as he asked casually if anybody had seen the sharks around; he'd just seen another two, and he'd wondered if they were the big fish we'd been whispering about to mum. 'They're man-eaters, too!' he added interestedly. We looked at each other and laughed at the folly of our secrecy, especially when we found out that Neil and Sandy had been talking about them all evening. It would take more than a rotten old shark or two to frighten them.

I had been considering our progress and proximity to the two small islands for the whole of the day. I looked at Douglas. He was well built and fit, and on him I pinned a hope that we might be rescued sooner rather than later. The weather had been a problem until now, but the waves were calming, and I hoped the following day would be even quieter. 'There are two out-islands north of the Galapagos chain and lying to the east, Doug,' I began in barely more than a whisper so that the others could not hear. He craned his neck in the darkness in order to listen as I continued, 'If the weather is fine tomorrow how do you feel about taking the dinghy and oars and as much of the rations as you need, enough for say two days, and seeing if you can reach them under oars to deliver an SOS?' 'Suppose they are uninhabited,' he came back guardedly. 'Then you can catch birds or fish, eat eggs and regain your strength and continue on to the main group of islands to the south; they would be clearly visible from there,' I asserted unknowingly. 'Our closest point of approach will be a little over sixty miles and you could cover that in two days easily, even against the current.' 'When?' came his reply through the darkness. 'Tomorrow,' I finished, giving him time to think it over. All the rowing he had done since Miami, and the expertise he had acquired with the dinghy, left me in no doubt that he could reach the islands. The question, however, was what he would find when he got there, and whether or not he would run out of water, if he had to go on to find the larger islands to the south.

During her night watch, I lay awake with Lyn and she told me how she could sometimes see her sisters Edna and Mary, after whom the dinghy had been named, sitting on the thwarts and pulling us towards safety. She talked to them in the long lonely hours when keeping her watch and they kept her company during the extra watches she stood, in order to allow Douglas and Robin a little more sleep. That night, however, the task of topping up became an exhausting half-hour marathon, which Douglas volunteered to assist with when required, as the forward flotation chambers were losing pressure rapidly, in fact almost as soon as we had stopped blowing.

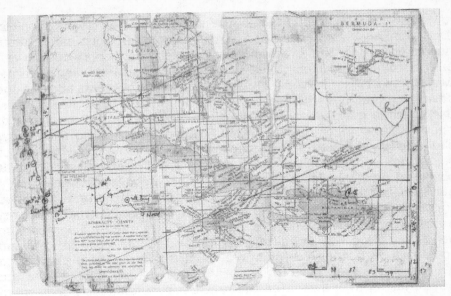

The map created by Dougal

Fifth day

Dawn brought with it a beautiful sunrise. We studied its rising orb in a mixture of quiet wonderment and deep reflection. The sea, now smooth in the gentle southerly breeze, reflected the beautiful colours of the Pacific with an incredibly intricate range of blues and reds that merged in ever-deepening arrays of stunning intensity. The morning clouds, little more than rounded tufts, ranged across the distant horizon with delicate tints of green and yellow mixed with multifarious shades of pink and orange, setting the whole sky ablaze with glorious colours suspended over a sea of the deepest azure blue, making the natural beauty of our surroundings truly breathtaking.

Another two flying fish represented the previous nights haul, one from the dinghy and the other from the raft, after it had flown in through the door during Robin's watch, with so much flap and slap that it had sounded more like a twenty-pound giant. Our harvest from the sea provided us with a two-inch strip of fish each for breakfast. Pacific flying fish are much smaller than their Atlantic brethren and in the Galapagos area the number of predators that prey upon flying fish gives one occasion to marvel that there are any left at all. As we enjoyed our breakfast, we were visited by another inquisitive turtle, which had approached the aft end of the raft where Douglas was keeping watch. It surveyed us with its bright yellow-and-black eyes, unblinking as it opened and closed its sharp hooked bill with menacing deliberate bites at the air. Brown in appearance, its leathery skin was covered with white scaly speckles and it bobbed its bony head up and down in the water only feet away from us. 'Dad, I'm going to have a go at catching it,' Douglas proclaimed, busily preparing the brass-ended bayonet connection of the raft paddle to use as a club. We watched in expectant silence as he waited for the right moment before raising the weapon and striking downwards across the back of its head. Its eyes immediately darkened as they filled with blood and it took off into the depths. It had no chance of surviving, yet still it escaped, making it blatantly clear that such a method on its own was never going to do the job.

'You know, Dad, that turtle clung on to its life regardless,' Douglas observed quietly. 'We don't think a turtle's life is worth considering, but the turtle does. Just because its death has become inevitable does not mean that it is willing to die here and now, or that it will not try to escape so it can have a few more hours of life.' I agreed with him. They were wild animals, after all, and fought back fiercely and could not be blamed for that. We couldn't expect them just to roll over and give their lives to us on a plate; we would have to find a way of taking their lives from them, whilst simultaneously preventing them from escaping.

Later that morning we allowed the raft to deflate at the towing end, where we had located the leak under the towing strap some three inches below the waterline. With Douglas holding the strain of the dinghy on the towrope, we doubled the floor back and managed to bring the damaged area into the body of the raft. Three small holes leaked air in an area of torn fabric under the strap, the result of *Ednamair* pulling too vigorously on the towrope in the strong breeze. We cleaned the surface and allowed it to dry in the hot sunshine, then after roughening the surface with some emery paper I tried to get the dried-out repair solution to stick in and around the small holes, but without success. We decided to try varnish as a substitute for glue. The sticky coats of varnish took half an hour to become tacky in the strong sun and after applying three coats to the raft as well as to the patches we stuck them together and waited a further hour for the varnish to harden without becoming brittle. Once inflated, the raft deflated even more quickly than before. Puzzled, I lifted the towing straps clear again. The patches seemed to have stuck so I asked Robin to inflate the damaged area again while I held it clear of the water. The pressure began to build until a telltale hiss of escaping air revealed itself from further along the side of the flotation chamber. I leaned over the doubled-up raft and found the hole, a quarter of an inch in diameter, worn in the fabric by one of the drogue trip ropes. No wonder we'd had to keep blowing! I plugged it with a rubber stopper and lashed the paper-thin fabric tight around the plug with nylon thread. By then the varnished patches had started peeling off so I stripped them off altogether and enlarged the pinholes in the fabric so that they were large enough to take a rubber plug. Once this operation was complete we blew up the chamber again, taking turn and turn about, whilst sitting in a row like the three wise monkeys. The chambers stayed inflated this time and we relaxed, happily relieved of our blowing routine, for a while at least.

After what passed for a lunch at midday, I caught Douglas's eye and nodded to the east. I was about to broach the subject of rowing when he interrupted me. 'Dad, I've thought of little else since you asked me.' His voice though trembling was assertive, and in a tone I had never heard from him before he said, 'It's risky and dangerous and ...' he paused for a moment, shaking his head, which was shielded by long shadows cast by the canopy under the remorseless sun, 'I've decided I cannot attempt it.' We exchanged glances and I knew instinctively I had let desperation cloud my judgement by foisting such a request on my young son's shoulders, for it would have been a fool's errand and would have ended in the deaths of us all. 'That's fine, son,' I concluded softly, trying to disguise the disappointment in my voice. 'Dad,' Douglas continued to stare at me, his eyes bright and clear as I turned my head towards the heaving seaway outside. 'Look at me, Dad, don't turn away. We may all die soon, and fingers may be pointed because I didn't agree to do it.' I made to refute such a possible allegation, but he lifted his finger to his lips in an effort to silence me. 'But Dad, I have made this decision because I think it is the right one. I've considered all the probable outcomes and I would rather die here with my family than die out there frightened, lost and alone, mourning the failure of what was always going to be an impossible task.'

Lyn, partially concealed by the shade, was listening too. 'Dad, I was nothing more than a lad a few days ago aboard the *Lucette*, but now I have had to make a decision that only a man should have to make. If, as a result, we are to die out here in the Pacific then I amongst us will die like a man, content in the knowledge that there had been a moment at least in my short life when I had acted like one too.' My face contorted in an emotional screwball as I reached my arms around my son's neck and hugged him to me. 'I'm so sorry to have burdened you with such a responsibility,' I whispered, truly repentant for my weakness and the lack of judgement I had shown. On the verge of tears, his voice heavy with emotion, my son's reply drove through me like a lance. 'Dad, now that I am a man, I want to be a man such as you!' Douglas had always lived in my shadow, always seeking reassurances from me in every decision-making aspect of his life. In a sweeping moment, he had broken that tie and realised that I was not the demigod he had always considered me to be, but just his old Dad who made errors and misjudgements like any other man.

Robin's blowing prowess was growing by leaps and bounds. Filling his lungs, he had learnt to blow with great gusto, improving his technique daily. I felt the exercise was doing him a lot of good, even though the loss of moisture it produced was a cost he could ill afford.

I worked out our noon position at 2 degrees and 6 minutes north and 230 miles west of Espinosa, using dead reckoning and making further adjustments for both wind and current. Whilst there was a fair measure of guesswork involved I could remember the currents from my ocean pilot books and estimated the force and direction of the wind, and hence the effects of leeway, from the sea state. There are precious few mile markers in the ocean, but I knew I would be able to check my position-keeping accuracy as the trade winds gave way to the doldrums and again when we sighted the Pole star on the other side of the equator. I had decided to stick to a longitude relative to the Galapagos, for it saved explaining to the others our position in terms of land. I also felt it pertinent to announce that we were now entering an area in which we might just see a passing ship. Robin had worked out, based on the assumption that twenty-five per cent of the French and New Zealand traffic took the rhumb-line route north of Galapagos, that there should be one passing through the area every two days. Unfortunately, his source data was based on my guesswork, which was none too knowledgeable in terms of shipping volumes.

During the afternoon we played Twenty Questions; Neil was particularly good at guessing the object, especially when Sandy had chosen it, even before many questions had been asked, whereas Robin was masterful at tracking down the objective with shrewd questions. Cumulus cloud built up again during the later hours of the day but the only visible shower of rain, falling from the base of the cloud in a grey curtain, missed us by miles. In an effort to buoy our spirits, I enquired if Robin would be interested in computing a statistical model of shower probability. He declined on the grounds that he would have to be supplied with the necessary data over a period of years as well as the correct theoretical bases so that his results could be meaningful, otherwise he could not accept responsibility for any decision that had relied on his determinations. Without fully understanding what he meant we teased Robin unfairly over his remarks, declaring that with or without his theoretical bases and highfalutin determinations, decisions had to be made in any event as the thirst and starvation we were suffering was anything but theoretical.

Amid great cheers, rain descended upon us just after dark, a heavy shower of short duration from which we collected half a pint of brackish yellow rubber-smelling water followed by a pint of fresh yellow rubber-smelling water. Our excitement subsided with the passing of the shower and we settled down again in our sodden clothing, feeling rich beyond measure because, for us, water was life itself. We rarely slept much now. The rising water levels in the raft afforded little comfort and were not conducive to sleep, besides which my mind seemed to be constantly monitoring our environment, listening to the sounds of the raft and the noise of the sea, as well as the movement of the fish and condition of the dinghy. When not observing such events I was thinking of ways of catching fish, of possible methods for straining plankton from the sea and of how to cover the raft canopy with sailcloth to exclude the filthy yellow dye from the water. When I had finished thinking, I would consider what might happen to us when the raft became untenable, as I felt sure it would do in the not too distant future. I was aware that Lyn lay awake during the nights too, and that her thoughts were never far away from devising methods of getting food and water into the twins' bodies and of helping them, and indeed the rest of us, to survive in the hostile and alien environment we were slowly coming to terms with. We now welcomed our call to go on watch, if only to relieve the burden of our furtive minds, for it allowed us to stop having to pretend that we were actually resting.

At about ten o'clock, the strange new sound of loud exhaling became discernible from the more usual noises of the ocean. We listened with bated breath as the source of the noise came closer and closer. Douglas, on watch, grunted from the door of the raft, 'Big whale and it's circling us.' Lyn and the children rolled their eyes in fear. The memory of the killer whales had grown more terrible with the passing of time and we all shared a fear that the raft was about to be attacked. With collective relief, we identified our travelling companion as a large and slow-moving sei whale, a species preyed upon by the killers. I tried to reassure Lyn that this one would not harm us for it lived by straining tiny plankton organisms from the sea. Nevertheless, she prayed with desperate appeal that we be spared a second attack. The whale surfaced many times around us during the following thirty minutes, often coming quite close. Even amid such nerve-jangling excitement, Sandy soon fell back into a deep sleep, and as the whale's venting blasts of foul-smelling breath coincided with uncanny accuracy with Sandy's snoring, we struck a common chord and laughed at their unmelodious duet.

A water leak developed in the forward compartment of the raft during the night, although the buoyancy compartment in the floor seemed undamaged. The influx of water seemed to come from the area where the dorado struck the raft most often, between the floor and side compartments, and made for yet more discomfort in circumstances that were already trying. The aft flotation compartment had also started to go soft for no apparent reason and I resolved to look for more leaks at first light.

Sixth day

This day started, for those of us not involved in watch-keeping, at the early hour of two in the morning when a noise like a sail in a gale, a flapping and slapping from aboard the *Ednamair*, announced the landing of a large fish. After miscalculating its flight path, it was desperately trying to put the error to rights. Quickly pulling the dinghy alongside the raft, I jumped aboard and fell on top of a huge dorado struggling in the bottom of the boat, its body arching violently as it attempted to escape. Hanging on with one hand to the part just forward of the tail, I pulled the knife from the thwart where it was kept and plunged it into the head just behind the eye and sawed desperately, finally severing the head altogether, then just to make sure that no reflex action would reactivate it I severed its tail as well. It was a beautiful thirty-five pound specimen, a monster amongst fish, and I quickly informed everyone of the joyful news. After washing the blood from my hands, chest and legs as best as I could in the darkness, I returned to the raft like an excited child at Christmas time, where I waited impatiently for morning to arrive. Just before daybreak, whilst we were still dozing quietly, a flying fish flew straight through the door of the raft and stuck Lyn full in the face. Now Lyn is a very steady and reliable person in a crisis, and seems to be able to do the right thing at the right time automatically, while less able people like myself are left floundering around wondering what should be done and in what order. On this occasion however her ear-splitting reaction to being slapped in the face by a wet fish in the early hours of the morning had us all scrambling around the raft looking for something akin to the Loch Ness monster, until the eight-inch leviathan was finally secured and made safe for breakfast.

There was no sleep for us after that and as soon as daylight had dispelled the shadows inside the raft I returned to the *Ednamair* to dress the dorado. I saved the liver and heart for breakfast along with its huge backbone, its head and some thicker pieces of white fleshed fillet from the back. The remainder I cut into long strips and hung from the stays, allowing them to dry in the sun. Our larder was off to a flying start in more ways than one! Later that morning, whilst cleaning the dinghy out, I found another flying fish lying in a tuck of the sail, which together with the other fare afforded us our first decent breakfast since *Lucette* had been so brutally taken from us. Lyn made us a raw fish stew, flavoured with lemon juice, onion and a concoction of fish liver and heart with small pieces of flying fish, marinated in lemon juice. It tasted truly magnificent and we followed it with our last orange, which was beginning to go bad, together with a sip of water. Our stomachs, unaccustomed to this bulk, felt quite full and afterwards we lay down to digest what had seemed like a banquet, finishing off with a section of backbone apiece, which we picked at with methodical precision. Robin gnawed at the head in good old-fashioned caveman style, while the rest of us first picked the bone clean then, under Lyn's direction, split the vertebrae to find tiny sacks of spinal fluid, full of protein and fresh water. Even Neil, who seemed to find his hunger more irksome than the rest of us, declared himself content.

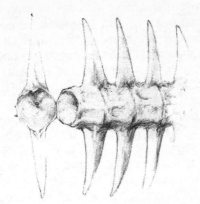

Fluid can be sucked from the spinal cavities of a fish

After breakfast, with the heads of two flying fish and some offal from the dead fish at my disposal, I went over to the *Ednamair* with the fishing line and some hooks, determined to have another go at the dorado. I tried a large hook first, casting well out from the dinghy to try to avoid the bait being eaten by the small scavenger fish which patrolled the sea around us. As I trolled the bait in towards the dinghy, the scavenger fish were onto it in a flash, their small mouths and sharp teeth making a mockery of the large hook as they tore the bait from it. The dorado followed the bait but made no attempt to strike, so I weighted the line with a sinker and, after baiting the hook again, sent it fifty feet down, avoiding the scavenger fish by casting well out. Tensely I waited for a strike but by the time it came, some fifteen minutes later, my over-tensed muscles were no longer ready for it. After a sudden slackening of the line, followed immediately by the slightest of gentle snatches, I slowly pulled in the bare end of line to discover both hook and sinker gone. Razor-sharp teeth had made short work of the nylon line, even cutting through the steel trace wire as if it had been made of butter.

I fixed a small hook on the end of the line, baited it with offal and returned to try and catch the scavengers, but my smallest hook was far too big to fit into their mouths and they merely ate the bait off it as soon as it entered the water. By midday I was tired of feeding the fish and returned to the raft with a few lumps of our midnight dorado for lunch. I felt we ought to eat the fish while it was still wet, for we wouldn't be able to eat it after it had dried until we had enough water to drink with it. I put our noon position at 2 degrees 40 minutes north and 240 miles west of Espinosa. There had been no ships and no rain, but Douglas's sharp eyes had detected a trace of cirrostratus cloud in the northern sky and we all knew from experience that this was a possible forerunner of weather systems and of storms, which could all bring rain. Douglas and Robin were busy investigating the influx of water into the forward compartment of the raft, and soon found the seepage to be coming in through a paper-thin section of fabric in the crease between the bottom and the side flotation chambers. Lyn had also found another small hole in the floor of the after section, which we were able to plug with a small piece of rubber. Later Douglas located the air leak in the after port side flotation chamber. Well under the water, it proved impossible to investigate without lifting the offending chamber completely out of the water, which would require turning the entire section upside down whilst we were still in it.

The sky darkened from the north as the afternoon progressed and I looked hopefully for signs of rain. The gentle layer of stratocumulus showed unmistakable signs of an occluded front, which was no longer active. It provided no rain on this occasion but we took heart from the simple fact of its existence. What was more, Douglas observed that it was travelling south, contrary to and high above the trade winds, in a direction away from the doldrums. With only seven pints of water left our spirits lifted at this most encouraging of signs.

The cloud belt sheltered us from the heat of the sun during the early hours of the afternoon, but as the skies cleared the radiated heat of the descending sun beat into the raft and we lapsed into a long spell of silent endurance. We sought scant relief by splashing water on what was left of our clothes and on the raft canopy, to reduce not only the raft's temperature but also our own body heat. Our clothing had suffered the effects of increased wear and tear right from the start, and Douglas had now discarded his tattered swimming trunks completely to ease the pain from the area of raw flesh around his buttocks and thighs, developed as a result of continuous contact with the salt water. Neil was similarly affected and Lyn had ripped the bottom section from her already torn housecoat, to protect his thighs from rubbing on the rough sailcloth, while preserving her own modesty by fabricating a rather ineffectual bikini from a separate piece of sail. My shorts had disintegrated completely, leaving me with only my underpants, whilst Robin and Sandy had managed so far to preserve their swimsuits intact. The boys had shirts and my top, though somewhat bloodstained, was still in one piece.

When the sun was at its zenith Douglas shared with the rest of us his discovery that by chewing and sucking on pieces of rubber band he had obtained from the sewing basket, saliva was created in his mouth, which in turn eased the burden of his thirst. The afternoon sun crept round to the port side of the raft, leaving us gasping in the torrid heat, until evening finally brought us respite. Lyn quietly arranged the bedding so that we should at least start the night with dry sheets and then passed the water round for sips. Our eyes followed the movement of the jar intently, as it moved from one to the other's lips, before being passed to the twins. Lyn saw that they had a mouthful each and, after wetting her own lips, placed the now empty jar back in its place. I watched the dark shadows under Douglas's eyes as he kept lookout for ships, his mouth working hard to try to retain the saliva and dispel the foul taste of thirst from his dry mouth. His face had become much thinner and the hollowness of his cheeks, clenched against the dryness of his palate, gave his head a skull-like appearance. Under the mounting pressure caused by the deteriorating condition of my children, I closed my mind and shut my eyes, trying to consider anew the problem of how to select and catch suitable fish without interference from the constantly attendant scavengers or sharks. I could only think of one answer, a spear of some description. I had seen plenty of fish spears on my travels, but their strength and design lay in a type of wood that was not available to me on the raft. It would need a reasonably thick shaft to provide sufficient strength and the point would have to be reinforced to give the softer wood at my disposal more penetrating power.

As the evening shadows darkened the inside of the raft, I opened another tin of water and decanted it into the jar. Lyn prayed quietly for rain and Robin, resting from a rapid spell of blowing, stared dully at the jar for a moment before turning his face back to the canopy, whence after sticking the tube back in his mouth he recommenced blowing with dogged determination. Douglas, sponge in hand, mopped up the seawater in the bottom of the raft while the twins helped break out the food boxes, ready for our last meal of the day. The breeze blowing gently from the south now died away, leaving the sea almost calm except for the marching swells produced by the southeast trades, whilst *Ednamair*'s sail hung limp for the first time since we had started our voyage north. We still had about 150 miles of northing to make before we would come under the influence of the doldrums weather system. With only six pints of water left, including the brackish stuff, I wondered if instead of reaching the Doldrums as we had planned we were in fact reaching the end of our road.

We each ate our small piece of fish in silence, and sucked at our small sections of lemon with an ecstasy of taste unequalled in my previous existence. We had one remaining lemon in the fruit bag and we each examined it in turn as though it were a nugget of purest gold, for in our diminished state it represented wealth beyond measure. Before darkness fell we sipped one last time from the water jar and lay down to ease the long hours of the night away dreaming of ice cream and fresh fruit with a detachment worthy of monastic meditation, as desire was subrogated to the rigours of self-denial. Meanwhile, slowly and relentlessly, the water seeped in beneath us, just as surely as the air seeped out from around us.

Seventh day

The windless night filled our ears with unaccustomed silence and in the quiet of the smooth calm swell the phosphorescent gleam of large dorado streaked from under the raft, to leap high into the air and land in bursting showers of green glowing fire, creating vivid displays rarely seen by man. It was the beginning of our second week as castaways and the foul dryness of our mouths aggravated the discomfort of our sleepless bodies, as we tried to ease the agony of our thirst, twisting first one way and then the other in a non-stop restless torment. Breathlessly we watched the gathering clouds obscure the stars, and as dawn paled the eastern horizon we looked on with excited expectation as droplets began to fall from the sky, and then whooped loudly in delight as the rain turned into a heavy shower, and gradually became a vicious downpour. Slowly the water in the pipe from the canopy ran clear and we filled our empty cans and spare plastic bags, as well as our bellies and our mouths until we could not force down another drop. We lay with our faces turned to the sky and let the pure fresh water cleanse the salt from our beards and hair; suddenly everything had changed from the shadow of the spectre of death to the joyful prospect of life and all by the advent of a shower of rain. We would make it to the doldrums now!

We lay uncaring, chewing strips of dorado and revelling in the absence of thirst; talking animatedly of good food and watching the bulging plastic water bags swing lazily from the roof of the canopy. What a difference that hour made and how good it felt to have water!

Douglas, lazily watching the dispersing clouds, suddenly sat up with a start, pointing excitedly towards the horizon. 'A ship! A ship! It's a bloody ship!' We crowded in a tense huddle at the door of the raft, staring in the direction of his pointing finger; a cargo vessel of about 6,000 tons was approaching us on a course that would bring her within a couple of miles of our present position. I felt my heart pound against my ribs. 'Get out the flares,' I stammered hoarsely, barely able to believe my eyes, 'and pass them to me in the dinghy, they'll see us better from there.'

A couple of miles was a fair distance, but on a dull overcast day like this, against a background of cloud and light rain, they should see us easily. I clambered into the dinghy and with hands a-tremble Douglas passed me the rockets and hand flares. My own hands shook uncontrollably too, as I ripped open a parachute rocket flare and, with a mute appeal to the thing to work, struck the igniter against the fuse. It spluttered and hissed, then roared off on a trajectory high above the raft, its pinkish magnesium flare slowly spiralling downwards leaving a trail of smoke in the sky. They couldn't fail to see it. I waited a moment or two, watching for the telltale shift in aspect that would confirm the ship was altering her course, then struck a hand flare and held it high above my head. The blinding red light was hot to hold and I pointed it away from the wind to ease the scorching heat being radiated onto my hand, as the red embers of the flare dropped into the dinghy. As the flare spluttered and died, I struck another, smoke from the first now rising in a heavy plume skywards. 'They must see that, surely?' muttered Douglas tentatively, doubt clearly evident in his every word, as he tried to catch what sun there was in the heliograph and signal an

SOS. I waited a little longer, my hands shaking as the blood in my veins slowly curdled. 'This chance might not come again,' I said to the anxious faces crowding the door of the raft, 'I'm going to use our last rocket flare and one more hand flare.' 'Fire it at the ship,' Douglas urged fiercely, pointing at its line of bridge windows. 'I cannot,' I stated flatly, 'they may be carrying explosives on deck and if the flare was to set her on fire then we could end up sinking them!' 'Huh, at least we would have some company,' came back his scoffed reply as he took up the whistle and blew loud SOS Morse signals across the water.

Douglas already sensed it was sailing on by, and for a moment I saw just how single-minded and ruthless he had become, for he was already prepared to consider his own survival at the cost of others. The thin veneer of civilisation had all but deserted him as he had come to terms with the brutal business of survival. 'No, we do things by the book,' I stated piously as we watched the second rocket flare soar and spiral its gleaming distress message high above us; desperately I struck the third hand flare and held it high, standing on the thwart whilst clinging precariously to the mast, no longer caring that I may cause it to capsize.

'Look, look, you bastards!' I shouted as anger and fear gripped my soul and sent my brain into a mindless swirl. 'Set fire to the sail!' Lyn's desperate plea reached me from the raft entrance. I stuck the flare to the sail but it only melted. The ship sailed towards us in an unfaltering line, getting closer by the second, its name *Straat Cook*, etched in black, clearly discernible along the white forecastle bulwark. We watched in wretched anguish as she slowly disappeared behind a rain shower, and when she reappeared her hull was already half obscured by the horizon. She was five miles distant and getting further away with every passing moment. The time was eleven o'clock. Crestfallen, my body wilted in capitulation. 'We dare not use another flare,' I stated hoarsely. 'They won't see it now and we have to keep something for the next ship.' Another minute ticked slowly by before we grimly surrendered to the awful realisation that we were being left behind. 'Stop whistling, son,' I whispered tearfully to Douglas, placing my arm around his tensely bunched shoulders. Disregarding my gesture, he blew obsessively on the life-raft whistle in long continuous blasts which pierced the air in loud mournful blasts. Submitting to the futility of his effort, he stopped blowing and began weeping profusely, quite unable to believe that we had been so near to salvation and yet so bitterly far.

'Don't leave us,' he pleaded pitifully after the vanishing ship, 'don't leave us here to die,' his deep guttural sobs reflecting our private and mutual thoughts. The others were crying too. How nice it would have been to be rescued just then. We were still fit and had not really suffered any irreversible damage or loss of life. Now it seemed to us that all was lost and we had just missed our best chance of getting home alive. A stunned silence ensued which was eventually broken with a feigned cheer from Lyn. 'It says in the instruction book that the first one probably wouldn't see us,' she recalled sadly, 'and I'd already told the twins not to expect anything,' she finished with a glance in my direction as she gathered the twins to her and comforted them. We stared at the dwindling speck on the horizon and felt so deserted and alone that it hurt. 'I'm sorry, lads,' I grated with sombre resignation, and returned to the raft tired and empty. 'We always considered that one of the most important tenets of good seamanship was to keep a good lookout.' 'Not on board that ship,' quipped Robin, trying to lighten our collective mood. In a bolstering of spirit we all agreed that the sailors aboard the *Straat Cook* seemed to be a pretty poor bunch of seamen.

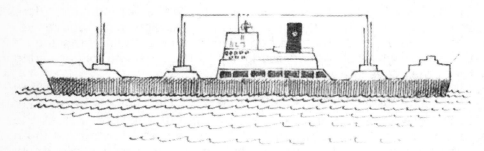

The ship that didn't see us

Our position was 3 degrees north and 240 miles west of Espinosa, which I calculated was almost 95 degrees and 20 minutes west. The date was Wednesday 21 June or, as Lyn reminded us, back home in England it would be midsummer's day. I surveyed our last three flares and the empty flare cartons bitterly. My eyes focused on the one smoke flare which was damp and wouldn't work, and in that instant a change came over me which altered my whole perspective of our dilemma. 'If those wretched bloody seamen couldn't rescue us, then we will have to make it on our own and to hell with them,' I proclaimed, for we could survive without help from them or assistance of any other kind. We would no longer depend on rescue from the likes of those, but set our minds on survival and on that aspect alone. 'If we are going to make it out of this, then we have to survive, and survive on our own!' I stated assertively, feeling strength and incredible resolve flood back into me, which lifted me from the abyss of depression and disappointment to a state of almost cheerful abandon. I felt the bitter aggression of the predator fill my mind. This was not our environment and the beasts around us would eat us if we failed. We would carve a place for ourselves amongst them; they had millions of years of adaptation on their side,

▲ The family all together in Bimini, just before Anne's departure.

▲ Anne on the ferry that took her to Nassau. She left us in Bimini to start her new life with Jeff.

▼ *Lucette* at anchor in Miami.

▲
Lyn boarding the seaplane in Miami to rejoin the family in Nassau.

◀ *Lucette* in dry dock in Miami.

The Robertson family meet the chief of the clan in Jamaica.
▼

► Rescue at last. Dougal and Douglas haul on the painter to pull the *Ednamair* alongside the *Toka Maru*.

Aboard the *Toka Maru* with the Japanese in Panama City.
▼

◄ Neil being carried ashore in Panama.

► Hidemi Saito, the boy who saw us from the *Toka Maru*.

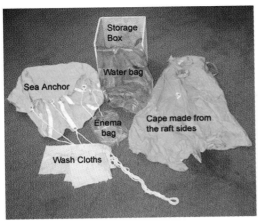

▲ Equipment saved from the dinghy.

Storage Box
Water bag
Sea Anchor
Enema bag
Cape made from the raft sides
Wash Cloths

▲ Douglas demonstrating the use of a cape made from the canopy of the raft, and the water bag that held the entire reserve of water.

Turtle fat with bag.

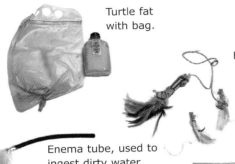

Fishing hooks.

Enema tube, used to ingest dirty water.

The heliograph used by Douglas in an attempt to attract the attention of the *Straat Cook.*

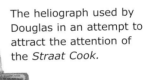

Articles saved from Lyn's sewing basket.
▼

Teeth from a shark we caught in the dinghy.

The 'little supper' made up for the twins every night on the raft.

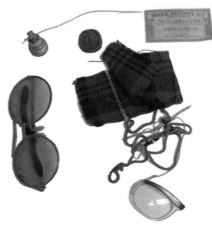

▲
Artefacts saved from the dinghy. The bag was used to hold fat, which the sun rendered into oil. We used it to rub on our bodies, to cover our sores, to drink when cold, and even as enemas, all to prevent dehydration.

Stores left over from the dinghy. ▼

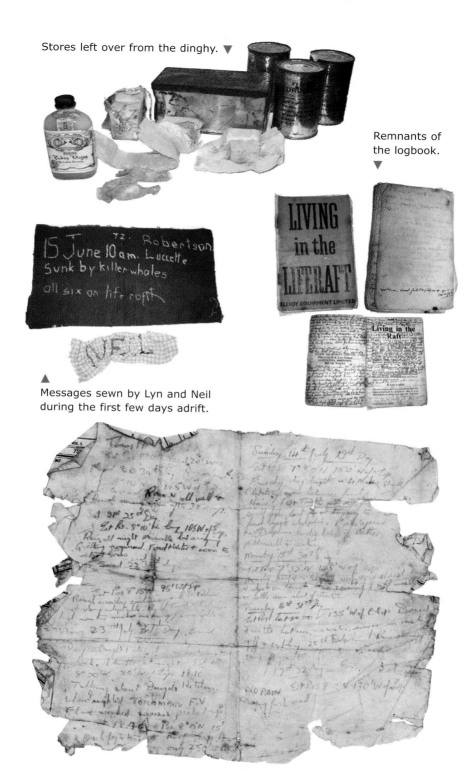

Remnants of the logbook. ▼

15 June 10 am. Lucette
Sunk by killer whales
all six on life raft

72. Robertson

NEIL

▲
Messages sewn by Lyn and Neil during the first few days adrift.

LIVING
in the
LIFERAFT
ELLIOT EQUIPMENT LIMITED

Living in the
Raft

▲ Extract from Dougal's log on the day of the rescue.

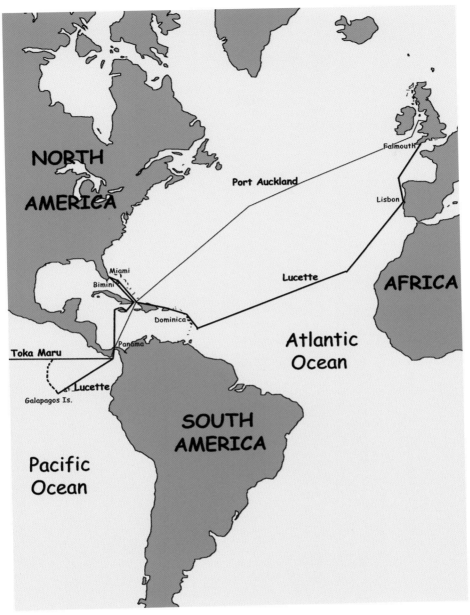

NORTH
AMERICA

Port Auckland

Falmouth

Lisbon

Miami
Bimini

Lucette

AFRICA

Dominica

Panama

Atlantic
Ocean

Toka Maru

Lucette

Galapagos Is.

SOUTH
AMERICA

Pacific
Ocean

▲ Map of the entire voyage.

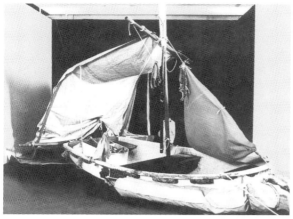

◀ *Ednamair*, fully dressed at the 1973 London Boat Show.

▶
Douglas with Valerie Singleton at the 1973 Boat Show.

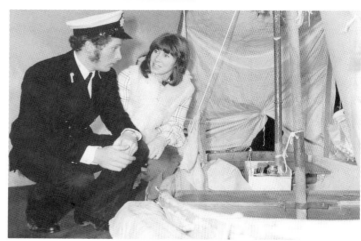

◀ The tanker *British Ambassador* in the Persian Gulf in 1975.

(Below left) Men away as *British Ambassador* sinks in the north Pacific in 1975. (Below right) The last night of the tanker. She did not survive until the morning.
▼

▲ Home at last: the survivors.

▲ The three sisters: Lyn (centre) with Edna and Mary, after whom the *Ednamair* was named.

▲ Lyn with Ali McGraw in Australia in 1991, during the shooting of the film *Survive the Savage Sea*.

◀ Dougal Robertson, author of *Survive the Savage Sea.*

▶

Lucette rounding a cardinal buoy in the North Sea in the 1920s, shortly after she was built. She appears with her transom stern, gaff-rigged sails and flat coach roof, all of which were redesigned following the fire in 1936.

but we had brains and some tools backed by a new-found resolve and determination. We would live for three months or six months from the sea if necessary but 'We would get these boys to land' as Lyn had said and if there was no other way we would do it on our own! From that instant on I became a savage, and 'the book' that I had so piously clung to, when considering Douglas's proposal of firing the flare at the ship, went out of the proverbial window.

We lunched on dry fish, a half biscuit and a tiny piece of glucose to cheer us up, followed by a good mouthful of water, after which I returned to the *Ednamair* to clear up the debris of empty flare cases and burnt powder. I busied myself with the cleaning up and re-stowed what remained of our worldly goods, and then thought long and hard about our new policy. Like a bolt out of the blue, a catchphrase blazed across my mind, 'Survival not rescue'. That was how I would alter my family's perception, a slogan to reset our expectations to survive to the very end, survive until we got to land, and if we were rescued it would be nothing more than an interruption to our survival routine. In that fleeting moment, it all became so clear to me and, returning to the raft, I shared my re-born vision with my family straightaway. With renewed enthusiasm I announced, 'From now on we have a new password. We forget words like rescue, for we can expect none, and we think of our existence only in terms of survival.' Lyn nodded immediately. 'What's the password for today?' she called to the twins. 'Survival,' they echoed and they seemed to understand that it was no longer a question of if, but more a question of when, we would reach land. Robin seemed to regard our change of attitude with mild indifference, but in Douglas's eyes I could see that the shadow of the ship's passing would haunt him for the rest of his days.

The wind rose from the south again and I decided to stream the sea anchor, to hold the raft in the shipping lanes for as long as I could. I was tempted to carry straight on, but rescue is after all part of the survival exercise and it would have been reckless not to maximise our chances when their probability seemed highest. In my heart, I considered it nothing more than paying lip service to the ordinary practices of seamen. In two days, the current would have carried us beyond the shipping lanes and we could then proceed on our voyage to the coast. With the sea anchor streamed and the sail reefed, I returned to the raft and settled down for a rest when an excited call from Sandy brought us all to the aft doorway. A huge hammerhead shark glided six feet below us and became entangled with the mushroom-shaped sea anchor for a moment. Its wicked eye leered up at us with a savage intensity as it watched our every move. The twins gazed down at it in fascinated awestruck silence, not in the least afraid, and discussed its more dangerous man-eating practices with Douglas as dispassionately as if they were visiting an aquarium on an afternoon outing.

10-foot hammerhead shark

Towards late afternoon we felt an unusually hard bump on the raft floor, quite unlike the quick thrust of the striking dorado. Douglas poked his head out of the stern door of the raft and found himself gazing at the large scaly head of a turtle. Its protruding yellow eyes set above its sharp hooked beak, it scrutinised us with a dispassionate unblinking stare. The day before I would have said, 'Leave it, we can't manage that,' but now things were different. 'We'll have this one,' I confirmed, indicating that we should try to land it aboard the dinghy. Douglas enthusiastically set about capturing his quarry, remembering his previous escapades. This time he snared the turtle's flippers with the rescue line from the raft and the beast, confused by its struggles, became ever more entangled in the line. With the turtle trapped, Douglas hobbled its flippers with tight loops of the cord and then tethered it with a rope something akin to a dog on a lead, before passing a second rope over the raft, which I made fast to the dinghy. Carefully avoiding the searching beak, Douglas freed the turtle from the rescue line and on his signal I pulled the struggling animal around to the *Ednamair*. Douglas quickly scrambled onto the dinghy and together we pulled the now belligerent turtle alongside. We twisted the turtle around until its back was adjacent to the dinghy, summoned our maximum strength and, gripping it by its back flippers, heaved it aboard in carefully timed unison. 'One, two and three,' it was surprisingly heavy and as it came aboard it tilted the dinghy alarmingly, which forced me to throw my weight to the other side in order to trim her. With a heavy bump and a thrashing of claws, the reptile was soon on its back in the bottom of the boat, all eighty pounds of it!

I put my thumbs up to the twins and Robin, who were watching intently from the raft and cheering excitedly. Avoiding the chopping flippers I studied the armoured amphibian with a farmer's eye. This was the difficult bit: just how was I going to kill it? Should I sever an artery or try Dougie's paddle on the head technique? I had helped to slaughter a few pigs and lambs in the past and leant on that experience to help in tackling the problem before me. With Douglas holding the beast in place, I grasped the pointed knife in my right hand and, putting a foot on each of the front flippers, held its beak with my left hand and plunged the knife into the leathery skin surrounding its neck, thrusting deep into the spinal column. With quick outward strokes of the knife to right and left, I cut both vein and artery in the grizzly act of execution. Deep red blood spurted into the bottom of the dinghy and gradually the beak and flippers ceased thrashing as the beast slowly bled to death. Apart from a few minor scratches I was unscathed, and as the approaching dusk gathered overhead I washed the blood from my hands into the bottom of the dinghy, careful not to spill any in the water. I didn't want to bring any more inquisitive sharks around, especially our hammer-headed friend, at least not until we had started moving again, for if they suspected that the blood came from the raft they could possibly attack the inflatable raft with disastrous consequences. Excitedly we discussed this substantial addition to our larder. Lyn recalled from the recesses of her mind that turtle livers were inedible so we decided to discard the offal rather than risk illness. Twenty-four hours previously, I would not have had the stomach for such a bloody business but the laws of survival were governed by the sternest of guiding principles. 'Survive or be survived upon' – such law was now our way of life. We would struggle and endure, and where our reflexes were not as swift as those of the animals and fish around us we had cunning and persistence; we were also developing new skills that seemed based on some deeply embedded instinct, all of which would improve with practice.

The wind steadily increased during the evening and the sea became noisy about the raft again. Inside, our bodies twisted and turned restlessly seeking a comfortable position, for only the twins were small enough to lie down full length on the floor. Water slopped around the depressions in the inflated rubber flooring made by our hip-bones and elbows, and the sound of the watch-keeper blowing up the flotation chambers became just another sound of the night for those of us trying to get some rest. To the watch-keeper however each stint was becoming an exhausting routine of bailing and blowing, which left our mouths red and sore and our hands stiff and cramped. It was at about this stage of the proceedings that tiny pimples, forerunners of much larger saltwater boils, began stinging not only our hands and feet but also our legs, arms and buttocks. With the need to catch not only our food but also our water, and pay ever increasing amounts of attention to the needs of the raft and dinghy, we were finding less and less time to look for ships!

Eighth day

As dawn broke, we awoke to the grim realisation that the ship had not seen us. As if reading our minds, Lyn called from her watch-keeping at the doorway, 'What's the password for the day?' The answer 'survival' was echoed by us all with surprising vigour as we set about the morning chores of mopping up and drying the bedding with a cheerfulness scarcely appropriate to our desperate situation. I went over to *Ednamair* to dress the turtle. It took me an hour and a half to remove the belly shell, sawing and hacking with the knife blade, which grew blunter as the shell seemed to grow thicker. Finally, with a bit of undercutting I managed to lift the shell off to reveal its entrails, allowing me to set about extracting the meat. It was evident that the turtle would have a poor killing-out ratio, less than thirty per cent, and its joints seemed to be located in the most inaccessible of places. It took me another hour to hack out the shoulder meat and the heavy red muscle surrounding the back flipper bones. I opened the stomach cavity and found, to my delight, a golden cascade of egg yolks. They hung like huge bunches of yellow grapes as I pulled them out, one ream after another. I cut some meat from the shoulder joint and then with a couple of dozen eggs placed in a dish returned to the raft with breakfast, where my family waited curiously for their first taste of turtle meat.

All of us eyed the raw meat with more than a little reservation. A grace of Robert Burns came to my mind and I quoted aloud:

Some hae meat and canna eat, some hae nane and want it,
But we hae meat and we can eat, so let the Lord be thankit.

Neil grinned and sank his teeth into a piece of red turtle steak. 'Good,' was all he managed after which we all set to with a will. We swallowed the egg yolks, bursting them like overripe plums inside our mouths, allowing their creamy richness to permeate our taste buds, savouring the flavour of the raw food as only starving people can. Robin declined the eggs on the basis that they were too rich for him but chewed vigorously at the tender meat, declaring that he enjoyed his steaks 'rare'. Douglas, Lyn and Sandy, after some initial hesitation, chewed at the pieces of meat with increasing interest, as initial rejection of the idea of eating raw meat gave way to a nodding acceptance of its taste. We washed it down with a draught of water and lay back, reflecting on our good fortune. If we could catch turtles and rain, we would survive all right. I thought of the fish spear again. With turtles and dorado, we would have wealth beyond measure!

I returned to the dinghy and carefully skinned the flippers and neck as well as the head, which Douglas wanted to keep for a souvenir, following which I carefully collected the offal into the shell ready to tip over the side once we had started moving again. Next, I cut the meat from the bones and divided it into small pieces, which I laid out across the thwart to dry in the sun. We had about twenty pounds of meat and bone altogether. *Ednamair* looked like the bloodiest of slaughterhouses, with strips of bloody meat and stacked body parts festooned about her. The dorado strips, which had almost dried to a turn, produced a very pleasant taste indeed. The huge turtle shell lay in the bottom of the dinghy, resembling a small bath, and we tried to imagine possible uses to which it could be put. My first thought was that I might be able to use a hard sliver to arm the spear, but the knife proved too blunt to shape the barbs and the shell itself was too brittle where it had dried out and not hard enough where it remained wet.

With the meat drying nicely, my return to the raft with another meal was hailed with shouts of glee, and lunchtime found us happily gnawing bones and engaging in light-hearted repartee. With the inside of the raft shaped like a cave, it was not difficult to imagine that we had slipped back a few thousand years in time, for not only did we look like cave dwellers, we were beginning to feel like we had actually joined their ranks.

I noted with interest that the temperature of the sea had risen by several degrees, the sign I had been watching for that would confirm we were no longer under the influence of the Humboldt Current. Our noon position, after a night at sea anchor in relatively quiet weather, had changed little from the previous day. I therefore recorded it in my 'log' as 3 degrees north with the longitude equal to a point 240 miles west of Cape Espinosa, the same as the day before. My actual logbook had of course been lost with *Lucette*, but I was keeping a scrap log, around the edges of the pages of the raft's instruction manual. At intervals during the afternoon, I crossed over to the *Ednamair* in order to turn over the drying turtle meat, hanging some on the stays and mast in order to make the most of every last bit of space available. Since we now had an interest in dry weather as well as rain, we comforted ourselves in the heat of the day with the thought that the drying turtle meat and fish would benefit, even if we didn't. Watch-keepers also had a dual reason for looking out for rain showers now, for the meat had to be brought under cover before it was rained upon, as getting it wet after the drying process had started would simply make it rot instead of dry.

Douglas and Robin had been investigating the influx of water into the raft again, plugging a small hole with a bobbin of cotton thread, which reduced the flow though it failed to eradicate it altogether. Even in the heat of the day, the flotation chambers had lost a great deal of pressure through the fabric and this had to be constantly replaced by blowing, in order to keep the raft as rigid as possible and so avoid undue wear from a combination of chafing, flexing and rubbing. Whilst I worked at providing and maintaining our reserves of food, Lyn and the boys worked hard at keeping the raft afloat and as dry as possible.

Lyn's day was full to overflowing, not only with keeping the twins occupied but also with tending to our various ailments, which were becoming more numerous with the onset of skin eruptions due to our limbs being constantly immersed in salt water. She insisted on a daily routine of leg and arm exercises for the twins, regardless of their protests, and saw that their bedding was dried each morning, in spite of the fact that it was soaked again shortly after it was placed over us. In our state of sensory denial, that initial feeling of snuggling down under dry sheets meant a lot to us. Only Robin had executed a bowel movement since the *Lucette* had sunk, and that shortly after joining the raft, so Lyn started agitating for a tube to be found, suitable for her to administer enemas, so that the unpalatable brackish water in the bottom of the dinghy could be absorbed rectally in the form of water retention enemas. Whilst I was perplexed at the engineering problems involved, I felt the idea was probably a good one, but as no solution presented itself the idea was temporarily shelved.

More serious was Lyn's anxiety over Neil's listlessness and his quicker deterioration in body condition than the rest of us, probably as a result of his initial bouts of seasickness. After much debate, we opted to allow extra rations for the twins, as long as the rest of us could obtain food from the sea. The emergency rations container was handed over to Lyn to be kept as supplementary rations for the twins only, for we all agreed that their digestions were less able to cope with the raw food, in the way that our adult bodies could.

As we lay down to rest that evening, we had resolved many of our doubts and anxieties, but more unsettling problems were already looming larger on the horizon. How much longer would the raft last? How often would we catch a turtle? How long could we do without vitamins, especially vitamin C, before bodily deterioration or scurvy set in? There were a thousand and one questions and no textbooks in which to look for the answers.

Ninth day

The southeast trade winds increased to a freshening force five during the night, keeping the watch-keepers busy with the bailer as the raft jerked uneasily between the sea anchor on one side and the pull of *Ednamair* on the other. The temperature of the seawater had grown noticeably cooler again, indicating that we were once more within the westerly set of the Humboldt Current. Although we had no means of steering the raft, we found it possible to slant the sail so that the dinghy pulled across the wind at an angle of about 45 degrees. This gave us course options ranging over some 90 degrees of arc, allowing us to steer from northeast to northwest and all points in between. We relied initially on observations of the sun and stars for orientation, and having found the relevant direction of the underlying swell, used it to record our course without reference to the sun, which climbed overhead at noon and became so high as to be unreadable. The wind too had started to become variable and unreliable, changing direction without being detected on several occasions. The wind had originally blown consistently from the southeast, but was becoming less constant and would continue to become less consistent in both strength and direction as we approached the doldrums. I discussed my methods of navigation at great length with Douglas, for I wanted to be sure that he was able to determine our direction and rate of travel on his own, in case for any reason I wasn't there to give it.

I estimated our noon position at 3 degrees 10 minutes north and 243 miles west of Espinosa. With our morning chores over, we lunched on a little dried dorado and some half-dry turtle meat, which tasted much nicer than the raw stuff, but required more water to digest it. We finished off with a small piece of onion, which left us with only two remaining. It made a pleasant change from our tiny piece of biscuit and Lyn, putting her culinary genius to work, managed to concoct 'egg-nog' from a dozen turtle eggs mixed with a cup of water, some glucose and a sprinkling of the dried yeast which we had rescued from the sewing basket. Robin had previously professed an aversion to turtle eggs but he drank his share of this mixture with relish; indeed, we all enjoyed the exciting new flavour.

The afternoon was baking hot, the sun's rays radiating through the double canopy with savage intensity, as we lay around in listless repose, waiting for the evening when the earth's shadow would shield us once more from the blazing orb. I was lying near the canopy door, my forearm seeking the saltwater coolness of the leaking floor, when my hand inadvertently brushed against the cotton plug we had used to seal one of the leaks. Impulsively I extracted it with a swift pull, allowing water to flood into the raft. Robin started up in alarm but I raised my arm to allay his fears. 'Come on, we're going to have a bath. You first, Robin!' I filled the bailer with cool seawater and poured it over his matted hair. 'My God, that's wonderful,' he enthused, as he revelled in the paddling pool we had created in the forward section of the raft. I sloshed water on all of them as they took turns to splash about like infants, pouring cool seawater over their heads as though under a cool mountain stream. The sharks might make it too dangerous to swim outside the raft but there was no reason why we shouldn't enjoy the cleansing effects afforded by the seawater inside it. After we had cooled down and revived our flagging spirits, the plug was replaced and the water bailed out again.

We all felt much better, and Lyn and the twins, busy with a pencil and some sailcloth, set about designing a greenhouse in which they were going to grow tomatoes when they returned to Staffordshire. Douglas occupied his mind with visions of roasted rabbit, which he had not seen or tasted since his childhood but was quite certain would be his ideal dish. We began to think seriously about food, not simply eating it but also growing and preparing it, right down to the tiniest detail. This led Robin and Douglas into a marathon memory game about Mrs Brown's shopping list, finally attaining a massive thirty-two articles, before Robin won largely by adding unpronounceable books on statistics to his list. I felt that their minds weren't suffering a great deal, even though their bodies were, for our sunken features had made our bones become a lot more pronounced.

The seas had roughened considerably during the afternoon, and by evening the raft corkscrewed heavily on the steep waves. *Ednamair* yawed and ranged under her reefed-down sail, persuading me to take it down altogether for the night, thereby easing the strain on the sea anchor rope at the other end of the raft. I checked the fastenings with the dinghy and felt thankful that we had the strong towing wire to hold us together. We were now making way in spite of the drag of the sea anchor, and my mind turned to the additional strain now being put on the aft towing straps, to which the sea anchor was attached. The drag had become considerable and the raft, though sealed as tightly as we could make it, shipped a lot of water as the seas broke over it on all sides. The floor had to be bailed every ten minutes to keep us from lying in water and the flotation chambers lost pressure so quickly that blowing them up was required on a non-stop basis. Later that night Douglas checked the rubber stopper in the forward flotation chamber and confirmed the nylon binding had cut through the heavily worn fabric around the hole. Carefully he bound it with tape, which reduced the air loss to tolerable limits until we could effect a more permanent repair in daylight.

The dinghy was still full of turtle blood and offal, which I dared not dump until we were moving at a reasonable speed for fear of a shark attack. The dinghy yawed sluggishly in the steep seas, shipping water over its gunwale during the long periods that it was caught broadside on. I decided that it was safer to risk collateral damage from the sea anchor than risk swamping the dinghy, so with Douglas's help I hoisted the loosely reefed sail once again, which involved us in some strenuous acrobatics, boarding the dinghy in rough and choppy seas.

With the tow reconfigured, Douglas and I sat awhile and took a breather. We talked quietly, Douglas still depressed by the failure of the ship to pick us up. He probably realised, more than Robin could ever do, what this meant in terms of our future prospects of rescue. The advent of autopilots, gyrocompasses and other modern electronic aids to navigation on ships had all but eliminated the presence of the human eye on the modern ship's bridge. The rubber raft and the fibreglass dinghy were poor radar targets and would not be picked up on radar screens except at very close range, and only then if they could be picked out from amongst the sea clutter. Indeed, if the standard of watch-keeping was as poor on other ships as on the one that had already passed us by, then we stood a better chance of being run down than picked up.

It was then that I noticed the wind had changed to blow out of the north. 'A change in the wind means a change in the weather,' I reiterated the old meteorologists' saying out loud. 'Do you mean rain?' insisted Douglas, his eyes shining through the twilight gloom. 'I'm not a prophet, Douglas,' I replied, 'but don't be surprised if it does.' His mood lightened and I struggled to suppress my own nervous pangs of excitement as we held each other's gaze and realised, in accordance with what had initially seemed an impossible plan, that this change in the wind heralded nothing less than our arrival at the outskirts of the doldrums.

Inside the raft, the water levels continued to rise, filling the depressions made by our body weight in the flaccid, deflated floor sections. Sleep became more and more difficult as the rising levels swilled about our waists. The cold water robbed us of our body heat and caused us to tire beyond the point of exhaustion, as we clung to the sides in an effort to stop our dozing heads slipping onto the floor and into the ever-deepening pools of water that were slowly beginning to link up and surround us. During the night, clouds thickened in the northern sky as another extensive occluded front passed over. Later, as the front cleared, the wind abated to a gentle breeze and the seas subsided. Heavy clouds obscured the stars for most of the night and, though no rain fell, we were afforded a more comfortable ride than we had expected the previous evening.

Tenth day

In the half-light of dawn, even before the break of day had faded the stars from the clearing skies, we tripped and housed the sea anchor, shook the reef out of the sail and continued on our way to the doldrums. We had paid lip service to the standard practices of rescue by remaining in the shipping lanes for as long as we could, but I felt that our present circumstances called for more than standard practice and was anxious that no more time should be wasted. We were still some distance from the rain area and our stocks of water were dwindling once more.

As soon as we were moving again, I left Douglas and Robin to locate and repair the leaks in the raft floor, and set to work in the dinghy with a new and resolute sense of purpose. I dumped the offal and bailed the blood out of the *Ednamair* as dozens of scavenger fish appeared from nowhere, the sea swirling as they fought to devour the scraps of coagulated turtle blood. In a few minutes, the now-familiar fins of four sharks were spotted as they patrolled the vicinity looking for the source of the blood. The sea boiled around me as one of them attacked and killed a dorado, the shark leaping its full ten-foot length clear of the water in a tremendous strike. Although they were our constant reminders of what lay in store for us if we failed, we could not help admiring the beautiful streamlined shape of these white-tipped sharks as they cruised close to the raft, in smooth unhurried serenity with their attendant bevies of pilot fish. Our admiration however, did not deter me from swiping one of them with a paddle when it came too close, forcing it to beat a hasty retreat. As if they had taken the hint we weren't troubled by any of the others, but thereafter we were never without at least one shark in attendance.

At 3 degrees and 30 minutes north and 250 miles west of Cape Espinosa, our noon position confirmed that the doldrums, a mere 90 miles hence, were well within striking distance and that the first leg of our incredible journey would soon be at an end. Again, high cirrus clouds moved contrary to the trade winds, their unsubstantial vapours conveying little more than hope to a desperate observer, but the signs were becoming more and more indicative of stormy weather ahead.

I turned my attention back to the dinghy, scraping out the turtle shell and collecting all the edible pieces from the flippers. The semi-cured meat had turned a deep brown colour under the heat of the sun and I took a little of it back to the raft, to spin out our luncheon of flipper bones and eggs. During the afternoon, one of the plugs in the bottom of the raft became dislodged and water flooded into the forward compartment, pouring through the much-enlarged hole. Douglas plugged the hole by ramming the dinghy instruction book, made of waterproof material, into it. A creditable use, we all agreed wryly.

While Robin bailed the compartment dry again I wondered how long it would be before the raft became uninhabitable altogether and we became entirely dependent on the *Ednamair* for our lives. There was no doubt in my mind that we would soon face the daunting prospect of leaving the raft, and it would most likely be sooner rather than later. The prospect of the six of us fitting into and living in the confined limits of the three-man, nine-foot-six-inch boat, along with our food and water supplies and other items of equipment, made me apprehensive indeed, for the slightest imbalance would bring the sea flooding in over her sides.

The kapok-filled lifejackets, originally used as pillows or for keeping our bodies from becoming submerged in the collecting pools of water, had become so saturated that I resorted to taking them over to the dinghy during daylight hours, where I placed them between the thwarts in order that they would dry out in the sun. In the meantime, we redoubled our efforts to search for leaks, especially one which eluded our increasingly intensive searches. We had narrowed its location to the aft section and it was the cause of much bodily discomfort indeed. I decided we had no alternative but to rip out the side screens of the raft to facilitate finding the leak, which was coming from somewhere under the flotation chambers. We set about this arduous and disconcerting task hoping to locate and fix the leak before darkness fell. Using the blunt-nosed raft knife Douglas cut large access flaps in the sides, whilst exercising great care to avoid accidentally cutting into the adjacent flotation chambers. Our search however turned out to be in vain.

Continuous contact with the salt water had aggravated our skin eruptions and we all suffered from an increasing number of saltwater boils, festering on our arms and legs, shoulders and buttocks. The extremities of our limbs stung with pain when brought in contact with the Dacron sail and other rough objects and were rapidly presenting additional health hazards, as the blood supply to our hands and feet was restricted. It was becoming clearer by the day that we had to keep out of the seawater in order to stop the eruptions spreading, but each day it was getting harder to stay out of the deepening waters that gathered in the bottom of the raft, which we could only do by balancing on the inflated thwart or the sides. The water was only a few inches deep but our body weight depressed the punctured floors to such a degree that the water now rose to our chests. We were still examining the fabric inch by inch when daylight faded, making further investigations impossible. We settled down to another uncomfortable night, the sound of the constant plying of the bailing cup broken only by the gasping and blowing of the watch-keepers as they struggled in chest-deep pools of chilly water to keep the flotation chambers inflated and the source of our salvation afloat.

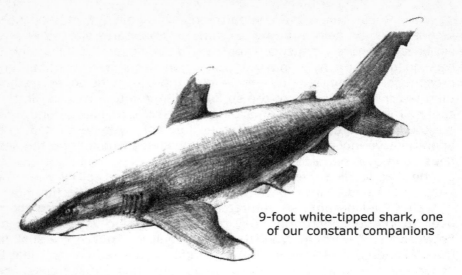

9-foot white-tipped shark, one
of our constant companions

Eleventh day

My morning inspection of the dinghy after a weary night of tossing
and turning, drying out and getting wet again, started with the
discovery that the petrol can had vanished during the night. Nobody
had seen it go and although I felt that we could have used the
container for water, the loss wasn't a tragic one, and was soon
alleviated by the discovery of two flying fish. We valued these tasty
morsels almost as much as the dorado did, and as long as there
were flying fish around then we felt sure that the bigger fish would
also remain with us. True, we had not found a way of catching the
dorado yet, but we might get lucky and another one land in the
dinghy, and I intended to start work in earnest on constructing a
spear. For breakfast we ate our last remaining scraps of onion, which
had unfortunately turned bad, and after a short rest Douglas and I
went over to *Ednamair* and dumped the scrapings from the turtle
shell and cleaned the inside of the boat thoroughly from the smears
of dried-on turtle blood, which adhered stubbornly in places. Douglas
gave it a final scrub with a crumpled piece of sailcloth and then we
secured the dried meat and fish in one of the boxes, placing a turtle
shell over it for a lid. We were ready for rain if it came, in more ways
than one, for we were down to twelve pints of fresh water once more
and would soon have to reduce our intake until another active front
passed over.

Our position at 4 degrees north and 250 miles west of Espinosa
seemed to be consistent with the sort of weather we were
experiencing. More occluded fronts, moving southwards from the
doldrums, passed over with ever greater frequency. Although rain
was still denied us, we were grateful for such signs in the upper
atmosphere, proof positive that rain lay ahead and not too far

distant. What was more, we were consistently moving towards the active fronts from which these occlusions emanated. We had all noticed that the seawater temperature had risen markedly again in the last twenty-four hours, indicating that we were finally free from the clutches of the westerly-bearing Humboldt Current. Whilst I could not be sure that we had crossed over the boundary of the counter-current until we reached the latitude of at least 5 degrees 30 minutes north, I felt it prudent to discount any further westerly drift in my dead-reckoning calculations. A moderate breeze continued to blow us northwards at a rate of 24 miles per day, and with an allowance for set and drift I hoped, indeed prayed, that we would be within the rain-bearing environs at the centre of the doldrums in a further two days. The spectre of a waterless week haunted us more than any other hazard, for water shortages left us weak, impotent and breathless from all but the slightest exertion. Lyn already knew that dehydration once started was difficult to correct, and not simply a matter of drinking extra water once it became available.

We had given up looking for the leak in the after section of the raft, and during the morning played Twenty Questions and talked about food. Robin described his travels in Ireland and I described my days as a youth with the Boy Scouts, camping and exploring in the Highlands of Scotland. The twins readily absorbed themselves in our adventures, and memories of our Sunday mornings abed at Meadows Farm brought reflective smiles across the faces of both Lyn and me.

Now that *Lucette* was gone, everyone wanted to return to their old lives in Britain. The twins listened avidly to my adventures as a youngster, walking in the mountainous countryside back home in Scotland. For them there would never be another *Lucette* and they were quite confident that when they grew up they would sail their own boat around the world, just like the Australian twins we had met on their ketch *Metung* in Jamaica. We remembered the *Lucette*'s gentle lines and robust build as we recalled the many adventures she had given us. The children felt perturbed that we had not completed our stated objective of sailing around the world, but I felt that the important objectives had already been achieved in widening the horizons of their minds. They were no longer afraid or shy about meeting people whose language and customs were different from our own, nor did they think that because they were different they were inferior. They were not frightened about the insecurities of life and had attained new self-confidence, so much so that they were more than able to hold their own in debates and debacles alike.

Robin puffed steadily at the flotation compartment. He was twice as good now as when he started, although there was still plenty of room for improvement. When Douglas took over, the valve positively squealed as he blasted massive breaths of air into the tube. The flotation chambers grew firm and rounded as the canopy's arched support became rigid under the increased pressure. It was late afternoon before Douglas spotted new clouds approaching in the distance. We watched ready and hopeful that the mushrooming cumulus clouds gathering on the horizon might bring precipitation in our direction.

Taking the spare paddle handle, I crossed to *Ednamair* and cut a piece of wood from one of the boxes and settled down to carve the head of a fish spear, which I planned to fit into the paddle handle shaft in the style of a harpoon. I was still whittling at the hard wood as dusk closed in. I didn't stop until the wood was smooth and streamlined into the shape of a barb, above which I had already carved two notches angled towards each other, ready to receive the armoured points of nails Douglas had extracted from the central thwart woodwork.

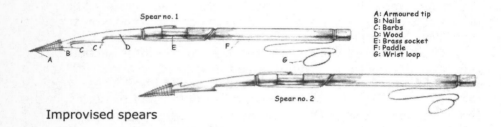

A: Armoured tip
B: Nails
C: Barbs
D: Wood
E: Brass socket
F: Paddle
G: Wrist loop

Improvised spears

Sleeping space inside the raft was now very cramped as we struggled to lie on top of the flotation chambers in an effort to keep clear of the water, now permanently gathered in the bottom of the raft. I decided to ease the situation by sleeping in the dinghy and took Sandy with me. It wasn't long after we had settled down on the hard fibreglass hull that we realised that the inflatable was much kinder to our bones, and as we clutched our sailcloth sheets around us we realised it was quite a bit warmer as well. We spent an uneasy night trying to find comfort for our tender, boil-infested bodies, finally snatching a few moments of exhausted slumber just before dawn. Our discomforts however were pure luxury compared to what the others had suffered aboard the raft. The routine of blowing and bailing had gone on through the night relentlessly, spurred on by the tyranny of survival's only alternative. I rejoined my worn-out crew, realising all too clearly that it was no longer a question of if but when we would have to abandon the raft. Life aboard was draining us of our reserves and as surely as it had saved us in the early days, now it was certainly killing us.

Twelfth day

Daybreak came slowly under a gloomy sky, typifying the more normal climes of the doldrums. I stirred to the harsh commands of self-preservation, my eyes scouring the sea as far as the distant horizon, before flitting to the sky and then back to the dinghy, searching vainly for signs of rain or a morsel of fresh food. I stepped aboard the raft to find Douglas blowing hard to inflate its aft section, which was sagged in a dismal droop, the archway support of the canopy having fallen to touch the floor. Despite all attempts to locate the source of the leak, the elusive puncture was probably getting worse with every passing wave, but since we couldn't find it we would just have to blow more often.

The morning routine of clearing the water and the saturated bedding from the raft was occupying more and more of our time, and as conditions worsened we were becoming slower in performing even the smallest of tasks. Lyn had to scold us all to get us to cooperate in clearing the raft and to tend to our sores. She cleaned the pus from our eyes and we groaned and snapped as she nagged us into the ordinary routines of body hygiene and exercise. Our raised voices and mood of restrained belligerence were rapidly brought to an end, however, when without warning it suddenly began to rain. We burst as one into a spontaneous cheer, only to fall silent a few moments later when as suddenly as it had started the rain stopped.

Lyn prayed that we might have enough rain to sustain life, and as the wreathlike cloud thinned and moved away, Robin commented about the power of Lyn's prayer. Frustrated at my helplessness, I felt anger surge through me at such a display of intolerance and fought hard to beat down the demons in my mind telling me to take inappropriate and savage revenge at such effrontery. Instead, I pointed out that the democratic freedom to worship was just as important as the freedom not to worship, and we could be spared his unsavoury remarks. Robin looked askance at me as the import of my tone rather than my words reached him, then, realising the demoralising effect of his throwaway comments, he gracefully apologised to Lyn and we all shook hands.

My spear was finished by the early afternoon and after varnishing the bindings of the nails located on the tip to produce a smoother point, I surveyed my handiwork with some misgivings. It looked the part, but whether it was strong enough for the task required of it we would have to wait and see. Even before it had been properly used in anger, I accidentally knocked the point against the mast and snapped the barb section clean in two. My language blistered the air as I fervently went to work on a second model, this time using a hacked piece of cypress Douglas had split from the central thwart for me, which was a tougher more stringy variety of wood. The absence of sun allowed me to work throughout the afternoon whilst the dinghy maintained a steady course in the gentle breeze and smooth glassy seas.

By late afternoon I had all but completed the components of my mark-two spear, and made ready to return to the raft. As I pulled on the towrope, I found to my surprise and horror that the shackle pin had worked loose and fallen out. I paddled back to the raft and reflected on our good fortune that such an event hadn't happened during the night or in stormy weather, for to lose the dinghy now would be to lose our lives. Not only were our food reserves stored in it, but also the refilled water cans, neither of which could be stored in the raft. I secured the end of the towrope to the towing strap and lashed the half hitches with twine, then took the small lifeline and secured it between dinghy and raft as a precaution against a repeat performance, for there were too many sharks around to go swimming after the dinghy if we lost it.

The bottom of the raft was now continually awash and our boils developed and spread at a disquieting speed, causing acute discomfort whenever we bumped into anything. To have even a piece of sail drawn across our skin resulted in minutes of searing agony, forcing us to move slowly and with caution to avoid unnecessary suffering. In the darkness, changing watch became an agonising and protracted exercise for everyone; it was obvious to us all that unless we could keep drier, we would become both unwilling and unable to do anything for fear of hurting ourselves. Despite the discomfort, bailing had to be carried out almost continuously, and when not bailing then blowing up the flotation chambers was the order of the day, a task that had become almost second nature to Douglas, who took on the brunt of this exhausting work.

Our talk no longer centred around the possibility of rescue, rather on how long it was going to take us to reach land and what sort of condition we would be in when we got there. Lyn talked quietly to the twins, of their grandfather's cottage on the quiet reaches of a small canal in Staffordshire and of how their grandfather, 'Old Pev', would have enjoyed hearing of our adventures and the different countries we had visited. The boys sat in restless repose as they tried to listen to their mother's words, the strain of concentrating a clear tax on their young minds as they struggled to adjust to life without water. Compounding our gloom, the sky had cleared completely by sunset, leaving no trace of a rain cloud in sight, as twilight deepened the velvet darkness of the Pacific night. Sandy and I decided to remain on the raft for the night and later whilst on watch, having completed my bailing duties, I observed a large fish splashing noisily beside the raft. I looked into the crystal depths and dropped my arm into the water, poised ready in the hope that coincidence would bring my hand in contact with the right part of the dorado, enabling me to haul it aboard. I managed to touch their backs a time or two but always in the wrong place. Being the eternal optimist, however, I felt sure that persistence would pay off and that sooner rather than later I would be rewarded with success.

As the minutes ticked by my focus slipped but I was suddenly brought back to the task at hand by a loud splash that burst the surface of the water, causing the whole raft to tremble as a large fish surged first alongside, then under our bodies. I relocated myself by the aft doorway and readied myself for the fish to jump a second time. Turning on its tail, it sprang from the water and collided against the side of the raft, just beneath my right arm. I dropped my hand and gripped fiercely, whilst pinning it against the soft fabric with my left hand. For a glorious instant I thought I had caught a huge bull dorado, then feeling the rough dry skin I looked down to behold the white belly and dagger-toothed jaw line of a five-foot shark, lying docile in my arms like a baby. Realising that one slash of those teeth would finish the raft in an instant, I dropped its inert form as if I had been holding a red-hot poker. As it hit the surface of the water, it snapped its savage jaws, struck the raft a powerful blow with its tail and disappeared into the night. Thankful for small mercies I resumed bailing, too shocked to speak. We didn't want to evacuate just yet, and certainly not in the middle of the night!

Thirteenth day

The bright sun rising in the eastern skies amplified our depressed mood after another wet and miserable night inside the raft. The discovery of two flying fish in the bottom of the dinghy together with one that had flown aboard the raft during the night did little to dispel the feeling of gloom, as we tucked into our meagre repast of half a raw fish each! Though the fish were very small, they were sweet tasting and contained fresh water, which reduced the amount we needed to take from the water jar. Though we were still on a voluntary system of rationing, I watched each person drink, more to reassure myself that they were taking their share than the reverse. On two occasions, Lyn put the jar to her lips to drink but did not draw. When I told her to drink, she protested that she did not need it and the twins could have her share. I knew the children needed her as much as their share of water, and put down the most compelling of ultimatums, none for anybody until she drank! Reluctantly she took the most meagre of sips imaginable from the bottle, returning my stare defiantly. Believing discretion to be the better friend of valour I decided to let the matter rest at that.

Looking with dread at the cloudless skies overhead, I took the three flying-fish heads over to *Ednamair* to use as bait, while I finished my second spear and the boys set about bailing, blowing and searching for leaks with stalwart determination. Dispelling the rigours of thirst, Lyn went about her morning chores, washing our clothes and drying the bedding followed by administering leg exercises to the twins. The scavenger fish quickly took the first head, requiring me to re-bait the hook with the second head and place it much deeper, hoping that the sharks would be elsewhere. To my surprise, I had a strike right away and a few moments later, a two-pound fish lay in the bottom of the boat, flapping to restrained whoops of delight and encouragement from the raft. I threaded the third head onto the hook and sent it deep again, admiring my catch as I waited for another strike. The captured fish flapped wildly in the bottom of the dinghy, so I took up the knife to put it out of its misery. I severed the head with a quick twist of the knife, but to my horror, as I pushed the steel blade into the flesh behind the gill slit, I heard a sharp click and was left holding a short stump of knife in my hand with the remaining six inches of blade left lying in the bottom of the boat. Unable to understand just how I could break such a stout blade by cutting a small fish's head off, I was still gaping when a second strike jerked my attention back to the line. A big one this time, it fought strongly and the line cut into my hands as foot by foot I pulled the fish in towards the dinghy. Robin and the twins watched excitedly from the raft door. I could see the fish now, a full twenty-pound blue fish of the mackerel variety, fighting and struggling as I dragged it to the surface. I pulled sharply to bring its silvery torpedo-like form towards the side of the boat. It rested awhile as I gently pulled on the line, guiding it ever closer. Suddenly the huge fish gave a mighty lunge into the air and was gone, the empty hook no longer curved but straightened by the dynamic force of the fish's leap. My disappointment was so intense and the pain from my crushed boils and fingers so severe that I would have wept had I the moisture to spare for tears. As my tattered emotions calmed, I put a larger hook on the line and baited it with some offal from the smaller fish I had caught earlier. I sent it deep again, determined that if I were lucky once more I would play my catch first and risk it being taken by sharks. The strike came almost immediately and slowly I pulled the line in. Unseen in the depths our dinner was taken a second time. The sharks had beaten me to it.

I had two large hooks left, and as I watched the long sleek shapes of the sharks glide slowly by I resolved to keep them for another day. Without warning, one of the sharks turned and with a rapid flick of its tail sped straight towards the dinghy, its ragged dorsal knifing the surface of the sea at a menacing pace. I grabbed the spear and struck savagely at its snout as it closed. Surprised at the contact, it flipped its tail wildly and dived deep, as two others cruising not far behind it kept a respectful distance, carefully watching and waiting for a change in the status quo. 'You'll not be having us for dinner today,' I snarled in their direction as I made the transit back to the raft with the newly caught fish for our lunch.

I found tempers frayed when I returned, with everyone being particularly uncooperative, as Lyn tried to get them to help with the drying of the bedding. Despite intensifying thirst, she insisted they all adhere to their set routines and complete their allotted jobs correctly. I turned to look at the twins. Neil, now painfully thin, together with Sandy was putting the odds and ends back into the raft pocket, after Lyn had cleared it of pieces of sodden wrapping paper and empty flare cases. Douglas and Robin moved lethargically in response to Lyn's chiding commands and my attempts at mediation brought Lyn and me into direct conflict, which quickly developed into a full-blown row. The others endured our fierce backbiting with stoical indifference, knowing full well the difference between inconsequential nagging and orders or instructions which had to be carried out for their own good, and where failure to comply could result in the loss of our lives. I looked at them all sternly. Our success depended on our ability to work as a team and I felt one way or the other I had to make them realise this. 'We all have to do things we don't like,' I said, still angry after my altercation with Lyn, 'and left to your own devices you would be dead already.' Robin opened his mouth to argue but I held up my hand to silence him and snarled with a savage intensity, 'If one of us dies because somebody doesn't feel like doing what they are told, then take it from me that somebody will be next.' Robin's startled eyes came into focus and Douglas stared blankly into space as if past caring. In our altered perspective, where we must kill or be killed and where death could strike us down at a moment's notice, a threat of such blatant and uncalled-for severity seemed almost normal, even expected. Robbed of my energy by the relentless thirst I sank back onto the thwart in reflective silence. Unable to rescind my admonitions, I pondered for a moment on how quickly our circumstances had toughened our outlooks, and wondered just how ruthless circumstances might make us, as the days ahead got even tougher and increasingly more desperate.

I didn't bother with working out our position that noon. After another unsuccessful attempt to find the water leaks, Douglas, Robin and I blew up the flotation chambers in turns, blowing hard for thirty breaths before passing the tube to the next man. Cumulus clouds began building into heavy clusters again and the probability of rain showers seemed good. Douglas in particular looked exhausted; always busy, he would finish one task then move right on to the next, without waiting to be asked. He seemed tireless, putting the whole of his energy into his work, but now deep shadows under his eyes betrayed the drain on his physical resources. I felt I could see the shadow of death behind his sunken cheeks. I put the thoughts of such a possibility behind me, for we could not get back to land without him, and the blow to our morale should he die would have devastating implications upon our collective effort. Lyn worked steadily at the other end of the raft, preparing the twins' little bit of extra food, as she carefully rewrapped the boxes in their waterproof bags.

Anxiously we watched the rain showers develop around us, counting as many as ten at one time, and when we finally realised they were all going to miss us we opened another tin of water for supper, to find to our horror it was only half full. Four pints left, plus two more that were brackish and foul. Despondency prevailed. Feeling thirsty and dejected, I suppressed the notion that salvation was slowly passing us by, lest my face revealed such thoughts to the others. I had become used to doing without sleep but there was little sleep for any of us that night and the youngsters could ill afford the loss. We listened to Lyn talking to the twins about their grandfather's cottage on the canal, about chickens, rabbits, gardens, anything to keep their minds from contemplating the absence of that most precious of minerals, water. My thoughts returned to Lyn's father, who had lived by the motto 'You've got to get up to survive'. I could hear his voice in my mind, repeating the phrase over. We were facing our greatest challenge yet as we struggled to stay alive without water, but guided by his inspiration I became determined to find a way to catch some fish, for from the fish we would get water and from that water we would get life. We passed the foul yellow stuff from the jar around for sips during the night, imagining ourselves lying in beautiful cool gardens, full of fruits and streaming fountains.

Once Lyn and the twins had fallen into a restless sleep I returned to the dinghy, and after much whittling and carving my mark-two version of the spear was ready to be tested. I decided I would try it on the dorado in the morning. I would have tried it there and then but the angle of strike was too deceptive in the dark. If there was to be no rain, we needed the water the fish contained otherwise we would die. I resolved that our water allowance should be reduced and toyed with the idea of distributing it in equal amounts to ensure that we all had a share. That quiet night marked the end of our second week afloat, leaving us moribund by thirst, with our stomachs panging from lack of food. Our tortured bodies stung in pain from the numerous boils and sores festering our bodies but we were alive and apart from our desperate need for water we were in surprisingly good fettle considering our circumstances.

Fourteenth day

The beautiful starlit night shone sparkles of twinkling light across the quiet swells, still reaching us from the distant trade winds, and seemed to mock our feeble struggle for existence in the raft. Entering our third week adrift, we found ourselves unceasingly tending to the maintenance of the life raft, which needed inflating and bailing in the forward section on an almost continuous basis.

Later that morning Sandy discovered the hole that had been leaking into the after section. It was surrounded by transparently thin fabric, worn gauzelike and threadbare by constant abrasion, my first glance confirming my worst suspicions that I was witnessing the beginning of the breaking up of the raft. I knew that it was unlikely that I could plug such a large hole, and yet if I didn't it could split wide open in the next heavy sea. I made a plug and inserted it into the hole, whilst Sandy held the tape ready to bind it in place. As I attempted the repair the hole split still wider and water flooded into the after compartment. I rammed the plug home in dismay, which impeded the ingress of the water, but left the raft in constant need of bailing at both ends. Apart from the discomfort, for we already had plenty of that, my only real opposition to leaving the raft was that it would mean abandoning the shelter afforded by the canopy. I decided to think of a way of fastening the canopy on to the dinghy to give us continuing shelter from the sun, so that when the time came to abandon the raft, it would be one less thing to worry about.

We had a sip of water for breakfast with no dried food to detract from its value, after which I crossed to the dinghy and tried once more to catch a dorado. The brazened heat of the sun's rays beat on my head like a club and my mouth felt dry like the skin of a lizard and full of my swollen tongue. The slightest exertion left me feeling quite breathless. I picked up the spear and took up my huntsman's stance by the side of the raft. The dorado were swimming deep down as if they knew I was looking for them. A bump at the stern of the raft attracted Sandy's attention. 'Turtle!' he yelled. This one was much smaller than the first, and exercising more care than previously Douglas plucked it from the ocean and he and Sandy manoeuvred it through the raft, keeping a tight grip on its beak as the others assisted with the claws and flippers, preventing them from damaging the fabric. I reached across the gap and took it from them, placing it inside the dinghy, where I tilted it onto its back without too much trouble. I studied the beast as it beat its flippers with powerful strokes onto the floor of the dinghy. Knowing for the sake of my family it must die, I studied the broken tools to hand and scratched my head in bemusement, wondering if I had sufficient strength left to penetrate the armoured skin and bone. I wrapped a piece of tape around the broken knife blade and fabricated a makeshift handle. Involuntarily closing my eyes, I made an incision deep into its throat. 'This time catch the blood,' Douglas croaked from the raft door. 'It should be alright to drink a little,' added Lyn in quiet desperation. I held the plastic bailer under the copious flow of blood which pumped out from the severed artery. The bailer filled quickly, requiring me to tuck the other container under the spurting neck wound as soon as it had filled. To an enthralled audience, I raised the cup to my lips and tasted the frothy red liquid cautiously. It wasn't salty at all! I tilted the cup and drained it. 'Good stuff!' I shouted, as though I had just consumed the elixir of life. 'Here, take some,' I offered to eager outstretched hands and passed the bailer full of blood, about a pint in all, into the raft for the others to drink. Lyn said afterwards she had imagined that she would have to force it down, for the sight of me draining the cup as my moustache dripped with blood had been truly revolting. I don't know what I looked like, but it certainly tasted good, and as the others followed my example it seemed my critique was unanimous.

I passed another pint across but it coagulated into jelly before it could be consumed. Lyn dissected the jelly in order to release the serum it contained, which she then mixed with the dried turtle and fish to form a rich stew-like gravy. My thirst relieved, I set to work with renewed energy, cutting my way into the turtle. Even with the restrictions imposed by having to use the broken knife, I still made quicker work of it than the first one, not only because it was smaller but also because, being younger, the shell was not so tough. The fact that I knew my way around the anatomy of a turtle helped a lot too.

The sky was serenely blue that afternoon and with our position decided as 5 degrees north and 250 miles west of Espinosa, I declared we had arrived at the official limits of the doldrums. Was this then doldrum weather? Was the 'Rhyme of the Ancient Mariner' correct after all with its 'Nor any drop to drink'? This was not the type of weather we had expected to find here and we had only four tins of water left, one of them half seawater – and if any of the other three contained short measure well, our only hope would be to catch another turtle. Pangs of self-doubt stabbed my gut once more. The idea that rain could be found in the doldrums had been exactly that, just an idea! It was too late to change our minds and impossible to turn back if we had got it wrong. All we could do now was wait, wait for it to rain or wait until we no longer cared.

The waiting dragged on inexorably, waiting to live, waiting for rescue or waiting to die, we knew not which – but waiting was the only option we had left. I looked around the raft at the remains of Robin and the Robertson family, their seawater-wrinkled skins covered with saltwater boils and raw red patches of exposed rash creeping across their bodies. They lay in the bottom of the raft, unmoving except to bail occasionally and then only half-heartedly, for the water in which we lay also cooled us in the heat of the day. Their bones showed clearly through their scanty flesh; our skeletal forms had become much thinner these last few days and our condition was deteriorating fast. The raft was killing us with its incessant demands, and with our 'Rain in the doldrums' trump card already played we could only wait and see what fate would bring. Douglas looked across at me, 'Do you think it'll rain tonight, Dad?' I looked at him and shrugged before studying the cloudless sky. 'I suppose it could do,' I breathed unconvincingly. 'But do you think it will?' he insisted. 'For heaven's sake, Douglas, I'm no prophet, nor psychic either,' I remarked unkindly, 'we will just have to wait it out.'

From the deep cavities under his brow, his eyes looked hopelessly at the inviting blueness of the sea. How could I comfort my eldest son when he knew as well as I that it might not rain for a week, and by then we'd all be dead? Unable to offer him hope I changed the subject, 'Let's hope for some fresh turtle for tea; we might be able to drink something from that.' I wondered if we could possibly live on turtles by drinking only their blood until the rains came.

Save for a little sip for the twins, we took no water that evening. In quiet whispers we talked of the dishes we'd like to eat in the gathering twilight. I chose fresh fruit salad and ice cream; Lyn, a tin of apricots; Robin, strawberries and ice cream with milk; Douglas, the same as me; Neil decided on chocolate chip ice cream; Sandy, fresh fruit, ice cream and milk, gallons of ice-cool milk. Later that night as Douglas sat motionless on watch, his silhouette etched sharply against the clear night sky, I heard his gravely voice call me across the raft. Then he was shaking my right shoulder as he summoned me from a restless half-sleep. In our time together aboard *Lucette*, I had grown used to being called from my bed to deal with emergencies or difficult situations of all types, but on this occasion things were different. Douglas had woken me to describe in detail a dish he had dreamed up during his watch. 'You take a honeydew melon,' he said, 'cut the top off and take out the seeds; that you use as the dish.' He paused to let me appreciate the scene. Moisture gradually formed in the bone-dry pit of my mouth. 'Chill it and drop a knob of ice cream inside, then pile in strawberries, raspberries, pieces of apple, pear, orange, peach and grapefruit, the sweet sort, then cherries and grapes until the melon is full; pour a lemon syrup over it and decorate it with chips of chocolate and nuts. Then,' he said with a dreamy expression on his face, 'you eat it!' 'I'll have one too,' I smiled, taking the bailer from him and squeezing his boil-covered hand in the darkness. I studied the sky to the northeast, where a faint film of cirrostratus cloud dimmed the stars, 'You know, son, I think it might rain by morning after all.' I could feel him relax in the darkness; then after a short pause his words came slowly, 'I'll be all right if it doesn't, Dad.' Sensing his mood I pleaded into the shadows, 'Don't let your bright light go out son, we need you now more than ever.' In reply, he simply returned my squeeze before sinking back into the chest-deep pools of water with the others, enduring their misery in gritty silence with the greatest of fortitude. I looked on with pity as the water covered my son's body; if he were lucky, he might get a few minutes sleep before daybreak.

Fifteenth day

I watched the clouds develop slowly and drift across the night sky, blotting out the stars one by one. Was it another occluded front? It was too early to say. Still shocked at the realisation that Douglas had with quiet courage already prepared himself for death, I knew that under the sweltering heat of the tropics, with so little water to sustain us, our lives were slipping away and time was fast running out for us all. As we sat and waited to realise our fate, I prayed quietly that my son would make it through the night, I prayed that my family and I would make it home, and I prayed that it would rain. We had done all that was humanly possible to do and were in God's hands once more. I watched the fish surge out from under the raft and even managed to touch one in a futile attempt to grab it. Suddenly the memory of the shark, still strong in my mind, caused me to draw back, and I returned to my bailing and blowing routine until Lyn took over. I pointed to the thickening cloud banking in front of a shimmering, orange-tinted dawn. 'Maybe we'll get something to drink out of that,' I stated more in hope than belief.

The sun sprang over the eastern horizon for only the briefest of periods, turning the sea from black to blue. With the passing of the dawn, my prayers were suddenly answered, for just after daybreak the rain began to fall. Gently at first, it rapidly turned into a mighty deluge as the huge thundercloud blanketed the sky from one horizon to the other. Beautiful, gorgeous rain poured out of the skies by the bucketful, beating down on our heads and splashing against our upturned faces. We leaned from under the canopy, to indulge in the sheer pleasure of this rare and most welcome of sensations. We laughed and cried in spontaneous joy and revelled in life's most precious jewel. The canopy of the raft had collapsed again during the night but we cared not. We saved a massive three and a half gallons and drank our fill besides. The wind from the south freshened a little, and as the weather cleared we all lay back relaxing to another new sensation, of being without the yearning, craving and mind-purging desire for water. Bailing and blowing went unheeded for the moment. We talked of the ship that didn't see us, for that had happened immediately after the last downpour. What a difference the rain made, cheering our spirits and lifting our hearts as the spectre of death, so near during the night, was banished to the backs of our minds. Douglas looked like a new man after he had guzzled his fill. 'Dad!' he blasted exuberantly, 'You remember when you asked me to row to the island,' he didn't wait for my answer, 'well if we can store up enough water like this then by heaven I'll row us all the way to America. In the dinghy we can make fifty miles a day, say five hundred miles in a fortnight – and you know what, we'll be home before you know it.' His eyes sparkled. I wondered what he would have said if I told him I had been thinking exactly the same thing.

The twins wanted to know more about the details of what such a venture would entail when Douglas, positioned by the open doorway, shrieked out in a voice of desperate dismay, 'Dad, the dinghy's gone!'

I was across the raft in an instant. I looked at the broken wire trailing in the water and the snapped polypropylene rope floating beside it. The dinghy was sixty yards distant, sailing away and taking our lives with it. I was the fastest swimmer, no time for goodbyes, to hell with sharks; the thoughts ran through my head as I dived headlong through the door, my arms flailing into a racing crawl even as I hit the water. I heard Lyn cry out but there was no time for talk. Could I swim faster than the dinghy could sail? I pondered the point as I lifted my head and sucked in huge draughts of air. I glanced sideways at the dinghy. The sail had collapsed as it yawed atop a distant crest, spurring me on to move my arms faster and kick even harder. My belly crawled as I thought of the sharks, and if they would get me before I gained the dinghy, but it was too late for second thoughts and my arms raced still faster in an all-or-nothing dash. I glanced again, only thirty yards to go but she was sailing through the water once more. I felt no fatigue or cramp in my muscles, my body felt like a machine as I thrashed my way through the sea, only one thought burning in my mind, the dinghy or us.

Suddenly I was there. With a quick heave, I flipped over the stern and dropped into the safety of the hull, tearing down the sail as my knees buckled from under me, leaving me prostrate across the thwart, trembling from head to toe and gasping for breath, my heart pumping like a pneumatic hammer. I waited until my senses returned then lifted my arm and waved to the raft, which looked incredibly fragile and inadequate as it buckled in the waves a few hundred yards away. Slowly I removed the stays and paddled back to the raft. It took nearly an hour before I finally nudged alongside, where Douglas greeted me with a hero's welcome and made me fast, whilst the long shapes of two sharks circled curiously in the depths below.

Exhausted beyond endurance, I slumped into the raft amidst excited chatter about how I had retrieved the dinghy. I lay on my back and slipped into a trance-like state, listening quietly to snippets of the conversation as they pieced together what had happened. 'I saw Dougal's body hurtle past me as he dived into the sea,' Lyn told the others, 'Then Douglas shouted a warning about the sharks and Neil shouted out for his Dad.' ' I just remember crowding to see past Douglas blocking the door,' quipped Robin. 'Dougal was cutting through the water faster than *Ednamair* was sailing, and I certainly couldn't have kept up a speed like that, for more than a few minutes at the most,' he added, his voice raised more in excitement than alarm. 'Nor I,' affirmed Douglas, 'the shark was close behind him, close to his right and his feet were threshing the water in a racing crawl.' 'Then we lost sight of him in the swells,' recalled Lyn as Robin had shouted, 'Don't panic – don't panic.' Their collective torment calmed a little once Douglas had informed them I had finally reached the dinghy. 'Good old Dad,' enthused Sandy as they reiterated Douglas's commentary a second time, adding more detail as they realised just how fine had been the line between success and failure, between life and death. They had for some time lost sight of me altogether and Douglas, craning his upper body, had struggled to maintain visual contact whilst keeping the others informed. As the raft slewed round more and more, Lyn had re-sighted me from the aft doorway. 'There, miraculously, I saw him, the dinghy like a cockleshell on the crest of a wave with Dougal paddling furiously, first one side then the other with such concentration and determination on his haggard old face. Relief flooded through me and I heard myself singing, 'There goes my love' from *Dr Zhivago*.

They all fell silent and I sensed they were all looking down on me. Unable to feel my own body I became aware they were holding my hands and smiling. As I flitted in and out of consciousness, I wondered for a moment if I had actually died, until Lyn mopped my brow with a wet piece of sail, my face still grey and ashen with exhaustion. She pressed the sipper jar to my lips. I shook my head but Lyn wasn't having any heroics. She made me drink, promising that none of the children would drink until I did. 'Touché,' I grinned, recalling my earlier ultimatum to her as she put a piece of glucose in my mouth. She cradled my head in her arms and my strength slowly returned. How frightened and desperate they had all felt, as they were forced to contemplate attempting the rest of the journey, cut off from their only real hopes of getting home: *Ednamair* and myself.

Once I had recovered, we inspected the wire and found it frayed under the plastic in two places. With Douglas's help I broke it in two places and removed the weakened length before rejoining it, which made the tow short enough to fasten a large nylon rope between the raft and the dinghy as a reserve line. Once the dinghy was secure again Douglas, Robin and myself put our cognitive powers to work by first figuring out and then rigging a sea anchor, which would automatically trip if the *Ednamair* broke away from the raft again, effectively stopping her from sailing away. We had not only closed the stable door this time, we'd hobbled the horse as well! I didn't relish a repeat performance of that swim, not ever.

Following the recent heavy rains, there was quite a lot of water collected in the bottom of the dinghy, mixed with some turtle blood from the sail and some seawater which I had spilled into the dinghy after my swim. As it was unpalatable Lyn urged we avoid wasting it by introducing it into our bodies in the form of an enema, as she had previously suggested. Douglas crafted a makeshift device by first stripping a piece of rubber tubing from the raft ladder and tapering the end with a scalpel blade, which he then fashioned into a makeshift enema tube. This we joined to the long bellows tube and Lyn made a funnel for the top from a polythene bag. Lyn expertly administered the enemas, first to myself as an involuntary guinea pig followed by Douglas and then the twins, finishing up by administering one to herself. I poured the water in for her amid much banter and backchat. Robin declined the offer. The idea of taking enemas was not so much to promote bowel movement as to allow us to absorb water which would be otherwise undrinkable. In the undulating raft, it was an undignified and hilarious procedure, requiring a steady hand and a lot of patience, but we managed it without spilling too much. We took between a pint and two pints each, which given the shrunken state of our stomachs was a lot more than we could have drunk.

Our noon position of 5 degrees and 15 minutes north and 250 miles west of Espinosa put us well inside the official limits of the doldrums. We had made the rain area and completed the first leg of our journey in fifteen days. I solemnly reflected that if we had stayed at sea anchor where *Lucette* had sunk and hoped for rescue, we would probably have all been dead. We had travelled over 400 miles and still had about 700 to go. What was more, we had as much, if not more, food and water than when we had started. Our condition was much worse, it was true, but we hoped that the recent increase in our water supply would help rectify that. We could not hope for an improvement in our living conditions, however, unless and until we abandoned the raft. I still had strong misgivings about our ability to fit into *Ednamair* along with our ensemble of stores and equipment. We would have about six inches of freeboard I recalled from when we had all been aboard her in the Galapagos; six inches wasn't much in the middle of the Pacific with sharks on constant patrol, and even if we managed to save flotation pieces from the raft it would be very difficult to support the dinghy with them. We couldn't afford to be swamped, not even once, for our water and stores would be ruined even if we managed to save ourselves. As I trawled through my mind listing the items which we required to take into the dinghy with us, I became perplexed in the extreme at the choices I would face should it not be possible for us all to fit on board. Deciding to cross that bridge if and when we came to it, I decided to initiate a propaganda campaign concerning the absolute necessity for instant obedience when we took to the dinghy, in order to maintain the correct trim. Rain had begun falling again and it settled to a steady downpour throughout the night. Douglas observed that we would need a canopy over the dinghy to keep the rain out rather than to catch it, if this sort of weather was to become the norm. I resisted the urge to whinge about the weather to the others, as was my British birthright, and was glad that on this occasion at least, the Ancient Mariner had been wrong after all!

Sixteenth day

The rain continued to fall all night long, and as we bailed the warm seawater out of the raft we were glad not to be spending a night like this one out in the dinghy. I went over to the *Ednamair* twice in the night to bail her out, for the rain was filling her quickly, and I shivered in the low temperatures of the falling rain. The raft canopy offered grateful warmth when I returned and the deep puddles of salt water in the bottom of the raft offered momentary relief after the chill of the dinghy. The others huddled tightly together on top of the flotation chambers, and tried to keep their legs and bottoms out of the water. Although we did not sleep we did get some rest, as the work of blowing and bailing went on around the clock. Our sores stung as we knocked them against the raft and each other, our eyes suppurated and our limbs had become permanently wrinkled and lumpy with boils. My backside was badly blistered from sunburn acquired on my turtle-dressing expeditions, which made it necessary for me to lie on my front all the time, punishment enough for another piece of carelessness. We languished in misery as the water rose to the height of our chests and sloshed about the inside of the raft. Slab-sided wavelets of cold seawater ranged across the inside of the raft and slapped us in the face as our heads dropped in snatched moments of precious sleep, and we clung onto the grab ropes even as we drowsed lest we slipped beneath the surface of the water and drowned. When morning came, we were tired and exhausted, with the prospect of another night already filling us with dread.

The rain continued to beat on the calm sea until mid-morning, when after a few desultory bursts of sunshine the weather closed in again and drizzled for the rest of the day. I decided to postpone the evacuation of the raft until the weather improved a little and I detected a distinct feeling of relief amongst the others at my decision. It wasn't until much later that I learned that my propaganda about trim had been so effective that my crew were too fearful to go into the dinghy at all! We had enough problems without adding cold to them as well, so we ate some dried turtle and fish, swilled down with plenty of water, which left us feeling a little more cheerful.

I reckoned we had made no progress in the windless weather, so I recorded our noon position as the same it had been the day before. During the afternoon, we talked at length about what we would have to do when the time came to take to the dinghy. We discussed which pieces of the raft we would cut out and which pieces of equipment we would take and where such essentials would be stowed. As evening closed in, the drizzle eased a little and the air became much warmer. We bailed and blew in the darkness in a non-stop routine, until Douglas suddenly lifted his head and stopped.

'Quiet!' We listened, intently, not even daring to draw breath. 'Engines,' he whispered. My stomach churned as I thought I could detect the faint beat of what might have been a propeller blade, growing louder and louder. I climbed into the dinghy with a torch but could neither see nor hear anything in the pitch black. I flashed SOS in Morse code around the horizon in all directions for a couple of minutes, but there was no answering light and after a further round of flashes I returned to the raft. We speculated on the possibility of it being a submarine bound for the atomic testing grounds near Tahiti, where we had heard before we had been sunk that a nuclear test was scheduled to take place, and then wondered exactly what sort of spy submarine would pick up survivors in any event. 'You know what, I think I might just decline,' Douglas had us all grinning at the prospect. As it turned out, it was a decision we did not have to make, for whatever it was, the sound soon disappeared without trace. The twins talked quietly in a corner about the sort of cat they were going to have when we returned to England, where they would keep it, what they would feed it on and how they would house-train it. Neil loved furry animals and could talk for hours on the subject. Douglas was back on roast rabbit and Robin was in rhapsodies over oatmeal porridge and milk. Lyn and I were just happy with plain old water, for it was just so good to have some!

That night will live in our memories as one of utter and abject misery. Our mouths became raw from the rough surface of the bellows tube and our lungs and cheeks ached with the effort of keeping the raft inflated. Because of the seawater on the floor of the raft, we tried to lie with our entire bodies on top of the flotation chambers, and because we lay on the flotation chambers we squeezed the air out of them ever more quickly. As we nodded into sleep, our faces dropped into the pools of water around us, causing us to wake with a start. The water continually absorbed our body heat and Lyn was terrified in case one of the twins should fall asleep face downwards and drown. Lyn remained in the water, giving up her turn to get dry on the thwart, in order to allow Douglas or Robin some additional respite. The dogged fortitude and quiet courage with which she endured the cold water was testimony indeed to her strong spirit and incredible willpower, as she did all she could to ensure the survival of our children. As the water seepages increased, we only had time to bail in the forward section of the raft, and even so we could not bail quickly enough to keep it dry; the after section became permanently flooded and totally uninhabitable. I estimated that we could probably keep the raft afloat for a few days more at most, but the effort involved was depriving us of all bodily stamina and our limbs suffered a massive proliferation of the boil-infested areas, which seemed to be spreading by the hour. It was clear to us all that we were pouring our lives away in the struggle to remain afloat. Our evacuation to the dinghy would have to be done and done soon. Death in the dinghy would come as a result of an error of judgement, a capsize perhaps, or through being swamped in heavy weather; either of these in my estimate was distinctly preferable to the deterioration of our physical and mental state, leading from sheer exhaustion into submission and certain death, if we remained where we were.

Seventeenth day

The rain stopped in the early morning just before daybreak and as the first rays of sun reached into the raft, probing our livid skin eruptions with warming fingers of light, I announced that this was the day I hoped we would transfer to the dinghy. I didn't expect a wave of enthusiastic support but I was more than disappointed by the absence of even the slightest display of interest, and surprised myself by asking the others if they would prefer to stay on the raft. Every morning they had declared they couldn't stand another night like the last one, but this morning the outlook was different for this morning made last night the final night, and the unknown suddenly yawned ahead. Robin demurred and said he was prepared to manage a few days longer, Lyn worried about the cramped conditions and trim, Sandy wanted to go, Neil didn't really care, and Douglas wondered if we wouldn't be swamped as the seas worsened. 'We can't keep this damn raft inflated for much longer in any event,' he stated grimly, 'perhaps another day at most – because with its demands on my moisture and energy it's bloody well killing me.' He looked away and shook his head as if finally admitting defeat. I studied his drained form; he had lost a lot of weight and looked drawn and exhausted from the practically non-stop round-the-clock puffing and blowing he had carried out over the last few days, in an effort to keep the raft's inflation tubes full. I felt, however, that as long as we could keep blowing we should remain in the raft.

As always, they left the final decision to me. It would be an irrevocable step and I fairly did not have the courage to make it. The sound of silence began to mount, impinging upon our minds and collective consciousness, with every second that passed. I was about to accede to the status quo, when without warning the floor in the forward compartment of the raft, which we had always regarded as the good half, came away along some two-thirds of its length, at the point where it joined the flotation chambers. The bottom literally disappeared from under us, leaving Douglas, Robin and Lyn floating in the water and gripping the lifelines inside the raft, to avoid being swept under the flotation chambers and away into the Pacific. Living in the raft would no longer be possible. In that moment my mind had been made up for me and there was not a second to lose.

'Right, the dinghy it is.' Live or die, we had to leave the inhospitable sanctuary afforded by the raft, and risk all in the open boat. Barely large enough for three persons, life in the dinghy would be cramped and expose us to a much greater risk from the elements of the open ocean. For the present, however, there was an even greater challenge, for we would each have to fend for ourselves as we risked the short crossing from the raft to the *Ednamair*. Only when, and only if, we had all successfully boarded the dinghy, would we be able to see how we stood.

In our weakened state, it would be impossible to haul our body weight out of the sea and over the gunwales of the dinghy. We had no choice but to board the dinghy from the top of one of the sections of the raft which was still inflated and intact. I set Douglas to cutting away the door pieces on the raft, from which he made capes to shield us from the wind and rain, and after we had prepared a small canopy Douglas and I dragged it through the water to the *Ednamair* and fitted it over the bow to offer protection from the sea and spray. I bailed out the rainwater next and then transferred the foot of the sail to the bow so that the dinghy would ride stern to the raft in order to facilitate boarding. I then proceeded to fasten the towropes with a strop to the dinghy's stern.

The next job was to clear the inside of the dinghy and make space. Over went the turtle shells, laboriously scraped and cleaned. Then came the lifejackets. I had given them careful thought. They were made of kapok and in their waterlogged state weighed about forty pounds each; I decided they wouldn't help us to keep afloat but it was quite conceivable that they might just cause us to sink, so over they went too. Various other trophies followed along with pieces of wood and lumps of metal that had been saved simply because they were there: empty flare cases, turtle flippers and the canvas valise for the raft, now relegated to a bulky lump of uselessness. Douglas had soon cut away all the useful pieces of rope from the raft and they were collected and stowed in the onion bag. I secured the bow canopy with more lashings and then returned to the dismembered raft, already partly submerged beneath the water, where Lyn and Robin gripped tightly onto the twins, herding them onto the top of the collapsed canopy and away from the encroaching seawater as it lapped at their heels on all sides.

With the raft and the dinghy as close together as we could get them, the twins were able to leap from the tubes of the raft directly onto the thwarts of the Ednamair, their young agile bodies balancing easily. Helping each other as they went, Lyn and Robin dragged themselves from the water onto the raft sides, whilst Douglas and I watched in fearful expectation of disaster. Step by agonising step, they inched their way precariously along the central thwart and then out onto the flotation tubes as the twins had done, heeding shouted instructions and guarded advice on each and every step of the way. When they were as close as they could get to the dinghy, they prepared themselves for the jump across the intervening gap. Lyn went first, followed closely by Robin, each received by the grasping arms of the twins. Douglas and I looked on aghast, lest either was to fall into the surrounding ocean, where they could easily be separated from us and in their feeble state be washed away or attacked by the waiting sharks. Douglas signalled the success of the transfer with an upturned thumb, as Robin got safely aboard. Though it looked full beyond capacity, our little boat still had freeboard for more. The moment of truth would come soon enough when I, as the last member of our party, would attempt to squeeze amongst the others and get on board.

With the raft now deserted, Douglas and I remained behind and began its demolition in earnest. We cut off the double canopy first and passed it over to the dinghy, followed by the precious knife. Making quick work of the worn fabric, we used the safety knife to hack off the canopy arch support, which we intended to use as a flotation collar. The main flotation chambers were leaking so badly that we decided they were not worth salvaging. We turned our attention to the grab lines, which Douglas hacked from around the raft, together with the rope ladders and other lines. To our surprise, a turtle poked its head up to view the proceedings so we caught it, slipped a rope around its flippers and passed it over to Robin to hold until we could deal with it. No point in passing up a good meal just because we were moving house. Maintaining our balance became ever more perilous as we dismembered the raft into sections. 'Damn it,' I heard myself shout, as in a moment of rash carelessness I accidentally sliced into the main flotation chamber with the safety knife. 'Quick, help me, I've cut the main flotation chamber!' 'I've got it, Dad,' came my son's startled reply as he plugged the gap with his hand and I re-arranged my grip, enabling me to hold the cut together to keep us afloat until he could pass the last of the loose material across to *Ednamair*. Under my instructions Douglas then carefully cut out the central thwart, which had a double-skinned flotation chamber, then as the floors of the raft tilted steeply downwards I saw, too late, the scissors slide through the hole at the edge of the floor and disappear into the depths. Moments later Douglas struggled to board the dinghy. The whole raft had now collapsed except for the forward floor piece, which though inflated leaked badly and would deflate steadily in about half an hour. Waist deep in water, I could remain aboard the raft no longer; unable to hold my footing, I slipped into the sea and headed for the stern of the dinghy, where inviting hands hauled me aboard. As soon as I was out of the water, we shoved the remains of the raft away, consigning it to the depths just as soon as it had lost what was left of its buoyancy. We then cast off the towing wire to sink with the raft but retained the nylon painter.

We all stared in silence as the remnants of the raft fell away behind us and drifted into the distance. The valiant little craft had served us well, and as its component parts either hung or floated around us we felt touched with sorrow at its passing, for when it was gone there would be little to protect us from the full force of the elements. Like being parted from the dearest of friends, we watched together as the bright yellow structure got smaller and smaller and its features slowly merged into a speck against the backdrop of the oily Pacific swells. Good old Siggi, his gift to us in Bequia had been our salvation and haven for over two weeks, and the pieces left over would still serve us as needs must. The raft had undoubtedly saved our lives when the *Lucette* had been sunk and reduced our need for water as we had sailed through the tropical heat of the trades. Without it, we would never have got this far and what was left of it would continue to keep us alive as we continued our journey towards land. I turned my attention back to the dinghy as Douglas and Robin corralled the overwrought turtle until we could find the time to kill it. Less than ten minutes later, the twins reported every last trace of the raft had vanished from sight.

CHAPTER 11

Incredible journey

Seventeenth day (continued)

We had abandoned the raft because life aboard it had become untenable, but now it had gone and we felt truly alone in the vastness of the ocean, the sense of desolation amongst the adults became even more acute and intense. The twins, however, settled happily into their allotted places in the bow, whilst Lyn and Robin sat on the centre thwart one each side of the mast. Slowly and carefully, I eased myself into position next to Douglas in the stern.

'Well, Mother, here's your ham tin,' said Douglas in a matter-of-fact tone, referring to her dream immediately prior to the sinking of *Lucette*. We all remarked on the irony as we took the sail down and streamed the heavy-duty sea anchor, to bring *Ednamair*'s bow on to the waves while we first killed and then butchered the turtle. Douglas and I heaved the unfortunate creature over the stern, securing its thrashing flippers and determined beak. So far so good, we were keeping good trim and even with the extra weight of the turtle aboard *Ednamair* rode the waves without dipping her gunwale or shipping any water; admittedly the waves weren't very big but it was an encouraging start nevertheless. Apart from Douglas, the rest of *Ednamair*'s crew had not yet witnessed my expertise with a butcher's knife, an omission soon put to rights. Douglas was quite eager to take his share in dressing the turtle, but he was still a little overzealous, and I dared not risk the knife being broken a second time. The serrated blade had more the appearance of a saw than a sharp knife, and while I managed to sever the arteries and catch the blood without spilling too much, it took a long time for me to hack through the tough belly shell. Stopping for a break midway through our labours, we indulged in our usual blood-imbibing orgy. 'The equivalent of a tea break, I suppose,' Robin observed, having become quite partial to it. Once he had finished his second cupful, we dumped the shell and offal overboard and ate some of the steak for lunch, before turning our attention to clearing up the boat. We sorted out the jumbled pieces of canopy and rope, and found homes for the pieces of sail, the spare sea anchor, rain capes and our meagre supply of stores. The flotation pieces we towed alongside, ready to be secured into position when we had prepared suitable lashings.

Our noon position I put at 5 degrees 20 minutes north and 250 miles west of Cape Espinosa (95 degrees and 30 minutes west) in order to reflect how little wind we had experienced in the last few days. The sea had become very calm and I decided to try our luck sailing bow first, steering with an oar, in order to make as much easting as possible whilst the seas were quiet. When the waves became too high for comfort, we would have to change the sail back to the stern again and sail backwards, presenting the most seaworthy part of the dinghy to the weather. While I made and secured a makeshift grommet onto the rudder pins to affix the steering oar, Douglas and Robin strung pieces of turtle meat from the rigging. Once dry we would be able to store the pieces and build up a reserve of food for the times when it was not possible to catch it fresh. Lyn and the twins were kept busy stowing what was left of our equipment and finding places suitable for the smaller items. We were all very careful not to change places to the opposite side of the dinghy without first warning of an intended move. Such movement could not be undertaken without first arranging for one or more of our group located on the opposite side of the boat to shift themselves simultaneously in order to maintain an even keel. In fact, with all the bottom weight, the dinghy was more stable than I had ever dared hope she would be.

The day remained overcast, sparing us the necessity of rigging a sun canopy or awning, until later in the afternoon. Instead, we concentrated on securing the flotation collar around the bow; lashing the ends of the long sausage-like float to the leeboard fittings, followed by securing the centre of the sleeve under the gunwale at the stem. With the contraption secured into place, if the dinghy plunged its bows into a sea, the collar would not only provide support but would prevent any waves breaking into the dinghy from ahead. We lashed the other float, originally forming the central divider in the raft, across the dinghy behind the central thwart and used it as an awkward backrest for the watch-keepers who would be seated there.

We now had more room to move around, so with Douglas balancing to maintain trim I moved to the bows and enlarged the spread of the canopy over the forestay, covering the dinghy from a foot or so forward of the central thwart all the way to the stem. I then lashed the sides of the canopy to the gunwale to form a tent, under which the twins at least would have some shelter. Most of the smaller pieces of equipment we stowed in the bows, while the water cans, cups and bailers were pushed under the stern seat. The box containing the dried fish and meat we then placed in the bottom of the dinghy, abaft of the central thwart. The twins tucked their small bodies under the canopy in the bow, whilst Lyn and Robin distributed themselves one each side of the dried stores box and Douglas and I sat on the thwart, leaning back on the float. As night fell, we tried to find comfort for our aching limbs, but whichever way we turned the unyielding wood and fibreglass gave little ease. For all that, there were undoubted and indeed blessed compensations. Our bodies were warm and dry out of the chest-deep water that had surrounded us in the raft, there was no blowing up to do except an occasional puff on the float and, on account of the calm seas, no bailing either. Even the assaults on our backsides from the sea's predatory inhabitants had stopped. Our bodies, protected by the fibreglass, had gained some peace even if it was at the cost of a little comfort.

In the arc of the cloud-strewn sky, the evening stars twinkled above us. On the raft, we had had only the overhead canopy to look at, which like the roof of a cave had protected us from the vast loneliness of the ocean. Like the far-ranging albatross and stately frigatebirds that soared around us, the sky was now our roof, the ocean our larder and the wind our power. The quiet beauty of the night brought back distant memories of our former life aboard the open decks of *Lucette*, as quiet zephyrs of wind left *Ednamair* idling at her sea anchor, awaiting the arrival of daybreak.

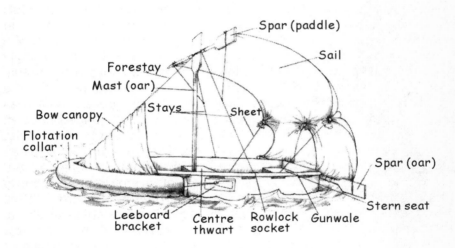

Ednamair under way

Eighteenth day

The night sky cleared and daybreak brought with it a beautiful sunrise of breathtaking splendour. Deep orange hues reflected from the close sparkling water, making me forget for a moment the precarious nature of our mortal tenure. A flying fish had landed in the dinghy during the night, which we sliced up and mixed with some fresh turtle meat and the pool of secreted juice, collected in the bottom of a piece of sail in which we had wrapped some of the undried meat. Mixed with some pieces of turtle fat, it made a very tasty dish indeed. A slight drizzle had occurred in the early hours so that the meat festooned about the rigging hung in limp damp strips, some of which, still uncured from the second turtle, had started to go bad. It didn't go offensively bad or stink, but simply disintegrated on contact with our mouths into a slimy gut-wrenching mess. There were of course no insects around to assist the process of decomposition, although we did observe a type of water-spider, skating on the surface of the flat calm sea. We also had the constant companionship of the storm petrels, delightful little birds which flitted endlessly over the ocean, dipping their feet into the surface of the sea whilst picking up pieces of turtle fat which we threw to them, earning themselves their South American name of 'walkers on the water'. British sailors affectionately knew them as 'Mother Carey's chickens'.

Frigatebird

Majestic frigatebirds soared across the sky at regular intervals, often working in pairs to catch flying fish, especially in cloudy or inclement weather. The flying fish seemed to shoal in this type of weather and it was quite common to see a frigatebird dive menacingly down onto a basking shoal, frightening them into flight in the direction of its partner, who was patrolling in a pre-arranged position waiting to pluck them out of the air. Flying fish that took to the air when attacked by dorado were treated likewise, often picked up by a swooping frigatebird before they could regain the relative safety of the water. On one occasion we saw a frigatebird and a dorado collide in mid-air, both in pursuit of the same flying fish. The frigatebirds, like the storm petrels, seemed to remain in flight over the ocean and were the most spectacular of our attendant bevies of feathered hunters, as they attacked their prey with dramatic hawk-like strikes.

Douglas took a particular interest in these birds and he and Lyn named each one of them. The largest they named 'Old Pev' after Lyn's father, as Lyn was sure his spirit was looking down on us through them. Then Douglas surprised us all with a spontaneous verse of poetry:

O sentinel of the southern seas, impervious to our plight
You soar aloft in majesty and hold us in your sight.

'That's quite good,' Robin opined. 'hmm – I hope to finish it before we get picked up,' Douglas responded. 'We won't be hanging around if you don't,' Robin assured him categorically, patting him on the back as he repeated trial phrases over in his head. 'Do you offer hopes of landfall ...' We all nodded in approval until Lyn brought a rapid close to the cultural proceedings with her offering, 'Or mourning for the dead.' 'Oh, I'm so sorry,' she asserted, putting her hand over her mouth, unable to believe what she had just said. The spell had been broken, however, and we all returned to our silent vigils, having so much to think about yet so little to say.

A new arrival in the form of a blue-footed booby visited us on this, our first morning in the dinghy, which was also our eighteenth day adrift. Circling curiously before landing on the sea not far from us, it preened its feathers and surveyed us with the rather comical expression peculiar to these birds. I caught my breath and shouted a stifled warning as we saw a shark nosing upwards towards the bird; the booby looked at me curiously then, sensing the presence of danger, stuck its head under the water. The shark, now only a few feet away, moved swiftly towards it but to my surprise the booby instead of taking off pecked at the shark's snout three or four times, forcing the fearsome fish to turn away. With the danger passed, it spread its wings and flew off. The shark was young and perhaps just curious, leaving me to wonder how the booby might have fared if it had been an older or hungrier shark. 'Still, it shows what a bit of determination can do,' remarked Douglas as the bird disappeared into the distance.

It had been cold in the night without the shelter from the canopy and we were all grateful for the soothing touch of the morning sun that gradually warmed our bones and thinned our blood, slowly heating our bodies until movement returned to our stiffened limbs. After sorting out the meat and discarding the slimy pieces, now so bad that even the scavenger fish weren't interested in them, we pulled the sea anchor aboard and reset the sail, still trimmed with the foot of the square sail sheeted to the bow. The light southerly breeze allowed us to steer in a northeasterly direction, using the steering oar to hold the dinghy on course. We were on our way again, and with 600 miles to go we were nearly half way to the coast!

Douglas and I had changed places with Lyn and Robin, a precarious business involving much bad language on my part and fearful reactions on theirs, as the tiny dinghy tipped dangerously and frantic yells of 'Trim' rent the Pacific air. The change was necessary to allow Douglas to swap steering positions with myself, for neither

Lyn nor Robin could use the steering oar or find the direction in which to steer, and although Douglas could scull expertly this was the first time he had used an oar as a rudder. As we settled down again, the dinghy made half a knot in the slight breeze and we talked of the north Staffordshire countryside where Lyn and the children had been born, and of the rolling hills and valleys in the Peak District. We all decided how nice it would be if we were actually sitting in a teahouse, drinking tea from china cups and eating hot buttered scones. The visions of the food were so real that our mouths watered in anticipation and I declared that when we got home we would open a café of our own. From that day onwards the café was to become our 'pièce de résistance' and our main topic of conversation. A kitchen-type restaurant located near the north Staffordshire town of Leek, it was to be called 'Dougal's Kitchen'. It presented a wonderful opportunity to discuss, describe and generally wax lyrical about all things food.

Our estimated noon position of 5 degrees and 30 minutes north and 245 miles west of Cape Espinosa recorded our first easting since *Lucette* had sunk and I felt that we were now far enough north to allow some set and drift for the counter-current, which ran east through the doldrums towards the Central American coast. At last, we really felt we were on our way home! The sores and boils on our limbs and buttocks had already begun to dry and while they were still badly inflamed, with many of them septic, the surrounding skin felt much better, with no further extensions to the infected areas. Our clothes had begun to disintegrate rapidly, though, giving rise to a new concern, that of avoiding sunburn on the hitherto unexposed parts of our bodies. My extraordinary contortions to avoid putting pressure on my sun-blistered posterior, supported by ample cursing and much colourful language, proved sufficient warning to the others to stay out of the sun. We would miss the warmth our clothes afforded us at night and this was a particular worry to Lyn, far more than any concern for modesty. Indeed our absence of clothing was never discussed in terms of modesty or morality, and while the capes that had been cut from the doors of the raft saved us many a night of misery by retaining a little of our body warmth, we never wore them during the day unless it rained. Douglas apart, our bronzed bodies still needed the protection afforded by our rag-like singlets, whilst we exposed the various parts of our distressed anatomy to dry in the fresh air.

We steered a steady northeasterly course for the rest of the day and then towards evening the wind freshened a little, building the waves to a sufficient height that they began to slop in over the square transom of the dinghy. With much manoeuvring to maintain an even keel, Douglas and I lashed the steering oar horizontally across the stern and brought the sail aft, sheeting it to either end of the oar thereby forming the lower boom. This move allowed the dinghy to ride bow on to the waves whilst sailing backwards, which minimised to an acceptable margin the danger of being swamped. Steering was performed by means of pulling the sail and yard down on the side the stern was required to move towards. This method allowed us to angle the dinghy across the wind by as much as 45 degrees provided the sea did not become too rough. The fore-and-aft trim was of much more importance now, for if the bow was too light it fell away from the wind, bringing the dinghy broadside on to the waves and into a vulnerable position. As the afternoon unfolded the wind increased, leaving me no choice but to rig a half-tripped sea anchor from the bow, which whilst hindering our progress, kept the bow pointed to the waves. We also repositioned the boxes, originally lashed onto the aft thwart, into the bottom of the dinghy, which increased our forward trim as well as our stability. As the wind diminished towards evening, and with the sea anchor still streamed, Douglas discovered that by simply lashing the sail into position *Ednamair* became self-steering, which allowed us to continue our watches as we had in the raft. Lyn insisted that I be spared the necessity of taking watches at night, for I was liable to be called out at all times and the heavy work of tending to the rigging and dressing the turtles was becoming most onerous in my exhausted condition. We agreed therefore that the night watches would be split between Douglas, Robin and Lyn, and that I was to be on standby at all times, day or night.

As the night closed in on *Ednamair*, a fragile and lonely speck alone in the vast reaches of the ocean, her crew arranged and rearranged their comfortless limbs in a relentless quest for sleep. Even so, we felt that we had conquered a major obstacle to our survival. Though we were yet to be tested, we felt at least that we were coming to terms with surviving in the dinghy without the insurance we had enjoyed in the raft.

Booby

Nineteenth day

Rain showers in the night caused us some discomfort and set our teeth chattering, as the cool blasts of geostrophic wind descended from the thunderclouds above us. Each and every member of the watch-keeping team was kept constantly busy as they bailed from beneath the inadequate shelter provided by the waterproof canopy, which we had stretched as far as it would go across the stern. Unfortunately it wasn't quite wide enough to reach all the way over. At the forward end the twins and I huddled under the bow canopy and managed to stay fairly warm and dry whilst the others were forced to battle the elements in quiet misery. Though their rain capes retained body heat during the night, they proved less useful at keeping them dry, when sitting on the open thwarts.

Cloud increased again during the predawn watches. Bright flashes of lightning appeared in the distance, giving way to continuous rain by daybreak. As the weather turned cold and the wind increased to a fresh east-southeasterly breeze, we were once again forced to stream the sea anchor fully opened, in order to stop us broaching. After reefing the sail, we set about preparing to collect some of the rain, in the earnest hope of increasing our water reserves. Our minds clung to the established methods we had already developed, as we stretched what was left of the old raft canopy over our heads and led the pipe down from the hollow in the centre, to a position where we could fill the empty tins in the bottom of the boat. In torturous agony, we held aloft the canopy with aching arms in order to increase the catchment area and suffered while the rainwater slowly trickled into our armpits and down our torsos, as well as into the empty tins. The rainwater still tasted of rubber, but the yellow dye seemed finally to have washed off. We all gained a certain amount of shelter from this method of collection, but it was certainly bought at the price of aching limbs and short tempers. The cans wobbled precariously on the sloping bottom of the dinghy and more than one was knocked over by the uncontrollable flapping of the canopy in the wind, spilling its precious contents into the bottom of the boat.

The turtle meat was also giving much cause for concern. The meat that had already dried we had stored in the box for safekeeping and it had become coated with a slight covering of fungus. The continuously damp atmosphere caused the hanging meat to sweat and we feared that we would not be able to dry the flesh of our last two turtles, which in turn would cause the meat to rot, rendering it not only inedible for the present but also useless as dry stores for the future. I decided therefore to dole out more of the fresh turtle meat than usual, saving as much as possible from our dry stores. The rain helped in some degree to keep the seas from building up to dangerous proportions and we took full advantage by topping up the water containers as well as our bellies. The relief of not having to worry about water was more than adequate compensation for the problems with the meat that the heavy rains had created.

The rain cleared after midday and towards two o'clock another blue-footed booby, younger then the first, circled the dinghy and alighted on the water, inspecting our strange appearance before deciding we were harmless enough. It flew around us again, then without warning swooped down, folding its five-foot wingspan in mid-air, and landed on Douglas's shoulder as he sat in the stern of the dinghy. Douglas, looking for all the world like Long John Silver, glanced sideways at the four-inch razor-sharp beak hovering just two inches from his right eye, then hastily averted his glance in case it pecked at him. The bird seemed quite unafraid, and while we admired its beautiful plumage and streamlined appearance we could not prevent our furtive minds from considering it as a possible alternative source of food. We spoke of what we knew about seabirds, concluding that they were salty, stringy and possibly full of lice. Having agreed that only in an extreme emergency would we consider these birds as a source of food, a small voice piped up from the bow, 'Not likely; if you pluck it I'll eat it!' We turned in astonishment to Neil, the source of the comment, and assured him that he could have some turtle meat if he was hungry. It seemed that the adults were being a bit too fussy after all.

Intermittent rain continued to fall for the rest of the afternoon. The seas, smoothed over by the sporadic precipitation, enabled us to half-trip the sea anchor and shake out the reefs in the mainsail and resume our course. The swells, still fifteen feet high and very dangerous in light of our small freeboard, put us in a position where there was no alternative but to remain in abject stillness, whilst remaining constantly alert and moving only with the utmost caution. A second chance after being swamped would be a meagre one indeed, for all our stores and fresh water would be ruined, to say nothing of the probable loss of life or limb from the waiting sharks. We had been well warned even whilst aboard *Lucette* that anything which struggles and splashes on the surface can attract and stimulate a shark attack. I returned to my ruminations about the usefulness of the float as a backrest for the central thwart as compared with its drawbacks as an obstacle when we changed positions. After the shortest of debates, we agreed its best function would be attached to the sea anchor, in order to provide us with a marker denoting the sea anchor's position. With the task completed, we all concurred that the increased room was well worth the loss in comfort. The evening brought a glorious rainbow and we gazed spellbound at the riotous bands of colour which suffused the sky and sea with the cloud into a brilliant and truly spectacular aura, combining breathtaking yellows, spliced with tongues of orange and red trailing into the far-off Pacific sunset.

Twentieth day

We all remembered Lyn's birthday. I often kidded her that America chose to be independent on July the fourth for that very reason. Dear Lyn, she had so much to put up with from us all and especially from me, which she bore with great fortitude.

We caught another turtle later that morning. It was a female but, alas, it had no eggs. It did bring fresh meat to the birthday menu, however, with dressing and carving the carcass occupying our entire morning. We all chewed the turtle bones at lunch and especially enjoyed the flavour of old dried turtle meat marinated in the fresh meat juices, mixed with a combination of dried dorado strips and fresh steak. Indeed, we feasted and then drank our fill of water in a muted celebration.

I estimated our noon position at 5 degrees and 55 minutes north, still 245 miles west of Cape Espinosa, which was a cautious estimate on my part, for I felt that we had made some westing since noon the day before, which negated the easterly drift of the current. *Ednamair* still rode to the combined sea anchor and float as we waited patiently for the seas to subside. We rested quietly in the afternoon and talked of all the nice things we had received on previous birthdays. After a long-drawn-out birthday tea, thirty minutes of slow chewing and sipping water, we sang 'Happy Birthday' to Lyn. It sounded a bit odd in a small boat in the middle of the Pacific as the familiar tune echoed across the waves of our watery wilderness, but it did our morale the world of good. As the quiet of the evening drew in, our singing repertoire expanded to include numerous other songs. Robin sang Welsh ones, I sang Scottish ones, and we all joined in with Lyn and sang English ones.

By twilight, the wind had dropped to the lightest of breezes. In the now peaceful atmosphere of another Pacific sunset, our voices boomed loud and clear and for the moment we felt almost at one with our alien environment, half believing that we could go on not simply surviving, but creating a way of life that had no objective other than life on the sea, from the sea. It came as something of a shock to realise that the twins, although they had joined in with some of the songs, had already concluded that this was in fact what had happened and that we were intending to go on living in this way, for months if not years. I decided that it would be good for them to see a record of our progress towards the coast and show pictorially exactly what my expectations were. I pointed to where we were on the chart and, trying my utmost to avoid setting their expectations too high, indicated when we might anticipate sighting land. We all talked at some length of the speed we might make, and when I mentioned, with a long stare in Douglas's direction, that once we were close enough we'd start rowing at night to make up for the loss of the counter-current, it sounded as if we were almost home. I tried to make the thirty-five days left to go sound like it was less than a month, whilst reminding my audience that one of the most dangerous attitudes we could adopt was that what lay ahead of us would be easy, in some way certain, or that the sea had suddenly become our friend. I knew from hard-won experience that where the land may be kindly to man, the sea was as impartial as the sky. I also knew that, in an environment where every other living creature had adapted and perfected its means of survival since the beginning of time, our chances of surviving amongst them lay in our ability to adapt our past experience and wisdom to our present circumstances. This, together with our ability to fashion tools, to help each other physically and psychologically, and to use knowledge as a weapon of offence as well as defence, were the attributes that would allow us to succeed in carving a living from the sea.

Even so, life in this harsh environment had moved from the realms of possibility, to become a matter of probability and even fact. 'We must get these boys to land,' Lyn had said back in those impossible days at the very beginning; for the first time I dared to let myself think that we might just succeed. As the realisation sank in, it was like a release from physical pain. I looked across the centre thwart to Lyn, crouched awkwardly in the bow, each arm tightly circling a twin, and wondered if I should share this revelation with her as a birthday present. As she looked back into my eyes, I not only saw her unfaltering love shining from them, but also the intuitive knowledge that my message had been received. After nearly twenty years of marriage, she could still surprise me.

The watches for the night were set as twilight deepened and the dorado flashed iridescent under the hull of the *Ednamair* in their endless pursuit of prey. These big fish posed one of the knottiest problems of our existence: how to get them from their present location in the water to a far more desirable location on the floor of the dinghy, only a matter of a few feet in distance but a massive leap in terms of expertise. It was becoming the obsession of my resting hours. The spear I had made was only strong enough to tackle the smallest of the dorado, but we seldom saw them, far less did they come within striking distance.

My thoughts became distracted as Robin stirred uneasily in his sleep, then suddenly he sat up and yelled, 'Where's the spike? We won't have any water left if we can't find it!' Douglas on watch looked closely at him. 'He's still asleep, it's all right Robin,' he soothed, gripping his shoulders and staring pensively back into his face through the pale moonlight. Robin lay back and twisted his long legs into another position, kicked Neil, pulled the sail cover off Lyn, and then jabbed his bony knees into my back. 'Ye gods!' I groaned and thumped away his offending knees with my fist; they moved with menacing certainty to kick Neil once more, and then as he turned over he dragged the rubber canopy sheet off the rest of us and thrust the food box into Lyn's chest. 'Robin!' we all shouted out in chorus. It was fifteen minutes before we had managed to settle down again, slowly squeezing ourselves into the available space, searching out places for arms and legs that had nowhere to fit. Since fifteen minutes was about the maximum length of time we could suffer such restrictions to our circulatory system, or the relentless press of the fibreglass on our sparsely covered bones and boils, all too soon it was time for Robin, poor lad, to move again.

Twenty-first day

As dawn approached the clear night gave way to cloudy squally weather, and in the early daylight hours *Ednamair* tugged impatiently at the float, with her sea anchor streamed to windward. Incredibly, it was the last morning of our third week adrift. 'Almost a month,' confirmed Robin as we counted the days back. 'Surely we can celebrate that,' he finished in the hope of a bit of extra food. Along with some extra turtle meat, we shared the flying fish that had come aboard during Robin's watch for breakfast.

As we re-stowed the water jar, the dinghy yawed sharply and Lyn pointed with an urgent cry to the float, drifting a hundred yards away from us trailing the broken sea anchor and rope behind it! We had a much smaller fair-weather spare, but it would not work effectively in rough seas; we couldn't survive without the rapidly disappearing sea anchor, and the float was our only hope if we were swamped. I quickly downed the sail and tried ineffectually to paddle our craft towards the bright yellow flotation tube. One of the paddles broke at the bayonet fitting, so I quickly substituted the oar from the foot of the sail. Douglas looked on with disdain as the paddles skimmed ineffectually over the water and the float and sea anchor receded further and further into the distance. His frustration finally got the better of him, and without a word I cleared the centre thwart and allowed him to take over. Douglas our champion oarsman started rowing with an oar to port and a paddle to starboard, each loosely tied to the gunwale with improvised grommets. An unequal combination in an unequal contest, he pulled our overloaded boat against both wind and weather with a gusto that the rest of us could only marvel at. The other oar was rigged as the mast and would cause chaos and much loss of time if taken down, so Douglas stuck grimly to his task without it, his wasted muscles bunched like whipcord as he thrust the dinghy forward with powerful strokes.

Fifteen minutes passed and still he rowed in a steady rhythm, gaining foot by foot against the buffeting waves. His breath came in harsh gasps as I encouraged him on. 'You're doing fine, Doug, we're half way – and gaining.' The float was still nearly a hundred yards away as I started to call out the distance to go, eighty yards, sixty, and so on. I could see that the effort was becoming a test of sheer endurance, but our eldest son steadfastly refused to give in. Gradually we drew closer until, after thirty-five minutes of rowing, I was able to secure the broken rope to the eyebolt in the bow of the dinghy. Douglas collapsed and sat gasping for breath on the centre thwart as Lyn hastily passed him some water and a piece of glucose from the ration box. I was grateful beyond words to have retrieved both float and sea anchor, for our journey without them would have been dangerous and maybe even impossible. I also realised that even with an oar apiece, Robin and I could not have accomplished such a task together, and that only Douglas's constant rowing practice had enabled him to perform such a feat now. It was a salutary lesson to us, too, in demonstrating how difficult it would be to retrieve anything or anybody lost overboard in rough weather. Douglas had demonstrated that he was still in good condition, though, and I felt cheered by the fact that when the time came to row towards the coast we would be able to do it.

Our examination of the sea-anchor rope revealed it had chafed through due to the constant action of the restless seaway. We spent some time making a substitute line strong enough to hold the sea anchor and float, for we were running short of suitable material which could withstand the constant chafing.

Our noon position I computed as 6 degrees north and 240 miles west of Cape Espinosa, which gave us all a boost, for our eastward drift was now evidenced on paper as well as – I hoped – in fact. The boys settled down to a game of Twenty Questions, which was followed by Robin telling us about his travels across Yugoslavia and Greece. While Lyn sewed diligently at our tattered clothing, I began fashioning a wooden handle from a section of the central thwart that I intended to secure onto the broken knife blade by a combination of lashing and a bit of designer carving.

The afternoon was overcast but dry and the hanging turtle meat now looked ready to be stored. As we gathered in the drier pieces and night fell, Douglas brought a sudden stop to proceedings with a startled cry, 'Flare, look a flare!' We scrambled to look in the direction of his jabbing finger, with our usual cries of 'Trim her!' as *Ednamair* tilted dangerously to one side. I didn't see it and Lyn wasn't sure but Douglas assured me that he had seen a green flare, a signal often given by submarines on manoeuvres, and with fingers demonstrating he confirmed he'd seen it go up as well as down. 'Shooting stars don't go up!' was Robin's immediate observation. We scanned the sea closely in the deepening twilight but we saw nothing. I brought out the torch and signalled in the appropriate direction but I felt that the sacrifice of one of our three remaining hand flares was unjustified, particularly if the submarine had merely surfaced to periscope depth and might not even be on our side of the horizon. We pressed our ears to the inside of the hull, straining every last fibre of our beings in an effort to detect the confirmatory beat of a large diesel engine. Alas, nothing transpired so I decided to wait a few more minutes and if no further signs of its presence were seen then we would have to write it off as another miss. We had become almost casual in our acceptance of this disappointment, to me a healthy sign that our thoughts were no longer centred on rescue as our main hope of survival.

The sea had quietened again with the lull of the evening and we had stopped shipping water, which allowed us the opportunity for some rest. We sat in surreal silence, enjoying the reprieve from the effort that had been required to keep the raft inflated, and rested our aching limbs, no longer throbbing from pain or inflamed from the constant immersion in seawater.

Twenty-second day

After a quieter night, during which I slept for over three hours, a most extraordinarily long time for any of us, the still hours of dawn brought with it another turtle. The usual frenzied scramble ensued, first to clear enough space to bring it aboard followed by some hasty repositioning into our allotted deployment, in order that we could perform the operation without getting bitten or swamped. I conscripted Sandy to help on this occasion, so Lyn transferred her position to the bows with Neil and the slaughter crew assembled, eying their new trainee with more than a little scepticism as they prepared for the gruesome and grisly task. With everyone in position the turtle, a big one by previous standards, was pulled to the side, beak snapping as it brandished its clawed flippers wildly. Douglas and I flipped it onto its back and slid it into position while Robin and Sandy trimmed the boat from the other side. Sucker fish, one nine inches long, dropped from the underbelly of the turtle and flapped wildly in the bottom of the dinghy, and though we had caught no fresh flying fish that morning, none of us could bring ourselves to try the grey jellified flesh of these repulsive-looking fish.

I had successfully fitted the new handle to the broken knife blade and could now impose much better control over the cutting edge. Nevertheless, it took considerable effort and dogged perseverance to locate the artery in the maze of tough tendons and wiry sinews which crisscrossed around the turtle's neck area like a finely wired loom. Its lacerating claws took their toll as we worked in the confined space, chopping hard against fingers and shins as it fought to escape its brutal end. Eventually I located and severed the artery, and as the blood spurted into containers held at the ready we braced ourselves to take our fill in swift gulps. We had to guzzle it quickly, because if we took too long it coagulated into a solid jelly-like lump. Lyn and the twins were less eager for it now that water was more plentiful, though Robin remained our champion vampire at three full cups.

The business of cutting open the heavy shell and making the careful incisions against the inside of the outer shell to extract the meat was heavy and exacting work. Many times I cut into my own numb fingers instead of the turtle. Douglas's strong arms helped me immensely, levering the shell and pulling the joints apart, which enabled me to cut in at the more awkward places. This particular one was a female and our expectation of eggs was met in full by a golden harvest of over a hundred yolks. Amongst excited chatter, we gathered the eggs into a bag whilst Sandy collected the deep yellow fat which lined the shell and placed it inside containers for processing into oil later. It was the largest turtle we had caught so far and we probably harvested twenty-five pounds of steak and bone from it, together with a mass of eggs and fat. Its carcass was so large that even Douglas struggled to extract the flipper bones, as he sawed with the blunt raft knife to sever the muscle and tendons from the bone.

Once he had finished, the shell and offal were quickly despatched overboard. We no longer worried about sharks for the dinghy was less vulnerable than the inflatable and we soon left the debris behind, whereas the raft, being towed by the dinghy, had to run the gauntlet of sailing right through it. Sharks cruised around us almost continuously since we had abandoned the raft, and after getting over the initial trepidation we had become used to seeing their stately progress, with their attendant retinue of pilot fish following in precise formation. We prepared a veritable feast for lunch and with the juice from the meat we mixed in a dozen turtle eggs, then cut up some mature dried turtle meat into small pieces and added it to the egg mixture. Lyn marinated the fresh turtle meat and the last of our dorado in this sauce, and after a hearty meal we lay back, our stomachs feeling full for only the second time since *Lucette* had been so violently taken from us. In fact, our stomachs had contracted so much that it now took very little to fill them, itself a blessing in disguise.

Our noon position I estimated at 6 degrees 20 minutes north and 240 miles west of Cape Espinosa, the result of a change in the wind to blow from the southeast, which had borne us before it since the early hours. It blew from an unusual quarter and made me more than a little apprehensive that we might well be blown right through the thin belt of the Doldrums if it kept up for too long. As the afternoon progressed, we spotted familiar cirrostratus cloud formations spreading wraithlike tentacles high up near the stratosphere. Building contrary to the wind at the surface, they were heading in a southerly direction, stretching long and broad icy fingers from far beyond the northern horizon. Before the hour was up, the thickening tentacles had grown steadily denser, snaking across the sky in vivid zigzags like the tracks of a busy railway junction, changing colour from white to a montage of orange, crimson, yellow and green.

My gathering apprehension turned to outright fear as dense vertical slabs of cloud amassed on the horizon. Like ragged cliffs hewn from solid rock, dark slabs of dense toppling cloud piled high into the upper atmosphere, and the sea beneath the tattered black cloud base heaved in a churning maelstrom of breaking whitecaps, a clear indication of the strength of the winds soon to be unleashed upon us. We watched with bated breath as deep yellow bolts of lightning flashed from the cloud base, and waited in silent contemplation for our time of trial. We had no choice, we would have to pit our skills against the elements that were about to descend upon us and in a destiny-defining moment I called everyone to attention to discuss how we could best avert this deadly new peril. 'We're in for some foul weather,' I confirmed to my worried crew, ordering an all-round check of knots and fastenings. 'We will have to fight for our lives,' I continued, reminding them gravely that vigilant attention to trim, accurate steering and the rapid clearing of incoming waves would all be paramount if we were to get through the approaching storm alive. We busied ourselves, nervously checking and rechecking the flotation-collar knots and fastenings as well as the sea-anchor ropes for signs of fraying. There would be no second chance if we lost any vital pieces of rig or equipment or if we were swamped.

I studied the faces of my fellow castaways, looking back at me as they listened intently. 'Whatever it takes, Dad, we aren't going to be beaten by a bloody storm,' Douglas's jaw line trembled as he spoke and I knew that if we failed to see the day through then it wouldn't be for the want of trying, or because I had been let down by my crew. With Douglas at the helm, we waited in escalating degrees of foreboding and dread for the storm to strike, and distracted our troubled minds by talking about Dougal's Kitchen late into the afternoon, discussing recipes for savoury pastries, which were to be served with hot soup of the old-fashioned home-made variety in the colder months of the year. Dougal's Kitchen not only allowed us to talk about food but the site for such a restaurant allowed us to roam at will around our home-town district of Leek, remembering all the vacant buildings and houses with nostalgic enchantment. The twins became increasingly interested as the wait continued, for nothing seemed more desirable to them in the face of the gathering storm than a beautiful hot Cornish pasty, followed by copious amounts of fruit and ice cream, consumed in the security of familiar and safe surroundings. Robin, with no personal knowledge of Leek to assist him, nevertheless joined in with his own recipes for good food and recounted an ensemble of his favourite dishes.

True to form, the late afternoon brought an end to our restless vigil as the last vestiges of daylight were swept from the sky by the sinister darkness of the heavy clouds moving overhead. Then the wind suddenly hit us with a strong blast from the north. In our precarious situation, with only a few inches of freeboard to play with, our demise hung on every wave and only the sharpest of lookouts, coupled with prompt and decisive action, would save us now. The sea around us exploded into cascading white-capped rollers and the squally blasts became more and more prolonged, forcing us to reef down the sail in order to ease the strain on the sea anchor and its triple combination of ropes. We still jerked uneasily at the end of the warp, plunging steeply in the short seas, which broke over the bow and sluiced into the dinghy in violent swirling eddies. Preferring to risk the rigours of the squalls rather than the breaking waves, we trimmed the dinghy so that the bow would ride a little higher. I shook out the reef just enough to allow sufficient speed to provide our craft with steerageway, which allowed young Dougie to keep *Ednamair*'s bow pointing directly towards the largest of the waves. Some of the more hazardous combers were breaking into perilous expanses of churning white water and running at right angles across the wind in a confused fashion, which on occasion caught us broadside on and rolled our craft precariously, allowing waves to repeatedly slop in over the gunwales.

As evening fell, the wind increased and gusted strongly, requiring me to take over the steering from Douglas, who was rapidly reaching the point of exhaustion. The dinghy yawed dangerously at times, leaving us gripped by the fear of an imminent capsize. The seas heightened as the evening advanced and grimly we prepared for the rough wet night that lay ahead, realising that there would be no sleep for any of us. By nightfall, the waves were slopping aboard ever more frequently and Robin, Lyn and Douglas had to bail continuously to clear the water gathering in the bottom of the dinghy. The rain came at about eight o'clock, and as the wind swung to the south it increased steadily in volume, until by ten o'clock a torrential downpour lashed our frail bodies. Lyn and Robin bailed in tandem whilst Douglas and I peered anxiously into the black night, trying to spot the breaking waves so that I could turn the bow to meet them. Occasionally a wave crest reared unexpectedly out of the darkness, catching *Ednamair* on the beam and flooding gallons of warm salt water into the boat, which sloshed back and forth in dangerous whirlpools as it mixed with the colder rainwater already forming a deep pool around our feet. Despite our non-stop bailing the water levels began steadily rising inside the boat as we fought against the elements in a battle that I feared we could easily lose. At eleven thirty, the wind shifted, and shortly after shifted again.

Our course made good became difficult to determine, my only guide being the long trade-wind swell which still ran up from the southeast, visible only intermittently in the brilliant flashes of lightning which illumined the sky at increasingly frequent intervals. I sat immobile as I had seen farm animals do, trying desperately to preserve my energy and retain a small part of dryness on my body by allowing the water to run off my head and shoulders in established paths. Gradually, as I moved to steer and observe sea and sail, I began to shiver, and soon became saturated beneath my cape, not only through the layers of my skin, it seemed, but right through my flesh and down to my very bones.

Twenty-third day

The torrential downpour kept up a steady drumming on both sail and canopy, hissing loudly as it struck the sea around us; the bailers scraped and splashed as they filled and emptied in a monotonous but reassuring rhythm. Lyn and Robin, on their knees under the waterproof sheet in the bottom of the boat, plied the bailers as Douglas tried to snatch some rest in the bow with the twins, but already the water had soaked them from beneath when an abnormally large wave had broken over the gunwales, temporarily overwhelming the bailers. At half past one in the morning, the wind eased and the rain began to fall vertically out of the blackness of the night. My particular burden became a little easier as the more frequent flashes of lightning allowed me to see where I was steering, and though the rain flattened the breaking waves they remained a serious danger to our little craft. The bailers' rhythmic beat scarcely altered in tempo as they scooped the rainwater into the sea.

At two o'clock the wind dropped completely and to our astonishment the rain increased in intensity and grew colder still, until I wondered if we were about to be assailed by hailstones. The bailers now plied with renewed urgency and increasing speed and I became so cold that I did not realise that the low-pitched groans emanating from our midst were actually coming out of my own mouth. Lightning hissed and flashed with a savage intensity and even greater frequency as thunder pealed deafeningly above us in a continuous reverberation of terrifying sound. Incredibly, the rain doubled and ten minutes later redoubled again, until a continuous frenzy of water poured out of the sky.

Above the noise of the storm I could hear young Sandy sobbing and Lyn praying while the rhythmic scrape of the bailers increased to a blur, as efforts were accelerated to keep pace with the rising deluge of water. Lacking a container, Douglas began bailing with massive scoops of his bare hands whilst the twins bravely fought back their tears and stretched out the bow canopy to keep it from spilling water into the boat. Everyone did what they could, and as our margin of safety narrowed every effort to minimise the ingress of water became vital. Unable to move, I sat frozen in place like a statue, the bitter chill seeping through to my very brain as my hands, numb with cold, clutched the sail ready to trim it the instant the next gust of wind struck. My eyes peered through the narrowest of slits into the gloomy night as bright flashes of lightning, in a perpetual state of discharge, made the clouds above us glow in a semi-permanent ruddy orange. For the first time since the storm had begun, the situation aboard the *Ednamair* started to look desperate and I wondered if our energy would last, as we struggled to maintain the frantic pace. My frazzled nerves took comfort and my spirit strength however, as I sighted the float up ahead, marking the position of the sea anchor. Just seeing it still there gave me the courage and revitalised my being so that I could keep on going, for it represented our only insurance should we be swamped.

My thoughts were suddenly interrupted. 'He's stopped moving!' Lyn's voice rose above the tumult, penetrating my consciousness from the darkness, as if she was calling from another world. 'Rub him, Robin! Rub the life back into him.' I became aware that Robin was kneeling in front of me, his arms stretched out towards my knees. Anaesthetised with the cold, I could no longer feel my limbs or my torso. Slowly he rubbed the feeling back into my body, his warming hands massaging my back and ribs, as I sat without moving until I managed to shout above the hiss of the rain that I could feel my limbs once more. We were in cloudburst conditions and there was no knowing what to expect next. Without warning a vicious downdraught of wind slammed into us from above, striking us like a hammer blow from behind and snatching the sail from my hand. I fought to control the dinghy and just as I thought I could not go on the rain lessened perceptively, allowing white-capped wavelets to whip up in angry splashes over our stern. The sea anchor swung our bow to meet this new threat.

'Sing!' shouted Douglas in a sudden moment of inspiration, 'sing to keep warm – sing for your lives!' We felt instinctively that he was right, for the reverberations not only warmed our bodies but, as the Christian martyrs must have done when facing the lions, we found the very act of singing charged our spirits in an ultimate act of defiance. In full voice, we burst into a wordless version of the Cuckoo Waltz. We sang everything from 'Those were the days, my friend' to 'God save the Queen', touching on Beethoven's Ninth and the Twenty-third Psalm on the way. The wind whipped the rain into our faces and stung our wretched skins, as desperately we fought to stay afloat. I gathered the sail into the reefed position to prevent it being ripped to shreds. The wind-thrashed sail now added a loud continuous flapping to the clamour of the rain and thunder.

Slowly and inexorably the water levels inside the boat began to rise. Stretched to the limits of our endurance, time was running out for the Robertsons. We needed a miracle and we needed it soon! The rain lashed us relentlessly from above, combining with the wind-borne spray and roaring spume of the waves as they surged beneath us, to form a reverberating non-stop crescendo. We all bailed for our lives but still the levels rose. Beaten practically senseless by the elements, I gradually felt my resolve soften and my will diminish as the conditions began to get the better of us. I was already considering how the end might come when my gaze caught Lyn's in a bright loom of lightning as it seared through the blackness of the treacherous night. A defiant light burned brightly in her eyes and held my stare, demanding that I not give up, demanding that I carry on, not just for myself but for us all. 'Bail!' I shouted to my weary crew, 'Bail for your lives!' Summoning reserves we didn't even know we had we turned to the bailing in an all or nothing frenzy. Then, without warning, the wind fell silent and the rain suddenly stopped. Our miracle had happened! Energised with hope I returned to the steering whilst the others continued to bail for all they were worth. They soon started to gain on the calf-deep water levels and eventually the familiar scrape of the plastic cups on the bottom of the boat could be heard again. The rhythm slowed perceptively as the squall eased and the spray lessened. I un-reefed the sail and steered the yawing bow back towards the waves again, only to find we were suddenly stern on to the swell: an instantaneous wind change of 180 degrees had occurred. My mind filtered through my knowledge of circular storms but I could not recall a storm cell like this one. Indeed, it had felt for the world like we were trapped inside a giant tornado. As suddenly as it had stopped just twenty minutes before, stinging sheets of rain returned in a teeming wind-borne deluge, to flay our exhausted forms as our battle to survive continued unabated until the predawn glow illuminated the eastern skies. Only then were we afforded some relief as the rain eased and the air grew slightly warmer, giving us hope that we were finally past the worst of it.

Dawn found us crouched under heavy rain and still bailing wearily in rhythmic scuffs with mechanical regularity. Occasionally one of the shattered bailers would stop for a moment, as their tired hands relaxed into momentary sleep. After a short pause, the scraping would start up again with renewed urgency in a half-remembered quickening of pace, as they tried desperately to make up for lost time, bailing in an exhausted trance-like sleep. I sat in the stern rigid with cold, able only to move my arms to trim the sail by turning my whole body through its centre either to the left or right, as *Ednamair* yawed to the vagaries of the squally winds. At nine o'clock, in the strengthening light of daybreak, Douglas relieved me at the helm. No sooner had I released the primitive controls to him than I collapsed onto the central thwart. As the rain finally began to lull, Lyn and Robin pummelled my frozen limbs and body back into life once again. Feeling gradually returned, and as the rain eased the wind fell light and the scrape of the bailing cups first slowed and then finally stopped. With the helm no longer manned we all slept as we knelt against the thwarts, exhausted but somehow afloat, occasionally waking to clear the small amount of water gathered in the bottom of the dinghy. Several hours passed before the rain spots became sporadic and light, splattering the glass-like surface of the sea in a scattered pattern of ever-widening, superimposed concentric circles.

Still numb from lack of sleep, we were woken later that morning by the sound of ankle-high wavelets sloshing to and fro inside the dinghy. Worn out, we had slept as the water steadily rose inside the boat to a depth of several inches, reducing our freeboard to a mere inch or two. We had only the quietness of the early morning seaway to thank for our salvation, as hasty action with the bailing cups reduced the water levels inside once more.

We returned to our rest, shivering as we chewed on strips of dried turtle meat and, as a special treat, a small portion of sea biscuit for a very late breakfast or an early lunch. It was warmer now, and as we huddled together under the sheet Lyn told us she had counted seven people in *Ednamair* during the night, stating that she had seen the vision of a presence rather than a person, positioned above and behind me, helping us to fight the storm. Although this was greeted with scepticism by the others, Lyn steadfastly maintained her belief in the vision, and indeed if this had helped us in the midst of that terrible storm then it certainly had made a great contribution to our survival. Given that our general situation was precarious enough, we had been to the brink of disaster and death many times during that night and failure by anyone of us to play our part would have meant annihilation for us all. For twelve long hours, we had tottered on the cusp of our own mortality, trapped in a half-world of the living and the dead. I wondered how much longer our weary bodies could have delivered what was demanded of them, or indeed how they would be able to continue to meet such challenges in the future.

I lay down to rest with the others, whilst I considered that 180-degree change in the wind and what manner of destruction it would have caused to a square-rigged ship caught in a similar situation. Taken aback and without warning, it would most certainly have been dismasted, and in such a storm what chance would remain for the unfortunate crew? In the same instant, I dismissed the thought from my mind, for they certainly couldn't have been any worse off than we already were!

Cloudy weather with intermittent rain continued throughout the day, the breeze rising through several squally spells to become a strong southwesterly wind, whipping the wave tops into a creamy foam, before prolonged and heavy showers beat the turbulent waters calm again. We sat shivering in the relentless rain, locked in abject misery and shivering torment, our near-naked bodies buffeted by the merciless wind and stinging spray. Exposed to these elements we had become completely exhausted. If it didn't stop raining soon, we knew we would not be able to go on. I heard an inner voice tell me I had had enough, urging me to quit, telling me to give up and die. I looked at my family and young Robin, struggling to deal with each setback with a stoic resolve that I could only admire. I took in a deep breath. I wasn't going to quit just yet; for the sake of my wife and my children I would gird my loins and see this nightmare through to the very end, refusing to give in until the last minute of the last hour of the final day.

I estimated, or rather guessed, our position that noon as 6 degrees 50 minutes north and 240 miles west of Cape Espinosa, for there had been many times in the night when our course and speed had been quite unknown to me. Douglas steered throughout the entire day, while the others took turn and turn about to bail the bottom of the boat dry so that Lyn, Robin and myself could rest. We dozed in a fitful half-sleep late into the afternoon. Our awakening was greeted with heavy banks of dark and threatening cloud covering the northern sky, which rolled threateningly towards us once again, bringing further bouts of rain with the darkness. We groaned and sang intermittently in the pouring rain, a moderate downpour by the previous night's standards, but heavy enough to keep Robin and me bailing like robots. Later the wind dropped to a dead calm and it became no longer necessary to steer. Lyn massaged our backs warm and Douglas and the twins rested in the bows trying to recover. Later we ate a supper of dried turtle, using the last of the eggs and as much water as we needed, drifting into a restless sleep whilst the twins snuggled up with their 'little supper' of emergency rations, which Lyn had started preparing for them on a nightly basis.

Twenty-fourth day

The steady grate of the bailing cups went on through the night. Side by side, Robin and I knelt under the yellow sheet of the raft canopy, our bony knees hard pressed against the fibreglass and our heads pushed against the thwart, as we unceasingly threw the water over the side. The steady beat of the rain on our capes only served to lull our senses and sleep, which would not come to my resting body before, tried hard to take me unawares now. I felt Robin lean against me as he too, dozed in exhausted slumber, only to jerk awake to the tyranny of the bailing cup. We could no longer feel any pain, our hands and limbs felt soaked to the bone and our skins, were a crumpled mess of nerveless wrinkles. We shivered and bailed and sang songs, any songs, to keep our circulation going, and when we were too tired to sing Lyn pummelled and rubbed our insensitive bodies, rejuvenating our circulatory systems and massaging life back into our frozen arms and legs.

The scrape and splash of the bailing cups grated on without a break, through the continuous and unrelenting downpour of rain, our hopes, our fears, our thirst, our despair, all forgotten in the emotionless limbo of anaesthesia brought about by exhaustion. Just as it was impossible to imagine how things could get any worse, a new and deadly hazard suddenly fell upon us. Vertical bolts of lightning speared downwards from the cloud base immediately above us, shattering the surface of the sea in exploding plumes of steaming water vapour and permeating the wind with the acrid smell of scorched air. Indiscriminate and deadly, like ethereal laser lances they punctured the sea around us. Thunder-less blue and white or sometimes deep yellow in colour, their blinding flashes seared the air, etching our cowering silhouettes against the insides of the dinghy, as we lay huddled together in the darkness, locked in frozen terror. Douglas's eyes rolled wide in fear as he struggled to hold my stare and groaned, 'If there is a hell on earth, Dad, then we are in it!' I hugged him to me, for I could not muster any words of comfort. Caught in a heavy deluge of mind-numbing rain and surrounded by fizzing bolts of lightning that shook the air, we felt like involuntary participants in a game of Russian roulette, scared out of our wits as we waited for the single strike of lightning that would fry us all in an instant. The minutes became hours as we continued to bail, scooping the water from inside the *Ednamair*. Cold rain kept falling from above and warm seawater flooded in over the sides, as our rattled nerves were too slow, or simply too tired, to alert us to the need to trim. Each minute seemed to last an eternity as the night slowly slipped by, draining us of every last vestige of strength and energy that we had left.

Dawn finally came to us, a silent witness in the eastern sky, its threaded wisps of silver light gradually strengthening to reveal Robin fast asleep, his kneeling body sagging and twisted sideways at an angle, jammed against the point where the dinghy's side met the central thwart, the bailing cup still clutched in his hand. Lyn knelt sleeping against the stern seat, her body pressed close to mine for warmth. My arm still moved in the motion of bailing until I realised that it had actually stopped raining. I sat back and sank into grateful oblivion. Death could have come to any one of us at this moment, without our knowledge or any offer of resistance to its coming. As we slept, Douglas returned to the steering and made the most of the southerly breeze as it strengthened during the morning. Sporadic shafts of gleaming sunlight awoke us later in the mid-morning and we chatted animatedly of the previous night's struggle, indulging in the euphoric aftermath of a job well done as we re-checked the rigging and fastenings, discovering in the process that one end of the flotation collar had come adrift. Thankfully, the sea anchor Douglas had worked so hard to retrieve had been up to the job and had remained intact, for without it we would have most certainly been swamped. We revelled in the quiet sunshine and our collective mood lightened as we reflected on our escape from the rage of the storm, and with a humble gratitude we gave thanks to each other and to the Almighty, for the courage and fortitude we had found to see us through.

As the day progressed, the boys' faces looked puffed and haggard, their slurring voices belying their assurances that they had had enough rest. We now ate our food without tasting and drank freely with veiled contempt for the water we had collected, rather than seeing it as a blessing from the sky. Our daydreams switched from ice cream and fruit to hot stews, porridge, steak and kidney puddings, hotpots and casseroles. The dishes steamed fragrantly in our imaginations, as we described their smallest details to each other. We could all but taste the succulent gravies as we chewed our meagre rations. The dried meat was rapidly being used up, and the hanging meat had developed a slimy film and was so unpalatable that I had to throw it overboard for fear we might be poisoned. Sickness of any description was a hazard we could not risk under any circumstances. It seemed that with the bountiful supply of fresh water our appetites had grown, requiring rations of the dried turtle to be severely reduced in case our larder become empty before the next catch. The clouds thinned towards noon and the sun finally broke through in the early afternoon. We greeted it like a long-lost friend, almost as welcome as the rain had been a week before, and spread soaked items of equipment to dry on the thwarts. Most of the first-aid kit was ruined beyond repair and my logbook, saturated almost beyond redemption, was carefully spread out to dry.

At 7 degrees 40 minutes north and 230 miles west of Cape Espinosa (95 degrees and 14 minutes west) our noon position placed us approximately halfway to land and we talked during the day of ways we might beach our boat when we made landfall, and discussed how we might light fires without matches. Our conversation turned to jungle lore and Indians. Robin frightened the twins by telling them that there were cannibals on the wild coast of Nicaragua where we might land. Their imaginations needed no stimulant to ferment their apprehension, and Robin, observing their grimaces, quickly backtracked and reassured them he was only joking. Douglas and Lyn had been discussing the possibility of making a net out of a piece of sail to catch plankton in order to vary our diet. It was decided to leave everything until the following day, however, for the sky had again darkened and we decided to snatch what rest we could during the day, in case we were required to work through the night again.

Our hearts sank as we prepared for another miserable night, but the rain when it came was light and intermittent and often nothing more than a drizzle, requiring the services of only one bailer and then only occasionally. Normal watches were resumed and we lay down to pass the night in dry discomfort, a relative luxury by recent standards. We had found the most comfortable arrangement to be Neil and Sandy lying lengthways in the bow, with myself in a V-shape across the gunwales of the dinghy, just forward of the centre thwart. The water cans were transferred from under the stern seat into the big wooden box, and this was kept lashed between the persons off watch, thereby allowing their resting or sleeping bodies to extend another foot as they lay on their sides on either side of it. The watch-keeper kept watch from a seated position on the centre thwart and all dry stores and food were transferred under the bow canopy right forward where they could be kept reasonably dry. The fish and bird life had been little in evidence during the past two days, although the dorado still weaved their patterns under the rain-spattered sea, but now, with the advent of drier weather, the sharks had returned in earnest. Lyn, taking the midnight watch, called me to deal with a large and frightening specimen, seemingly intent on knocking the bottom out of our little craft as it approached in menacing silence. I slammed it with the business end of the fish spear on its next transit and it skulked off with a sudden swish of its giant tail and a dramatic burst of speed, to seek a less spiteful playmate. The rest of the night passed peacefully enough, with the rain stopping before midnight and the clearing skies offering a greater promise of a better day to come.

Twenty-fifth day

Daylight brought welcome sunshine and clear blue skies. A flying fish had landed on the sail during Douglas's watch and he had made a catch any cricketer or baseball player would have been proud of, his quick hands trapping it against the pliant fabric of the canopy before it had time to slide off again. The twins had half of it each for breakfast while we chewed a small piece of dried turtle meat. The larder was becoming too bare for comfort, prompting a debate whether it was better to eat up the remains of the dried turtle and risk not catching any more, or whether to spin it out and risk it going bad in the damp weather.

Our deliberations were interrupted when a nicely sized female turtle popped its head up to have a good look at us. We cleared the space between the stern seat and the centre thwart, so that Neil could get aft from the bow to do his share with this one. The turtle bumped heavily against the bottom of the boat, and tensely we waited to see if it would surface within reach. Douglas grabbed at the shell and I grappled with a back flipper, until we had manoeuvred its back against the side of the dinghy. 'Trim!' came the shout from Lyn as water streamed over the gunwale whilst we wrestled the reptile inboard. Neil and Robin leaned outwards on their side to counterbalance the sudden increase in weight as it cleared the water, then in urgent unison 'Trim!' was again shouted as the giant specimen flopped into the bottom of the dinghy, negating the need for the counterbalance previously provided. Flippers, claws and beak thrashed and snapped as we first secured and then slaughtered our unfortunate victim. It quickly stilled as its bright red blood gushed into waiting containers held at the ready. We had found that we could sharpen the stainless-steel knife blade on the back of the broken raft knife if we persevered for long enough, the sharpened blade making it easier to effect the kill, as well as making the butchering of these beasts a little less arduous. Robin and Douglas imbibed their usual portions of blood but Lyn and Sandy declined, preferring to draw the serum out of the coagulated blood to drink as a sort of gravy. Neil, like me, drank as much and ate as much as was offered of anything, good, bad or indifferent, as long as it wasn't salty.

Douglas expertly extracted the flipper bones while I rested from my labours, having dissected the main part of the shoulder muscles. Neil collected the fat and a small harvest of eggs and looked on interestedly as, following Lyn's suggestion, I cut out the heart and we dumped the entrails overboard. Two hours later, our bodies covered in blood, we gazed in satisfaction at the large turtle steaks hanging from the stays and set about cleaning up the boat as well as ourselves. Our tattered clothing, mine in particular, was now very bloodstained with both turtle blood and some of my own, the result of cut fingers and clawed forearms endured during numerous kills.

With our good fortune in catching food since abandoning the raft, we had steadily improved in condition, and our sores and boils showed significant signs of clearing up at last. Although the storm had taken a heavy toll of our energy reserves, we generally felt much more rested than during the frantic bailing and blowing marathons required in the raft. The cramped conditions in the dinghy often gave rise to bitter reproach and argument, however, when tender limbs were trodden on or kicked. We had also developed an instinctive awareness of the feel of our boat and became instantly aware when a small change in the angle of heel required one of us to move in order to correct the trim, which we did almost subconsciously.

I determined our noon position as 7 degrees 23 minutes north and 225 miles west of Espinosa, which again aroused talk of the coastline of Central America and our most likely landing place. With the rain clouds gone, we cowered beneath our makeshift capes as the fiercely strong sun beat down on us relentlessly once more. Whilst we were loath to curse the sunshine, we all knew that heat like this would kill us as surely as the heavy rains of the day before had almost done. Douglas and Robin discussed the problems of rowing in the hot sun, and as the afternoon progressed we poured seawater on each other to ease our discomfort in the equatorial heat. We all agreed that we would probably only be able to row at night and during calm and overcast days.

As the afternoon sun shifted across the northern horizon towards the west, three red-footed boobies flew close by, then one of them landed on top of the oar which served as our mast. Our friend was quickly joined by the other two, and they all three perched on the paddle used as the uppermost spar for the sail, one on each side of the first. We all looked at Neil but he shook his head and pointed to the turtle meat with a smile, 'We hae meat and we can eat.' His eyes sparkled brightly from within their deep dark sockets, formed by the sharp outline of his skull, for his face had again thinned remarkably in the last few days. The boobies made a fine figurehead and we watched them with delight. Preening their feathers, they held out their beautiful wings with tails outspread, eying the meat speculatively. They could get their own food easier than we could, so we decided that our hospitality didn't extend to a free meal and politely tipped them off their perch, sending them on their way.

The evening brought quiet seas with calm weather, and a glorious sunset just before twilight bestowed a peacefulness of the spirit upon us. We sang the old songs of Scotland, which the children loved to hear, for they carried a story with them. We sang Welsh songs with Robin, whose Welsh inheritance did not, alas, extend to the musical traditions of the Welsh people. Lyn sang Brahms's Lullaby as a special nightcap for the twins and, as twilight deepened and watches were set, Douglas broke our contemplation with 'This mighty ocean is your home, no walls or fences halt thy roam.' We looked on impassively. 'The next line of my Ode to the frigatebird,' he explained with upturned palms, as if we should have known. Lyn and I smiled as she resisted the urge to add a line of her own, recalling all too vividly what had happened the last time.

As a family unit, I felt that we had already gone beyond thinking in terms of survival. We had started living from the sea as an adopted way of life, for not only were we surviving, we were improving in our physical and mental condition. As we settled to rest, I pondered the philosophies advocating 'at sea' living. To my mind, there was little prospect of man developing a cultural relationship with the sea, in the way that he has done with the land. The predatory feelings which are brought to the fore to make living possible in this primitive style would suppress the emotions as well as the appreciation of beauty and intellectual debate. For ourselves, however, we had stopped thinking of rescue as the main objective of our existence; we were no longer subject to the daily disappointment of a lonely vigil, or to the idea that help might be at hand or was even necessary. We no longer had that helpless feeling of dependence on others for our continued existence. We stood alone, immersed and at one with the wondrous beauty and brutality of the raw nature that surrounded us, not merely inhabitants but indeed citizens of the savage sea.

Twenty-sixth day

The calm of the previous evening was short-lived. Cloudy, squally weather came up from the south, and *Ednamair* tugged at the half-tripped sea anchor and bludgeoned her way towards the northeast once more. Rain showers peppered the surface of the sea as they followed the squalls and we huddled under our capes and flimsy sheets for shelter, the bailers scraping their monotonous rhythm, interspersed with random spates of more rapid activity, as the water level rose and fell. The rest of the night remained quiet, however, and save for Robin and Douglas, who took the night watches, the rest of us managed to get some sleep.

Towards dawn the wind and sea got up and on several occasions *Ednamair* yawed alarmingly, threatening to broach, as she span sideways under the mighty bursting wave crests that reared high above her starboard side. The sail repeatedly collapsed as the dinghy's bow fell away from the wind, only to snap full again as we were caught in the grip of successive windy blasts that caught us with their full force, as we traversed the unsheltered summits of the wave crests. Under first Douglas's and then Lyn's more reticent coaxing, *Ednamair* was straightened out to meet the seas head on, and when it seemed certain that the rearing crests would smash down and swamp us, our little craft just rode up and over them and the roaring wave tops disappeared like magic beneath us.

Lyn woke me in the strengthening light to say that she could no longer see the float even with the assistance of the monocle Douglas had constructed for her from a lens belonging to her broken spectacles. I lifted my head above the bow canopy and searched the area of sea where the float should have been; there was no sign of it. I reached forward under the canopy and pulled at the sea anchor rope, it was slack. The heavy-duty sea anchor and float were gone and I wondered what sort of fish could have taken it so quietly. There were quite a few I could think of, but the cleanly severed anchor rope and trip line told me nothing. Although we were making better speed than with the float and sea anchor streamed, the possibility of broaching to with our six-inch freeboard became too risky, urging me to rouse the others to assist with streaming the much smaller spare sea anchor. We just had to hope against the odds that we would not encounter any more storms like the one we had recently suffered, for lacking the heavy-duty canvas construction of our previous version, the flimsy fabric of the spare sea anchor would not last for very long in anything but the smoothest of seas. I set the drogue to the semi-tripped position and attached it with two ropes, one of them a thick piece of unravelled polypropylene, which would certainly give most predators indigestion. This rope also had the advantage of floating on the surface, enabling us to see it more clearly by day and by its phosphorescent trail at night.

Squally weather conditions continued throughout the day, with Douglas and I alternating at the helm to steer *Ednamair* through the worst of the seas. Our noon position of 7 degrees 30 minutes north and 210 miles west of Cape Espinosa gave us encouragement to take advantage of the favourable southwesterly wind, for though we were suffering from the buffeting that the dinghy was receiving, we were also making good progress in the right direction. Later we started shipping water in increasing quantities as the waves became even higher, sporting large rolling whitecaps that crashed about us on all sides, so we opened out the sea anchor and hove to, with our sail reefed down to avoid being swamped altogether. There was little rest to be had as I insisted we all keep a sharp look out for the occasional giant swells, which sometimes ran at right angles across the crests of the wind-driven seas and were a perilous danger to our open craft.

Towards evening, just as Lyn had finished her routine of tending our various skin ailments and ensuring that the twins performed their muscle-toning leg exercises, a strangely uncomfortable feeling came over me. At first, I thought I was going to be ill, then, looking hastily around and grabbing a piece of sail cloth, I realised that for the first time in twenty-six days I was about to have a bowel movement! The experience was exhausting and left me weak and trembling for almost an hour afterwards, but the satisfaction of knowing that my body was again functioning normally was encouraging. An hour later Douglas followed suit, and though he was the last person to display signs of physical weakness the effort left him weak and helpless, suffering massive muscular contractions in his stomach for hours afterwards. This event went some way to relieving Lyn's concern, for whilst the others including herself showed no real signs of discomfort, she felt there must come a time when our bodily functions should revert to normal, in order to avoid being poisoned by the retention of body waste, as our increased intake of solid food was maintained. She therefore planned a second course of enemas for herself and the twins the following day.

Robin once again declined the services offered. I considered being more insistent with him, for the dangers from internal cramps or an intestinal blockage could have had fatal consequences and were an unnecessary risk, especially whilst water was still available for enemas. I weighed this against the effects of challenging his natural reserve and how that in itself might adversely affect his chances of survival. On balance, I decided that while he maintained all the outward appearances of good health, I would leave him in peace but keep a close eye on him. As Robin had the largest physical frame in our group, I purposely gave him larger rations of food than the others so that his body condition would be maintained similar to our own. I also felt that, as the only person outside our family group, he could be watching for any signs of discrimination against him, a natural enough fear in his situation, so I tried to ensure that he was never given grounds for such thoughts. Often I incurred the wrath of the others as I doled out our meagre rations. Robin's strong strain of human sympathy made up in many ways for his practical inabilities, and his unshakable belief in our eventual rescue and our ability to survive until then was a spur to my own determination.

We talked into the night of various ways of cooking omelettes, pancakes, chapattis and oatcakes and put them on the teatime menu for Dougal's Kitchen, then lay back stretching and re-stretching our twisted limbs and listened to the rough seas surging around the dinghy's hull as she pitched in uneasy restraint at the curb of the sea anchor each and every yard that we made comforting us as it brought us a yard closer to the end of our relentless torment and a yard closer to home.

Twenty-seventh day

The rough southerly wind, which had blown throughout the night, had kept us awake and in a high state of anxious alert until daybreak, forcing us to steer *Ednamair* through breaking seas whilst constantly keeping her bows pointed in the direction of the white-capped rollers. As dawn approached the seas quietened in the dying wind and with a half-tripped sea anchor we steered an east-northeasterly course into the shimmering rays of the stupendous orange and red sunrise.

Sandy and Neil slept heavily in the quiet of the morning, after yet another night of discomfort and unease had denied them any rest or comfort in the pitching bow of the dinghy. Exhaustion had overtaken them at about four o' clock and they had slept until eight, only to be awakened with stabbing hunger pains fuelling their instinctive urge for food. After a welcome breakfast of turtle meat and eggs, Lyn set about the morning routine of airing the pieces of sail which we had used as bedding, a simple task in the quiet sunshine but practically impossible in the present weather conditions, where heavy deluges of spray lashed our tired forms.

Later that day, as the sea calmed, we spread the remaining turtle meat out to dry and brought out the tins of turtle fat, now swimming in beautiful golden oil, in order that the refining process from fat to oil, brought about by the action of the sun, could continue. With a dipper apiece Lyn and I skimmed the surface and collected the valuable oil drop by drop, taking great care to avoid any sediment, until we had filled a small plastic jar with the golden fluid. We then filled one of the empty water cans as well, collecting about two pints in all. We now had not only a medium which Lyn proposed to use for enema purposes but also, like the apothecary's panacea for all ills, a health-giving liquid that could be taken internally, rubbed on externally, used as a lubricant for tools, or even used to smooth the breaking wave tops should the need eventuate. Lyn administered a small water enema to the twins and herself that afternoon without result, all the fluid being retained, so she decided to try them with a turtle oil enema the next day. In the meantime she rubbed a little of the oil on our sore parts to make them impervious to the salt water and to minimise the risk of developing pressure sores, for in our cramped uncomfortable conditions we had difficulty in keeping the weight off our buttocks and bony parts. My sunburned backside was now healing at last and I was able to lie on my back again without breaking the skin on the burnt patches or healing scars.

Our noon position of 7 degrees 33 minutes north and 190 miles west of Espinosa put us another twenty miles nearer land for the day's run. I decided to try my latest version of the spear that afternoon, and took up a position on the centre thwart with weapon poised, watching the dorado swoop to and fro under the boat. Tensed in position with every muscle poised ready to strike, I waited patiently for the right fish at the right moment, an exercise in both persistence and endurance. Indeed, to hold the spear poised, ready to thrust with all the power I could muster at an instant's notice, was an exercise in reflex action which civilised men have long forgotten. At about three o'clock in the afternoon one of the smaller dorado, about ten pounds in weight, flashed under the boat and turned on its side, disturbing the small fry which sheltered under a piece of sheet trailing in the water. The white underbelly of the fish showed clearly only about two feet below the surface of the water and I thrust at it with all my strength, feeling the armed point strike the fish and penetrate. With a sudden jerk, I felt the spear tip break, then a moment later the fish was gone. Ruefully, I surveyed the product of my afternoon's work. It had broken at the barb again, requiring me to find an alternative way to catch them that would successfully overcome the inherent design weakness in my spear.

Discouraged by the failure of my efforts thus far, I sat back and considered the options. As we all brainstormed and debated the design, from fastening a line to the spear tip to ruing the loss of the fine gaff I had left aboard Lucette, an idea suddenly came to me. Could Douglas's strong arms straighten a hook and make it into a spear tip? I considered the matter in silence, until another solution came to me in a blinding spark of joyful exhilaration. The tip would be the fishhook. 'That's it!' I yelled gleefully. I didn't need a spear after all, what I needed was a gaff, and I could make one too! It would mean that I'd have to strike upwards instead of down but I felt sure it would work. As I explained my plan to Douglas and Robin, we set to work immediately cutting grooves and notches in the right places on the spearhead and paddle, working steadily until the cooling air heralded the end of the day.

The sunset was another magnificent exhibition of tropical splendour, a glorious montage of blue, green, orange and gold, gradually melting into the surface of the sea, where it was reflected skywards in indescribable and breathtaking beauty. 'It's strange, Dad,' remarked Douglas, and I felt sure he was about to deliver another line of his poetry, 'It's strange that such beauty can exist amid such danger.' I had to agree it was a paradox indeed that we could appreciate such beauty as we stared into the face of our own mortality. As we sat in a thoughtful silence, we considered that we had been adrift for almost an entire month and were all still alive. Not fit and maybe not healthy, we remained tired and exhausted, starving and thirsty, but despite all the privations we were alive and still kicking. Where there was life there was hope, hope that we would catch more food, hope that we would catch more rain, hope that the weather would remain calm and, dare I even think it, hope that soon we would make it back to land.

The evening's chatter centred around Dougal's Kitchen, with enthused zest as we sensed we were on the verge of a breakthrough with our latest fish-catching device. We would serve coddled egg and cheese pasties, with minced beef pasties to a special recipe of such savoury goodness that our mouths watered in imaginary delight. Surely the public would flock in hundreds to sample these beautiful delicacies! Why, we wondered, had nobody thought of them before? We enjoyed the thought not only of ourselves consuming these beautiful pasties, but also of the hungry farmers on market day thronging the homely precincts of our eatery and wolfing large quantities of food, at a modest profit to ourselves of course!

As darkness advanced upon us, we settled down to the discomfort of another night with warm thoughts of savoury odours and satisfied customers, whilst our own miserable bones made harsh contact with the unyielding fibreglass hull, resting awhile in one position until 'pins and needles' warned us of restricted circulation or cramp locked our muscles, making immediate movement imperative. With movement came the inevitable chain of disturbance to the others, and when the movement stopped the boundary lines denoting our allotted spaces were checked and rechecked in a ritualistic manner, more akin to a pack of dogs or wolves than a huddle of desperate human beings.

Twenty-eighth day

The weather deteriorated during the night watches, until by morning a rough southerly swell was rolling up beneath us, tossing *Ednamair* in a twenty-foot cycle of uneasy movement. A small cross-swell made for much discomfort, as the crests slopped aboard with each dip of her bows, making it necessary for us to bail continuously. The sluggish lift gave me cause for concern. Calling Douglas to take over the helm, I exchanged places with the twins in the bow and detached the bow canopy so that I could examine the flotation collar. As I leaned over to examine it, a wave washed right into the dinghy.

'Knife!' I yelled, stretching my hand behind me, as I observed an even larger green-crested roller bearing down on us. I hesitated, caught in two minds as to whether I should replace the canopy to try and shed as much of the incoming deluge as possible, but the knife had already been thrust into my hand, leaving me no choice but to cut the ropes which held the flotation collar to the bow. The collar dropped heavily into the water as the bow rose high in the air, sending the breaking sea creaming past beneath us. Quickly I cut the other lashings and then poked my finger into the non-return valve of the waterlogged collar. Water spurted out from the sleeve and a cursory examination showed a series of holes where the rope lashing had chafed the fabric to a gauzelike mesh. It was clear that, far from keeping us afloat, the flooded collar had in fact been holding us down. *Ednamair* had been trying to keep afloat with a millstone round her neck! We detached the collar completely and lifted one end into the boat, slowly draining the water out of the other end, until the ten-foot sleeve lay crumpled and empty at our feet. Taking a length of fishing-line, I folded the leaking end up and lashed it firmly with the heavy nylon cord, until it was airtight again. Douglas made short work of inflating it, his massive breaths quickly making it firm and tight. Fully inflated once more, Douglas, Robin and I secured it to the plunging bows with strong tape instead of rope, to try and avoid a repetition of the chafing. Once we had finished, the dinghy rode easily again as the float controlled her pitch and protected her bows from the breaking seas. With the canopy refastened, we snuggled down again with very little water being shipped inboard, affording the watch-keepers a rest from their bailing duties at last.

Raft knife

Turtle knife

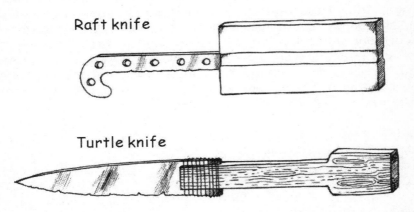

Tools of the trade: turtle knife consisted of broken blade of kitchen knife with an improvised handle

Our noon position, at 7 degrees 40 minutes north and 180 miles west of Espinosa, indicated a good day's run of nearly fifteen miles with the sea anchor streamed fully open. As the wind and sea eased in the afternoon it became unnecessary to steer, enabling us to make the sail fast, and with the sea anchor half tripped we resumed our progress to the northeast. Robin played host to our own version of a popular radio programme, 'Desert Island Discs', that afternoon and a fine talent he had for the job too. I was elected to be the radio and with rather less aplomb I sang or hummed the chosen tunes whilst the others listened. Our choices of recordings surprised each other, as well as ourselves, for we now placed different values on music than mere entertainment or nostalgia. The youngsters chose much more serious music than either Lyn or I had expected and while I tried to sing as many of the classical pieces selected as I could remember, I had insurmountable difficulty with most, such as Elgar's *Enigma Variations* for Robin, music to the ballet *Coppelia* for Douglas, Bizet's *Symphony in C* for Lyn. Beethoven's *Violin Concerto* was my own choice; I could not recall a single note, and yet I had last heard it played as recently as our visit to the San Blas Islands, when its vibrant chords had been as familiar to me as my own right hand. I did manage to recall others, like *Finlandia* for Robin, Lalo's *Symphonie Espagnole* for Lyn, Beethoven's Ninth and Mussorgsky's *Night on a Bare Mountain* for Douglas. Recordings of Scottish songs were favourites too, with Douglas and the twins mouthing the words with me. We attempted an old Welsh ballad for Robin but settled on *Those were the days* by Mary Hopkins instead. Lyn's choice of Wagner's *Siegfried Idyll* was also mine, for we had often listened to it together during our courting years back in Hong Kong. My attempt to sing it nearly ended in tears, but I managed to swallow the lump in my throat, at least for the first few stanzas. Neil chose the Mexican folk song *South of the Border*, a popular watch-time song aboard *Lucette*, and Sandy the theme song of *Dr Zhivago*. We finished off with 'Cool clear water' for Lyn followed by her own rendition of 'I'll take you home again, Kathleen', which like my Twenty-third Psalm she had chosen for childhood memories. Vocal recordings were popular, not all of which were songs. Lyn wanted readings from Dylan Thomas, whose

> *Do not go gentle into that good night*
> *Rage, rage against the dying of the light*

she often voiced to coach us through times of storm and stress. Douglas requested Gerard Hoffnung's after-dinner story 'The Bricklayer', which raised chortles and chuckles aplenty as, responding to the demands of my audience, I just made up large sections of it as I went along. I wanted a good Scots voice to read Robert Burns to me. Selections of books included some obscure works on statistics for Robin, the *Oxford Book of Verse* for Douglas, Chekhov's plays for Lyn, and a comprehensive study of marine, plant and animal life for Neil and Sandy, so that we might know what it was that we were seeing and eating.

We had had our fill of culture by teatime and turned to the tantalising thought of rowing for the coast when we met calmer weather. We had no rowlocks for the oars, so we would have to rely on Dougie's strength once more to make thole pins or fashion grommets to use in their place. There was no wood strong enough but Douglas thought we could use the U-shaped steel tube from the raft bellows. Lyn found it under the stern seat and I handed it to Douglas. 'Exercise your muscles on that,' I challenged, 'I want it broken at the bottom of the U.' I could hardly believe my eyes as Douglas flexed his incredible biceps and pulled at the bar with all his might. It moved imperceptibly at first, before straightening with a sudden give. We then watched his eyes virtually pop as it straightened fully and then bent in the opposite direction. Three more times Douglas bent and straightened the bar, before it snapped at least an inch more to one side of the U than the other. 'Sorry,' he gasped, grinning all over his face as stars flashed across his eyes from the sheer strain of the task.

We tried the pins in the rowlock sockets. They fitted onto the thwarts quite nicely and with a grommet lashed to them to take the oars we felt we were all set. All we had to wait for now was a good supply of water. We couldn't row without fresh water in much larger quantities than we had been used to, which meant a large container had to be found, which we simply didn't have, or did we? It was Robin's idea that made me realise we did: the flotation collar! Bringing his analytical skills to bear, Robin suggested that if it was to be calm enough to row, it would by definition be calm enough to do without the flotation collar; and the collar could hold enough water to get us all the way to the coast. I pitted his idea against the dangers presented by our reduced freeboard, for if only nine inches of water accumulated in the bottom of the dinghy it would add enough weight to make swamping almost unavoidable in anything but the smoothest of seas. On balance, our need for water swung the argument, and I decided that when the time was right the flotation collar would be dispensed with, cut up and made into a water container. We went to rest with hope in our hearts, with no rage at all against the dying of the translucent hues of yet another beautiful tropical sunset, for the wind was fading away as the darkness cloaked us, bringing with it the tantalising prospect of a gentle night.

Twenty-ninth day

We made good headway before a gentle westerly breeze that had held steady throughout the night. With the sea anchor tripped, *Ednamair* made over a knot to the east-northeast as she sailed once more into the ragged reflection of the rising sun that marked the beginning of our fifth week adrift. The ascending elliptical shape shimmered in the strong refractive airs, changing into a large perfectly round globe before altering its colour from red to orange and then bright yellow, as it lifted clear of the horizon to guide our daylight progress and restart the hard unyielding business of survival with all its harsh routines.

I had barely started work on my gaff when, looking down into the sea past the flashing blue-green and gold of the dorado, I spotted the menacing brown shape of a shark. It was the first small one I had seen since my short-lived escapade with the one on the raft. This one was of a manageable size, though. We had caught a flying fish in the night, but it was only a very small one, so rather than eat it I opted to put it on the large hook and, weighting the line heavily, cast it well out to clear the attendant scavenger fish. My baited hook drifted down past the shark and at first I thought he was going to ignore it, but as the bait fetched up on its line, the shark turned and nosed towards it.

Douglas stretched across the dinghy from my usual place beside the thwart, 'What the hell do you think you are doing, Dad?' 'Catching a shark,' I replied calmly as the shark nosed a little closer. 'You're bloody mad,' he yelled, sitting up quickly. Robin too was sitting up apprehensively and Lyn said, 'You mustn't.' 'Good old Dad,' chorused Neil and Sandy from the bows. 'I'm having him,' I confirmed, tongue in cheek, and watched tensely as the shark approached the bait; the moment I felt him contact I would have to strike, for if he got the nylon line between his teeth he would bite through it like butter. He hovered over the morsel but would not bite. We watched as the shark turned away and with an air of resignation, I jerked the line upwards, intending to bring it in and at least save the bait. Suddenly I felt the slightest contact and with tingling fingers I jerked the line upwards swiftly. In the same instant the line exploded into action: somehow I had actually hooked him! He fought with alternate periods of listless acquiescence and galvanic action, twisting and plunging savagely in an almighty effort to rid himself of his snare. I was afraid of the line breaking but I feared more the arrival of a larger shark, attacking the one I had hooked. With Douglas helping me man the line, we slowly hauled him to the surface, the line cutting deep into our hands as the pressure built. Lyn sat apprehensively in the stern, paddle held ready to fend off its snapping jaws.

The shark broke the surface in a burst of white water, struggling savagely for a few moments, before plunging back into the deep. I deliberately let him range on the line, allowing him to tire before attempting to land him into the bottom of our boat, for we needed him to be nigh on exhausted before releasing him in the midst of our unprotected legs and feet. 'A five-foot mako,' Douglas, our resident shark expert, confirmed, 'and guess what, he's hooked right through the eye!' Armed with this valuable knowledge, I knew there was no escape for him as he resurfaced in a plume of spray. 'We'll have him this time,' I grunted, my hands aching as the line cut deeply into the heel of my hand. All too quickly he was alongside and I realised I had no idea what to do next. 'They can't move once out of the water,' shrieked Douglas, 'let's haul him out and cut his head off before he can bite any of us.' It sounded fine in theory but one mistake and one of us would lose a leg or a hand in an instant. 'Be ready to take the line, Robin,' I asserted hotly, 'I'm going to grab his tail and pull him in backwards.'

Excitement rose to fever pitch and Robin and Lyn looked on in trepidation, for they had the biting end to contend with and one mistake could be fatal. The shark surfaced again, then like something akin to a dog on a lead he just lay alongside as if waiting for us to act. Gingerly Robin took the line from Douglas as I quickly leaned over and grabbed the shark's tail under the water. 'Trim!' I bellowed to the twins who were already leaning out on the other side of the dinghy. Its harsh skin gave me a good grip, and with a quick pull I hauled the shark out of the water and held him prostrate over the gunwale. 'Cut off its head...' Douglas's animated shriek spurred me onwards. I stabbed repeatedly into its head and eyes, as it lay in trancelike stillness, overhanging the deep blue ocean. Without warning it winced and snapped the air with its razor-sharp teeth. 'Lift it inboard by the fins,' I directed to Robin and Douglas as I redoubled my grip on its tail. Robin lifted the struggling fish inboard and Lyn promptly rammed the paddle into the gaping jaws, which clamped shut in a vicelike bite. Knife in hand, I leaned forward and stabbed it through the other eye. The shark shuddered and then lay still. 'Cut its bloody head off,' Douglas repeated insistently, gesticulating the appropriate sawing motion across its neck whilst jerking the tail from my hand. I stabbed the knife into the slits of the gills behind the head and sawed away at the tough skin until the head was severed. 'Right, you can let go now,' I stammered, as I finally wrenched the head from its lifeless torso.

5-foot mako shark – quite an armful

Vanquishing such a powerful adversary left us all exhilarated. Douglas took the head from me and hoisted it aloft like a trophy. We had turned the tables on our most feared enemy: sharks would not eat Robertsons but Robertsons would eat sharks! I had spoken too soon, however, for the severed head, snapping with powerless jaws, closed its mouth on Douglas's hand with sufficient strength to puncture the skin and draw blood. With our celebrations brought to a premature end, I quickly gutted out the internal organs to leave a solid thirty-five to forty pounds of fish, with very little waste apart from the head. We breakfasted on the liver and heart, then Robin, much to the chagrin of his shipmates, picked up the head and, eyeball to eyeball, gnawed off the flesh whilst carefully avoiding the teeth. He relished it, tearing the flesh away with his hands and teeth with the gusto of a wild dog.

Lyn noticed the stomach sack of the shark contained hard lumps, and curiosity soon got the better of her. I slit the stomach sack open to reveal several semi-digested flying fish, which tasted like meat baked in a casserole dish, and was the closest to cooked food that we had tasted in weeks. I cut generous strips of white flesh from the almost boneless carcase. It was tougher than the dorado but juicier and we chewed the moist strips of shark meat with great relish. Our larder now began to look full once more. Long strips of shark swung from the forestay while the remains of the turtle meat continued to dry nicely. I cut out the jawbone from the shark's head while Lyn and the twins cleaned the spinal column. When *Lucette* had sunk, we had lost all our Indian jewellery from the San Blas Islands, the prettiest of which were the shark's teeth and backbone necklaces. Now we grinned at the thought that we had the raw materials to hand and time to spare to start making our own.

Our noon position of 7 degrees and 50 minutes north and 160 miles west of Espinosa evidenced our improved progress, and though the weather became overcast and unsuitable for drying the shark meat it at least afforded us shade from the glaring sun. I set to work on the gaff once more, whilst Douglas steered, and Lyn and Robin tended the hanging fish and meat. Robin had become rather edgy these last two days and now under Lyn's exacting instructions he became wistful and petulant, leaving jobs unfinished and making little attempt to put things right when remedies were brought to his notice. Whilst I chided him and re-checked his work to ensure it had been completed, I felt he was beginning to suffer from the onset of dehydration, for he was the only one amongst us who had not had the benefit of a water retention enema.

During the afternoon we had discovered to our dismay that the water which Douglas had decanted from one of the unopened tins had been foul. I checked the other four, only to discover to my horror that of the remaining cans one more was unpalatable, being full of black sediment, and one was brackish, where salt water had trickled in from the seawater that had washed in over the stern. There was still a gallon and a half of water in the plastic bag we had made from the float, so we were not in immediate danger from a shortage of water, but I was only able to relax after I had checked its contents. Much to my relief, I was able to confirm to the others that it was still sweet enough to be palatable, and secure in this knowledge we settled down to our various chores once more. Lyn had found a foot of stout copper wire in her sewing basket and I was getting the germ of an idea about constructing a more efficient gaff than the model I was currently fashioning.

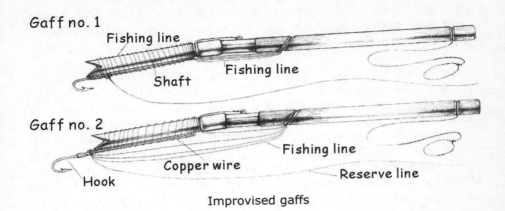

Improvised gaffs

Lyn had given the twins a small turtle-oil enema in the early afternoon to try to ease their blocked systems, and now Sandy was responding. Our nickname for the bailer which we had used for urinating had up to now been 'the pissoir'. There had been no need for a receptacle of any other sort in our constipated conditions but now, after a short conference in the bow, Neil shouted, 'Quick, pass the shittoir, Sandy wants to go!' Sandy's experience was not nearly as exhausting as Douglas's or mine, and Lyn thought that the turtle oil had helped in this respect. As we watched the pieces of shark swinging against the clearing sky in the evening, we felt some satisfaction that with the turtle meat already in store we had enough food to last us for over a week. Additionally we still had some of the emergency rations, which were reserved for the children's 'little supper', to help them cope more comfortably with the rigours of the night.

Thirtieth day

The gentle breeze fell to a flat calm during the night and at dawn the promise of another dry day was reflected in the magnificence of the suspended dawn skyline. The limpid blue of the sea flashed as powerful dorado sped under and around *Ednamair* as the simultaneous cry of 'Turtle!' from both Robin and Sandy heralded the arrival of food. We shifted hastily into our positions, clearing the dinghy for action. A large stag turtle nosed curiously at a trailing rope and in the next instant Douglas, with a swift grab, had secured first one then both back flippers. A wild struggle ensued, for this was a tough one, and with painful lacerations to our hands we finally landed him in the bottom of the dinghy, lifting our feet like we were treading on hot coals as we attempted to avoid his lashing flippers. Having secured him, Douglas held one flipper and pressed shut his snapping beak whilst Neil and Robin held back a flipper apiece, allowing me to keep both hands free for the coup de grace. The tough hide made it difficult work, all of us sustaining cuts and bruises to our legs before the deed was done and the turtle's carcass lay unmoving at our feet.

It was well past noon by the time the meat was hanging and the shell and offal dumped. It had been tougher work than usual, but the meat was a good deep red, and tastier than we had previously sampled. Neil helped collect the fat and Douglas did his stuff on the flipper bones. Robin had finally been persuaded to help Neil collect the fat but he didn't seem to have much of a will to complete the job. I suggested he raise his water a little and see if it made any difference to his productivity. We nursed our wounds as we cut and tore the meat into small pieces and hung it in the rigging, where it slowly dried in the hot sunshine. The shark strips were still occupying the rigging, and since there was no wind I took the sail down and spread the small pieces of meat across the stern seat and the centre thwart, forcing us all to crouch in the bottom of the dinghy, where our limbs became even more cramped and distorted as they overlapped in the greatly reduced space.

Dorado: male (with high forehead) and female

We lunched well on shark and fresh turtle meat, though, nibbling at pieces of turtle fat for afters and crunching the bones in order to extract the rich marrow from their centres. We were all blessed with strong teeth, and although the rest of our anatomy suffered in varying degrees, our teeth remained clean and plaque-free, without any external assistance from brushes. Our diet obviously suited them!

The sun shone fiercely all day, but we suffered it gladly for the drying meat and fish needed every minute of it. The quicker it dried the better it cured, so we poured cups of salt water over each other to keep cool and turned the meat over at regular intervals. Our heads pulsed in the blazing glare until later in the afternoon the heat of the sun cooled, providing much-needed and welcome relief. We collected in the dried meat and stored it in the sailcloth bag in the hope that, weather permitting, a further day's drying on the following day would finish the job. With the food safely put away, we returned to our usual places, Douglas steering, Robin and Lyn seated on the thwart and the twins lying over me in the forward compartment.

Talk soon returned to Dougal's Kitchen and lamb stew. Our conversation was almost immediately interrupted, however, by a powerful stench, the source of which we could not immediately ascertain. Neil was lying over Sandy who was lying over me and it wasn't long before I felt warm droplets of putrid diarrhoea dribbling onto my body from above. Sandy was covered and I admonished him with vitriolic chastisement. Surely he must have felt the need to go. 'Why not use the shittoir,' I said, as he had done just the day before. 'I don't know,' he replied in heartfelt embarrassment. Even Neil remarked that he must have felt something before it happened. 'Not a thing,' assured Sandy, wiping down his soiled body with seawater and a piece of sailcloth. It was then that he noticed Neil was covered in it too. Realising that Neil had been lying above him, Sandy soon worked out that it was his twin brother and not himself that was the culprit! The turtle-oil enemas had been more effective than we had dared hope. As the sea was calm, I flooded the bottom of the dinghy with a couple of inches of water and we all enjoyed a late bath time as we cleaned not only ourselves but also the insides of the boat. The vile stench remained with us for the rest of the night, however.

It was only when I was making up the log for the day, and was about to enter up the small change in our position since noon, that Neil leaned across to me and whispered, 'Hey, Dad, put this in your log. On the thirtieth day Neil had a shit.' I looked to see if he was serious; he grinned an impish smile and smirked, 'It's right, so put it in.' Well it was after all a remarkable incident, and as well as the more routine remarks that was what the logbook was for. I duly made the entry in the log to the raucous laughter of the others.

While our skin problems were slowly improving, both my own and Douglas's hands had become a mass of hacks and cuts. Every time we caught a turtle, I usually collected one or two cuts to mark the occasion and this, aggravated with sticking fishhooks into myself, brought the combination of cuts and old boil scars to a pitch where I looked like a victim of some ancient Eastern torture. After the initial sting of pain, these cuts gave me very little soreness and I wondered if the salt water anaesthetised them in some way.

Evening threw quiet shadows over the sea and we re-packed the drying food under cover for the night. Lyn placed the small pieces of turtle in one section of the bamboo sewing basket while the shark strips, now emitting a strong odour, were placed in a separate piece of sail. The sea was almost mirror-calm and loud splashes broke the unaccustomed silence as dorado leapt after flying fish and sharks leapt after dorado. A louder splash made the sea foam nearby, as a larger predator, identified by Douglas as a small pilot whale, attacked a dorado, which leapt desperately into the air in order to escape. Large black fins surrounded us for a few moments as the rest of the pod passed by, causing our hearts to beat rapidly as we monitored their erratic progress. The fins of the large sharks were never far away either, but we ignored them as long as they left us alone.

Dougal's Kitchen came back into the conversation as we chewed our strips of shark meat. Robin described the various catering systems and the range of menus he had encountered on work placement but we decided to stick to a minimum of uncomplicated dishes. Pasties served in cold weather, supplemented with sheep's-head broths and ham-bone stock, lentil soups and a special sort of Scotch egg together with cold chicken pasties and iceberg lettuce salads in the summer. In order to accommodate our expanding appetites, we decided to open a small private room catering for special dinner parties, and here we really let ourselves go with curries, shish kebab, stroganoff, exotic Chinese foods, thick steaks and luscious salads.

As dusk descended, the evening planet Jupiter reflected a sinking path on the calm surface of the sea, whilst the star I knew to be Antares in the constellation of the Scorpion gleamed a warm red in the firmament above us. I was observing the Southern Cross and its pointers to the south when Douglas called excitedly to me from the thwart: 'I can see it Dad, look!' I twisted my head round quickly and adjusted my gaze, following the direction of his pointing finger. 'It's the Pole star!' he uttered as if talking to a child. Like a giant signpost in the heavens, it twinkled its beckoning light at us for the first time since we had been wrecked. We were unlikely to see the Pole star south of 5 degrees north latitude, so this welcome sign confirmed our latitude and verified our distance run of some 400 miles to the north. We were back in the northern hemisphere and, strangely, we felt we were also back amongst friends.

Thirty-first day

Ednamair lay quietly under the brilliance of the night sky. Long phosphorescent trails streaked the sparkling surface of the sea, as marine life darted in profusion around us. Deeper down, large patches of glowing green fire chased swiftly in pursuit of smaller quarry, while scattered areas of luminescence glowed brightly and faded again in response to some unidentified stimulus. It seemed the whole world of marine life was abuzz beneath us, locked in spectacular but deadly combat, in the struggle to survive. Dorado patrolled the vicinity of our little craft with brilliant moonlight reflecting from their silver scales, as occasionally they lay quiescent on their sides, showing their pale underbellies.

A sudden splash followed by a heavier bump under the keel indicated the presence of a much bigger fish and Robin, on watch, grabbed a paddle and poked at it through the darkness. I leaned over the side just in time to see a huge shark, its tattered dorsal fin gliding by at the height of our shoulders as it cleared the underside of the boat and then bumped us with a second bone-jarring strike. I grabbed the broken spear and thrust at it on its return, striking the monster across its back, and though it gave no sign of alarm when the blunt point made contact it didn't return. It was the biggest specimen we had seen, longer than the dinghy and as wide at the head, but thankfully it made no further attempt to attack us.

Dawn found us in our usual state of torpor, half-awake after a night of restless movement to ease our sore and aching limbs. I sorted the drying strips of turtle and shark and chided my weary crew into action, then we re-hung the various portions of turtle and fish back on the rigging. Crouching in the bottom of the boat once again, we begrudged the diminished space but surveyed the profusion of meat with certain satisfaction. We were starting to build a reserve of food again, which would be useful if our initial landfall was inhospitable or if for any reason we ran out of turtles. I eased my cramped and twisted posture and turned to watch Robin pour the water from the plastic bag into the drinking jar, after which I watched him carelessly refasten it. Lyn and Douglas were busy preparing a breakfast concoction of various marinated strips of meat and fish. Alarm bells began to chime in the deepest recesses of my mind but I knew not why.

My thoughts were interrupted by the cry of 'Turtle!' from Neil as he felt it bump under the bow. The next moment saw us fully alert, hurriedly clearing the stern area as the unfortunate amphibian investigated our fibreglass hull. We were now expert turtle catchers, and our teamwork was a smooth sequence of coordinated movement as the turtle was swung aboard, flapping wildly like its predecessors. The fresh meat from this turtle would allow us to preserve the meat from the last one, which would materially augment our reserves. We set to work with a will, Douglas performing the execution and the others carving off the joints of meat. We needed a substantial reserve of meat if we were to start rowing, for working oarsmen get hungry as well as thirsty, and at the end of it all we had to be fit to cope with the emergencies that were bound to arise when we made landfall. To die through weakness at such a point would make our present struggle a futile gesture against fate.

Lyn assisted in stripping out the shell blubber and expertly removed the fat covering the intestinal wall. The fat was stuffed into a plastic bag and hung on the rigging, where the sun would render the fat into oil. We enjoyed a luncheon of fresh turtle steak and meat juice, with the now coveted marrowbones handed round for chewing afterwards. The marrow's taste differed with each turtle and the bittersweet taste of this one provoked a wide variety of comments. We speculated on the possibility that residues of strontium were stored in the marrow, transferred by marine life from the French atomic testing grounds in the ocean current sequence running into this area. It mattered not, for living continuously on a knife-edge had blunted our fear of the more remote threats to our welfare and we gnawed with vigour, grateful that our teeth were our own and able to withstand the onslaught of such primitive usage.

It was not until the shell was finally disposed of that we discovered the plastic water bag was empty. Having been tied into place by Robin, it had been knocked from its lashing by the struggling turtle. I literally shook with anger as I absorbed this new information and fought back my shattered emotions as I came to terms with the fact that almost all our water, in an unseen moment of lapse, had been lost. I turned unjustly on Robin with bitter acrimony and rebuked him for his carelessness. There had been reason enough to regard Robin's practical skill with suspicion, and with an important thing like water there was little excuse for my neglect to see that the water bag had been safely stowed. I, like him, had grown careless in the new-found relief from anxiety about our reserves of food, and was now faced with the brutal consequences. I lifted the bag amid a stony silence, blood dripping from its crumpled emptiness, and handed it to Robin. 'Better wash it out with salt water,' I growled, biting my lip as I fought to control my anger. 'See that it's rinsed before you fill it in the next rain.' 'I will, Dougal, if it's the last thing I ever do,' he replied quietly, his eyes meeting mine in quiet understanding as Douglas added an oath of support for Robin. 'I saw him tie the knot, Dad, and I saw the extra turn in it and I was just too bloody tired to say anything.' 'We're all exhausted and mistakes are bound to happen,' I rasped, fully aware that unless we refilled the bag and quickly then this self-inflicted wound could spell the end for us all. 'We'll make sure it's refilled together,' Douglas finished to Robin as they solemnly exchanged glances in a silent pact.

Our noon position of 7 degrees 55 minutes north and 145 miles west of Espinosa only served to illustrate how little ground we had covered over the last two days. The added worry of a water crisis changed our relaxed mood of complacency in the morning to one of impending doom by the afternoon. The loss of the water bag was serious indeed, for it left us with only eight pints in the tins, and two of these were foul. I could see no signs of rain and set to work immediately to finish work on the gaff. If we were to run out of water only turtle or dorado could save us. Turtle came only when it suited them but the dorado and other fish were there for the catching and it was on these that I had to concentrate.

The hot sun beat down on us during the afternoon, drying the parts of the fresh meat we had hung in the rigging and curing the already half-dried meat spread on the thwarts. We stoically endured the blistering heat, seeking shade from pieces of sail placed over our heads and obtaining coolness from evaporation by rinsing our clothing in the water and placing it on our naked bodies. Evening clouds of the altocumulus type spread across the evening sky, affording no prospect of rain, as we packed away the dried shark, which had begun emitting a sharp savoury smell like that of smoky bacon. As the afternoon progressed we became more and more depressed by this sudden new threat to our existence, which was in the form we had dreaded the most. We had had a good day in the food stakes, but food was no use without water.

The dorado were moving close to the surface, in a calm and placid sea, persuading me to try my latest version of my gaff immediately. I had fastened a barbed fish hook with repeated turns of the heavy nylon fishing line, bound into place with two separate lengths of the hundred-pound breaking strain cord. I then fastened the line from the eye of the hook to the grooves cut into the shaft of the paddle handle. Douglas put his muscles to use once again, binding it tightly to the spear shaft and making the whole weapon as rigid as possible. I also took the precautionary step of fastening a reserve line from the hook directly into the boat, which in a moment of absent-mindedness I secured to the mast. I lowered the business end of the gaff over the side and waited for a suitable fish to come within striking distance. They were not in the least alarmed by the presence of the weapon and swooped around *Ednamair* in their usual profusion. I was poised ready to strike and an air of expectancy hung over us as we cleared away the box of water cans, in anticipation of my landing a fish. Slowly I turned the hook in the direction of a small female when, with almost no warning, a medium-sized bull dorado shot over the gaff. My hair-trigger reaction was almost instinctive and I struck upwards into the fish. The sudden weight of the fish on the hook made my heart leap. 'Look out!' I yelled as I jerked the gaff upwards, bringing the fish into the boat with an almighty thud, followed by a rapid-fire slapping and flapping of fins as our intended prize struggled for its life. Just as I began to relax, there was a sudden heavy pull on the handle, followed by a loud ripping sound, and then the fish was gone. Having leapt over the side with our hook still attached, it then broke the reserve line clean in two as though it had been made of cotton. I looked at the broken line as if in a trance, before cursing myself out loud for being such a fool. The reserve line should not have been fastened at all, it should have been held by one of the others, ready to pay out in the event of just such an occurrence. I studied the gaff and looked at the flayed ends of the lines securing the hook. The double line had actually parted close to the hook where it had been bound to the shank of the spearhead. The design fault lay in the structure being too rigid for the materials I had available. I looked around the boat, observing the disappointed faces of the others, and thought I detected an attitude of scepticism at the sheer temerity I had shown in even thinking I could secure one of these powerful fish with such ludicrous equipment in the first place. Unrepentant, I settled down with the knife in the gathering twilight and stripped off all the broken nylon before securing fresh line in its place. I had one hook left, and if that were lost then we would have to depend on turtles entirely. Darkness closed in with the new gaff unfinished. We settled down quietly for the night, silent and with leaden hearts under bitter clouds of despair and disappointment.

Lyn took Douglas's watch that night and being unable to sleep myself I sat with her. We talked quietly of the farming life we had left behind us back in England. In conclusion, Lyn expressed her wish that we return to our lives of farming once we got back home. The old frustrations and anxieties of our life together on the farm welled up within, compelling me to tell her that I would never go back to a despairing life of nagging and bitterness, engendered by the twin poisons of poverty and hardship that to me had epitomised the farmer's lot in the United Kingdom. I told her there was more to living than the brutish existence we had shared before *Lucette*, and that if we were fortunate enough to make it home then I intended that life, for me at least, would change. I had found a new person in myself during the last few weeks, a person that would no longer accept fate as inevitable, a person who recognised that choice, and the will to follow it, was one of the single most powerful elements of life. 'Dealing with the issues we have had to face since the shipwreck has given me the courage to make much more daring decisions about my life,' I continued, my tone raising to ensure my words bridged the darkness. 'In these weeks I have learned to listen and not just to speak. Even now I feel the power of life over death, of living and not just existing; I have touched the pulse of life itself and I never want to let go of what I have found!'

The intensity of my voice began to frighten Lyn and she felt that my desire for a new life did not include her. Her hushed tones rose an octave as she protested about the lack of water and electricity I had forced her to tolerate at Meadows Farm. She asked how exactly I expected to live such a life of ideals, when basic requirements could not be provided. Our conversation rapidly turned into a full-blown argument. I found that even the simple process of talking of those times brought back the bitterest memories as I realised our life of doing without, and of long hours of toil, day after day, had first eroded and then finally crushed the happiness from our existence. The barrier of bitterness, expunged with the voyage of the *Lucette* and the nearness of death we both felt on the raft, rose unexpectedly to divide us. Before the woken eyes of our children, Lyn wept as I flung savage recriminations at her for the years of nagging and misery I felt she had inflicted upon me. The assault did not last long, and soon, exhausted of my energy reserves, I lapsed into the booming silence of arid repentance, finally asking and receiving her forgiveness. The declining moon illuminated our brief reconciliation before we lay down to recuperate and preserve the saliva in our parched dry mouths.

Thirty-second day

After a night of breathless calm and brilliant starlit beauty, the sombre hours after moonset brought a morning of hot sun and a cloudless vibrant blue sky. I worked feverishly on my second gaff and soon had it ready for use. This model featured a triple nylon line leading from the hook eye direct to the grooves in the handle so that on striking, the hook would have freedom to swivel within the limits of the arc permitted by the short line. I felt sure that this time it would work unless the line itself was faulty. We were down to six pints of water now and with no prospect of rain or a passing turtle some alternative source of water had to be found, and quickly, for the effects of thirst and dehydration were already beginning to take effect.

We had finished breakfast and I was about to clear the stern of the dinghy prior to making another attempt with the gaff when Douglas spotted a patrolling turtle in the distance. He pointed to the scaly head surveying us from fifty feet away and we hurried to clear a space. 'Another one!' shouted Sandy, pointing to the starboard bow where a stag turtle had appeared near the anchor rope. I was toying with the idea of killing them both, when the stag turtle suddenly spotted the other, a female. There was no hesitation; in an instant the stag joined the female, mated, and then they both disappeared beneath the surface. Desperately we scanned the surface for signs of their return but they had both vanished. I had always assumed that the turtles had sought our company because they thought *Ednamair* was possibly a little island. After this event, however I realised that they were in fact seeking us out as a prospective mate. I made a mental note that we were unlikely to capture any females with eggs while there were stags around and turned my attention back to the gaff.

The boys were looking very disappointed, and as I manipulated my improvised fish catcher they resigned themselves to some more of my fooling about. Lyn was particularly cross, both at our losing the turtles and at the additional hardships brought about by my fruitless fishing escapades, and she nagged us all with bitter reproach, starting a long and pointless harangue about the conditions to which she had been subjected throughout our married life. She continued about how I had failed to provide the normal civilised amenities on the farm, how the roof had leaked, how the stove hadn't worked properly, and of the years we had made do without electricity or a telephone, as well as the lack of money. She then continued with how such living had resulted in the neglect of the children's education and a non-existent social life. The whole gamut of bitterness and frustration as the wife of an overworked and underpaid hill farmer rose up within her, and I snapped and snarled back at her with equal savagery until she burst into tears.

Without warning, Douglas suddenly stood to his feet, gripping our makeshift mast just beneath the point where it flared out to form the blade of the oar. 'Shut up before you kill us all,' he bellowed to Lyn and me in desperate anguish. 'Sit down before you tip us over,' I spat back at him, raising my hand in admonishment, but he slapped it down. Water slopped dangerously in over the gunwale as he adjusted his grip upwards. His eyes burned with a savage intensity as he held my glare. To my dismay I realised he knew exactly what he was doing, for I dared not move an inch from my present position, because if his hands moved up the mast by more than a fraction we would capsize instantaneously. 'You're killing us all with your bloody arguing,' Douglas continued without remorse. 'If you want to die then let's all die together – right now; all I have to do is lift my hand to the mast head and it's all over. Is that what you want? Because your stupid arguing will kill us all just as certainly as your bloody bickering will.'

'OK, Douglas, OK – you've made your point,' I stammered in shocked realisation. 'You as well, Mother,' he demanded harshly without moving his hand from the mast. 'I'm sorry, kids,' sobbed Lyn in a renewed bout of weeping, her dehydrated body unable to afford her even the luxury of tears as her form trembled in frustrated torment. Robin comforted her quietly with a reproachful 'Oh! Come on now' in my direction. I was unrepentant, however, and looking crossly at her sniped, 'Lyn, if you don't stop nagging, I'll leave you and go back to sea.' My astonished onlookers stared at me in wide-eyed reproach whilst Douglas, having brought an end to the arguing in spectacular fashion, relocated himself in the bottom of the boat. A long period of stony silence ensued.

After an even longer period of reflection, during which I added a few finishing touches to the gaff, we cleared the boat once more for fishing. I handed the reserve line to Douglas and told him to make sure that, if the fish broke loose from the gaff and took the hook, he was to give it plenty of slack and play it slowly. Tensely I watched the dorado swoop beneath the *Ednamair*, my muscles aching as they hunched in tensed poise, ready to act on a split-second reflex. 'Shut up,' I snarled unfairly in Lyn's direction as she talked to the twins. 'How the hell do you expect me to concentrate with you gossiping away!' Several large fish cruised around but they were over the forty-pound mark, too big a risk both for ourselves and for the fragile gear. A smaller dorado slanted under the keel, so I lowered the gaff a foot deeper into the water. I could feel the silence as we all waited in an expectant hush. A larger bull swooped towards the smaller one and then with a sudden swerve turned right across my striking path. It was far too big to tackle but I could not stop my impulsive urge as I jerked the gaff upwards into the pectoral flesh of the giant fish. The swift upward lunge with the hook was followed immediately by a powerful surge of weight, then astonishingly by a gleaming arc of silver flashing through the air. Pandemonium ensued as we fell on the wildly struggling fish trapped in the bottom of the boat. I grabbed its tail and cut it off with two swift strokes, then groping forward severed its head; it was ours!

We looked at the twenty-pound fish with a combination of disbelief and incredible glee. 'Thank you, my love!' I looked in astonishment at Lyn, now all smiles and said, 'Do you mean to tell me that this bit of fish can change you from a ...' 'Yes,' she interrupted, smiling sweetly, 'come on, what are we waiting for?'

I grinned as we turned to dress the fish carcass. We ate a little of the flesh for lunch but concentrated mainly on the juicy liver and heart. After I had cut the flesh away from the backbone we severed the vertebrae and sucked the spinal fluid from the cavities. Robin, chewing at the head, found that the large eyes were nearly all moisture, and by sucking them like giant sweets he had soon reduced them from an inch in diameter to something the size of a small pea. The gaff had worked and worked well, but in the scramble the copper wire which held the hook rigid for striking had broken, so I abandoned fishing for the rest of the day, happy beyond words that at last we had found a way to reap a harvest of not only food but also water from the sea.

We celebrated our arrival at latitude 8 degrees north and 135 miles west of Espinosa by not having any water with our lunch, and prepared to spend a hot afternoon, cooling each other by repeatedly dowsing our bodies with streams of seawater whilst intently watching the developing cumulus clouds for signs of precipitation. We had laid out the drying turtle to complete its curing process and had hidden the pieces of fresh dorado away from the sun, to retain as much of its moisture as possible. Our hopes of rain developed with the clouds, and when we saw a shower falling in a black curtain on the horizon we opened another tin of water to ease our tortured mouths. Four showers passed us by without even coming close, and as the light westerly breeze ruffled the surface of the placid ocean the clouds diminished in size and drifted away to the northeast. We sucked the moisture from the raw fish until there was nothing left in our mouths but fibre. We spoke of dishes we would serve in Dougal's Kitchen on a hot summer day. Cold consommé, fresh fruit salad and ice cream, a dish we dwelt on for quite a while, together with long, long drinks of cool fruit juices. At teatime, succulent slices of tomato on toast or in sandwiches, pancakes écossaise or chocolate- and coconut-covered sponge cakes. With five pints of water left between six of us, we had much need to use our imaginations, which supplied us with increasingly vivid hallucinations of food stacked in ever-increasing quantity and splendour.

I quietly told Lyn and Douglas that we must impose self-rationing upon ourselves, only taking sips of water from now on, supplemented when possible by the moisture we could obtain from the fish. The spectre of thirst had already settled on Douglas's face, his eyes more darkly shadowed deep into the depths of his skull sockets. He took the news without complaint, however, knowing that as our options reduced the road to survival would become harder still. Robin seemed to be in better shape physically and he was paying more attention to detail concerning the work he was given; even so, the thought of that wasted gallon of water preyed unremittingly on his mind. Lyn was untiring in her ministrations to the twins, tending their eyes, their skin ailments, and massaging their legs with turtle oil as well as exercising their limbs. She bathed us when we were hot and rubbed us when we were cold and saw to it that the sheets were as clean and dry as they could be. With that job done, she nagged and badgered us into cleanliness, where every move had become an effort beyond belief.

I decided to overhaul the gaff in the cool of the following morning and then tried to rest. My mouth was dry and foul tasting as my enlarged tongue searched my gums for saliva and found none. With eyes shut and lips pressed firmly together, I thought of a long cool draught of milk. As if by magic, I felt saliva moisten my mouth, and my desire for water eased a little. It was going to be a hard night, for sleep would not come to ease the burden of our thirst. The boys' distress increased likewise, for with no relief from their misery afforded by the precious hours of night-time oblivion, they tossed and turned restlessly complaining at each other for usurping an extra inch of space or the tiniest fold of sheet. Robin's muttered delirium was interrupted only by the sipper jar, the sole mediator which won unequivocal approval, as it circled its eager patrons only twice during the night.

Thirty-third day

I set to work at daybreak, the calm sea showing barely a ripple as the windless dawn hung like a pink curtain in the clear eastern sky. Shafts of sunlight reflected from our parchment-dry skins, revealing our eyes having sunk visibly overnight into deep pits, surrounded by dark-ringed sockets. Without clouds there could be no rain, and an air of depression descended on us as one. I overhauled the gaff carefully, testing the tension of the lines and adjusting the angle of the hook, now closer to the end of the spear shaft on the shortened length of copper wire. We cleared the space in the bottom of the dinghy to give room to work and took down the sail so that in the event of a catch I could have a clear swing inboard.

Slowly I lowered the gaff into the crystal-clear water, my nerves taut and muscles trembling with expectation. Dorado swooped close by under the stern, six of them turning in graceful unison as they swerved slowly in tight formation alongside the dinghy. I struck desperately and missed. 'That was not the way to catch fish,' I voiced my thoughts out loud and, realising the hopelessness of such an approach, forced myself to relax as the fish scattered in tantalising profusion around us. Lyn handed me a sip of water, wetting my mouth and allowing my nerves to quieten. A single female cruised six feet down, rising slowly as she approached us. I angled the hook towards its path and suddenly there were two more, close by and gliding up from the bow, right across the line of strike. The gaff swung as I felt the hook bite then detach and hold again as the lines took the strain. 'Look out!' My shout was unnecessary as the fish, twenty pounds of bone and muscle, performed a graceful arc into the bottom of the dinghy and thrashed wildly at our feet.

There are two places to catch and hold a dorado, one where the tail joins the body, and the other at the eyes. Placing the thumb and middle finger in the eye sockets and pressing firmly seems to have a paralytic effect on the fish. To try to hold these very strong and slippery fish in any other way would end up in simply assisting the dorado back over the side and into the sea. A dorado's whole existence depends on its ability to leap after flying fish, and the simple two-foot hurdle formed by the side of the boat proved to be no obstacle, as they fought against us, desperately attempting to flap their way to freedom. The moment to relax came only after the fish was dead; lack of vigilance at any time before that would allow for an easy escape. Knife in hand, I held the gaff clear to try to avoid it being damaged amid the mishmash of struggling arms as Douglas, Robin and Sandy each grappled with the fish. Finally, Douglas held it still by gripping hard into its eye sockets. I dropped the gaff and caught the tail, our knuckles bruising on the fibreglass as the fish lashed its imprisoned frame. A few seconds later, we surveyed the long blue and gold body as it turned to silver. Even in death, it remained a thing of great beauty. I disliked killing these fish even more than the turtles, but likes and dislikes did not enter into the survival stakes; eat or be eaten was the law of survival at sea, and our choice was clear.

'Right – we'll have two more,' I announced, still panting with exertion. 'We need the water they contain.' My blood-spattered hands readjusted the hook on the striking end of the gaff. The ideal place to plant the hook was in the area under the body in the first six inches behind the head. The fish was then compelled to swim towards the pull of the gaff, whereas if the hook was inserted too near the tail the powerful thrusts would take the fish away from the direction of pull, with a considerable increase in dynamic tension, resulting in the probable breaking of the lines. The second dorado of the morning came aboard five seconds later, a smaller one this time and hooked much too near the tail, but it had practically collided with the gaff the moment I lowered it into the water. Luckily, it hadn't been one of the larger specimens.

We rested a little after the demise of this unexpected bounty and looked at the two shining fish, lying in the blood-spattered water in the bottom of the dinghy. 'Clear them forward a bit,' I instructed Douglas, 'we don't want to be slipping on them when we bring the next one aboard.' It was with great care that I lowered the gaff for the third strike. Five minutes grew to ten, ten to fifteen, and my shoulder muscles began aching with tension as the boys fidgeted in their places, but I was wiser now that we had two in the bag. I wasn't going to risk our last hook on a risky strike; it would have to be in the right place in the right fish. A magnificent bull dorado suddenly surged under the keel, about twenty or maybe even thirty pounds I guessed. Swiftly I struck at it, skimming its side, but failed to plant the hook. To my surprise a female, attracted by the flash of the bull's sudden evading tactics, swam straight towards me. I struck upwards and felt the hook give as it sank home, then fear gripped my heart as I felt something snap. I shouted a warning to Douglas, holding the reserve line, then risking all or nothing I heaved it into the boat. The hook parted from the fish as it landed in the bottom of the boat, and Sandy grabbed its tail as I fastened my fingers in its eyes, its mouth snapping at the heel of my hand with rows of needle-sharp teeth. It was a mammoth twenty-five pounder and we surveyed our catch with satisfaction as its struggles died away, the pigment rapidly changing colour in its iridescent scales. I felt we could certainly get enough water from these fish, thereby avoiding the necessity of opening another tin of water until the evening. They would also provide some enjoyable eating.

On examination, Douglas discovered the gaff had one of the three lines from the paddle handle broken. When the strain had come on the hook the tension had been unevenly distributed, but the two remaining lines had fortunately been strong enough to take the strain. As we gutted the fish Lyn investigated the stomachs and found two recently swallowed flying fish packed inside. We added these to the livers, roes and hearts and ate before sucking the eyes and the spinal fluid, then cut some of the flesh into strips for drying later. We also kept enough wet fish in reserve for meals during the rest of the day.

We had established a certain amount of security at least, with forty pounds of fish drying and a good quantity of turtle meat already dry. We needed only water now but, alas, it looked as if we were going to have to depend on what we could extract from the fish. The sun rose in the cloudless sky as the day advanced and the sea, now mirror-calm, reflected the glare of the sun under our pieces of sail to such a degree that by noon we wilted in the furnace of the sun's rays. Listless and weary, we poured salt water onto each other's parched bodies and clutched pieces of sail and canopy over us to escape the direct rays of the sun whilst we sweltered in the oven-hot shade. All afternoon we poured water on the sails, hoping to stop the heat conducting through and radiating into our bodies. By the onset of the afternoon, several small fleecy cumulus clouds appeared, but gave no sign of developing into clouds of rain-bearing capacity. Pinned down by the heat, we left the fish to dry, unheeded and untended.

I simply allowed a ten-mile easterly drift for the day's run; we were going nowhere of our own volition, and the weather was suitable neither for rowing nor for sailing. The sun crept slowly down to the western horizon, which now assumed the appearance of a clean-cut, dead-straight line in the calm seas, having lost its more usual lumpy appearance as the calm deepened. There was hardly a sign left of the trade-wind swell from the south. We tracked the sun's progress inch by inch, our drought-stricken mouths silently counting the minutes till the sun would set and allow us our next sip of water, a prerequisite to moving around for circulatory relief and exercise. Carefully I opened a tin of water and decanted it into the jar then, taking the mug, I measured out a small mouthful each. Eyes gazed fixedly at the jar as the mug was passed round. I made sure each had an equal share and swallowed; the time for rationing had arrived. A small piece of wet fish constituted our supper and a moody silence prevailed, our talk stilled by the need to conserve the moisture in our mouths.

Douglas's deep-set eyes searched the horizon, not for ships but for the high-reaching cumulus of a rain cloud; the skin of his cheekbones was drawn taut, sharply etched against the white sail. I was worried at the steady deterioration I had observed in his condition since the onset of the current heat wave. Suddenly I was aware he was returning my stare. 'Forgive me, Dad, I just can't go on anymore.' His brow dipped and his voice became barely more than a whisper through the half-gloom of the approaching twilight. His mouth, swollen out of shape, was full of blisters and his energy all but spent. The effects of dehydration and thirst racked his body and gripped his very spirit. I reached for him in the darkness and held him close to me. 'You can't give up now, Doug,' I stammered, fighting back impotent tearless sobs. 'We need you, son, we need you to help row us back to land.' I squeezed his arms as if to accentuate the inert strength stored within his thick limbs and his eyes refocused. 'When, Dad?' he grated with a pleading look in his eye. 'As soon as the rains come,' I replied, hoping against hope that my stated reliance on him would shake him back into survival mode, as he weighed the odds. 'OK,' he whispered, 'I won't let you down.' I sat there holding his arm, our bond deep and unshaken. 'I know you won't my son – now try to get some sleep.'

Later that night Robin stirred from his slumbers, muttering to himself, then sat bolt upright talking aloud in semi-delirium. I decided I had been too hard with the rationing and ordered up a midnight feast, carefully measuring another sip of water each. With mouths moistened, *Ednamair*'s crew settled quietly to rest again. An hour later, Douglas, who was on lookout, excitedly called me to look at a ship's lights on the horizon. I asked him to look carefully again before I disturbed the sleeping twins and the disappointment crept into his voice as he saw the light fade and disappear. There are many explanations for these lights, the most common on a clear night being that of a star, refracted to several times its normal size, appearing momentarily on the horizon through a gap in the cloud layer just before setting or after rising. Thirty seconds' scrutiny usually serves to discount the illusion. I had not dismissed the other more disturbing explanation, however, for it was possibly an apparition borne of severe thirst. Both Lyn and Robin called me on their watches to verify the same illusion, which I asserted, in public at least, was due to the setting of different stars.

The beauty of the starlit night was not lost on us, even in our arid physical condition, and we gazed in rapt silence at the breathtaking grandeur of the brightly twinkling stars, glowing in the depths of the Milky Way. We were very small fry indeed in these oceans of space. I could hear Lyn's voice quietly praying as I dozed but then, as I looked into the limitless heavens I could only think of FitzGerald's verse from the 'Rubaiyaat of Omar Khayyam':

And that inverted bowl they call the sky,
Where under crawling coop'd we live and die,
Lift not your hands to it for help, for it
As impotently moves as you or I

Not because I thought the verse was apt but because I liked the rhythm of the words and their assessment of our relevance in the universe. The night crept slowly on through the muttered delirium of Robin's dreams and the twins restlessly turning, as they searched fruitlessly in their quest for ease, which in truth only water could bring.

Thirty-fourth day

As daylight approached, we all lay sleepless and un-rested. We scanned the small cumulus waifs coming up from the south for the possibility of rain; it seemed the upper atmosphere had wind even if it was calm at sea level. The water jar was empty and we eyed the remaining four tins with longing. As soon as there was enough light, I repaired the broken line on the gaff and we cleared the decks for fishing. Robin, Sandy, Douglas and I sat in the stern section as Lyn spoke reassuringly to Neil in the bows. My mouth was sore and raspy, dry and foul tasting, which bothered me and distracted my attention from the task at hand, as I tried unsuccessfully to work up some saliva. My eye caught Lyn's as she motioned with her hand in a gesture of drinking and pointed to Neil. I couldn't see him but the thin shank of his leg told me what Lyn was trying to say. 'Let's have sippers before we start,' I responded quietly. 'Otherwise I won't be able to concentrate.' Robin opened the can with sheer alacrity and Douglas poured it with ritualistic care into the water jar. I measured out a ration, a mere half-inch in the bottom of the mug, then passed the jar to Lyn. 'Hold on to that,' I rasped with a confirmatory nod of my head, 'we don't want it broken.'

I turned once more to the fish and found myself gazing at a twenty-five-pound female dorado about to go under the boat whilst two enormous bull dorado lazily eyed the *Ednamair* as they glided past. They looked between sixty and eighty pounds apiece. I waited for the smaller fish to return and angled the hook in readiness; it came with a rush, flashing from under the keel at high speed. I jerked the gaff towards it in a belated reflex action, then as I watched it turned sharply in a right angle after the bulls. My hook struck with a satisfying solidity and then detached from the end of the gaff with a heavy jerk. I pulled sharply and the fish flew in a graceful arc into the bottom of the dinghy. 'Grab it!' I yelled as it thrashed amongst a forest of legs and arms. Sandy dropped to his knees and groped after the slippery body, Robin stuck his legs out like a soccer player trying to keep his hands off the ball and the fish, with a great leap, used his knee as a stepping-stone before vanishing with a splash over the far side of the boat. I cursed them all generally and Robin in particular. 'Why in hell's name can't you keep your bloody knees out of the way?' I snarled, disregarding the fact that there wasn't any place else for him to put them. 'In future use your hands, and,' I added maliciously, 'it doesn't matter if the bloody fish bites you. It'll have hold of you, even if you haven't got hold of it!' Robin gazed at me unhappily with mute reproach and tucked his knees awkwardly into the side of the dinghy.

I lowered the gaff again after readjusting the hook and waited for my nerves to quieten. Slowly I relaxed and watched another formation of fish approach. Gleaming arrays of blue and green edged with gold and silver swam by, but none were in the right place to risk a strike. Twenty minutes later I was still waiting, nerves stretched to the limit, angling the hook towards the flash of the fish, as I tried to assess the size and direction of their trajectory before I risked a strike. A fifteen-pound female suddenly came down from the bow. I struck at it and missed but the fish, attracted by the flash of the hook, turned sharply back towards the gaff. My second strike was accurate, an inch behind the head and under the belly; a second later our breakfast was aboard. Douglas dropped the line and had it by the tail almost as it came over the gunwale and the knife finished its struggles a few seconds later. It wasn't a big fish but it would have to do. I cut up the flesh and handed out pieces of spine to suck. The twins had an eye apiece and the rest of us chewed at the liver and roes.

The white-hot disc of the sun beat mercilessly on our little craft that morning. Lyn and I continued to bicker at each other until Lyn dissolved in a fit of impotent sobs. Robin, acting as conciliator with only the best of intentions at heart, became trapped in the irrationality of our arguments and was promptly used as the deflective butt of our wrath. I had to admire his resilience as he tried a less direct approach than Douglas had used, in an effort to curb my own and Lyn's unfortunate antics. The bitter reproaches were interrupted by the shout of 'Turtle!' from Douglas and our quarrels were forgotten in the flurry of clearing the necessary space and getting the trim right. The turtle bumped the side of the boat and Douglas reached down and grabbed it. As I waited for him to swing it aboard, the lengthening silence made me anxious. 'Come on, let's have it!' I demanded. 'It's gone. It was a massive stag and somehow it slipped from my...' Douglas's voice tapered into silence, contrite with confused misery. 'You what?' I yelled. 'Why the hell don't you leave it to me if you can't manage!' Furious, I slapped his knee with my open palm. 'That's right, hit him, you big bully!' Lyn's voice shrieked from the bow. We stared at each other in frustrated silence before I slowly lifted the box of empty water cans down off the thwart and lashed it back in position. We spent the rest of the morning contemplating our own misery, without even the benefit of companionship to ease our thirst.

Noon however brought gathering cumulus in the southern sky and our position of 8 degrees and 5 minutes north and 120 miles west of Espinosa (93 degrees and 20 minutes west) restored a little sweetness to our bitter thoughts. I announced that we should now be about 380 miles from the coast, two-thirds of the way home, and if rain came we would be able to make it in eighteen more days by rowing at night. The early afternoon found us chewing pieces of wet fish to moisten the dryness of our mouths and ease the leathery texture of our tongues. Reluctantly I opened another can of water in order to wash our mouths clean of salt residues from the fish, which had been stored in sailcloth moistened with salt water. We watched the rain showers develop, staring at the falling curtains of rain many miles distant with hypnotic intensity, as we each willed out loud for them to head in our direction. It had already been our experience to have a shower spend itself before reaching us, so we resisted the impulse to indulge in drinks all round as a large curtain of rain crept towards us. By four o'clock, we knew it must hit us, and as the sky darkened the relief brought saliva unbidden to our mouths. We passed the jar round for an un-rationed sip and then as large isolated drops fell around us we turned our faces to the sky, our parched mouths wide open to catch the first lifesaving drops as they fell, quenching our thirst and washing the encrusted salt from the sail and the canopy.

The raindrops grew in size and intensity as the main curtain of rain approached. We eagerly sipped at the puddles of brackish water gathering in the sail then, just as the full weight of rain was almost upon us, the heavy downpour fell to a sparse patter of drops. We gazed blankly at the retreating sheets of driving rain, churning the water only a few hundred yards distant, as it disappeared into the distance at a faster speed than we could ever hope to muster even if we were able to give chase. Desperately we scooped the remaining pools into the cans, keeping separate the water collected from the rubber bow canopy, which was brackish and unpalatable. It was half an hour before we silently folded the sail into the stern and slumped back in our places. After a quiet word with Lyn, I passed her the brackish tin of water and she administered it by enema to the twins. We had collected a little water at least, some in the cans and some in the drinking jar. I gazed resentfully at the distant curtain of rain then shrugged; some water was better than none! I brought out the gaff and sat watching the fish swoop under the dinghy. 'Come on,' I said to Robin and Douglas, recumbent in the bottom of the dinghy. 'Clear away and stand by for a fish, if we can't get water one way it'll have to be the other.'

Thirty minutes later, I was still waiting for a fish to swim within striking distance. A large bull dorado glided temptingly close but the smaller ones kept a respectful distance. 'Change places,' I grunted to Robin, who carefully eased across to maintain our trim. Two minutes later, I struck at a twenty-pounder and felt the sense of relief flood into the marrow of my bones as the fish thrashed wildly on the floor of the dinghy. Sandy, his face contorted with pain, gripped desperately at its tail whilst my fingers sought and found the eye sockets before I plunged my blade home. I cut my thumb in the haste to finish it off and was still nursing my wound when I noticed Sandy was weeping and holding his knuckles. He had held on like a limpet despite the beating his skinned knuckles had received between the thrashing fish and the side of the dinghy, as it beat through its final death throes. I put my arm around his skeletal form and comforted him, wondering how it was that Sandy, at only twelve, had so much determination and practical common sense.

As we sucked our drops of spinal fluid and ate the pieces of wet raw fish in silence, the clear evening sky held out no prospect of rain. Lyn prayed again. It seemed to lift her burden of worry and anguish for the twins and helped her to feel less alone. 'Our Father, which art in Heaven, hallowed be thy name.' Her voice was quiet as we listened to her repeat the Lord's Prayer after putting the twins to rest. Robin suddenly choked on a piece of bone and Lyn quickly gave him some biscuit and a piece of wet fish. It seemed to do the trick and we settled down to wait the night out.

Thirty-fifth day

The early hours of the predawn morning saw us watching in an expectant hush, as extensive banks of dark thundercloud massed in the southern sky. The great billowing cumulonimbus mushroomed up to the very portals of heaven itself as they slowly blotted out the stars above us. Impenetrable grey with tattered black bases, the solid ballooning edifice of cloud seemed cast of concrete, as it advanced towards us. Bright flashes of lightning accompanied by loud thunderclaps made us shiver involuntarily and the brightening dawn was turned back into night as the towering cloud base bore down upon our helpless craft. We felt the pores of our mouths tingle with the stress of anticipation, as the saliva failed to generate in our parched palates. I passed the jar round with a quiet caution. 'Sippers only, till we know for sure.'

This time the dawn did not fail us. Amid tears of gratitude and whelps of joy, a huge deluge of rain fell upon us. An hour of wonderful bountiful, heavy and beautiful rain. We filled the containers and tins as well as the plastic bag (Robin's privilege) then filled our shrunken stomachs to uncomfortable distension. Robin felt redeemed now that the plastic bag was full once more. We were able to take water from it by means of a spout which Douglas had fashioned in one corner of the bag, thereby precluding the tying and untying of the neck when dispensing its contents, which eliminated the risk of a repetition of the previous loss. Lyn gave us all another enema and to our surprise we all, including Robin who had refused the enema treatment, had bowel movements shortly afterwards, holding on to each other as we perched on the gunwale to perform. We gorged dried turtle meat again, and now that water was available the older savoury strips of turtle steak from the bottom of our larder were most welcome after so long a diet of wet fish. We devoured the reeking strips of the dried shark, which had a much stronger taste than the dried dorado. Its tangy, tongue-biting flavour was distinctively savoury and even quite pleasant, so long as there was plenty of water to wash it down.

The cry of 'Turtle!' just before noon had us scrambling to clear the stern area of the box full of water cans. The head of a curious female turtle bobbed into view a few yards from the starboard bow. We licked our lips in anticipation of eggs for lunch, then, as I remembered Douglas's difficulty with the last one, I called out that nobody was to touch it until I could get to it. Robin, who was nearest, called out that it was well within his reach and that he could capture it easily. 'Robin,' we echoed in unison. 'Change places, Robin,' I said, 'it's better to be sure.' Lyn joined in urging him to leave it alone but with a new-found confidence he reached over and grabbed its protruding flipper. Seconds later the turtle was gone from his ineffectual grasp. I could hardly believe it had been so stupidly lost, and anger surged through me in a rising wave of red mist. I turned on Robin and struck him with my open palm. The air turned blue as I heaped my full and unadulterated anger upon him in the form of a string of uninterrupted expletives. 'Why the hell didn't you do as you were told?' I barked, fixing him with a fierce glare. Robin rubbed his face where a red mark was forming from the contact with my hand. 'It's a good job we aren't on a rugby field, else it'd be a different story,' he stammered rhetorically. Instead of letting things go, I succumbed to a second bout of anger as waves of debilitating fury swept over me again. 'If this had been a rugby field I'd have broken your bloody jaw,' I snarled, my hand reaching for the paddle handle. 'If you disobey an order again I'll hit you with this,' I growled, my whole body trembling with rage. He looked at me with a contrite expression and muttered something about dropped catches at cricket. I felt helpless under such a conflict of wills. I did not want his explanations, just an assurance that he would not refuse to obey my orders in future. How could I persuade this young man that not only his, but the lives of my wife and children, depended on our ability to hunt and catch food as a team? He knew and acknowledged that Douglas was much stronger than himself, and had witnessed with his own eyes how he had been unable to hold the last turtle. He had been told to leave this one alone and had deliberately disobeyed. When confronted with his irresponsibility, he sought refuge in the cricket field, failing to observe that the rules of survival had far more dire consequences than the rules of cricket; if you dropped a catch in this game, you starved and died! I turned away in disgust. 'Put the things back again,' I ordered uncaringly, staring fixedly out over the sea, my face distorted beyond recognition by the foulest of deep-set scowls. The water cans and bric-a-brac from under the stern seat were re-stowed in position. I looked at Robin, opened my mouth to deliver a lecture, then shut it again. At twenty-two, I could hardly expect to reform him in his unpractical ways, but I made a mental reservation to be ready with a paddle first, if he reached for another turtle.

Our noon position of 8 degrees 10 minutes north and 115 miles

west of Espinosa showed little progress, and with rain once more in
the offing my thoughts turned to rowing again. We needed more
food reserves, particularly turtle, and a larger water storage
capacity. My eyes went to the flotation collar and as a matter of
routine I leaned over and checked the fastenings. A tiny spurt of
water from under the rope prompted me to investigate further; it
was half full of water again, this time from a hole chafed in the other
end from the one we had repaired previously. After the collar had
been inspected, we established the presence of not one but five
holes, two in the middle and three in the valve end. After untying
and emptying the tube, I lay back to rest and tried to think my way
out of this new dilemma. I could not see any possibility of repairing
the holes, but with no flotation collar, our lives remained balanced on
a razor's edge with no support for us or the dinghy if we were
swamped in rough weather. I looked at the holes again and sat
awhile, racking my brains to find the answer. There was none,
except the possibility of trapping some air in the sleeve by bending
the tube over and lashing it in the middle as well as the end.
Unfortunately, we didn't have any suitable line left, except the fishing
line. It was time to implement Robin's original idea. 'Hand me the
knife,' I called to Douglas. With quick strokes, I cut the tube in half
where the two holes had been. I now had two pieces, each five feet
long. I fastened the piece with the good end to the centre thwart,
open end up, and lashed it in position. 'This,' I declared, 'is our
reserve water tank. It'll hold about seven gallons and as soon as we
have it washed and half filled we'll start rowing towards land.' I
looked at the other piece. If we were swamped, it was big enough to
support the weaker swimmers whilst Douglas and I attempted to get
the dinghy afloat again. I felt delighted with this compromise and by
evening had almost forgiven Robin his behaviour of the morning. I
suddenly felt alarmed: if Robin rowed he'd be sure to drop the oar
over the side; couldn't fail! There would have to be a foolproof
fastening on the oars.

Projected rowing fixture

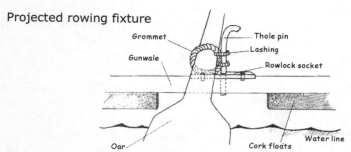

As the twilight deepened into night, the faint breeze from the
south ruffled the surface of the sea and I warned the watch-keepers
to be on the alert for squalls later on. With no flotation collar, and
only the flimsy reserve sea anchor to prevent us broaching, rough

weather could mean the end for us. Only Douglas and I shared the full import of this knowledge; I felt it would be an unnecessary burden to the others to labour such a point as we drifted inexorably eastwards into the quiet of the night.

Thirty-sixth day

During the midnight hours, the wind slowly rose from the south. At first it was a fine gentle breeze, then the wind blew with increasing force until the breaking tips of the waves gleamed in the darkness. This was the first day of our sixth week afloat, and the *Ednamair* pitched and yawed, shipping more and more water over the midships section. I set Douglas steering her into the waves, while I opened the sea anchor out and adjusted the trim of the dinghy to keep a high weather side. The squalls strengthened and Douglas and I stood watch on watch, helping our tiny boat through the violence of the rising seas. Lyn and Robin were still unable to steer, so they took over the bailing when required. I felt uncomfortable without the assurance of the flotation collar and prepared a strangle cord on the water sleeve, enabling me to make it into an airtight float very swiftly if such an emergency arose. The squalls brought rain of an intermittent and moderate intensity, which made the night both cold and uncomfortable. We bailed and sang songs to keep warm, the memory of drought too recent for us to feel churlish with the weather. Collecting rainwater became difficult in the strong wind but we managed to gather enough to rinse the salt out of the sleeve, and then put over half a gallon of good fresh water into it, before the rain finally tailed off into a drizzle. The wind eased with the rain and dawn found us shivering and huddled together, eating dried turtle and strips of putrid shark to comfort our sodden skins.

Each day had now acquired a new objective. We had to try to gain as much as possible over our reserves of stores and water, until there would be enough in reserve to get us to the coast. I looked upon each turtle and dorado as the last. Our continued supply of dorado was far from certain, for if I lost our last hook by an error in the strike, then the gaff would be ruined. It only needed a split-second delay with the strike to make the difference between a dynamic pull of about 80 pounds and one of 180, with the consequent breaking of the unevenly tensioned lines, and I knew in my heart that it was only a matter of time before just such a mistake would occur.

Lyn washed and mended our gauze-thin clothes, which now had the appearance of aged aboriginal garb. Douglas had only his shirt left and Lyn tried in vain to sew his shredded undershorts together, in an attempt to make him presentable for when we reached land. Lyn's housecoat, now in ribbons, was more ornament than use, and my tattered underpants and vest were stiff with turtle blood and fat. Robin and the twins were in rather better garb, for their labours made fewer demands on their clothing. I suppose we would have been thought a most indecent lot back amongst civilised society. Robin and I had beards with unkempt moustaches hanging over our upper lips, whilst scars from our saltwater boils covered our arms, legs and buttocks and were scattered across other parts of our anatomy, intermingled with claw marks from turtles as well as cuts and scratches from other sources.

The adults were not desperately thin but the twins, Neil in particular, had become very emaciated. Knee cramps troubled us from time to time but generally speaking, apart from Sandy who had developed a hollow bronchial cough which Lyn's expert ear had detected the day previously, we were in a better physical condition than when we had abandoned the raft. Lyn informed me that she feared Sandy had possibly contracted a form of static pneumonia resulting from our prolonged confinement in the dinghy and that we would have to monitor his condition continuously, for such illnesses had been known to result in death after only a few days. Many of our sores had healed and our bodies were functioning normally again. We were eating and drinking more, and our ability to gnaw bones and suck nutrition from them increased with our knowledge about the easiest ways to eat them. We were no longer just surviving, but were improving in our physical condition. As I looked around at our little company, Neil also gave us cause to worry, for his thin physique made it difficult to determine whether he was improving or not, and he seldom complained unless in real physical pain. Lyn was careful to see that his supplementary diet was kept as high as possible, which I supplemented with scraped bone marrow to add to their 'turtle soup' (a mixture of pieces of dried turtle, meat juice, water, eggs when available, and fresh or dried fish).

Our thirty-sixth day ended much as it had started: wet, cold and windy, with seas slopping into *Ednamair* as she bounced in the steep short waves, the bailer's familiar scrape and splash remaining the constant companion to the helmsman, hunched on the stern whilst peering at each wave in order to determine its potential danger to our unprotected craft. Robin, trying to snatch forty winks whilst off duty, suddenly sat up with a cry of distress. 'There's no meat on my bone!' he shouted in wide-eyed dismay. Then, looking at the thumb he had been sucking with a puzzled expression on his face, he lay down to sleep again, leaving the twins chortling in the bows for an hour or more afterwards.

As they drifted off to sleep, Sandy's rest became interrupted by increasingly regular bouts of coughing, which left him gasping for breath and totally exhausted. I whispered quietly to Lyn and Douglas through the darkness that if his condition did not improve markedly by the next day then the need to start rowing would become imperative, with or without reserves of water.

Thirty-seventh day

Our gratitude at the arrival of the dawn lent warmth to our bodies, and the heavy night showers slackened to a few scattered drops, allowing Robin and Lyn a respite from bailing. At least the sea had been calmed by the heavy beat of the rain, easing the burden for both Douglas and me when steering through the night. Lyn and Robin worked together, bailing whenever the breaking waves broached our defences. Daylight made the helmsman's task a lot easier, for we could then see well in advance the high waves or rogue swells which might upset our boat, allowing plenty of time to take compensatory action. Breakfast of dried turtle, dried fish and plenty of drinking water heartened us all, after which Lyn set indefatigably about her morning chores, handing the sheets to Robin who maintained a running commentary as he stoically held them in position to dry. Douglas, smiling at Robin's antics, honed away at the turtle knife, bringing it to a better edge, for it couldn't exactly be called sharp any more, whilst the twins laid out the dry stores under the canopy to air them. This helped remove the light fungal growth that had started to appear on them in the damper atmosphere we were encountering. Sandy's coughing eased a little with the daylight but I had already decided that we would start rowing eastwards as soon as we had tested the viability of Douglas's rowlock mechanism.

As the sky cleared we brought out the fish strips and fastened them to the forestay, following which we refastened the plastic bag containing the turtle fat, now swimming in golden oil, which we harvested into a separate bag and hung on the rigging out of the way. During a reshuffle of limbs, the bag was accidentally squeezed and its slippery contents spilled into the bottom of the boat. It took over an hour to clean the greasy oil from the bottom of the boat. Later Douglas took pity on Robin's uneducated fingers, and patiently instructed him in the art of tying hitches and knots, until our activities were brought to a halt with the cry of 'Turtle!' I eyed Robin and Douglas grimly. 'This one's mine!' I seethed with a prolonged glare. We cleared the stern of the dinghy quickly as the turtle bumped alongside; it was another stag and a good-sized one. I leaned over and caught hold of the shell, and then adjusted my grip in an attempt to secure its back flipper. He fought strongly. 'Grab his flipper'! I barked to Douglas who sat opposite me not daring to move. After a moment's hesitation, he caught the flapping back flipper but as the turtle threshed around, he was forced to let it go again. Sensing it was about to break free the turtle bolted into the deep, pulling away in a desperate frenzy of flippers and splashing water. In an almighty battle of mind over matter I refused to let go, the strain coming onto my whole body as my arm stretched to maximum extension and beyond. The gunwale dipped under the water and my arm felt like it was about to be wrenched from its sockets, as the edge of the shell cut deep into my wrist. With an all-

or-nothing heave, I jerked the turtle back to the surface and Douglas secured its flipper once more. As its struggles eased, we got our hands to the beast's shell and seconds later it was hoisted aboard.

As it lay on its back in the bottom of the dinghy, beak snapping and flippers going like windmills, I gasped for breath from the exertion and wondered if we were just growing weaker or if this was a particularly strong turtle. Perhaps a bit of each, I thought, as I watched Robin grasp its flailing flippers with both hands. Taking up the knife, I insisted we get on with the grizzly business at hand and started the three-hour struggle, pausing frequently for rests at each stage of the butchering process. After slitting the turtle's throat, it sometimes took as long as half an hour before the next stage could proceed, depending on when the bleeding stopped. We still drank the blood, even though there was now plenty of drinking water, in order to derive all possible nutrition at our disposal. Finally, when the job was done and the dripping meat hung from the stays, we stopped for a meal of dried dorado and fresh steak soaked in the delicious meat juice, which greatly restored our flagging spirits.

The estimated day's run, which put us at 8 degrees and 15 minutes north and only 95 miles west of Espinosa, indicated a speed made good of over 1 knot with the sea anchor fully open, which gave us further cause for satisfaction.

The chart revealed that we were now approaching the direct route between Panama and Hawaii, making the possibility of sighting a ship greater than of late. The indifference with which this little snippet of information was received was a source of satisfaction to me, for the distinct lack of interest shown by all indicated that our hopes were pinned on making a landfall and there would be minimal distress if a passing ship ignored us. We had no bailing to do in the afternoon, for the seas had diminished and the sea anchor was again half-tripped, allowing better progress to be made. The discomfort from the lumps of meat swinging from the rigging, and my insistence that the thwarts should also be used as drying space for the turtle meat, made us cramped and irritable. Already tired from the rough night, Douglas and Robin started bickering over the position of the box between them – an inch either way was a matter for grave dispute – and then Robin and the twins continued the debate over the territory under the centre thwart. Lyn and I, in harmony for a change, decided that if they could still find the energy to argue then, with the possible exception of Sandy, they must be getting stronger rather than weaker.

After a meal of fresh turtle meat and water, we chewed a bone apiece and talk returned to Dougal's Kitchen. Percolated coffee and good quality English cheeses. 'Oh, how my mouth waters for the sharp taste of a Cheshire cheese!' remarked Lyn as we debated the use of paper plates and how they might remove some of the drudgery out of restaurant work. The use of manufactured flavours came in for a lot of criticism, in that they were used to enhance the flavour of material which bore very little resemblance to food, and that subtle differences in flavour were fast becoming a part of restaurant history. The cry of 'Turtle!' quickly brought us back to the doldrums and we gazed at the very small specimen which had been investigating the sea-anchor rope. It wasn't much bigger than a soup plate and we decided to let it grow. As it came alongside Robin tipped it up by its shell and hauled it on board. He passed it to Douglas, who handled it like a small pet until it sank its beak savagely into the thumb of his left hand, drawing blood. 'Aaargh!' his sharp yell cursed the airwaves and after checking it was nothing more than a deep scratch we couldn't help but tease him, telling him to leave the little thing alone.

Some time later, as the sun began to set, a larger female turtle came close and the temptation to have eggs for breakfast was too great. We would have to dress it in the dark but there was a moon later and besides we could now do the job blindfold. After insisting I take a back seat, Douglas and Robin caught and hauled the creature aboard, and five minutes later Douglas was drawing the blood from its neck arteries. Under the cloak of darkness, he sawed around the shell and quickly sought the egg clutches on either side of the intestines, only to find none. My disappointment was intense, prompting me to join the search. Douglas checked again to make sure, confirming there were definitely no eggs. Feeling much aggrieved, I set to work in the dark, feeling my way around with knife and fingers, cutting the meat away from the shell and severing the various knuckle joints joining the flippers to the body. In need of a rest, I retired and let the others continue the butchery, which they completed in a record time of two hours.

With the onset of the night Sandy's coughing had began to bring phlegm from his lungs and seemed to be getting worse as the night progressed. He finally drifted off to sleep, finding temporary solace for a couple of hours, until another bout of coughing racked his body back to the world of the waken.

We spent the rest of the night talking quietly, of the distance we could row in a night and how long it would take us to reach the coast. I estimated that at 350 miles it was about fifteen days away, and that if the weather allowed us to dry our present stocks of turtle meat we should have nearly enough dry food to see us home. Douglas was quick to point out that once the mast was taken down it would be more difficult to dry the meat and a substitute support would have to be found for the canopy. We still had well over three gallons of water in store and the night sky looked heavy with rain cloud. A good rain would allow us to fill the sleeve, maybe even tonight! A vague excitement stirred within me as I decided that if rain did come we would fit the thole pins then make and test the grommets in the morning, ready to start the third and final phase of our incredible journey back home.

I settled my head uncomfortably against the centre thwart and drowsed a little, moving my cramped limbs to ease the pressure on my buttocks as the twins' legs lay heavily across my midriff. Finally, I gave up attempts to sleep and stuck my head out beside the end of the canopy, looking at the gaps in the clouds, trying to assess what the night sky held for us. The back of my head found comfort against the gunwale and I drowsed in a sitting position, my eye catching the glow of the moonrise as I looked around the horizon from time to time. A terrific blow on the back of my head suddenly stunned my senses and made my head flash with pain, seeing stars that were not part of the firmament. Lyn's cry of 'Shark!' dimly penetrated my singing eardrums. I turned my head in time to see the huge man-eater loom out of the darkness towards us, its triangular fin rushing at the dinghy before scraping heavily under the keel. Identifying the tail fin as the one which had struck me such a blow on the previous run, I grabbed the paddle to show the beast we still had some fight left. Savagely I thrust the brass socket at its head and felt it jerk solidly as it made contact. The massive beast dived deep, leaving me to make the flattened brass socket round again.

Thirty-eighth day

Daylight dispelled our disappointment over the lack of turtle eggs from our last kill, and after a breakfast of raw steak and the flesh of a scavenger fish, which I speared on the end of the knife and marinated in the meat juice collected overnight, we felt more able to see the day through.

It hadn't rained much and I still had a good-sized lump on my head where the shark had left its mark. A small shower, followed by some drizzle, had increased our water reserves by a pint and the overcast sky gave little prospect of a good drying day, nevertheless we hung out the meat in small strips to make the most of it. A large oceanic white-tipped shark cruised nearby with an escort of eight pilot fish in symmetrical formation across its back, lending it the appearance of an underwater fighter plane. I prepared the gaff while Lyn and Robin sorted out the turtle meat for drying and the twins readjusted the canopy and handed out some strips of dried dorado, which needed a final airing before they could be permanently stored. We now checked over our considerable amount of dry stores every morning, to ensure that they were in good condition.

Again, Sandy's coughing had eased with the passing of the night, but I had already decided that, with the successful trial of the grommets and rowlocks, we would draw up a rowing rota later that morning. Days lost now could prove fatal later on, if Sandy's condition deteriorated or spread to the rest of us.

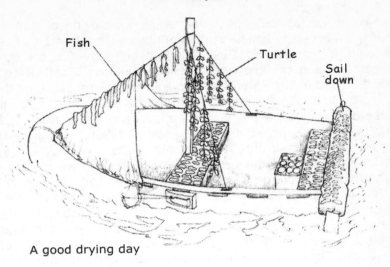

A good drying day

The fish strips quickly went damp and soggy in the humid atmosphere, and we noticed that if we allowed them to compact the small pieces of turtle meat warmed up, as if affected by some kind of spontaneous combustion. The dorado were reluctant to come near the *Ednamair* with the shark still cruising around, but after both Douglas and Robin had made repeated swipes across its head with the paddle it withdrew to a safe distance. I planned to land another two dorado that morning, one for eating immediately, which would allow us to save the turtle steak for drying, and the other to augment our already burgeoning stocks of dried fish. Taking up my usual vigil over the gunwale, I angled the gaff towards two dorado bulls that seemed a little too large to be likely prospects, when a large female shot by close above the hook. I struck swiftly and missed but at that instant a smaller bull of about fifteen pounds followed the female's track and literally impaled itself upon my hook, which sank into its flesh in a perfect strike! The fish flew into the dinghy with unerring precision and it was secured and killed in the space of a few seconds.

Feeling very pleased with ourselves, we admired the high forehead of the bull while Douglas gutted it and I made some small adjustments to the nylon lines, which hadn't borne the strain evenly. I directed Douglas to retain the offal, for I had noticed that although the dorado didn't eat it, they gathered round curiously as the scavenger fish fought to get a share. I had the idea that even a good fish could be taken unawares at this time, so I had Robin throw some offal over the side, just ahead of the gaff. The scavenger fish rushed in a boil of foam and spray as they fought over the scraps, while the dorado swooped close by. I chose a twenty-five-pound female dorado and struck. The hook sank home, then with a ripping sound the lines snapped one after the other and the gaff went light. I looked swiftly at Douglas but he was already pulling in the reserve line slowly. 'Didn't feel a thing!' he exclaimed. My initial reaction was one of extreme dejection, for the escaping fish had taken our last big hook with it. There would be no more fresh dorado. Despite our best endeavours, the nylon lines must have been cracked and both Douglas and I had failed to notice. The tensions in the lines must have been different too, or they would have broken simultaneously. The disturbed water had also probably distorted my aim, but it was no use being wise now; there wasn't another hook to be wise with. My spirits picked up a little as I realised that our stocks of dorado exceeded those of turtle meat and we had enough of both to get us to the coast, even if we caught no more fresh turtle to supplement our rations. We still had another small hook to use for inshore fishing if required and I could always try to stab for another scavenger fish. After all, we had been fattening them up for a while now, with our regular jettisoning of turtle and fish offal.

I estimated our noon position at 8 degrees 21 minutes north and 85 miles west of Espinosa, another twelve miles nearer to land. It was not a great boost to our morale but I pointed out that throughout all the time we had been adrift we had either been becalmed or the wind had been favourable. There hadn't been a day yet when I had had to record an adverse run. The calming seas also indicated that we might soon be able to row, although the heavy cross-swell, building in height since mid-morning, would have to diminish before we could start. Lyn bathed the twins that afternoon and after their daily exercises and a half hour apiece on the centre thwart to spread their limbs, they retreated under the canopy as a heavy shower threatened.

The dorado we had caught in the morning now swung in wet strips from the forestay while the drying turtle meat festooned the stays and cross-lines, which we had rigged to carry the extra load of meat from the two turtles. Douglas continued working on the thole pins, binding them with rope before creating two canvas sleeves to save wear on the oar shafts, whilst the rest of us set to work to fashion a new flotation piece. Robin and I took the unused piece of sleeve and started to bind one end shut with the spare fishing line. The clouds grew thicker as the afternoon advanced; it was going to be a wet night again and perhaps we would be able to fill the water sleeve at last. Seven gallons of water seemed like wealth beyond measure in our altered circumstances and changed sense of values. I chopped up some dried turtle meat for tea and Lyn put it with a little wet fish and marinated it in meat juice. She spread the dry sheets for the twins under the canopy and then prepared their little supper. After a short debate on rowing techniques, during which Douglas agreed he would try rowing just as soon as the swell had settled, we talked once more of Dougal's Kitchen and if it should have a wine licence. As we pondered the delights of Gaelic coffee, my eye, looking past the mast and sail, caught sight of something that wasn't the sea. I stopped talking and stared in dumbfounded silence as the others all looked at me. 'A ship,' I said. 'There's a ship and it's coming towards us!' I could hardly believe it but it seemed solid enough. 'Keep still now!' I yelled in the sudden surge of excitement, as everyone moved to the edge to get a better look. 'Trim her! We mustn't capsize now!' Reluctantly they all sank back into their places.

I felt my voice tremble as I told them that I was going to stand on the thwart and hold a flare above the sail. They trimmed the dinghy as I took up my position. 'Right, hand me a flare and remember what happened with the previous ship we saw,' I reminded to my children's upturned faces in case we were to be subjected to a similar outcome. They suddenly fell silent, recalling the terrible despondency when our signals had gone unheeded the last time we had sought rescue. 'Oh God!' prayed Lyn, 'please, oh please, for the sake of my children – let them see us.'

I could see the ship quite clearly now, a Japanese tuna fisher. Her grey and white paint stood out clearly against the dark cross-swell. 'She looks like a great white bird,' Lyn whispered to the twins, their faces lighting in excitement. I estimated she would pass within about a mile of us at her nearest approach. I relayed the information as my crew listened intently, the tension of not daring even to hope of imminent rescue building like a tangible, unbearable wall of pressure, whilst extending a cloud of expectant unreality amongst us. My eye caught the outlines of two large sharks a hundred yards to starboard. 'Watch the trim,' I warned. 'We have two man-eating sharks waiting if we capsize.' I waited a short while longer. The ship was getting closer with each passing moment. I had to hold back igniting the flare so that she would be at her closest when it was fully alight.

Time went by in long, slow and agonising seconds, then suddenly I could wait no longer. 'OK, I'm going to light the flare now. Have the torch ready in case it doesn't work,' I rasped, unable to quash the vein of hope rising in my voice. I gasped as I ripped the caps off the pyrotechnic, pulled out the striker and struck the primer. Like a huge match, it first smoked and then spluttered before it sparked into life, the red glare illuminating *Ednamair* and the sea around us in the gathering twilight. I could feel my index finger roasting under the vibrant fire emitted from the tip of the flare, forcing me to wave it to and fro in order to escape its searing heat. Its bright light shone a brilliant red, radiating outwards in the calm air, then, unable to bear the fiery heat any longer, I threw the flare high into the air and we watched in silence as it curved in a brilliant arc and dropped into the sea.

'Hand me another!' My voice was hoarse with pain and excitement and I felt sick with apprehension, as the ship surged in the swell ahead of us. The second flare failed to light. I cursed it in frustrated anguish, as the priming substance chipped off instead of igniting. 'The torch!' I shouted, 'get me the bloody torch.'

Six pairs of eyes strained through the gathering gloom to get a better look at the approaching vessel. Senses were on high alert as every nerve fibre strained to detect the slightest change in aspect of the approaching vessel that would indicate she had seen us. The ship continued to plough through the quartering seas, her bow headed in a direction that would take her well clear of our position. As the ship pitched and yawed in the oily swell, maintaining her course and speed, the children returned to the bottom of the boat, clutching the sides in white-knuckled dread, as they sensed that too much time had elapsed for the vessel to respond. 'Look, for Christ's sake, look,' Douglas implored, his voice trembling, as the muscles in his face and neck twitched in involuntarily spasm. We continued to stare in nerve-jangling doubt as the ship began to draw abeam. Douglas started blowing on the whistle again; long shrill tones pierced the expectant silence as we all hoped against hope that we would be spotted. Slowly excited whoops turned to desperate sobs, as the realisation dawned that we were about to be left behind a second time. My shoulders drooped in defeat as I resigned myself to eking out our life aboard the dinghy. 'Damn them,' I remorsed, cursing my helpless impotence as the ship continued on a course that would take her past and clear.

'Dad, look,' Douglas and Sandy chorused, interrupting my morbid thoughts, as they pointed fervently in the direction of the ship. Its aspect had altered markedly and its bows were now plunging into head seas creating flurries of spray. Barely able to look, my heart beat the inside of my chest wall like a tightly skinned drum as my grimace turned to a beaming smile; she had begun to alter her course, only slightly and not directly towards us, but nevertheless a distinct and definite alteration. Hope sprang in my heart but words deserted me as we watched the vessel continue to adjust her course in the seaway, each of us daring for the first time to believe that our incredible journey might soon be at an end. The approaching ship corkscrewed in the rolling swells as we witnessed another large and substantial alteration to her course, followed by a prolonged reverberating blast on her whistle. At last there could be no doubt, she was on her way to save us.

I flopped down onto the thwart and in a glorious moment realised that our ordeal was over. Tears welled up within me as the suspended belief, held in case we were left behind once more, was suddenly relaxed to the reality that we were about to be rescued and returned to the real world, from which we had been so brutally extracted six weeks before. The sounds of the wind and sea became interspersed with the sound of weeping from the bottom of the boat, where Lyn and the twins sobbed in joyful abandon. 'We're not crying 'cos were sad,' insisted Neil between sobs, 'we're crying 'cos we're happy.' Stumped by his perceived contradiction he returned to the ecstatic clutches of his mother, unable to find words that would adequately describe his happiness. Douglas, with tears of joy in his eyes, hugged first his mother and then me in a bear-like embrace. Robin laughed and cried at the same time as he slapped me on the back and shouted 'Wonderful! We've done it. Oh! Wonderful!'

I put my arms around Lyn, feeling the sharp tears of relief stinging in my eyes. 'Looks like we'll get our boys to land after all,' I confirmed as tears ran down my cheeks in blessed release. As we revelled in our sudden and unexpected salvation, the fishing boat glided to a stop, less than a hundred yards abeam. Japanese sailors lined the railings, gaping in a mixture of awe and disbelief at the fragile cluster of humanity that appeared before them, crowded into the confines of such a small boat, so painfully thin and weak yet still clinging so strongly to life. Death I surmised could have taken me easily then, for I had become caught up in a euphoric daze and knew that I would never again experience such a pinnacle of contentment.

CHAPTER 12

Safety

The high flared bows of the *Toka Maru* towered over us, pitching and rolling in the uneasy swell. We poured our entire supply of turtle oil on to the sea to try to smooth it, as the dinghy rocked violently in the cross-chop of waves and swell, deflecting from the steel wall of the ship's side. As they drew near, the Japanese seamen lined the rusting white bulwarks, craning their necks to get a better view. They pointed towards our emaciated children, lying quietly in the bottom of the boat and then, with urgent shouts, a group of them broke into a hubbub of commotion, throwing heaving lines in our direction. More lines followed, snaking through the air and splashing into the water, tantalisingly close but just beyond our reach.

After what seemed like an eternity one of the lines landed right across our midst. I handed the dirty oil-laden fibre with thrill and exhilaration whilst Lyn passed us what remained of our clothes. Douglas, without the benefit of any trousers or underwear, smiled wryly at the thought that his naked form was somehow more acceptable in appeasing his mother's desire for modesty, once he had a shirt on. The rise and fall of the dinghy was too great to make the line fast so I gripped it tightly, and we were pulled alongside to the bulwark door now opened in the ship's side. We could scarcely believe our eyes as eager hands reached down and hauled us bodily from our little boat. Compared with each other we didn't look too bad, but now as fit young men assisted us onto the bulwarks we could see our bodies were painfully thin; swollen knee and elbow joints were connected to sticklike limbs, and protruding rib cages made our skeletal forms look weak and feeble.

Neil was the first to leave, closely followed by Sandy. 'Come on Douglas, you next,' I grinned in delight as Douglas hesitated, waiting for his mother to pass in front of him, but to do so would have resulted in a precarious trim, and the sharks were still waiting. *Ednamair* bumped heavily as the swell flung her against the side of the ship. With aching arms, I wound the line tighter around my wrist. 'Right, Lyn, on you go,' I urged, no longer sure how long I would be able to keep us alongside. Lyn's legs kicked out as she was hoisted aboard. 'Come on, Robin.'

I looked at the deserted hull of *Ednamair* and with sudden longing in my heart knew that she must come too. I threw the polythene bag containing the dried turtle, and my logbook and one or two of the trinkets from the sewing basket onto the deck of the fishing vessel, then passed the line round the mast, bringing its end with me as I too was lifted to the safety of the solid wooden decks.

Lyn, Douglas, Robin and the twins lay prostrate along the deck and I wondered what was wrong with them, until I too tried to walk and discovered my legs were too weak to budge. I clutched the bulwark for support, then, to my dismay, saw the Japanese sailors cast off the *Ednamair*. It was clear they intended to leave her drifting in the ocean. I gestured wildly, for no one spoke our language, that we must have the boat as well, but they shook their heads and held their noses. We were oblivious to any smells and couldn't discern the redolence of the drying fish and turtle meat still hanging on the rigging, which to them must have been overpowering. I leaned out over the bulwark, trying to catch the masthead and something in my appeal must have reached them, for at a word of command from the bridge they brought boat hooks to bear and lifted *Ednamair*'s stern up to the deck. I grasped at the handles to help them but they motioned me away, then in a swift series of hacks, cut all the lashings that secured the mast and the canopy as well as the oars and sea anchor, before tipping *Ednamair* upside down and emptying her entire contents into the sea. With a final heave, *Ednamair* was brought on deck. The suckerfish which we had thrown over after peeling them from the underbellies of the turtles were still clinging to the fibreglass bottom and were washed away, as the hosepipe and brushes got to work in the capable hands of the Japanese seamen. We smiled and thanked them at every meeting of our eyes. They returned our smiles with nods of approval, unable to communicate with words, instead relying on the innate ability of humans to supersede the constraints of language when seeking true understanding.

9-inch remora or suckerfish

My blistered finger smarted painfully from the burn of the flare as I staggered to the companionway leading to the bridge. Pulling myself up with my arms, I greeted the captain of the *Toka Maru* at the starboard bridge door and thanked him warmly in sign language, for the efficiency of his crew in spotting us. We could only gesture for

I had no Japanese and he no English, but gestures were more than adequate. I hugged him in my arms as my eyes flashed him a message of gratitude much deeper than the thanks I proffered.

I produced my logbook and we went into the chartroom to check positions and to give details of who we were and where we had come from, for as far as I knew we had not as yet been reported missing. We were picked out of the ocean in position 8 degrees 15 minutes north and 90 degrees 55 minutes west. My estimate of 8 degrees 20 minutes north and 92 degrees 45 minutes west, without sextant, chart or compass wasn't a bad guess after thirty-eight days adrift in the crosscurrents and opposing trade-wind drifts that complicate this part of the Pacific Ocean. My estimated latitude was good, only five miles out, but my estimated longitude, though a hundred miles out, was even better for we were a hundred miles nearer to land than I had prudently estimated and we would have reached the coast five days sooner than I had predicted! We had travelled over 750 miles by raft and dinghy and had about 290 miles of our journey left to go. We would have reached the American coastal shipping lanes in ten more days and the coast in fifteen. Laboriously, I drew in on the chart the position of our sinking and pointed out on the calendar the date we had been sunk. I drew a small picture of *Lucette* and the killer whales, followed by a list of our names and nationalities, so that our worried daughter Anne and other relatives would soon know we were safe. The captain nodded his understanding and after shaking hands once more he wrinkled his nose and pointed at my tattered underclothing, shouting enthusiastically 'Showa! Showa!' I could well imagine the powerful odours emanating from my blood- and grease-soaked rags, though I was completely unaware of the smells myself. The only part of our bodies that seemed in no need of cleaning was our teeth. Throughout they had remained plaque-free and smooth to the feel of our tongues.

I tottered back towards the foredeck, where my family and Robin were seated with their backs against the hatch coaming; in their hands were tins of cool orange juice and on their tired and haggard faces beamed looks of blissful contentment. I picked up the tin that Lyn had put to one side for me, smiled my thanks to the Japanese, who grinned broadly back at me, and lifting my arm yelled 'Cheers!' to our group of astounded onlookers, who continued to stare and marvel at us, still not quite able to believe the rescue they had so bravely and efficiently effected. We each savoured the taste of that beautiful liquid and vowed we would remember it to the end of our days. I looked at the twins – the juice seemed to be reflected in their bright eyes and their smiling lips – then suddenly my legs gave way and I flopped down onto the deck, still gripping my can of juice to prevent it from spilling. We all laughed at my awkwardness as I crawled beside Lyn and sat down, putting the can to my lips to suck on it like a child at the breast. I thought how lucky I was. An hour ago I had been ready to accept death; now I was being re-born!

The Japanese crew carried the twins to the four-foot deep hot seawater bath, whilst beckoning Robin and Douglas, who stumbled along behind on uncertain and shaky legs. Immersed in the warm water, they soaped and lathered their bodies, wallowing in the luxury of hot bubbling soapsuds, scrubbing at the brown scurf which their skins had developed. It would take many such baths for the ingrained discoloration to disappear altogether. Later Lyn and I luxuriated in the warmth of the deep tub. The ecstasy of not having to protect boil-covered parts of our anatomies from solid contacts was a relief beyond measure and the simple joy of soap lathering in hot water felt to us all like one of the greatest luxuries of civilised mankind. New clothes had been laid out for us from the ship's stores, and the kind concern shown us by these smiling warm-hearted seamen was almost too much for our shattered emotions to bear. How cosy to have garments that were soft and dry. With the tingling sensation of cleanliness came awareness of the rags we had taken off; poor worn, done things, they had kept the sun off our backs and had held the moisture next to our skins to keep us cool, as well as keeping us warm when the night winds lashed our rain-soaked bodies. Now destined for the broad reaches of the Pacific, we watched as they were tossed overboard, thankful that our bones were not inside them.

On our return to the foredeck, there on the hatch lay a huge tray of bread and butter and a strange brown sweet liquid called coffee steaming its aroma across the deck. I thought back to all that had happened since I had last attempted a cup of coffee aboard *Lucette* just moments before the sinking. Our eyes gleamed as our teeth bit into these strange luxuries and in a very short space of time the tray and coffee pot were empty and our stomachs full. So full in fact that we couldn't squeeze in another drop, for we all felt as if we had swallowed footballs.

We tried to settle down to sleep on the tarpaulins and flags spread out on the deck inside the fo'c'sle for us. But the unaccustomed warmth became a stifling heat, and we were not used to the vibration of the engines. Indeed, the whole attitude of relaxation and freedom to move around was so strange that sleep would not come, exhausted as we were. I lay thinking strange thoughts of our life in the sea, like a merman suddenly abstracted from an environment which had become his own and then returned to a forgotten way of life amongst strangers. I felt lonely for the sea and for the uncomplicated issues at stake there, until I realised that my thoughts had for so long been centred on devising ways to reach land that I had forgotten what I would do when I got there. In fact this unexpected interruption of our plans, the destruction of our painfully acquired stores of food and water, together with the sudden abrogation of the laws governing our survival, the tyranny of which still dominated our minds, was all rather overwhelming. We would need more than just a few days to readjust to civilised channels of thought.

At about midnight, we could stand it no longer and staggered out on deck to seek the familiar cool night air, where we stood and enjoyed the starlit skies and the gently rolling swells of the ocean. Robin, lucky man, at least could sleep. The junior watch-keeper, Hidemi Saito, a personable young man who could speak one or two words of English and had a phrasebook for the more usual situations, came along the foredeck and after enquiring about the cause of our unease brought us a second meal, a noodle congee with small pieces of beef. The flavour was enchanting. He then plied us with sleeping pills, which didn't make the slightest difference to our mental turmoil. Robin appeared just in time to finish off the remainder of the congee and we brought our pieces of bedding out on deck and rested under the stars.

In the days that followed, we indulged in the luxury of eating and drinking wonderful food, the meals growing in quantity and sophistication as we slowly adjusted to life aboard. The familiar figure of the cook Sakae Sasaki became the symbol around which our whole existence revolved, as he bore tray after tray along the foredeck in our direction. Copious amounts of bread and butter, spinach soup, prawns, fruit juices, fried chicken, roast pork, tinned fruit, fermented rice water, coffee and a special treat, ice tea with lemon and real ice. The assault upon our stomachs seemed unending and even when they were full we still felt hungry, a most frustrating sensation! During our twenty-one days after the sinking of the raft, our bones and bodies had grown to form the shape of the dinghy against which we had lain. Each morning we ached after lying in contact with the flat and unyielding deck, after which we luxuriated in the deep hot seawater of the giant bath then groaned under the burden of indigestion from the excessive intake of food, finishing each day by trying to relax in the cool of the tropical night. Daily we exercised our swollen ankles and weakly legs as we learned to walk once more. The Japanese crew took the twins to their hearts and showered them with kindness. They made gifts of clothing to us all, as well as soap and toiletry requisites, towels, notebooks and pens. They delighted in watching the twins draw, write and play together. Lyn and I studied their work too, examining their pictures of killer whales, turtles and the *Lucette* with interest. The start of their long programme of rehabilitation was just beginning.

During the voyage to Balboa on board *Toka Maru*, we talked with the Japanese crew members, in drawings and by means of a phrasebook, of our separate voyages. Theirs had been from Japan and ours from Britain via Panama. We mused at the remarkable coincidence which had brought us together in those timeless wastes of the Pacific, a story in itself illustrating the occurrence of the improbable set to confound the expert. Robin, a well-qualified statistician, had never lost hope of being rescued, whilst I had calculated the chance of being rescued to be so small that it could be discounted. A case of the statistician adopting the attitude which rightfully should have been mine and of my adopting an attitude which ought to have been his!

Toka Maru, a 300-ton motor fishing vessel, had left Japan on 4 April 1972, bound for the fishing grounds in the south Pacific, normally a round voyage of about three or four months. She had developed engine trouble and lain in Honolulu for forty-three days while the trouble was put right, then resumed her journey to the tuna fishing grounds situated approximately 8 degrees south of the equator. Fishing had been slow, and finally, running short of oil, she had been ordered to Manzanillo in Mexico to refuel. *Toka Maru* had passed unseen, well to the west of us, when her orders were changed and she had been instructed by her owners to proceed to Panama, thus bringing her on a convergent course with the *Ednamair*. Although the watch-keepers on the bridge had already spotted us, they had decided that a tiny craft like *Ednamair* couldn't possibly sustain life at such a distance from land. It was not until our distress signal was seen that, in the words of Hidemi Saito, 'After yelling to alert the captain I dived for the automatic steering and came full speed to the rescue.' For those who believe that a higher intelligence directed the movements of our craft, there is much evidence to sustain their belief. For those on *Ednamair* like myself, who simply believe that coincidence has a very long arm, we can only accept our meeting with *Toka Maru* with humble gratitude. Had our paths not crossed in the middle of that boundless ocean, literally in the middle of nowhere, the outcome of our ordeal could have been tragic indeed.

It took four days for *Toka Maru* to reach Balboa, by which time we had to some extent regained the use of our legs and Sandy's cough had all but vanished. In those four days, Captain Kiyato Suzuki and his wonderful crew brought the milk of human kindness to our tortured spirits and peace to our savage minds. They also removed the bitter canker of revenge from my character, locked in my heart since the *Sagaing* had been bombed by their Imperial war machine in 1942. Then the Japanese had taken the lives of my young family. Now, thirty years later, in a bizarre twist of fate, those same countrymen had saved the lives of myself, my wife and my children, bestowing upon me that most valuable of gifts, the ability to forgive. With many years of hurt swept away and their forefathers' debt settled in full, I felt the liberation from pain like a tangible wave of blessed release. These kindly fishermen represented a new generation of Japanese, whose character bore no resemblance to the ogres in my memory, for they proffered only friendship to us. Their humanity regained my respect for their nation and their kindness my respect for its people. If for no other reason, our voyage aboard the *Lucette* had served me this one great purpose.

Lyn and I watched as Douglas and the twins talked and drew pictures with their new-found Japanese friends, Lyn and I felt that they too had become citizens of the world. They were already communicating without the help of language, in the sure knowledge that men and women of other nations and races had hopes, fears and ambitions which were not so different from their own. Douglas smiled across to us, 'and thoughts return to where you ply, lonely sea, Pacific sky – that's the last line of my Ode to the Frigatebird,' he grinned widely. 'Write it down, son,' I beamed, happy that he would be able to finish his poem as he had promised in those despondent days when all had seemed lost.

During the short passage back to Panama, we had plenty of opportunity to scrutinise and debate our journey back to the living, and our discussions became revealing and intense, as we sat amongst the blankets of our temporary home in the forecastle.

Whilst we had executed many man overboard drills we had never once practised an abandon ship procedure. In hindsight, we should have held realistic practice drills regularly, and should have had more than one set of emergency stores and water stored in containers ready for a speedy getaway. High-sounding phrases about leadership, duty and discipline sounded very impressive in the raft's instruction book; the perils of boredom, apathy and idleness were emphasised therein with great reverence. In real terms we all knew that knowledge was leadership, common sense was duty and the practical observance of survival laws was discipline; any departure into the realm of orthodox authority or social rank suggested in some survival manuals we considered specious nonsense, and the crass idiocy of creating work for 'idle' hands we felt we had exposed as such.

The ability of different personalities in a group of people to blend would always be dependent upon the circumstances of their being together. What may work ashore or in the workplace may not hold up in the close confines of a yacht or under survival conditions, where every small chink becomes exposed. As skipper and father aboard *Lucette*, the family already considered me an unforgiving despot, a situation polarised still further in the raft. Lyn, unable to get her way by negotiation, often had to resort to emotional blackmail to get me to listen, and the children all too often performed their duties through fear of retribution rather than desire. Robin joined our group and like the omega wolf in a wolf pack became a convenient scapegoat when things went wrong. Robin, much to his credit, recognised this and more often than not went along with his given role in stoic silence. He had signed up for a life of adventure, not a fight for his life, and what had been hard for us to bear had been a lot harder for him. He had been a necessary and important member of our group, focusing our attention away from the ever-present doom and gloom that hung over us.

During my time as a castaway, I became increasingly despotic, causing resentment and ill will amongst my crew. Whilst I considered this very necessary for the survival of us all, I did feel that I had been unfair to Douglas and to Lyn in the ruthless and dismissive way I had dealt with them, ignoring the fact that they were standing shoulder to shoulder with me and providing expertise and strength that I simply did not possess. Robin I had been particularly unfair to, especially in the later stages, for he was alone, without the support of his family, trapped in an alien environment and a desperate situation. Robin's cheery nature and chirpy chitchat was an important element in our survival over such a long time, and his ability to manage the abuse thrown at him indicated just how strong and versatile in character he really was. Ideas like sailing to the doldrums rather than staying put were a matter of consensus and did not originate with me alone, nor did the idea of catching turtles, which came from observing Douglas's initial attempts. I had been eager to listen to and where necessary adapt the suggestions and ideas of the others, though we all agreed that my single-minded determination and unwavering focus was pivotal to our success. Where time permitted, we often discussed options and sometimes took many days to make decisions, especially if their outcome would determine whether we should live or die.

The system of self-rationing, which we used for saving water, was much more successful than imposed rationing could have ever been, and I'm sure that most castaways would have behaved similarly in the same circumstances. Rationing, when introduced in the later stages of our trip, was done so as to ensure that everyone took their share of water, and it used up our reserves much more quickly.

Cannibalism, traditionally called 'the custom of the sea', was never considered and we all agreed that if we ran out of food or water then we were quite prepared to die together. Self-denial lies at the very core of fortitude, and inner strength together with unshakable resolution motivates the castaway in his determination to survive. There were lapses from this harsh code, sure enough, but they were soon restored with an appropriate word and the spirit of comradeship, which was a far more important factor in our survival than any imposed discipline. It was the consensus amongst us all that our spirit of comradeship enabled us to bear the extremes of emotional torture and physical discomfort imposed upon us, even to the point where individuals risked or considered the sacrifice of their own lives to assist in the survival of the others.

Discomfort, we decided, was the most devastating destroyer of morale. Only a deep understanding of the need to share discomfort reconciled the sufferer to their pain and prevented them from attempting to better their lot at the expense of the others. In our case, Robin probably suffered more than any of us in this acceptance of the survival laws. He barely had time to recover from his initial seasickness aboard *Lucette* before he was abstracted from the routines of shipboard life and thrust into the melting pot of practical application aboard the raft. We others, including the twins, had learned to live with the sea aboard *Lucette* and come to terms with the harsh laws of survival even as far back as the farm, whereas such rules had been thrust on Robin with a savage cruelty that offered only dire alternatives. Added to this was his isolation in the midst of our long-standing family attachments. To his credit he soon abandoned the carefully fostered prejudices acquired in the course of his education and came to understand that survival was the hardest school in life, for there were no failures!

When debating our differing characters and how they assisted in the survival process, we felt that the most valuable attribute was a well-developed sense of the ridiculous, allowing us to laugh in the face of impossible situations and even spectacular failures. Such ability also permitted us to come to terms with the setting aside of civilised codes and mores, which hitherto had been our guidelines in life. Similarly we felt that a pompous adherence to precedence, the assertion of physical superiority or the inability to abandon prudish reserve were traits as deadly as thirst or starvation in the confines of a survival craft. Recognition of these simple cornerstones helped us all to adjust to the realities of our dilemma.

Lyn's adjustment to survival was made so much easier for her by her deep knowledge and experience of life-and-death situations which she had come across in her nursing career. Even so, her agony and desperation as a mother watching the swift deterioration of her children detracted immensely from her personal ability to cope. She resented it deeply when she noticed that I gave Robin larger portions of food than the other adults, even after I had explained my motives in so doing. Her spirit of self-sacrifice was so dominant that it may well have led her to an early death, with the terrible knock-on effects that such an event would have had on the twins, until I insisted on introducing water rationing to ensure that she took her share. She did not really believe that we could reach land until, in the later stages, our food and water reserves had accumulated in sufficient quantities, such that the remainder of our journey seemed at least theoretically feasible. Apart from the agonies endured during the sinking, her worst moments occurred when she realised that we could not return to the Galapagos Islands in the first few days after we had been sunk, and when she thought that I might not succeed in reaching the dinghy after it had broken loose. Her greatest fear was when we transferred from the raft to the *Ednamair*. She persisted in thinking that her premonitions of the disaster were valid, in which she dreamt of us all sailing on the sea in a ham tin. Lyn remained convinced that a spiritual presence assisted us in the worst of the storms, and that her prayers were more effective than her prodigious feats of physical endurance and relentless concern for our creature comfort, to say nothing of her expert nursing care. She was adamant also that the only reason we were all saved was because the *Lucette* took with her the baby's caul which she had saved from her midwifery days.

Douglas's worst moments were during the sinking when he thought his life was about to end by being eaten alive, and during the first two days, when he feared we might not reach the rains in time. After we had rigged the dinghy and completed our first day's run in the raft successfully, he realised we had a fighting chance, which bolstered his spirits and restored his will. Despite the terrible disappointment of missing the ship, his fear of death by thirst and dehydration only reinforced his determination to help me in every way he could. He didn't mind Robin having a little more food and resented that he couldn't do even more of the work than he did. The time of most extreme duress for him was during the electrical storm in the dinghy, when he feared that the indiscriminate lightning could have killed us all at a stroke. He took more and more work off my shoulders as time went by, until he was performing most of the heavier tasks, such as hanging the meat, raising and lowering the sail and extracting the flipper bones from the turtles, as well as a multitude of smaller tasks, including sharpening the knife and checking the lashings and sail fastenings. Never afraid to have a go, he didn't fear failure and contributed in the creative phase of many of my own ideas and achievements. He was also a great source of inspiration with unexplored ideas, such as making nets from sailcloth to strain plankton from the sea, and devising methods of propulsion should the winds have left us or become adverse. I could not have been blessed with a better assistant. His experience did not make him afraid of the sea, for following in my footsteps he was already intending to apply for a cadetship in the merchant navy as soon as we got home.

I hesitate to ascribe independent thoughts to the twins and would not attempt to determine how much their presence made our survival necessary. Their influence over our behaviour undoubtedly increased our tolerance of each other, and the simple fact of their presence amongst us prevented differences of opinion, discomfort and the unbalanced share of the work from escalating into something more serious. Neil felt happier in the inflatable and Sandy felt better in the dinghy. They weren't quarrelsome at any time and although reluctant at times to exercise their limbs, they always took an interest in the work of the boat and the catching of food. They didn't think of dying; indeed, when Lyn tried to assuage their fears by explaining that without water they might go into a long sleep they thought she meant just that. Looking back on their experience, they thought it was all rather exciting.

Robin never doubted that we would reach safety, and felt that we were capable of existing indefinitely on *Ednamair* until rescue or landing. His sense of security grew rather than diminished as time went by, and his confidence in our ability to support ourselves from the sea and ultimately reach safety remained unshaken. His worst moments occurred when I disappeared whilst trying to recapture the dinghy and when we abandoned the raft for *Ednamair*, the fear that we would be unable to trim the dinghy efficiently enough to prevent swamping having been communicated to him a little too well. As he became accustomed to living in the dinghy, he not only regained his confidence in our ability to survive but his confidence grew stronger, as our food and water position improved.

Amongst the successes we enjoyed there were many failures. When one failure followed another we refused to give up, recalling the saying, 'You haven't failed until you have stopped trying.' Despite all the odds and the many setbacks, we never stopped trying. With necessity being the mother of invention, and finding ourselves in an environment where money could not buy a solution at any price, we discovered to our surprise that our inventive abilities increased beyond measure, finding life-saving solutions with just the materials we had to hand.

Our story has all but run full circle. It started with our adventure aboard *Lucette* and the desire to enrich the lives of the children and change our lot in life, and finished with the story of our yacht's destruction. I suppose that had we not survived, we would have all simply vanished without trace as others have done before us, with hardly a ripple to show in the maelstrom of world events. It would probably have been pointed out to grieving relatives that in a fifty-year-old yacht anything could have happened – and only the few who knew her would have paused and wondered. My heart still grieves that *Lucette*'s fine hull was so wantonly destroyed, and I am grateful that she took as long as a minute to sink; other yachts of more modern build would have succumbed in much less time, taking their unfortunate crews with them. In spite of what may seem my sceptical appreciations of her crew, I will go on record and state that I could not have been cast away with five more tolerant and stout-hearted people, bonded together with a deep love of life, which they were ready to sacrifice for each other. Were it not for them, it would have been so easy for me to have just given up and gone down with my beloved *Lucette*.

We arrived in Panama at four o'clock in the morning of 28 July 1972. *Toka Maru* eased her way under the Bridge of the Americas and entered her berth in Balboa. The popping of flashbulbs from the cameras of the world press, mixed with shouted questions and the rush and bustle of television cameras and radio reporters thrusting microphones under our noses, made us wonder if the broad silent reaches of the Pacific Ocean were not to be preferred! An oasis of peace was imparted to us by the able management of the situation by Mr Daly, the British Consul in Panama City, and under his care and protection we were conducted through a short press conference and had photographs taken with our Japanese saviours. Lyn and the children wept as they said 'goodbye' in newly learned Japanese: 'Me-na-san, ka-za-ku, sy-an-ara' (Thank you, we shall not forget, farewell). Our meeting, like ships in the night, had occurred quite by chance, an uncanny coincidence of time and space that had saved our souls. We had shared unique and special moments, forging an affinity and rapport with these men that we would remember for the rest of our lives. Now our time together was over. It was time for us to return to our world and they to theirs. We hugged our last goodbyes and took our leave, in the full knowledge we would not see them again. They had given us back our lives and we would never be able to repay them for that.

The gathering melee of news reporters, delighted to have such a demonstration of emotion on our return to civilisation, allowed us to go in peace and we were whisked off to the large American-style Hotel 'Executive' in downtown Panama City. It was five a.m. before we were safely ensconced, and we immediately resumed our pursuit of allaying the insatiable hunger of our bodies, by consuming large quantities of steak and eggs, with pancakes and waffles on the side and ice cream to follow. Douglas and Robin had three 'steak and egg' breakfasts each that morning, only one of which was supposed to satisfy a rancher!

Medical examinations, conducted with care by the staff of Santo Tomas Hospital in Panama City, found us to be anaemic, in spite of our bloodthirsty practices. but already recovering from the after-effects of severe dehydration, one such being the inability to walk. Sandy had contracted a slight bronchial pneumonia, which was treated with antibiotics without requiring his admittance to hospital, and Neil had suffered more generally from the effects of dehydration than the rest of us. Our legs were subject to swelling when exercised too much and we were told to resume normal activity slowly. Blood pressures were not exceptional and pulse rates, although high, were attributed to the strain of overloading our digestive systems and our continuing sleeplessness, for I could still only manage two hours a night. We had all lost a terrific amount of weight, between twenty and thirty pounds each, from bodies that weren't fat to start with, but subsequent examinations disclosed no lasting ill-effects either external or internal.

During the ensuing days in Panama, we received cables and telephone calls from our friends and relatives from all parts of the world, offering and giving help to us in our time of need. It was an experience of friendship which augmented the kindness of our

Japanese friends and made our rehabilitation all the more possible. Robin flew back to England a few days later whilst we waited to board the MV *Port Auckland* in Colon harbour, planning to return home at a more leisurely pace. On our day of departure we waved goodbye to our good friends the Jensen family from the Club Nautico Yacht Club, as we settled along the ship's side rails. Looking on with still more tears in our eyes, Lyn and I watched as our children leaned across the heavy teak woodwork waving their arms enthusiastically, pleased beyond measure that they were finally 'on a steamer home'. Anne was waiting back in England and soon we would all be together again. Even as I leant on the heavily varnished rail I felt the chills of an uncertain new world opening up before us, as I tried to balance the loss of *Lucette*, and our entire savings, with the wealth and depth of the experience we had gained, which could not be measured in terms of money.

Our odyssey, born and planned so long ago back on Meadows Farm, had all but ended. Instead of the adventure I had promised them, I had put my wife and family through a horrendous ordeal, which had so nearly resulted in their deaths. Despite the eventual successful outcome, Lyn and I remained racked with guilt, which a thousand apologies to our children, and indeed to each other, could not relieve. We had risked the lives of our children, and had put them through a life-scarring nightmare to save them; we had lost everything we owned. For reasons they probably didn't fully understand, the children had relished the trip aboard *Lucette*. Now that they were safe, even their experience adrift would not have been swapped for anything. Douglas told me even before we had reached Panama that he would thank me every day of his life for giving him such an adventure, and Neil stated in a moment of shipboard boredom that he preferred it on the raft. Indeed, in perhaps one of the most remarkable paradoxes of all, we found that we all missed the clarity and simple values encountered whilst living on the edge, as the very act of living had felt so much more rewarding when death lay in wait around every corner. Indeed, life's true worth can often not be realised until one is confronted by the spectre of death.

As a family, we would have to try and start over, viewing the loss of our money and entire asset base philosophically, accepting that there was a ticket price for every ride. Whilst the kids had lost out on their education they had each gained degrees with honours in the university of life, and whatever their futures held in store for them now, I knew they would meet adversity with courage and face life's challenges without fear or preconception. This, at least, was an ace I could keep. My family would not carry the burden of an unfulfilled destiny on their shoulders, nor could their adventure be designated a one-off magical experience. They had swum with great whales and whole schools of dolphins, they had dived on stupendous barrier reefs that teemed with every imaginable form of marine life, they had visited many historic sites and unique peoples, in far-off and inaccessible lands. They had discovered forgotten outposts of empire and ancient ruins, explored shipwrecks both old and new, and trekked along deserted island paradises.

Happy to have saved my children and happy to be able to forgive the deaths of my wartime friends and family, I cupped my chin in my hands and rested against the rail gazing seawards. My thoughts returned to the loss of our classic old schooner and I turned to behold my boys once more, joyfully recounting their sea-borne adventures, still vivid and alive in their hearts and minds. Taking Lyn's hand in mine, I realised our journey had not just been a trip of exploration to foreign lands but a unique and unrepeatable passage through the experience of life, and that in many ways, though her mortal remains lay entombed beneath the restless waters of the Pacific Ocean, the last voyage of the *Lucette* would never end.

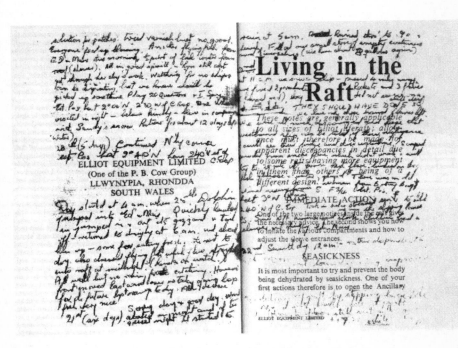

Part of the log in the raft handbook

Epilogue
1975: Amen to the *Ambassador*
Douglas Robertson

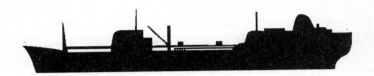

I joined the *British Ambassador* as a navigating cadet in Saudi Arabia on Christmas Day 1974. Trying to berth in a stiff breeze, the inexperienced pilot collided with the newly built jetty and demolished the mooring pontoons even before the concrete was properly dry. Following threats of seizure and even arrest the owners paid for the damages and it was several days later, after the completion of makeshift repairs, that we were allowed alongside once more, where we took on a cargo of just over 50,000 tonnes of crude oil destined for the port of Long Beach on the other side of the Pacific. Sailing just before new year, the *British Ambassador* entered the crowded Malacca Straits in early January 1975.

As we passed the bright lights of Singapore a Korean fishing boat not unlike the *Toka Maru* exploded just half a mile ahead of our position and was soon afire from stem to stern. Contrary to the custom of the sea, our newly promoted captain commanded that we sail on by, forcing a sister ship over six miles ahead of us to return in a race against time to effect the rescue.

Two days later, halfway through the morning four-to-eight watch, I called the captain from his slumbers to witness two men standing on a submerged platform in the water, waving madly in order to attract his attention.

'They are probably fishing,' he stated dismissively as the ship was ordered once again to sail on by.

Horrified, I said that fate would strike back for such flagrant disregard for the safety of life at sea. In fact those two men were the first of the Vietnamese boat people, and two years later a Maersk line ship – belonging to my future employers – picked up over 4,000 such individuals in what was declared the largest uplift of castaways in history.

Two days after rounding the northern point of Luzon, the *British Ambassador* encountered heavy weather as she struck out on the great circle route towards the United States of America. On the nineteenth day after leaving Saudi, fate did indeed strike back.

Just before lunch on a sunny morning the engineer's alarm began to ring and I reported to my muster station on the bridge. The captain sent me below to find out what the fuss was about. My heart skipped a beat when I entered the engine room to discover the ship's engineers scurrying about their tasks with a deep sense of urgency. The plates were awash and water was already flooding into the lower levels of the machinery flats and making them impassable. The chief engineer was below the plates and shouting for a bandage. A large-diameter condenser intake pipe in the ship's bottom had fractured and a serious leak had breached the vessel's watertight integrity. The second engineer shouted in my direction, asking me to help him shut the sea valve. We both struggled with the heavily corroded valve wheel, then became alarmed at the ease with which it turned. A few seconds later the spindle fetched up against its stop but the water flooded into the ship with undiminished force.

'Get back to the bridge and tell the captain to send out an SOS,' came the chief's desperate utterance as he witnessed the failure of the sea valve.

Events suddenly took on a dramatic new turn as the electricity generator exploded with an almighty bang and a blaze of flames. Thankfully the rising water levels soon put it out but it was clear that the situation was deteriorating by the second. By the time I got back out on deck the ship was dead in the water and had come to a stop with the wind gusting at force 10 or more. White-crested waves sloshed down the windward railings and up onto the decks. I rushed forward to the bridge and delivered my breathless and somewhat disjointed report.

'What's up with the old gaffer?' chortled the old man dismissively as I burst onto the bridge, but on hearing my words his jaw dropped as he realised his first ever command was about to disappear from under him.

'We are sinking and the chief reckons we should send out an SOS,' I confirmed to my disbelieving captain.

'Take me to him,' was his reply, his tone changing from that of mild amusement to one of ice-cold seriousness.

Not until the captain had seen the damage for himself was a Mayday actually sent out. 'Mayday, Mayday, Mayday, this is the *British Ambassador* calling Mayday, Mayday, Mayday.'

Our distress call shattered the early-morning airwaves and sent my pulse racing as I realised that the sea was about to test my survival skills for a second time. An American T2 tanker of World-War-II vintage answered our call. Her name was *Fort Fetterman* and she advised she would be in position the following day by late afternoon. Thirty-six hours didn't seem long in vastness of the Pacific but there was already serious concern aboard that the *British Ambassador* would not stay afloat for much longer than that, at best.

All hands were turned to in order to secure tank lids, cofferdams and access hatches in an attempt to maintain what little watertight integrity remained. I was detailed the job of sealing off the accommodation and porthole deadlights, which I carried out alone in the terrifying darkness of our sinking ship, aware that she could go at any moment. It took over four hours to complete this task, which undoubtedly prolonged our time afloat as we waited for the rescue ship to arrive. As the afternoon progressed our own ship continued to settle by the stern and the out-swung lifeboats to windward were stove in on their davits by the high seas, which left us with only two remaining lifeboats, one motorised and the other equipped only with oars.

Towards evening all the crew moved what food and stores they could find to the central accommodation and as night fell they huddled in the eerie silence of the saloon in what was now a dead ship. Chicken soup was heated on top of the ships emergency kerosene navigation lamps as we watched and waited the night out, ready to leave at a moments notice should the order to abandon ship be issued. Daylight revealed the ships decks to be steeply inclined by the stern and the engine room section aft completely flooded.

Both officers and crew tried to hide their apprehensive faces as the endless waiting continued past noon. The captain informed all aboard that we would take to the boats before nightfall if we had not already been picked up as deteriorating weather conditions made it unsafe to remain aboard. The wind was blasting the stricken vessel at force 12 and more, and heavy seas swept across the decks as the ship lay ever lower in the water. True to her word, the *Fort Fetterman* arrived just after 1500 hours. But her lifeboats were unsuitable to effect any sort of rescue, and the cries of euphoria soon subsided as it became clear that the only effective means of escape remained with our own boats – a task that in such weather conditions seemed increasingly less viable with each passing minute.

The second officer was detailed to assemble a working party to launch the remaining motorised lifeboat from the afterdeck and take half of the crew to the waiting ship, then return for the rest of us. The boat, fully loaded with crew members in bright red lifejackets, was lowered away amidst nervous shouts. On hitting the water she snatched heavily at the bowline securing her in the meagre shelter afforded by the ship's lee side, before snapping it clean in two. Seconds later the boat was cast off from her falls and the frightened castaways made their way through towering seas to the waiting rescue vessel. It took over an hour to cover the gap between the two vessels and on arrival abeam of the *Fort Fetterman* the appalling weather conditions made it impossible to maintain station alongside so that the crew could disembark. Large cargo nets were hastily rigged down the sides of her hull but the high waves slammed the frail lifeboat into the heavy steel structure of the rescue ship, making the operation both difficult and perilous.

The officers' wives went first, clinging desperately to the heavily knotted cargo nets as they hauled themselves towards the safety of the deck. The second officer's wife was caught by the watery deluge of a wave rolling across the deck from the windward side and, unable to maintain her grip under the cascading torrent crashing down on her from above, lost her grip and was swept over the side. Without a thought for their own safety, two of the able seamen dived over the side and rescued her, saving the young woman from certain death.

After fifteen minutes of keeping the boat alongside to allow the disembarkation to continue, the lifeboat began to break up, large cracks appearing in the bow and stern sections. Suddenly a large wave rolled clear across the deck and poured into the crumbling boat, swamping it right over the gunwales. A mad scramble ensued as the last remaining men raced up the safety net to escape the sinking survival craft, which was totally submerged on the end of its painter. It had to be cut away to drift helplessly at the mercy of the wind and sea.

The captain adjusted his binoculars and looked on helplessly from the quiet of the *British Ambassador*'s starboard bridge wing. It was clear that a second such rescue attempt to save the remainder of the personnel on board would not be possible. With both windward lifeboats useless we wallowed beam-on to the rising waves, and with only the midships rowing boat left to leeward the situation began to look ominous for the rest of us trapped on board. Just after 1600 hours the *Fort Fetterman*, with her survivors all accounted for, wished us luck and departed for the sanctuary of land, leaving us alone and vulnerable at the mercy of the elements. The *British Ambassador* was settling deeper and deeper in the water and it would only be a matter of time before we would be forced to evacuate in whatever way we could. We made more hot soup, using the rapidly diminishing stocks of paraffin in the navigation lights, and passed what paltry rations we could find amongst the thirty-four men left on board, fully aware that lack of food and water was soon going to become a serious issue if help did not arrive soon. As darkness approached, the captain ordered continuous use of the emergency radio to issue Morse-code SOS messages into the ether in the hope that a rescue ship would find us before it was too late. As an emergency measure we also swung out our last remaining lifeboat and prepared it for immediate launching. That night we slept in various clusters in close proximity to the lifeboat, ready for an instantaneous getaway should the command to abandon ship be given.

In the vibrant nightlife of distant Tokyo, seamen from all over the world drank and made merry in the many bars of the city, enjoying some well-earned shore leave. A group of young Germans were especially joyous, having docked after a successful but tough salvage operation aboard their purpose-built ocean-going tug *Arctic*. Their enjoyment was bought to a swift end, however, when the shrill whistles of their call-back alarms were sounded by the ship's captain. They had ten minutes to get back to the *Arctic* or their ship would leave without them. Our distress call had at last been received.

Dawn found us cold, tired and hungry, but our spirits were lifted by the news that our SOS had been answered. The *Arctic* was already under way and proceeding at double-full-ahead, risking all to get to us before we sank. It was a race against time, and her estimated time of arrival was 1700 hours that same day. If the weather didn't deteriorate and she was not delayed then we felt for the first time that we might just make it. Close watch was kept on the *British Ambassador* all day, for we felt she could go at any moment. With over thirty castaways aboard the drinking water was rapidly running out and we had to make do with only a mouthful of chocolate for breakfast and the last of the lukewarm chicken soup for lunch. Our only morsel of comfort was that if things got too dire there was an ample supply of beer and whisky from the ship's bonded store, which was located midships and was still above the level of the rising seawater. At least we would drown happy.

As the afternoon progressed the aft accommodation slipped lower and lower into the sea. During the early evening the tank lids were smashed open by the heavy rollers that crashed continuously across our decks. The air became acrid with the smell of sulphur as the crude oil began to leak onto the surface of the sea, irrefutable proof that slowly but surely our aging ship was beginning her descent into the depths of the Pacific Ocean.

My thoughts returned to the last time I had tried to cross this magnificent ocean. I had been shipwrecked then, and now on my second attempt I was about to be shipwrecked again. In the most uncanny of coincidences, my life was to be at the mercy of the sea for a second time in less than three years. I took comfort, however, from the knowledge that distress messages had been sent and acknowledged. The balance of probability of life over death was decidedly more in my favour than it had been the last time I had been cast adrift.

Tension amongst the crew mounted as the waiting continued. Waiting for the first signs of the rescue ship to appear over the horizon; waiting for the first signs that our own moribund vessel was commencing her final downward plunge to the seabed; waiting for the anxious shouts that would signal us all to the last remaining boat. Worried frowns and fretting silence dominated the mood until at last a shout suddenly announced sight of the *Arctic* approaching from the northwest. Cheers drowned out the roar of the sea as we welcomed our saviour with grateful thanks. The *British Ambassador* was settling visibly by the time the tug came alongside. Much to our relief she launched her own boats and under the cover of darkness rescued every last man. The German crew welcomed us on board their ship and supplied us with thick steaks and cold beers, reviving our flagging spirits and calming our beleaguered nerves. The onset of darkness, however, delayed the towing operation until daybreak the following day.

Daylight finally revealed our old tanker, hull down in the water with an oil slick some twenty miles long and three miles wide trailing out behind her. The weather had moderated a little, and with millions of dollars in salvage at stake the captain of the *Arctic* was anxious to get the tow connected as soon as possible. I was one of the boarding party of volunteers who re-boarded the sinking ship to assist with the connecting of the tow. A huge steel hawser was hauled out to the forecastle of the *British Ambassador* with the intent of making her fast and towing her to Japan. The work was strenuous and demanding as the four-inch hawser was winched up to the bulwarks and the tow taken under control. At some 3 knots our progress was slow and matters were complicated by a telegram from the Japanese Air Force. They were refusing us entry into their territorial waters on the grounds of pollution. Their point was fair even if their ultimatum was not, for their cable stated that they would use whatever means appropriate to deny us entry, including the use of airborne bombs to prevent us proceeding to a Japanese port. I was beginning to wonder if I was indeed reliving my father's life. Was it really possible that I was about to be bombed by the Japanese, as he had been aboard the *Sagaing* some thirty-three years before me?

'We will cross that bridge if we get to it,' sighed the salvage tug's captain as he scanned his uncooperative charge with his binoculars. The *British Ambassador* swung across our fore-and-aft line first to port and then to starboard in the lumpy seaway, requiring us to slow to the speed of 1 knot. As evening approached, the dreams of an easy bounty began to fade as the sinking tow began to trim excessively by the stern. Later that night all hands were mustered on deck as the *British Ambassador* slowly turned over on her side and under the cover of a light rainsquall slipped beneath the waves and disappeared from view. Busy crew members took up heavy-duty buzz saws and worked at a frantic pace to sever the tow cable before she pulled us under as she went. The date was 13 January 1975. The position was 25 degrees north, 137 degrees 45 minutes east.

Feeling strangely alone, we all whispered a last amen to the *British Ambassador*, wondering how it could be that such a ship could founder in the modern age of shipping. It seemed that the sea, far from being tamed by man, was as demanding as ever of his respect and relentless to exploit any break in his vigilance.

After transferring her survivors to the Japan-bound *British Holly*, the *Arctic* was able to claim for her severed tow cable but lost her right to salvage when the *British Ambassador* sank. A subsequent enquiry revealed structural failure as the cause of the sinking. No lives were lost, and the crude oil was apparently reabsorbed by the environment. It seemed that the only losers, for once, were the insurance companies.

Ode to the frigatebird

Oh sentinel of the southern seas, impervious to our plight,
You soar aloft in majesty and hold us in your sight.
Will you still be with us in the desperate days ahead?
Do you offer hopes of landfall, or mourning for the dead?

For many weeks you've led the way, beating wings, unblinking stare,
Immortal spirit with us now, we turn to you with bended brow.
Thy jet-black plumage, graceful sight, keeps eerie vigil through the night;
Now seems to us that all is lost, as in this little boat we're tossed.

This mighty ocean is your home; no walls or fences halt thy roam.
'Neath opalled wings to life we cling and wait to see what fate will bring;
With humble prayers, thy warriors we, place our faith in destiny.
God give us courage, oh! armour me, that we survive the savage sea.

A ship – a ship, we voice the cry, oh frigatebird don't let us die;
Our pinnacle of contentment soared as eager hands hauled us on board.
Now we rejoin the human race and sadness falls upon my face;
Farewell my friend, I'll ne'r forget thy black-green feathers bold and set.

On moorland hill now curlews fly, for many years have passed us by;
Long remembered are those days, o'er curling wave where dolphin plays;
Now life's harsh conflicts bend my will; and your inspiration guides me still
As thoughts return to where you ply, the lonely sea, Pacific sky.

Composed by Douglas and Linda Robertson

Appendix 1
The SY *Lucette*

Lucette was originally built to the order of a Major Noott in 1922, in a boatyard known as Kings of Burnham on the banks of the River Crouch in Suffolk, England.

In accordance with the highest standards of the day she was fabricated from top-quality materials with a contemporary gaff-rigged sail plan. Her planking was of pitch pine, 1.25 inches thick, and her frames were of doubled grown oak. Such frames were formed as the oak trees were growing by bending the boughs into shape so that the grain of the wood extended longitudinally throughout the entire length of the piece. Her long keel was finished with a three-ton lead cap and all the fastenings in the hull were made of copper. Though heavy, this gave the hull additional strength, making her very suitable for the rigours of extended ocean cruising.

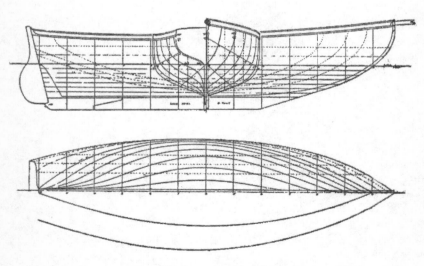

SY *Lucette*: original line plan

Her original specifications are indicated in an extract from the 1930 edition of the *Lloyds Register*:

LLOYD'S REGISTER OF YACHTS, 1930

1	2	3	4		5			6	
Consecutive No.	Yacht's Name.	Type. Rig.	TONS.		Dimensions			Build	
Offficial Number.			Registered Net & ross.		T.M.	Br'dth.	Depth.	Builders.	Where.
Signal Letters.	Material of Build.	Sailmaker.	Thames Measurement.	Length	O.A.	Head-room.	Draft.	Designers.	When.
					W.L.	Sail Area.			
3318	Lucette Wood	AuxSch	8.72		39.3	11.4	6.1	W.King & Sons	Burnham-on-Crouch
146650	Par.Mot.	Cranfield,22	12.83		39.5	6.2	5.0		
			19		36.0	923		N.E.Dallimore	1922

8	9	10	11 Classification. 12	
Engines and Boilers. Particulars and *Builders*.	Owners	Port belonging to.	Port of Survey.	Character for Special Survey.
			Other Classifications if not L.R.	Date of last Survey.
Alterations, etc.				Equipment Letter
Parrafin Motor 4Cy.3 1/2"-4 3/4" *Bergius.GLS.24*	Major A. W. Noott	London		

The first overseas cruise undertaken by the owner was a trip to the Baltic Sea by way of the Kiel Canal in 1927. Even then she was known to be something of a slowcoach and her broad flat transom gave her an ungainly appearance when viewed from aft. This mini-adventure was recorded in a book by her American skipper A F Loomis called *Fair Winds in the Far Baltic*, which was published in 1928 by Ives Washburn of New York. It is of specific interest as it was done at a time when the Zuider Zee was open and Amsterdam a coastal port.

On reading Loomis's book I soon discovered a few remarks with which I could readily concur – one such being a quote from an eminent sail maker of Cowes who said that 'she would go a long way but take a lo-o-o-ng time to get there'. When first seeing her himself, Loomis's own comment was that although 'high sided and bluff-bowed, she nevertheless gives the impression of great seaworthiness'.

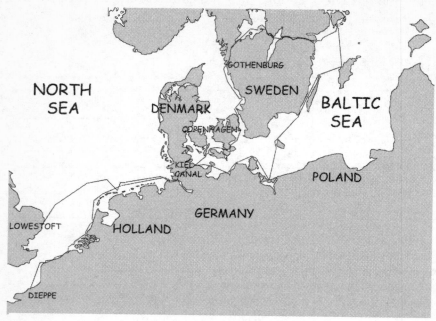

Voyage to the Baltic in 1927

Lucette with her original gaff-rigged sail plan

Voyage plan 1927

Table of distances: Lowestoft to Stockholm

From	To	Miles	Hours under way
Lowestoft	Cuxhaven	280	61
Cuxhaven	Brunsbüttelkoog	15	2
Brunsbüttelkoog	Kiel	55	9½
Kiel	Albuen Point	46	8½
Albuen Point	Petersvaerft	49	9½
Petersvaerft	Copenhagen	53	9½
Copenhagen	Helsingör	20	4
Helsingör	Halmstad	40	8
Halmstad	Gothenburg	85	17
Gothenburg	Lilla Edet	40	6
Lilla Edet	Brinkebergskulles	16	4½
Brinkebergskulles	Bromö Sund	59	10½
Bromö Sund	Karlsborg	46	14
Karlsborg	Berg	35	8
Berg	Söderköping	27	9
Söderköping	Saltsjöbaden (Stockholm)	94	19
		960	200

Table of distances: Stockholm to Dieppe

From	To	Miles	Hours under way
Saltsjöbaden	Nynäshamn	30	7
Nynäshamn	Visby	78	13½
Visby	Kalmar	95	19½
Kalmar	Rönne	90	21
Rönne	Swinemünde	70	12
Swinemünde	Warnemünde	126	19
Warnemünde	Holtenau	76	10
Holtenau	Brunsbüttelkoog	53	8
Brunsbüttelkoog	Cuxhaven	15	2½
Cuxhaven	Ijmuiden	205	34
Ijmuiden	Hook of Holland	35	5
Hook of Holland	Zeebrugge	55	7½
Zeebrugge	Ostend	10	1½
Ostend	Calais	42	6½
Calais	Dieppe	78	13
		1058	180
	TOTAL	2018	380

Average speed Outward Bound,   4.8 knots.
Average speed Homeward Bound,   5.9 knots
Average speed Entire Voyage   5.3 knots

During this trip *Lucette*'s voyage was blessed with fair winds, which they took with them, and despite near-disaster on the constantly changing tidal flows of the Texel Sands off the coast of Holland, their adventure left a lifelong impression on her crew and they remembered it with pleasure. After escaping the shifting sands of Texel *Lucette* recorded a distance run of 35 miles in five hours, proving even then that with the right wind she could make as good a speed as any cruising yacht of her era.

In 1936 *Lucette* caught fire alongside and much of the saloon was burnt out. New owners took advantage by refitting the saloon with a deck cabin and replacing her large counter with a finely pointed canoe stern, thereby adding some four feet to her hull length. At the same time her rather undersized gaff rig was converted to the triangular Bermuda style more typical of a modern-day yacht and the sail plan was increased in size by the addition of a three-foot boomkin aft.

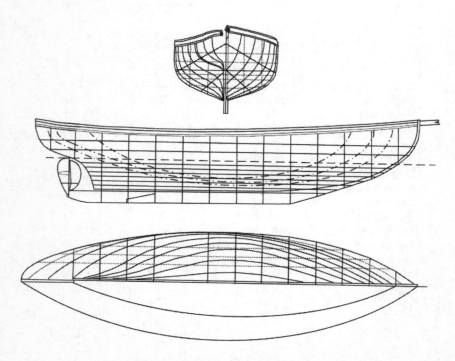

SY *Lucette*: Line plan after refurbishment

Lucette spent the war years on the south coast of England. It is thought she was involved in the Dunkirk evacuation, though no documentary proof is available. After the war she made passage to the Mediterranean where she chartered out of Gibraltar and the Balearics, eventually finding a home in St Angelo, Malta, from 1965 to 1968. Here she was chartered by the British Army for adventure training, providing seamanship and navigation practice for parties of up to eleven on round trips to Catania in Sicily. After this *Lucette* was moved to Valletta, also in Malta, where she was laid up for a long period of time until she was purchased by Dougal for his round-the-world voyage.

Lucette with her new sail plan and canoe stern

Dear Mr. Robertson,

        I appreciate that you and your family have been
subjected to a surfeit of publicity recently and must have suffered
endless idiot questions and comments about your experiences aboard
Ednamair. I hesitate to intrude further on your privacy; but it occurred to me that it is just possible that you may not know that
Lucette figured in a book written many years before yours by one of
her original owners. Having said that, I must confess that I can
remember neither the title nor the author as I read it some fifteen
years ago when my step-father, Douglas Moxey, was owner of Lucette.
The book must have been written before the mid-thirties when she
acquired her canoe stern because I recall a drawing or photograph
of her showing a steep transom.

        My recollection of the book is extremely hazy,
but you might be interested to know that Lucette had several near-
misses early on in her career (in the Baltic, I think); and reading
your account of her extraordinary demise reminded me that, in my
experience also, she courted catastrophe on a couple of occasions.
Rather ignominiously, she was gutted by fire while overwintering in
Santander with a caretaker aboard. Not much beyond the hull survived.
And we almost lost her with all hands trying to get into le Palais
harbour, Belle Ile, in very dirty weather. The engine, a decrepit
14 h.p. Kelvin, failed at a critical moment when we were broached-to
with no sea-room at all and only a storm-jib to lug us inelegantly
to safety (we had lost the use of the mainsail earlier that day when
a gooseneck sheared and mast and boom parted company -- no chance of
making running repairs in that weather). The Kelvin went over the
side soon after, to be replaced by a Coventry-Victor which never gave
us a moment's trouble.

        I don't propose to bore you with an account of our
voyages aboard Lucette. In all they consisted of a fairly uneventful
cruise from Salcombe to the Aegean, spread over several of my school
holidays. Incidentally, you had worse luck in the Bay of Biscay than
we. We always had Genoa-weather there and were twice becalmed (on one
occasion I dived over the side, under the keel and up into the embrace
of a Portugese Man o' War). It is simply that you don't forget the
craft aboard which you learned to sail, suffered and mastered seasickness, stood your first night watches; and -- even though she was
never as good to windward as I hoped -- I'll always remember Lucette
with affection.

        A final note. Should you ever be tempted to resume
your interrupted voyage, did you know that Lucette had a sister-ship
(a ketch as I recall)? I last saw her in La Rochelle harbour thirteen
years ago. She may be afloat still -- probably is if she was built as
well as her sister.

        My congratulations on your survival; my sympathy
for your loss of a fine old lady.

                        Yours,

                        Bob Franklin.

Previous owner's letter

Appendix 2

Voyage plan,
27 January 1971 – 31 August 1972

Date	Departure port	Miles	Days en route	Arrival port	Date	Days in port	Vessel
27 Jan 1971	Falmouth, England	930	11	Lisbon, Portugal	6 Feb 1971	14	*Lucette*
20 Feb 1971	Lisbon, Portugal	720	8	Las Palmas, Canary Islands	1 Mar 1971	27	*Lucette*
28 Mar 1971	Las Palmas, Canary Islands	2,580	33	Bridgetown, Barbados	1 May 1971	8	*Lucette*
8 May 1971	Bridgetown, Barbados	120	1	Admiralty Bay, Bequia	9 May 1971	5	*Lucette*
14 May 1971	Admiralty Bay, Bequia	160	3	Portsmouth, Dominica	17 May 1971	5	*Lucette*
22 May 1971	Portsmouth, Dominica	90	2	English Harbour, Antigua	26 May 1971	4	*Lucette*
30 May 1971	English Harbour, Antigua	200	2	St Thomas, US Virgin Islands	1 Jun 1971	16	*Lucette*
17 Jun 1971	St Thomas, US Virgin Islands	530	3	Matthew Town, Great Inagua	20 Jun 1971	2	*Lucette*
22 Jun 1971	Matthew Town, Great Inagua	45	1	Little Inagua	22 Jun 1971	5	*Lucette*
27 Jun 1971	Little Inagua	45	1	Matthew Town, Great Inagua	27 Jun 1971	4	*Lucette*
1 Jul 1971	Matthew Town, Great Inagua	120	1	Crooked Island, Bahamas	2 Jul 1971	1	*Lucette*
2 Jul 1971	Crooked Island, Bahamas	90	1	Conception Island	3 Jul 1971	Over night	*Lucette*
3 Jul 1971	Conception Island	50	1	Cat Island	4 Jul 1971	Over night	*Lucette*
4 Jul 1971	Cat Island	25	1	Little San Salvador	5 Jul 1971	2	*Lucette*
6 Jul 1971	Little San Salvador	90	3	Nassau, New Providence	9 Jul 1971	10	*Lucette*
19 Jul 1971	Nassau, New Providence	50	2	Great Stirrup Cay	21 Jul 1971	1	*Lucette*
22 Jul 1971	Great Stirrup Cay	135	2	Miami, Florida	24 Jul 1971	124	*Lucette*
23 Nov 1971	Miami, Florida	45	2	Bimini, Bahamas	25 Nov 1971	8	*Lucette*
2 Dec 1971	Bimini, Bahamas	45	1	Miami, Florida	2 Dec 1971	54	*Lucette*

(Continued overleaf)

Date	Departure port	Miles	Days en route	Arrival port	Date	Days in port	Vessel
25 Jan 1972	Miami, Florida	45	1	Cat Cay	26 Jan 1972	Over night	*Lucette*
26 Jan 1972	Cat Cay	110	1	Nassau, New Providence	27 Jan 1972	6	*Lucette*
2 Feb 1972	Nassau, New Providence	120	3	Exuma Cays	5 Feb 1972	1	*Lucette*
6 Feb 1972	Exuma Cays	525	5	Kingston, Jamaica	11 Feb 1972	17	*Lucette*
28 Feb 1972	Kingston, Jamaica	80	1	Port Antonio, Jamaica	1 Mar 1972	14	*Lucette*
15 Mar 1972	Port Antonio, Jamaica	630	7	Colon, Panama	22 Mar 1972	3	*Lucette*
25 Mar 1972	Colon, Panama	20	1	Portobello, Panama	25 Mar 1972	5	*Lucette*
30 Mar 1972	Portobello, Panama	10	1	Isle Grande	31 Mar 1972	1	*Lucette*
1 Apr 1972	Isle Grande	10	1	Nombre de Dios, Panama	2 Apr 1972	1	*Lucette*
2 Apr 1972	Nombre de Dios, Panama	30	1	Porvenir, San Blas Archipelago	3 Apr 1972	32	*Lucette*
5 May 1972	Porvenir, San Blas Archipelago	70	1	Colon – Panama Canal transit	6 May 1972	10	*Lucette*
16 May 1972	Colon – Panama Canal transit	35	1	Panama City	17 May 1972	Over night	*Lucette*
17 May 1972	Panama City	900	15	Galapagos	1 Jun 1973	12	*Lucette*
13 Jun 1972	Galapagos	200	2	200 miles west of Cape Espinosa	15 Jun 1972	at sea	*Lucette*
15 Jun 1972	200 miles west of Cape Espinosa	350	17	Doldrums	2 Jul 1972	at sea	Raft
2 Jul 1972	Doldrums	400	21	Doldrums	23 Jul 1972	at sea	*Ednamair*
23 Jul 1972	Doldrums	600	4	Panama City	27 Jul 1972	28	*Toka Maru*
24 Aug 1972	Panama City	4,200	7	Liverpool, England	31 Aug 1972	home	*Port Auckland*
Total miles travelled		14,405					

Appendix 3
Glossary of sailing terms

Abeam: to the side of the vessel, at a right-angle to the fore-and-aft line

Beam ends: The vertical sides of the hull, usually midships

Beat: To sail to windward

Boom: A wooden support for a sail where one end is attached to the mast

Broach to: To turn accidentally sideways into the wind and sea

Coach roof: The roof of the deckhouse forward of the deck saloon

Counter: The part of the vessel's stern that is above the waterline

Dead reckoning: Determination of position from course steered and distance run

Drogue: Water parachute or similar object used to reduce leeway when hove to

Fo'c'sle: Cabin nearest the bow

Freeboard: Distance from the water to the top of the side of a boat

Garboard strake: The hull plank next to the keel

Genoa: Large jib-like sail used in light winds

Grommet: Strong circle of rope

Gunwale: Top corner / edge of a boat where the side meets the deck

Gybe: To turn the boat (generally while sailing downwind) by bringing the wind around the stern

Heave to: To stop sailing a desired course and to steer to wind and sea instead

Heel: The angle leant over by a vessel when in the seaway

Jib: Loose-footed triangular sail forward of the mast

Leeboard: A dagger-like board that is sunk into the sea when beating to windward to reduce leeway

Leeway: Sideways motion of a vessel due to wind

Luff: Leading part of a sail

Luff up: When sailing upwind, to bring the bow of the vessel closer to the wind

Reach: To sail with the wind approximately abeam

Reef: To reduce the sail area by making the sails smaller

Rhumb line: A straight line on a Mercator projection chart which in reality is a curved line

Schooner: Sailing vessel with fore-and-aft rig and mainmast nearest the stern; *Lucette* was a staysail schooner

Sea anchor: Device to restrict leeway, usually in the form of a water parachute

Seaway: The part of the sea being sailed through

Set: Direction (of current)

Sheet: Rope attached to lower corner or corners of a sail, used to fasten the free end and alter its shape

Spar: A wooden support for a sail where both ends are unattached

Stays: Supports for mast

Stem: The bow; the front end of a vessel

Strake: One of the long planks forming the side of the boat's hull

Swell: Waves caused by distant winds

Tack: To turn the boat (generally while sailing upwind) by bringing the bow through the wind; also refers to the orientation of the vessel in relation to the wind: 'on starboard tack' means that the wind is coming from the starboard side

Thole pins: Upright supports to which an oar may be attached

Thwart: A crossways seat in a small boat

Transom: The stern of a yacht where it is bluff rather than pointed

Trim (of vessel): Fore-and-aft manner in which a vessel floats in the water

Trim (of sails): To alter the shape of the sail with the sheet to stop the wind from spilling

Yaw: Action of the bow moving from side to side when making way

Afterword

Apart from the dreams, which lasted for over twenty years, lives returned to 'normal' for the Robertson family after they had returned home aboard the MV *Port Auckland*. Dougal wrote his book *Survive the Savage Sea*, which became a worldwide best-seller in over twenty languages. He went on to write another book called *Sea Survival*, which has since saved the lives of many castaways, offering tips, charts and remedies gleaned from his time on the Pacific.

'Dougal's Kitchen' never did open, and neither Dougal nor Linda ever fully recovered from the guilt their feat of endurance had burdened them with. Dougal moved away from the family home aboard a yacht he had purchased from his publishing endeavours, never again to cross the world's great oceans but simply to revel in the more simple enjoyment of pottering about in boats along the sun-drenched reaches of the Mediterranean.

Linda, true to her words in the dinghy, returned to farming and created a renowned pedigree herd of Limousin cattle, with the able assistance of both Neil and Sandy. The bloodstock lives on to this day in many herds throughout the UK.

Robin took up his career in finance and settled down to family life with his wife and four children, stating that he never again wished to be far away from food.

Anne and Jeff lasted a surprisingly long time before they finally split, she to find true love and he to return home and get married.

Douglas, true to his wishes, went to sea, only to be shipwrecked a second time aboard the SS *British Ambassador*, also in the mid-Pacific. Undaunted, he went back to sea and attained the rank of Chief Officer like his father before him, before relinquishing his life on the ocean wave. With both father and son shipwrecked twice, Douglas has since pointed out to his own sons that this is the sort of family tradition best avoided in future! Douglas had come to terms with his own death many times whilst a castaway and now considers the rest of his life a gift. No longer restricted to thinking in straight lines, his outlook to this day remains unburdened with the sense of each day's weight, spurred instead with the knowledge of its wonder and the realisation that it is indeed a gift to be alive. His feelings about their survival epic are perhaps best summed up in the poem 'Ode to the Frigatebird', which he started writing upon those Pacific wastes.

Neil is keeping his mother's ideals alive, farming in the English midlands. He is happily married with a family of four children.

Sandy is a boat owner and lives with his wife and four children aboard the MV *Ocean Dawn*. Whilst he makes short hops to Spain and France he hopes one day to follow in his father's footsteps and cross the great ocean to the Caribbean or even perhaps sail around the world.

The dinghy *Ednamair* and its artefacts are currently housed in the National Maritime Museum in Falmouth, Cornwall, having been well cared for by Edna Beaumont for over 20 years. There is a website called survivethesavagesea.com, where further information and pictures can be seen.

After drifting for many days, during which much of her valuable war cargo was salvaged, the *Sagaing* eventually sank in the waters of Malay Cove, where she lies to this day. A memorial to the *Sagaing* can be found at the merchant navy memorial in Tower Hill, London.

Dougal died in 1991, shortly before the film of his book was released, and his obituary is displayed in the Clan Donnachaidh museum in Pitlochry, Scotland, together with the letters written on the raft by both Douglas and Neil. Linda, who never stopped loving him, died in 1998. They are survived by four children and eighteen grandchildren, whose lives were touched forever during that Sunday morning rumpus in the family bed at Meadows Farm, when Neil in all innocence uttered those inexorable words, 'Daddy's a sailor, why don't we sail around the world?'